Election, Atonement, and the Holy Spirit

Princeton Theological Monograph Series

K. C. Hanson, Charles M. Collier, D. Christopher Spinks,
and Robin A. Parry, Series Editors

Recent volumes in the series:

Koo Dong Yun
*The Holy Spirit and Ch'i (Qi):
A Chiological Approach to Pneumatology*

Stanley S. MacLean
*Resurrection, Apocalypse, and the Kingdom of Christ:
The Eschatology of Thomas F. Torrance*

Brian Neil Peterson
*Ezekiel in Context: Ezekiel's Message Understood in Its Historical
Setting of Covenant Curses and Ancient Near
Eastern Mythological Motifs*

Amy E. Richter
Enoch and the Gospel of Matthew

Maeve Louise Heaney
Music as Theology: What Music Says about the Word

Eric M. Vail
Creation and Chaos Talk: Charting a Way Forward

David L. Reinhart
*Prayer as Memory: Toward the Comparative Study of Prayer
as Apocalyptic Language and Thought*

Peter D. Neumann
Pentecostal Experience: An Ecumenical Encounter

Ashish J. Naidu
*Transformed in Christ:
Christology and the Christian Life in John Chrysostom*

Election, Atonement, and the Holy Spirit

Through and Beyond Barth's Theological Interpretation of Scripture

MATTHIAS GREBE

Foreword by
DAVID F. FORD

◈PICKWICK *Publications* · Eugene, Oregon

ELECTION, ATONEMENT, AND THE HOLY SPIRIT
Through and Beyond Barth's Theological Interpretation of Scripture

Princeton Theological Monograph Series 214

Copyright © 2014 Matthias Grebe. All rights reserved. Except for brief quotations in critical publications or reviews, no part of this book may be reproduced in any manner without prior written permission from the publisher. Write: Permissions. Wipf and Stock Publishers, 199 W. 8th Ave., Suite 3, Eugene, OR 97401.

Pickwick Publications
An Imprint of Wipf and Stock Publishers
199 W. 8th Ave., Suite 3
Eugene, OR 97401

www.wipfandstock.com

ISBN 13: 978-1-62564-204-2

Cataloguing-in-Publication Data

Grebe, Matthias.

Election, atonement, and the Holy Spirit : through and beyond Bath's theological interpretation of Scripture / Matthias Grebe, with a foreword by David F. Ford.

Princeton Theological Monogaphs series 214

xxii + 290 p. ; 23 cm. Includes bibliographical references and indices.

ISBN 13: 978-1-62564-204-2

1. Barth, Karl, 1886–1968. 2. Election (Theology)—History of doctrines—20th century. 3. Atonement. 4. Holy Spirit. 5. Bible—Hermeneutics. I. Ford, David, 1948–. II. Series. III. Title.

BT111.3 G822 2014

Manufactured in the U.S.A.   11/04/2014

To my Fathers

neque enim Pater iudicat quemquam sed iudicium omne dedit Filio
   —St John 5:22

Contents

Foreword by David F. Ford   ix

Preface   xi

Acknowledgements   xvii

Abbreviations   xx

Introduction   1
1. The Pastoral Motivations of this Study and the Nature of the Problem
2. The Task of the Study
3. The Method of Study
4. An Outline of the Study

1   Election, Rejection, and Exegesis   10
Introduction
1. The Pastoral Concern with Election
2. Re-locating the Doctrine
3. The Basis of Barth's Doctrine of Election: God's Self-Revelation
4. Jesus Christ: the 'Electing God' and the 'Elected Human'
5. *Simul Electus et Reprobatus*: God's *Yes* and God's *No*
6. Barth's Typological Exegesis of Leviticus 14 and 16
Conclusion

2   Jesus Christ the Elect: Through and Beyond Barth   66
Introduction
1. An Exegetical Challenge to Barth's Doctrine of Election
2. Barth's Typological Interpretation Revisited
3. An Alternative Typology
Conclusion

3   The Covenant, Humanity and *das Nichtige*   100
Introduction
1. The Covenant
2. Humanity
3. *Das Nichtige*
Conclusion

4   Jesus Christ the Judge: Through and Beyond Barth   145
Introduction
1. Atonement in the Early Church
2. The Reformed Backdrop of Barth's Theology of Atonement
3. Barth on *Cur Deus Homo*?
4. Jesus the High Priest
5. *Jesus is Victor*: The Conquering of Sin
6. *Existenzstellvertretung* in the New Testament
Conclusion

5   Election, Atonement, and the Holy Spirit   199
Introduction
1. Election and Universalism
2. The Eternal Spirit and the Mortal Soul
3. Humanity, Freedom, and Faith
Conclusion

Conclusion   247
1. Problems with Barth's Exegesis
2. Beyond the Binary Impasse of the *Yes* and *No* in Christ
3. Pastoral Implications: Limited Atonement and Universalism
4. Systematic Implications: The Economic and Immanent Trinity
Concluding Remarks

Bibliography   261
Subject Index   273
Name Index   281
Scripture Index   285

Foreword

KARL BARTH'S DOCTRINES OF ELECTION AND ATONEMENT ARE SURELY among the greatest achievements of Christian theology. They also contain some of the deepest and most daring biblical interpretation ever written. And throughout his works Barth challenges his readers to explore, test, and if possible improve on how he understands Scripture. Matthias Grebe has taken up this challenge.

Dr Grebe both appreciatively sounds the depths of Barth's doctrines of election (or predestination) and atonement (or reconciliation) and also perceptively examines biblical passages that are central to them. The result is a fascinating variation on Barth's understanding of salvation that is based on Dr Grebe's own fresh interpretation of Scripture.

Nor is that all. In chapter five he goes beyond his Cambridge doctoral dissertation, that I had the privilege of supervising, to extend his discussion by relating it to the Holy Spirit and to ordinary life. Here Barth's radical (and rather neglected) theology of the Holy Spirit is drawn upon to face squarely such difficult issues as human freedom and the possibility of salvation for all. The distinctiveness in being Christian lies, as in Barth, not in Christians being the only ones to be saved but in the specificity of the gift of the Spirit to them.

This is a book that immerses readers in good theology and invites them further and deeper into theological, biblical wisdom on some of the most demanding issues in Christian thought.

David F. Ford
Regius Professor of Divinity and Director
of the Cambridge Inter-faith Programme
Lent 2014

Preface

"Mache die Dinge so einfach wie möglich—aber nicht einfacher."
   Albert Einstein

"Es ist schwieriger eine vorgefasste Meinung zu zertrümmern, als ein Atom."
   Albert Einstein

TRADITION HAS IT THAT IN 1770 WHEN MOZART WAS FOURTEEN YEARS old, he went to Rome and listened to Allegri's *Miserere* in the Sistine Chapel during Holy Week. It was forbidden under threat of excommunication to make a copy of the papal music, but after the service the young Mozart was able to transcribe the piece entirely from memory.[1] Some time later, Mozart met Charles Burney, a British historian of music, who bought the manuscript from him and took it back to London. When the piece was published the following year, the Pope ordered the young musician to appear before him, but rather than excommunicating him, he praised him for his accomplishment.

Regardless of this story's historicity, and whether or not Mozart truly possessed an eidetic memory, this anecdote illuminates something of the task of the theologian. For a musician to hear a piece of music and transcribe it can be thought to be analogous to a theologian's 'hearing' the Word of God by reading Scripture and writing down the interpretation for teaching and preaching. Though these two tasks share certain outward similarities like transcription, they are also deeply divided by inner dissimilarities when it comes to the method of interpretation. Whereas it might be possible for a musical genius like Mozart to transcribe a piece of music accurately having only heard it once, the task of theology is a somewhat impossible, limited,

1. See Vetter, "Mozarts Nachschrift," 144–47.

and paradoxical one. Impossible, because the theologian is wrestling with Scripture, the subject matter of which is the transcendent God, and the task of theology is to interpret his self-revelation, which depends on God and is only possible *ubi et quando Deo visum est*. Limited, because the theologian is bound by certain restrictions. The Word of God is dynamic, constantly exceeding human capacities. Even if God chooses to unveil himself in Scripture, with our limited minds and our human words it is never fully possible to comprehend or encapsulate what we hear and read about God in his Word. Paradoxical, because, as Karl Barth famously said: "As ministers we ought to speak of God. We are human, however, so we cannot speak of God. We ought therefore to recognize both our obligation and our inability, and by that very recognition give God the glory."[2] Therefore, "all theological thought and utterance is *theologia viatorum* and thus 'broken' [*gebrochen*] and 'piece-work' [*Stückwerk*]."[3]

Furthermore, theology "has to be reapplied to the situation of the day if it is to give life."[4] It is not the words of the Bible that have changed but the situations in which they are heard. "Some may wish to repeat a past theology, but this is not possible. The context has changed, and what is actually communicated and understood today can be very far from the original meaning."[5] Therefore, every generation has to grapple anew with the great theological questions and re-interpret pivotal Christian doctrines. Unlike a musical transcription therefore, theology does not simply involve restating a received body of knowledge. It also needs to be re-contextualised for every generation and reconfigured through ever-new expressions across time. Thus every theologian must apply the Reformation principle of a return *ad fontes*—to the text—to avoid remaining in a static tradition and instead to continue the Church's dynamic message of Jesus Christ. Theology is a constant process of re-examination and re-engagement with Scripture.

As David Ford observes, it should be the purpose of basic theological Christian academic theology to describe the world in the light of a scripturally-informed picture of God that has been painted anew for every generation and culture.[6] Barth reminds us that we have to return constantly to Scripture because "critical scholarship of theology itself stands in constant

---

2. Barth, "The Word of God and the Task of Ministry," 186.

3. Barth, *Church Dogmatics* III/3, 294. Volumes of the *Church Dogmatics* will hereafter be cited as *CD*.

4. Hooker, *From Adam to Christ*, 10.

5. Ford, "Introduction to Modern Christian Theology," 1.

6. See Ford, "Epilogue," 761.

need of criticism, correction and reform."[7] Theology is not only an academic discipline, but, as Barth points out, "a function of the Church,"[8] providing ecclesiastical self-examination and interpretation of the Bible for the Church today. The continued life of the Church depends on her ability and willingness to "hear the voice of Scripture [. . .] and on whether Scripture compels the Church continually to return to it."[9]

However, if theology has an obligation to inform the Church, it appears to be falling short in its delineation of two crucial doctrines: election and the atonement. These two doctrines, which together Barth claims are the "sum of the Gospel,"[10] should unite Christians. But the dominant mainstream views on both election and the atonement split believers and have triggered bitter divisions, with parties questioning each other's commitment and even faith.

Furthermore, in order for theology to be life-giving there are two challenges for every 'new' theological idea explored and endorsed, particularly in the academy. First, academic theology is always at risk of being only fully understood within an academic setting. Thus the first challenge for theologians, if their ideas are to be useful and give life to the Church, is to ensure that those ideas are communicated as comprehensibly as possible. At the same time, it is vital to avoid the opposite error—that of oversimplifying simply to give quick answers to difficult questions.

Secondly, as Bruce Chilton warns, any "progress in theology is difficult to attain. One might imagine that one should build directly on the foundations of consensus, and extend our knowledge in that manner. But the foundation of theology is the study of texts, and the understanding of texts is prone to change. Theologians must therefore keep a wary eye on the foundations upon which they build, lest their castles be left in the air; every act of theological thinking should grow from the bottom up."[11]

The varied understandings of key texts can obstruct consensus in theology. And yet, theology is best done in conversation. When this dialogue does not take place, the stronghold of various doctrines and opinions (often safeguarded by a small minority who thereby position themselves as the 'gatekeepers of orthodoxy') becomes a difficult one to penetrate with new ideas. This has both positive and negative implications. Though it means that certain doctrines are retained and defended in order to maintain

7. *CD* IV/3, 881.
8. *CD* I/1, 3.
9. *CD* I/2, 691f.
10. *CD* II/2, 3.
11. Chilton, *Isaiah Targum*, xi.

orthodoxy, this might also mean that in some circles there is almost no scope for revision, correction, or challenge. Once a particular doctrine is perceived as being scripturally informed (and is thus widely embraced as 'orthodox'), it can become a pillar of a certain theological framework, even if the scriptural foundation is disputed. By this point, however, the doctrine might be established so strongly in the tradition that it eludes all challenge simply because such questioning is immediately interpreted as a direct attack on the integrity of Scripture. The result of this approach is that, within the particular tradition, self-examination, critical engagement with outside opinion, and genuine re-engagement with Scripture are sometimes forgotten. As we shall see, this has occurred with the doctrines of election and the atonement.

However, if we are to acknowledge, as Barth tells us, that all theological thought is *Stückwerk*, then theology would benefit from the example of the history of science. Einstein's new insights required him to leave some (though not all) of Newton's thoughts behind.[12] In order to achieve progress in theology, we need to remember that the key to understanding a hermeneutical circle may sometimes require leaving older, less accurate biblical interpretations behind.

Karl Barth was aware of the difficulties of attaining progress in theology as well as the reality that any life-giving theology needs to rest on a biblical foundation. When reading Scripture, he was confronted with a 'strange new world' which caused him to change his theological starting point to one focused on the text of the Bible itself. This new engagement with Scripture was therefore the main impetus behind Barth's reconstruction of the doctrine of election, and though Barth was aware that he had radically departed from his Reformed tradition and was criticized for his new approach, he felt that the authority of Scripture compelled him to do so.

Likewise, the following study, driven by that same authority, will also say *No* to certain prevailing understanding of the doctrines of election and atonement. The *No* that is uttered must ultimately be viewed as a positive *Yes* to a challenging but hopeful new perspective. As Karl Barth said when

12. For the paradigm shift in science and the implications *for* and impact *on* theology, particularly contemporary pneumatology, see Wolfgang Vondey, "The Holy Spirit and the Physical Universe." Vondey argues in the abstract of his article that "a methodological shift occurred in the sciences in the 20th century that has irreversible repercussions for a contemporary theology of the Holy Spirit. Newton and Einstein followed fundamentally different trajectories that provide radically dissimilar frameworks for the pneumatological endeavor. Pneumatology after Einstein is located in a different cosmological framework constituted by the notions of order, rationality, relationality, symmetry, and movement. These notions provide the immediate challenges to a contemporary understanding of the Spirit in the physical universe."

interviewed late in his life for a documentary: "Actually, by nature I'm not spoiling for a fight. [. . .] Someone who forcefully says 'yes' also needs to say 'no' with the same vigor."[13] It is important to emphasize, however, that the *Yes* that this present project offers does not intend to boastfully promote itself at the expense of others. Another prominent churchman has perfectly expressed the spirit in which this study is intended to be read when he wrote, "winning is a word not about succeeding so that other people lose, but about succeeding in connecting others with life-giving reality."[14]

It is by following Barth's example and applying the method exemplified in the *Church Dogmatics* that we can re-examine the doctrines of election and the atonement for a new generation and culture.

Matthias Grebe
Bonn, Lent 2014

---

13. Barth, *JA und NEIN–Karl Barth zum Gedächtnis*, video.
14. Williams, *Silence and Honey Cakes*, 32.

Acknowledgements

THIS BOOK WOULD NOT HAVE BEEN POSSIBLE WITHOUT THE GREAT ASSIStance of a number of individuals and institutions, all of which require special thanks and acknowledgement for their generosity, encouragement and kind support.

In a break with tradition (which for some reason nearly always places the author's spouse at the very end of a long list of acknowledgements) first and very much foremost I would like to thank my wife, Victoria. Her ceaseless encouragement and constructive criticism, and her indefatigable spirit and willingness to take risks have made me a better theologian, a better Christian and a better man. I must also say thank you to my parents, Wolfgang and Ellen Grebe, and to my parents-in-law, the Revd Andrew and Ann Corke—sources of endless inspiration, critique, love, prayer, and support both in and out of the academic process.

To my *Doktorvater*, Professor David Ford, I owe a special debt of gratitude. For his time, encouragement, and wise counsel I am exceedingly thankful. I will always be grateful that at the beginning stages of my doctoral studies he redirected me back to my early interest in the atonement, encouraged me to include more exegesis, and finally supervised a thesis that evolved in ways that neither of us could have anticipated. David's pedagogical method is almost Socratic—like a 'spiritual midwife' he has guided me through the labor pains of first finding my *Thesis* and finally giving birth to the *Überthese* (thesis of the thesis). In introducing me to Scriptural Reasoning, his contagious desire to remain in constant dialogue with the Scriptures has undoubtedly finessed the blending of systematic theology and exegesis in this work.

The book was written alongside training for ordination in the Church of England at Ridley Hall, Cambridge, where my pastoral tutors Revd Dr Philip Jenson and Revd Dr Paul Weston, and principal, Revd Canon Andrew Norman were a constant support. Revd Dr Mark Scarlata and Revd Dr Rob McDonald are two men of great faith, intellect, and friendship who served as a constant reminder that these qualities need not be opposed. The same is true of Revd Nabil Shehadi, to whom I am deeply grateful for letting me preach on the atonement during my placement at All Saints Church, Beirut, and for encouraging me to combine a life in the academy and in Church ministry. The community at St Barnabas Church, Cambridge, and particularly the great fellowship at Cluster 2, never let me forget that theology should be both informative and formative.

Indeed, it has often been said that it is outside the library that the 'real theology' occurs. This has manifestly been the case in Cambridge, and my gratitude is extended to members of the Ford Home Seminar and the community at Tyndale House for their willingness to engage with numerous contentious questions. Attending and delivering papers at the annual conferences of the Society for Biblical Literature and the Society for the Study of Theology has also allowed me to test out various ideas.

Some journeys go back much further than is initially obvious, and more people have contributed to this book than they know. Revd Fred Ritzhaupt first encouraged me to study theology and it was his sermons that taught me what it really means to be co-heirs of Christ and know God as *Abba*. During my time at Tübingen, Professor Bernd Janowski introduced me to the Old Testament cultic atonement and Professor Otfried Hofius taught me about how this became the background for the Pauline understanding of the death of Christ. Not only has their exegesis on the atonement manifestly influenced the content of a thesis on the cultic atonement, but their approach towards a *gesamtbiblische Theologie* also underlies the biblical hermeneutics of the cultic texts here. I was also fortunate enough during my studies to discuss my work with Professor Peter Stuhlmacher and Professor Hartmut Gese, who in some ways might be said to have started the Tübingen School of the atonement with his essays on biblical theology.

A number of people were instrumental in me coming over to Cambridge in 2007. Early plans to apply to Cambridge were fostered through a chance meeting with Revd Dr Greg Seach and Professor Tom Greggs at Tübingen. Thanks too to Professor Christoph Schwöbel and Dr Jens Adam for their support at this time. During my early years in Cambridge I was fortunate enough to have my MPhil dissertation supervised by Dr Simon Gathercole, and I would also like to thank Professor Sarah Coakley for her guidance during the first year of my doctoral studies

A major part of this research was undertaken during a semester at Princeton Theological Seminary in 2011, where I received a very warm welcome from Professor Iain Torrance and was able to mine the excellent library at the Center for Barth Studies. I benefited greatly from informal supervision by Professor Bruce McCormack and a lecture series on Barth (as well as numerous post-lecture chats) from Professor George Hunsinger, who also encouraged me to write about Barth's understanding of the cultic atonement. No list of acknowledgements of those inspiring individuals at PTS would be complete without my mentioning Ronald Chicken—conversation with this exceptional friend continues to be extremely formative.

In December 2011, it was my pleasure to introduce my formidable dialogue partners Dr Ashley Cocksworth and Dr Robert Leigh to 'Tübingen hospitality' when we visited Professors Eberhard Jüngel and Jürgen Moltmann and had an opportunity to discuss our work with both. Our earlier visit to the Barth-Archiv in Basel afforded us the chance to hear some firsthand anecdotes about Barth from Dr Hans-Anton Drewes, and our further correspondence has proved extremely fruitful. Not only was I able to look through the collection of Leviticus commentaries housed at the archive, but Dr Drewes kindly sent me various sections with Barth's own annotations.

Further sincere appreciation is reserved for those who assisted throughout the project. Dr Matthias Gockel's feedback and suggestions have been invaluable over the years. Michael Bigg and Revd Dr Mark Scarlata scrutinized various exegetical sections, and I am grateful to Dr Ashley Cocksworth, Revd Andrew Corke and Dr Richard McLauchlan for proofreading the entire piece. It need not be said that any remaining errors of style or content are entirely my own.

Financially, this research would not have been possible without the support of the Master and Fellows of Christ's College and the Faculty of Divinity in Cambridge, and particularly the trustees of the Levy-Plumb Fund for the Humanities and the Hedley-Lucas Fund. The Cambridge European Trust and the Kurt Hahn Trust (also at Cambridge), the Sarum St Michael Educational Charity and the Foundation of St Matthias, and the generosity of the former Bishop of Salisbury, Rt Revd David Stancliffe, also deserve special mention.

The conversion of my doctoral thesis into a final book manuscript would not have been possible without support from the DAAD, and during this stage I was also very fortunate to begin my post-doctoral research at the University of Bonn under Professor Andreas Pangritz. Final thanks to Pickwick Publications for accepting the title into their Princeton Theological Monograph Series, and especially to Dr Robin Parry for his exceptional editing eye.

Abbreviations

Works of Karl Barth

I/1	*Church Dogmatics*, vol. I, part 1 (Edinburgh: T. & T. Clark, 2nd ed., 1975)
I/2	*Church Dogmatics*, vol. I, part 2 (Edinburgh: T. & T. Clark, 1956)
II/1	*Church Dogmatics*, vol. II, part 1 (Edinburgh: T. & T. Clark, 1957)
II/2	*Church Dogmatics*, vol. II, part 2 (Edinburgh: T. & T. Clark, 1957)
III/1	*Church Dogmatics*, vol. III, part 1 (Edinburgh: T. & T. Clark, 1958)
III/2	*Church Dogmatics*, vol. III, part 2 (Edinburgh: T. & T. Clark, 1960)
III/3	*Church Dogmatics*, vol. III, part 3 (Edinburgh: T. & T. Clark, 1960)
III/4	*Church Dogmatics*, vol. III, part 4 (Edinburgh: T. & T. Clark, 1961)
IV/1	*Church Dogmatics*, vol. IV, part 1 (Edinburgh: T. & T. Clark, 1956)
IV/2	*Church Dogmatics*, vol. IV, part 2 (Edinburgh: T. & T. Clark, 1958)
IV/3	*Church Dogmatics*, vol. IV, part 3: first half (Edinburgh: T. & T. Clark, 1961) and vol. IV, part 3: second half (Edinburgh: T. & T. Clark, 1962)
IV/4	*Church Dogmatics*, vol. IV, part 4 (Edinburgh: T. & T. Clark, 1969)

CD	*Church Dogmatics.* Karl Barth. Translated by G. W. Bromiley and T. F. Torrance, 4 vols. Edinburgh: T. & T. Clark, 1956–75.
KD	*Die Kirchliche Dogmatik.* Karl Barth, 13 vols; München: Chr. Kaiser, 1932 and thereafter Zürich: EVZ, 1938–65. Individual volume abbreviations as above.

Others

AUSS	Andrews University Seminary Studies
CCEL	Christian Classics Etherial Library
CNTC	*Calvin's New Testament Commentaries.* 12 vols. Edited by D. W. Torrance and T. F. Torrance. Grand Rapids: Eerdmans, 1959–72.
CO	*Ioannis Calvini Opera quae supersunt Omnia.* 59 vols. Edited by Wilhelm Braum, Edward Cunitz and Edward Reuss. Corpus Reformatorum: vols 29–87; Brunswick: C. A. Schwetchke and Son, 1863–1900.
DOTP	*Dictionary of the Old Testament: Pentateuch.* Edited by T. Desmond Alexander and David W. Baker. Downers Grove, IL: InterVarsity, 2002.
DTIB	*Dictionary for Theological Interpretation of the Bible.* Edited by Kevin J. Vanhoozer et al. Grand Rapids: Baker Academic, 2005.
EKK	Evangelisch-Katholischer Kommentar zum Neuen Testament
EncChr	*The Encyclopedia of Christianity.* Volume 1: A–D. Edited by Erwin Fahlbusch et al. Eerdmans: Grand Rapids, 1999.
HSCP	Harvard Studies in Classical Philology
HThR	*Harvard Theological Review*
IJST	*International Journal of Systematic Theology*
Inst.	John Calvin, *Institutes of the Christian Religion.* 2 vols. Edited by John T. McNeill. Translated by Ford Lewis Battles. Philadelphia: Westminster, 1960.
JAOS	*Journal of the American Oriental Society*
JBL	*Journal of Biblical Literature*
JR	*The Journal of Religion*
JRTh	*Journal of Reformed Theology*

JSJ	*Journal for the Study of Judaism in the Persian, Hellenistic and Roman period*
JSOT	*Journal for the Study of the Old Testament*
JThS	*The Journal of Theological Studies*
NIDOTTE	*New International Dictionary of Old Testament Theology and Exegesis*. 5 vols. Edited by William A. VanGemeren. Grand Rapids: Zondervan, 1997.
NIGTC	New International Greek Testament Commentary
NTS	New Testament Studies
NZSTh	*Neue Zeitschrift für Systematische Theologie und Religionsphilosophie*
PTR	*The Princeton Theological Review*
SJTh	*Scottish Journal of Theology*
SP	Sacra Pagina
SPCK	Society for Promoting Christian Knowledge
TDNT	*Theological Dictionary of the New Testament*. 10 vols. Edited Gerhard Kittel and Gerhard Friedrich. Translaed by Geoffrey W. Bromiley. Grand Rapids: Eerdmans, 1964–76.
TDOT	*Theological Dictionary of the Old Testament*. 15 vols. Edited by G. Johannes Botterweck and Helmer Ringgren. Translated by David E. Green and Douglas W. Grand Rapids: Eerdmans, 1975–2011.
TLOT	*Theological Lexicon of the Old Testament*. 3 vols. Edited by Ernst Jenni and Klaus Westermann. Translated by Mark E. Biddle. Peabody, MA: Hendrickson, 1997.
TRE	*Theologische Realenzyklopädie*. 36 vols. Edited by Gerhard Krause and Gerhard Müller. Berlin: De Gruyter, 1976–2004.
WBC	Word Biblical Commentary
WMANT	Wissenschaftliche Monographien zum Alten und Neuen Testament
WUANT	Wissenschaftliche Untersuchungen zum Alten und Neuen Testament
WUNT	Wissenschaftliche Untersuchungen zum Neuen Testament
VT	*Vetus Testamentum*
ZAW	*Zeitschrift für die Alttestamentliche Wissenschaft*
ZDTh	*Zeitschrift für dialektische Theologie*

Introduction

Then beginning with Moses and all the prophets, he interpreted to them the things about himself in all the Scriptures.
   (Luke 24:27)

THE RELATIONSHIP BETWEEN THE DOCTRINES OF ELECTION AND ATONEment is key to understanding the Christian faith, and the person and saving work of Jesus Christ. However, despite their centrality, these doctrines are not undisputed in the history of the Church, nor is there a unanimous view regarding the Church's teaching of them.

1. The Pastoral Motivations of this Study and the Nature of the Problem

The teaching and preaching of the cross has always played a central role in the life and growth of the Church. The question 'Am I one of the elect?' strikes at the heart of the issue of personal salvation and captures the essence of what is means to be a human being made in the image of God. However, when it comes to the issues of *how* Jesus achieved salvation and *who* gains from his death ('Who did Christ die for?') believers disagree amongst themselves, as do academics. Questions such as 'What do these doctrines say?' 'What is their biblical justification?' 'What is their relationship?' and 'What do they mean to me?' are often raised by scholars, clergy, and laity alike.

The doctrine of election (or rather, the concept of predestination) has always been a point of disagreement in the history of the Church from the Reformation onwards. Those who espouse a limited atonement must wrestle with the implication of the Calvinist theory of double predestination, that a God who loves all humankind predestines some of his creatures to hell. On the other hand, those who espouse a universal atonement must explain the apparently clear statements by Jesus in the Gospels that, for some, hell and the "gnashing of teeth"[1] will be a reality.

These two ways of viewing the doctrine of election are linked with two particular views on the atonement: rather than asking 'Why or for whom did Jesus die?' a more specific question is raised—'Did Jesus die for the sins of the entire world or only for the sins of certain chosen individuals?' This is the question of universal or limited atonement. The questions of election and atonement thus seem to be very closely related to each other and are in fact interdependent.

The doctrine of double predestination is linked with limited atonement and the doctrine of universal election with universal salvation (universalism). The argument is as follows: if Christ died for the sins of the entire world then it logically follows that all people must be saved. Many people seem to be content with this answer. God loves the whole world—the Bible even indicates that God wants all to be saved (see 1 Tim 2:4). So, if God loves the whole world, Christ must surely have died for the sins of the whole world and hence all are saved. Others, however, question this, saying that this is not in accord with the New Testament account of the afterlife. Since, they argue, the Bible clearly talks about a punishment of the sinner in hell, then Christ can only have died for the sins of the elect. Only those people who were predestined for heaven are the ones for whom Jesus bore the sins on the cross. Otherwise the cross would be rendered insufficient (because, as they argue, some people do go to hell) and the logical conclusion of this would be that God wanted to save all people but was defeated in his objective, which seems an absurd proposition. They therefore argue for a 'limited atonement,' a doctrine that explains that on the cross Christ bore the sins only of the elect. In this way they try to safeguard the 100 percent effectiveness of the cross. They argue that although this does not indicate any limitation of the infinite value and power of Christ's atonement, nevertheless "while the value of the atonement was sufficient to save all mankind, it was efficient to save only the elect."[2] All the sins Jesus bore were for those who would definitely go to heaven and thus none of his sin bearing was in vain.

2. The Task of the Study

This book is tasked with resolving the logical problem of the relationship between election and atonement. In doing so, three principal themes will

---

1. Matt 8:12; 13:42; 13:50; 22:13; 24:51; 25:30 and Luke 13:28.
2. Boettner, *The Reformed Doctrine of Predestination*, 152.

emerge: (1) sin bearing; (2) the relationship between God's being *ad intra* and God's works *ad extra* (the relationship between the immanent and economic Trinity); and (3) divine sovereignty and human responsibility.

1. Those understandings of election and atonement that advance double predestination or universalism would benefit from a fresh exegesis on cultic Old Testament texts. I seek to demonstrate that these understandings both rest on a false premise, that is, a wrong understanding of sin bearing. Following Barth's typological approach but not his conclusions, it will be shown that Christ did not bear sins in the way the Azazel-goat did (by bearing them upon itself and thus taking divine punishment). Instead, we will see that Christ was a sin offering and did not, therefore, bear sin on the cross. This understanding will offer a doctrine of universal atonement that frees the doctrine of limited atonement from its otherwise logical conclusion, that some of the sins that Christ bore on the cross were borne in vain. I will show that it is possible to argue for a universal atonement (Christ died for the entire world) without it logically having to conclude with a universal salvation (not all are saved) and that it is possible to take seriously the passages about God desiring all of humanity to be saved without rejecting the passages about the judgment upon sinners.

2. The dissatisfaction many people have with certain atonement models raises questions such as 'How can a loving God pour out his wrath upon the sinless Jesus?' and 'How can a loving Father punish his Son?' In the Gospel of John, Jesus says, "Whoever has seen me has seen the Father" (John 14:9). If Jesus in *person* reveals the Father then his *actions* must unveil the being-in-act of the veiled God. Therefore, the immanent and economic Trinity must be congruent, and God's being *ad intra* must match his works *ad extra*. This raises the questions of how we should interpret the death of Jesus in history and what this reveals about the nature of God. This book asks how God is being revealed through his being and actions and will demonstrate that the death of Jesus on the cross must be seen as God's most loving act. It is on the cross that the love of the Father for humanity is most fully revealed as that of the *Deus pro nobis*.

3. My re-examination of the relationship between election and atonement, in relation to Christ's obedience and suffering and his cross and resurrection,[3] seeks to emphasize both divine sovereignty and human

---

3. Richard McLauchlan, "Poems from Holy Saturday," writes "that any account of the Christian narrative that cancels or forgets the suffering of the Passion is a false one," 96. He highlights the importance of Holy Saturday as a vantage point from which these sufferings may be appropriately viewed. Drawing on the work of Alan E. Lewis, McLauchlan claims that any account of the Christian three day Passion narrative, which is too keen to read the story solely from the perspective of Easter Sunday runs

responsibility. This examination looks to avoid falling into the extremes of either limited atonement or universalism. By distinguishing between a penultimate and ultimate Word of God, one risks creating another kind of a *Deus absconditus*, which is what Karl Barth so fervently tried to avoid and correct in his reading of Calvin. Though God has to have the final word in salvation, I shall seek to show that the final decision over humanity is seen on the cross, in the *Deus revelatus*. God is love, and human responsibility demands a corresponding human decision in faith and obedience, to accept the offer achieved by Christ in order to participate in the triune God by the mediated presence of the Spirit.

3. The Method of Study

Our primary dialogue partner in this book is Karl Barth. Although not always agreeing with Barth and at places challenging some of his biblical interpretations, this book engages with his *Church Dogmatics* (hereafter *CD*) in order to reflect on the doctrines of election and atonement. It looks at how these doctrines appear in the *CD* and examines them systematically and exegetically. For Barth, the doctrine of election is the "sum of the Gospel"—it reveals God's love for humanity and in this way, reveals *who* God is.[4] In addition, the doctrine of atonement tells us *what* God does, the outcome of God's love for humanity, since "in his works He is Himself revealed as the One He is."[5] What Barth is essentially describing is the unity of Christ's person (being) and work (activity) and he therefore sees the doctrines of election and atonement as intimately related.

Barth's re-working of the doctrine of election is considered to be one of the most important innovations in twentieth-century theology. However, as Bruce McCormack has argued, in Barth's theology the doctrine of election has replaced the traditional Protestant notion of double imputation and because of this, forensicism has become "the frame of reference that

---

the risk of a 'cheap triumphalism' which neglects the terrible events which preceded this day of joy. Although Christ's suffering is central to the doctrine of atonement in this study, I have chosen to highlight the relation between the doctrines of election and atonement, focusing in on the cross and resurrection. However, we ought not to forget the importance of the silent second day of the Christian *Triduum*, and the reader should keep this in mind as we proceed through this study. For further insights on this important day between these two events see von Balthasar, *The Glory of the Lord Vol. VII*, esp. pp. 228–35; *The Von Balthasar Reader*, esp. pp. 148ff; and *Mysterium Paschale*, esp. ch. 4, and Lewis, *Between Cross and Resurrection*.

4. *CD* II/2, 3.
5. *CD* II/1, 260.

is basic to the whole of his soteriology."[6] Barth's doctrine of the atonement (expressed predominantly through judicial terminology) is therefore more forensic than the traditional understanding due to the character and role of his doctrine of election. Barth was responsible for initiating a unique christological revision in theology and his *CD* opened up a new understanding of the doctrine of election, avoiding the dilemma of the 'horrible decree' of God selecting some people for heaven and others for hell. Nevertheless, I seek to show that Barth did not draw some of the implications of his ideas about election and atonement through to their logical conclusions.

Barth understands exegesis to be superordinate [*vorgeordnet*] to dogmatics and he therefore emphasizes that "*die Exegese, die Norm ist für die Dogmatik.*"[7] This study is grounded in Barth's own insistence that "*Dogmatik daher beständig durch die Exegese zu korrigieren* [*ist*]"[8] and takes up Barth's challenge in the small-print of §35.2, where he encourages his readers to test his systematic thought through a close engagement with his exegesis rather than simply criticizing his doctrinal claims.[9] I will argue that Barth's version of forensicism creates a number of problems. This book will deal with these problems with particular reference to *CD* II/2 and *CD* IV/1, and offer an alternative exegesis of cultic texts (Lev 14 and 16) to test Barth's claims. While many commentators acknowledge Barth's innovation in this area, few have attempted to offer a correction "from within" Barth by using his own method.[10] This book aims to build upon Barth's method and apply a 'correction' to some of his thought, working through and moving beyond Barth. These exegetical adjustments to his doctrine of atonement will be predominately developed with the help of the atonement theory of the Tübingen School and the interpretation of Jewish scholars of these cultic texts. This re-working of Barth's thought will seek to demonstrate that the 'sum of the Gospel' does not merely comprise the doctrine of election but requires election to be taken *together* with the doctrine of atonement; both doctrines communicate that from eternity and in history God is the loving *deus pro nobis*.

Barth's *CD* has been compared to a musical composition resting on the *leitmotif* of the story of the God-man Jesus Christ and the covenantal fellowship between God and humanity in and through his atoning work on the cross. Hans Urs von Balthasar famously likened Karl Barth's entire *CD* to

6. McCormack, "Justitia Aliena," 192.
7. Barth, "II. Dogmatik und Exegese," 153.
8. Ibid.
9. See *CD* II/2, 366.
10. Ford, *Barth and God's Story*, 93.

a theological symphony.[11] Mirroring much eighteenth-century symphonic structure, the *Church Dogmatics* is permeated by the binary of God's *Yes* and God's *No*. In fact, Barth's entire doctrine of election can be seen to follow a sonata form of introduction, exposition, development and recapitulation:[12] §32 introduces the doctrine of election; §33 gives an exposition of the basic theme and content of the doctrine in a binary structure, election (Dur/major) and rejection (Moll/minor) in Jesus Christ; §34 develops this further with the help of new examples (Israel and Church); and §35 recapitulates this in the light of what has already been said about the binary theme of election and rejection with regards the individual. Where the composer uses "counterpoint, changes in harmony, key, rhythm to keep the movement interesting, the theological composer uses references to the same theme in older treatments, arguments with contemporaries, surprising implications, ethical consequences, all to the same end, developing the themes while sustaining interest."[13] This is particularly evident in the exegetical small-print of §34 and §35. Barth's doctrine of reconciliation shows a similar binary structure, though this might initially seem elusive due to the length and detail of the section in the *CD* dealing with this. §57–58 introduce the doctrine; §59–63 (*CD* IV/1) and §64–68 (*CD* IV/2) represent a long section in which exposition (humiliation and exaltation) and development (Holy Spirit and the community) are intertwined; and finally §69–73 (*CD* IV/3) brings together and recapitulates the basic themes of humiliation and exaltation from the middle perspective of the Mediator, united in Jesus Christ.

Like Schubert's eighth symphony, however, Barth's *CD* remains 'unfinished': at Barth's death only a fragment of *CD* IV/4 had been published and the planned final volume on redemption was never written.[14] One might suppose that these musical parallels in structure and thematic development might be accidental. However, Barth's love for classical music, in particular Mozart, is well documented, and a portrait of the Austrian composer still hangs in his study at the same level as a portrait of the Genevan theologian, Calvin. Von Balthasar suggests that not only was Mozart's music beloved by Barth, but that it also informed his theology and shaped the style of the *CD*. "One will do well to keep in mind Mozart's melodies while reading Barth's *Dogmatics* and Mozart's basic style when searching for Barth's basic intention. It is in this way that one should read, for example, those pieces

---

11. See von Balthasar, *The Theology of Karl Barth*, 59.
12. See Stoltzfus, *Theology as Performance*, 112.
13. Gill, "Barth and Mozart," 409.
14. See *CD* IV/4, Preface.

that seem like the powerful finale of a symphony: the end of Barth's doctrine of election."[15]

4. An Outline of the Study

As mentioned earlier, the overall task of this book is to give an exposition of Barth's doctrines of election and atonement and to investigate the systematic implications of his exegetical justification of the doctrines, focusing particular attention on Barth's typological exegesis. I shall challenge Barth's exegesis and seek to show that (in contrast to Barth) a cultic rather than a forensic interpretation should be emphasized when looking at the death of Christ. The structure of the argument has a circular (or rather a chiastic) movement, taking the reader from God's being in eternity to his action in history, and back to eternity. It is divided into five chapters:

Chapter 1 begins by highlighting the important influence of Pierre Maury on Barth's thinking on election, a christocentric approach which Barth incorporates into his 'system,' making it part of his own theological method. After dealing with the pastoral concerns about election in the theologies of the sixteenth and seventeenth centuries, the personal questions of salvation and Barth's negation of a *decretum absolutum*, the chapter then shows how Barth has relocated the doctrine of election within the doctrine of God, highlighting his actualistic ontology. Before giving an exposition of Barth's doctrine of election, we discuss the basis of the doctrine, God's self-revelation in Jesus Christ. There follows an examination of Barth's use and radical transformation of Calvin's doctrine of double predestination in *CD* II/2. Barth's christological shift is to make Jesus both the electing God and the elected human being, the subject as well as the object of election. This exemplifies the binary structure seen in God's *Yes* and *No*, the positive election and negative rejection on the cross, and reveals the underlying question of this book: whether Jesus can be both the elect and rejected of God. The implications of Barth's view of election, and further criticism of this view, will be discussed and answered in the subsequent chapters. The following section gives an exposition of Barth's typological exegesis of the cultic texts of Leviticus 14 and 16 found in the small-print of §35, and emphasizes that Barth's exegesis—in which he identifies all four animals as a type of Christ, symbolizing his election and rejection—is in line with the exegesis of some of the Church Fathers. The chapter ends with Barth's challenge to the reader to surpass his argument.

---

15. Von Balthasar, *The Theology of Karl Barth*, 28.

Chapter 2 takes up Barth's exegetical challenge and applies it to his doctrine of election, proposing a correction from within using Barth's own methodology, thus correcting Barth with Barth. Here the concept of *Existenzstellvertretung* (a vicarious offering of one's life as an equivalent substitution for the forfeited life of another) is used as a paradigm to explain the significance of cultic atonement and to provide a plumb line to assist us in our engagement with Barth. After looking at the verb *kipper*, the sacrificial rites, the role of the blood and the Day of Atonement in which the various rituals converge, the notion of sin removal is explicated. Our conclusion is that it is not the first goat, the sin offering (*ḥaṭṭā't*), that bears sin, but only the second goat (for Azazel) that bears the iniquities of Israel into the wilderness. Chapter 2 then revisits Barth's typological exegesis and gives an explanation as to why Jesus should only be identified with the first goat, the sin offering, and therefore should be seen solely as the elect and not the rejected. We will see that this has further implications for Barth's dialectical method.

Chapter 3 discusses themes that arise in *CD* III—the covenant, humanity and *das Nichtige*—and uses them as three lenses to focus our investigation upon specific questions. The covenant is discussed because chapter 4 will argue that the goal of the atonement is the re-establishing of the covenantal fellowship with God, and thus it will challenge the notion of Jesus being a covenant-breaker. An examination of Barth's treatment of humanity is important because this will address questions raised in previous chapters regarding Christ's human nature in relation to humanity's human nature. It will also help to understand the death of Christ with regard to his hypostatic union, which will be discussed in chapter 4. In §50, where Barth deals with *das Nichtige*, we read about Barth's ontology, of being and non-being, and the dialectic of *Yes* and *No*. Here Barth gives further insights into his understanding of the negative aspect of election, the cross. All the material discussed and all the questions raised in this chapter will be considered in the next. However, rather than taking these questions consecutively, they will there be used as focal points to challenge Barth's view of atonement.

Chapter 4 begins with a short exposition of the view of the atonement taken by the early Church and an evaluation of the *Christus Victor* and Christ as Victim models. It then highlights Barth's Reformed background to the doctrine of atonement and identifies some problematic aspects in Calvin's view of this doctrine. Next, Barth's doctrine of the atonement in *CD* IV/1, including his understanding of the Anselmian question *Cur Deus Homo?*, is expounded with special emphasis on §59.2 'The Judge Judged in Our Place.' We will discuss the forensic fourfold *pro nobis* (including Barth's small-print, where he spells out his ideas on this topic in cultic terms). Our conclusion will be that a cultic understanding of the atonement should be preferred over a forensic one. After a section on the accurate understanding of sin and sin removal, in which we conclude that Jesus did not *bear* sin, but conquered it on the cross, the last section of chapter 4 contrasts Barth's view of the atonement with the concept of *Existenzstellvertretung*; I seek to show that 2 Corinthians 5:21 is in fact not "unbearable," as Barth claims, but that Christ's death on the cross reveals not only that God is love, but also that God's action is love. Hence our conclusion is that Jesus is not punished on the cross by bearing sin and enduring the wrath of the Father, but that as the active Judge he himself condemns sin in the flesh. Therefore the atonement should not be seen as a punishment or abandonment of the Son by the Father, but as a Trinitarian event in which Father and Son, rather than being opposed to one another, work perichoretically together for the salvation of humanity.

Chapter 5 finishes with concluding thoughts on the doctrines of election and atonement and the Holy Spirit's role in Christ's saving work on the cross. Since the outcome of our exegesis is that Jesus is only the elect and not the rejected, we will discuss the questions of rejection and *apokatastasis* at the end of the book, together with the pastoral implications of Barth's risking the creation of a new *Deus absconditus*. Furthermore, we will discuss the relationship between the notion of bearing sin and the Spirit's role in the atonement, and how humanity is given a new immortal resurrection body to fellowship with God. The work of the previous chapters highlighted the fact that God has spoken only a *Yes* over Jesus Christ, the only true elect, and that rejection is spoken against sin *through* Christ (and we therefore concluded that Christ does not bear sin). The final section of chapter 5 will then explore the consequences of those who do not make a corresponding human decision by faith and accept Christ's saving work but reject the objective work of Christ. The questions that we are seeking to answer are: how does humanity participate in the subjective work of the eternal Spirit, and which individuals are involved in this?

The conclusion will seek to demonstrate that since Jesus Christ is not the passive 'Judge Judged in Our Place' but the active 'Judge Judging' sin and thus rejection is not the Father's *No* over against the Son, but the *No* of the Father through the obedient Son against sin, that this understanding gives a fuller Trinitarian understanding of the atonement, more in harmony with the understanding of a corresponding work of immanent and economic Trinity.

I

Election, Rejection, and Exegesis

For he chose us in him before the creation of the world to be holy and blameless in his sight. In love he predestined us to be adopted as his sons through Jesus Christ.
   (Eph 1:4–5)

Introduction

THE DOCTRINE OF THE ELECTION OF GRACE IS THE KEY TO KARL BARTH'S *Church Dogmatics*,[1] indeed the key to his entire theology.[2] According to Gloege, most of the elements of the later doctrine of election are already present in the second edition of the *Römerbrief*, ready to be used "like dynamite that only requires a fuse."[3] Gockel[4] investigates Barth's christological revolution of the doctrine of election,[5] which took place between 1936 and 1942[6] and shows that Barth's 'second' and 'decisive revision' of the doctrine was sparked off in June 1936. Barth heard a lecture on 'Election and Faith,'[7] given by the French pastor Pierre Maury during the *Congrès international de théologie calviniste* in Geneva.[8] Maury's impact was "quickly

---

1. *CD* II/2, 1–506.
2. See Gloege, "Zur Prädestinationslehre Karl Barths," 78.
3. Ibid., 80.
4. Gockel, *Barth and Schleiermacher*, 158–97.
5. For the revision in the doctrine of election see also Gloege, "Zur Prädestinationslehre Karl Barths," 78–85.
6. Gockel, *Barth and Schleiermacher*, 158–64.
7. Maury, "Election et foi."
8. See Maury, *Prädestination*, 15–16 and McCormack, *Karl Barth's Critically*

registered in Barth's lectures in Debrechen, Hungary (September 1936),"[9] and the central point of Barth's christological revision, "the correlation of election and reprobation with the crucifixion of Jesus,"[10] appears for the first time in *Gottes Gnadenwahl* (1936): "God's decision, as it has been made once and for all in Jesus Christ, is our life's predestination."[11] This was the "germ cell"[12] for his later exposition of the doctrine, as one commentator has called it. McCormack comments that "[t]hese lectures set forth the basic viewpoints which would govern the massive treatment of the theme of election in *Church Dogmatics* II/2."[13] One year later, Barth also referred to the christological centring of the doctrine and the thesis that God "actively chose to take on Himself reprobation and condemnation"[14] in his Gifford Lectures (1937) at the University of Aberdeen, where he discussed the Scots Confession.[15]

We first encounter Barth's original and widely influential ideas on election in chapter 7 (§§32-35) of the *CD*, the opening chapter of II/2, *The Election of God*. What Barth does in *CD* II/2 is to formulate a christocentric doctrine of election, wholly in terms of the person of Jesus Christ,[16] which in turn leads to a critique of the Calvinist model of election with a *decretum absolutum*[17] and a polemic against the idea of a *Deus absconditus*.[18] McCormack comments that "[w]hen the history of theology in the twentieth century is written [. . .] I am confident that the greatest contribution of Karl Barth to the development of church doctrine will be located in his doctrine of election."[19] The locus of my argument in chapter 1 will be §§32-35 on the doctrine of election and in particular the election of the individual in §35, *CD* II/2, in which Barth argues that Christ is both the elect and the rejected.[20]

Realistic Dialectical Theology, 455.

9. Gibson, *Reading the Decree*, 25.

10. Gockel, *Barth and Schleiermacher*, 202.

11. Barth, *Gottes Gnadenwahl*, 26.

12. See Stoevesandt, "Karl Barths Erwählungslehre," 110.

13. McCormack, *Karl Barth's Critically Realistic Dialectical Theology*, 458.

14. Gockel, *Barth and Schleiermacher*, 202.

15. See Barth, "Gottes Entscheidung und des Menschen Erwählung," 94-103.

16. On the right understanding of christocentrism in Barth's theology see McCormack, *Karl Barth's Critically Realistic Dialectical Theology*, 453-55.

17. See Maury, *Prädestination*, 9. For a concise outline of Calvin's doctrine of election see Nimmo, "Election and Evangelical Thinking," 29-31.

18. See Jones, *The Humanity of Christ*, 78.

19. McCormack, "Grace and Being," 92.

20. See *CD* II/2, 306-506. For the subsection 2. 'The Elect and the Rejected' of §35

Barth reaches this conclusion in the course of his challenge to the Reformers' views of predestination and their elaboration of a doctrine of an abstract Christ—a doctrine that Barth sees as ultimately non-christocentric. In looking at John 1:1f. and employing Calvin's concept of double predestination,[21] Barth observes a coexistence of both rejection and election in the person of Jesus,[22] who is fully divine (this aspect dealing with the condemnation on the cross) and fully human (exalted into community with the Triune God); both elector and elect.

Thus, the teleological view of election and reprobation is preserved and given a new focus in Jesus Christ.[23] The definition of the second and final revision of Barth's doctrine of election is a location of the gracious choice in Jesus Christ, and a uniting of the dialectical *Yes* and *No*, election and reprobation, in him.[24] Barth revises the Reformed concept of double predestination, going beyond the binary of Calvin's two groups of elected and rejected[25] and makes Jesus Christ the single reprobate.[26] Thus, it is Jesus who is the rejected one,[27] and in his rejection sinful humanity is thereby elected so that no human being is any longer the object of divine condemnation and reprobation.

This chapter will challenge this view. In fact, the underlying question investigated in this book is whether Jesus can be simultaneously both the elect as well as the reprobate. The first part of this chapter will outline and investigate Barth's doctrine of election as it appears in *CD* II/2 and highlight the binary structure of election and rejection in Christ. The second part of the chapter will give an exposition of one small-print exegesis of Barth's in §35, a typological reading of Leviticus 14 and 16,[28] texts which are part of

---

see pp. 340–409.

21. Calvin writes "we say that God once established by his eternal and unchangeable plan those whom he long before determined once and for all to receive into salvation, and those whom, on the other hand, he would devote to destruction," in *Inst.* III. xxi.7, 931.

22. See Maury, *Prädestination*, 16.

23. See Goebel, *Vom freien Wählen Gottes und des Menschen*, 30. Goebel writes that the doctrine of election has a "teleologische Ordnung: die Erwählung des Menschen zum Leben ist das Ziel der Erwählung des Sohnes Gottes zum Tode am Kreuz," 30.

24. See Gockel, *Barth and Schleiermacher*, 203.

25. See *Inst.* III.xxi.5–6, 926–30 and III.xxii.11, 946f.

26. See Gockel, *Barth and Schleiermacher*, 205.

27. See Maury, *Prädestination*, 33.

28. See *CD* II/2, 357–66.

Barth's exegetical backbone for his dogmatic reflection in the large-print of the doctrine of election.[29]

1. The Pastoral Concern with Election

In the sixteenth and seventeenth centuries the question that dominated the debate on election was the human dilemma about personal assurance of salvation and the individual's relationship with God.[30] The dispute between Lutheran and Reformed theologians was left unresolved.[31] For the Reformers, and particularly Calvin, the doctrine played a significant role when confronted by pastoral questions concerning salvation, such as 'How can I be sure about my salvation?'; 'How do I know that I am saved?'; 'How do I know that God loves me and that I am not a child of wrath?' For Calvin, the doctrine of election highlighted God's divine grace as revealed in Jesus Christ.[32] He "gravitated toward an understanding of predestination as the focal point of soteriology,"[33] and insisted that individuals should put their trust solely in the salvific work of Christ. Thus, contrary to the general perception, Calvin's approach to the doctrine of election arose from a desire to comfort believers confronting crises in their personal faith and troubled with questions about personal assurance of salvation.[34] "The fact that [. . .] the firmness of our election is joined to our calling is another means of establishing our assurance. For those whom Christ has illumined with the

---

29. "In Barth, there is a sense in which the relationship between exegesis and doctrine is more straightforward to navigate. The *Church Dogmatics* presents small-print exegesis and large-print historical-dogmatic reflection side by side, so that Barth's hermeneutical approach is often on display either close at hand or by wider reading in the *Dogmatics*," in Gibson, *Reading the Decree*, 25.

30. "Barth hat in seiner Erwählungslehre Bezug genommen auf die reformierte Kontroverse des 17. Jahrhunderts zwischen Infra- und Supralapsarismus über die 'Frage nach dem obiectum praedestinationis' (136.157) und dabei der supralapsaristischen Auskunft, der erwählte Mensch sei der homo creabilis et labilis 'das *relativ* größere Recht' (150) zugebilligt gegenüber der infralapsaristischen Mehrheitsmeinung von Dordrecht, die besagte: obiectum praestinationis sei der homo creatus et lapsus," in Goebel, *Vom freien Wählen Gottes und des Menschen*, 36. See also *CD* §33, 127–43.

31. See here Kreck, *Grundentscheidungen in Karl Barths Dogmatik*, 189.

32. Calvin writes "We assert that, with respect to the elect, this plan was founded upon his [God's] freely given mercy, without regard to human worth," in *Inst*. III.xxi.7, 931.

33. Muller, *Christ the Decree*, 23.

34. See here Hays: "No one can say that Calvin's heart is not in the right place. [. . .] Calvin himself seems to mourn the necessity of this 'dreadful decree,'" in Hays, "Blessed be Egypt my people," 30.

knowledge of his name and introduced into the bosom of his church, he is said to receive into his care and keeping."[35] Thus, for Calvin, election "is irreducibly connected to soteriology and its pastoral comfort in the life of the believer."[36]

Yet the pastoral problem with Calvin's doctrine was (and continues to be) that it "often failed to provide the very comfort it promised"[37] and instead made believers even more uncertain about their salvation. Furthermore, this view could represent a loving God as a malicious tyrant who seems arbitrarily to choose some to be saved and others to be damned.[38] As a Reformed theologian, Barth recognizes the importance of the doctrine of predestination but is also aware of the difficulties it raised—the disconnect between the pastoral intent of the doctrine to comfort and the way it functioned in practice, its outcome and impact on believers. Barth believed he had rediscovered the positive force that the doctrine of election could have when understood correctly. He takes an idea that for many had come to appear arbitrary and examines it fully in light of Scripture, pointing out that it did not refer to God's arbitrary choice of individuals, but instead to his divine grace revealed in Jesus Christ. Barth's view of predestination is that it was intended to emphasise God's eternal decision to be gracious towards humanity and above all that it reveals that God loves humanity and that God is love. Barth's revolution in the doctrine of election in Reformed thought is to "replace Calvin's version of double predestination with a universal election."[39]

Although drawing on "Calvin and the subsequent Reformed tradition"[40] (and hence also on Augustine),[41] Barth re-examines Scripture and sheds new light on the doctrine of election, radically transforming it. He sees Christ not simply as a "mirror"[42] [*speculum*] of human election as

35. *Inst.* III.xxiv.6, 971.
36. Gibson, *Reading the Decree*, 170.
37. Mangina, *Theologian of Christian Witness*, 68.
38. See Hays who writes that Calvin adopted double predestination to "answer the question *Why when the gospel is preached, do some believe and others not?*" in Hays, "Blessed be Egypt my people," 30.
39. McCormack, "Grace and Being," 93.
40. Nimmo, "Election and Evangelical Thinking," 31.
41. Gunton writes that "Calvin's doctrine of election is materially the same as Augustine, Anselm and Aquinas," in Gunton, *The Barth Lectures*, 112.
42. *Inst.* III.xxiv.5, 970. Calvin writes that "in him, as in a mirror (*speculo*), we may behold God's fatherly love towards us all, since he is not loved separately, or for his own private advantage, but that he may unite us along with himself to the Father," in *Comm. John* (*CNTC*, vol. 5, 97); *CO* 47, 342. Furthermore, Gibson explains that

advocated by Augustine and Calvin[43] (which Barth argues would make Jesus an "instrument,"[44] independent and separate from the divine primordial decision [*Urentscheidung*][45] to be the *Deus pro nobis*) but also as the basis (the means as well as the content) of the whole doctrine. The concept of Christ being the 'mirror' of election was not enough for Barth to deal with the troublesome implication of Calvin's view,[46] namely to give an answer to the question of assurance of salvation ('How can a person know that he or she is among God's elect?').

Barth's doctrine of election removes any possibility of Jesus Christ not being involved in God's decision and precludes any decree that bypasses Jesus Christ, a *decretum horribile*: "The decree of God is not obscure, but clear. [. . .] This decree is Jesus Christ, and for this very reason it cannot be a *decretum absolutum*."[47] Thus the election of Jesus Christ leaves no room for uncertainty or a hidden mysterious decree of God to elect some and condemn others—there is no *decretum absolutum* besides Jesus Christ, who is the ultimate *decretum concretum*.[48] According to Barth it is the Triune God himself who elects himself in Jesus Christ, and in this way Barth brings election out into the light, firmly grounding it in the knowledge of Jesus Christ and anchoring it in the Gospel. Indeed it can be argued that Barth's entire undertaking in the *CD* is directed against the notion of a speculative and abstract "God in general."[49] Thus Barth makes the doctrine of election "the sum of the Gospel,"[50] because it is here that we see that God loves humanity: "If Jesus is only elect and not primarily the elector, what shall we really know at all [. . .] of our election?"[51] The doctrine of election is therefore at the heart of Barth's systematic undertaking, because it demonstrates God's

---

"Calvin's Christ is clothed in a range of metaphors which describe his relationship to the doctrine of election: Christ is a book, in whom all the elect are written; Christ is a mirror, the place we look to see our own election; a guardian, protecting the election given to us by the Father; and a pledge, guaranteeing our election," Gibson, *Reading the Decree*, 4.

43. See Gloege, "Zur Prädestinationslehre Karl Barths," 81.
44. See also Nimmo, "Election and Evangelical Thinking," 32.
45. *KD* II/2, 82.
46. See *KD* II/2, 60ff.
47. *CD* II/2, 158.
48. See *KD* II/2, 108. See also Gloege, "Zur Prädestinationslehre Karl Barths," 27–29.
49. *CD* II/2, 49.
50. *CD* II/2, 3.
51. *CD* II/2, 104.

love for humanity and hence is "wholly the gospel," the "very essence of all good news."[52]

2. Re-locating the Doctrine

However, McCormack argues that Calvin's mistake was not only that he divided humanity into two camps but also that his concept of who and what God is was itself mistaken.[53] Therefore the difference between Calvin and Barth is to be found at a much deeper level, "at the level of divine ontology."[54] He explains that there is a clash between the different categories with which Barth and Calvin are working, Calvin's being what might be called an "essentialist ontology" and Barth's an "actualistic ontology."[55] McCormack shows that this change is first and foremost a revolution in the doctrine of God itself, since Barth is working with a different ontology to earlier theologians of the Reformed tradition.[56]

For Barth, the question 'Who belongs to the elected?' (or 'To whom does election apply?') is secondary. The primary questions for Barth are always 'Who is the God who elects?' and 'What does God reveal about the nature of election?'[57] Unlike Calvin, for whom it was part of the doctrine of the Holy Spirit,[58] Barth treats the doctrine of election within his doctrine of God,[59] and so (just as in the *Göttingen Dogmatics*)[60] he locates the doctrine

---

52. *CD* II/2, 13f.

53. On these two camps, Calvin writes: "We call predestination God's eternal decree (*aeternum Dei decretum*), by which he compacted with himself what he willed to become of each man. For all are not created in equal condition, rather, eternal life is foreordained for some, eternal damnation for others. Therefore, as any man has been created to one or the other of these ends, we speak of him as predestined for life or to death," in *Inst.* III.xxi.5.

54. McCormack, "Grace and Being," 97.

55. See ibid., 98. For further reading on Barth actualistic ontology see Nimmo, *Being in Action*, passim. Nimmo gives an excellent introduction (pp. 4–12) where he explains that Barth's actualistic ontology is "grounded in the eternal election of Jesus Christ," 10.

56. See McCormack, "Grace and Being," 93. For an excellent exposition of the Triune nature of God see Williams, "Barth on the Triune God," 147–93.

57. See McCormack, "Grace and Being," 93.

58. See here Gunton, *The Barth Lectures*, 114.

59. See Goebel, *Vom freien Wählen Gottes und des Menschen*, who writes: "Barth hat die Erwählungslehre als einen notwendigen konstitutiven Teil der christlichen Gotteslehre—im Unterschied zur Tradition (vgl.82.100)—konzipiert und lociert," 28.

60. Gockel, *Barth and Schleiermacher*, 164.

of election at the end of the section in the *CD* on the doctrine of God and before the section on the doctrine of creation. He looks at it christologically, making Jesus Christ both "the Subject of election and its Object,"[61] both true God and true man, in whom God reveals himself.[62] Through this move, Barth finds his *Punctum Archimedis* for all further theological thinking on the doctrine of election.[63] Barth envisages neither an abstract concept of God nor an abstract concept of humanity. For Barth, the person Jesus of Nazareth in history is the sole basis of election. What is fundamental to Barth's "actualistic doctrine of election is the insistence of Barth that Jesus Christ is not only elected man but is also electing God."[64] Von Balthasar points out that earlier theologians often "misconstrued the Christological basis" of the doctrine of election witnessed in the Bible and failed to "contextualize election as part of God's relationship to Christ,"[65] seeing election as an individual occurrence between an isolated human being and an abstract and thus terrifying, absolute God. However, what Barth presents in his doctrine of election is the election of the Son of God who is not only the object of God's election but also the subject of that election from all eternity.

Traditionally it was the Father who was seen as issuing the eternal decree and the function of the Son was to respond to the Father (rather than being part of the decision). Jüngel points out that "God's being is *in movement* from eternity"[66] and the eternal election of Jesus Christ implies a divine decision concerning "God's being-in-act,"[67] which becomes manifest in "the temporal history of Jesus Christ [which is] the fulfilment in time of God's eternal resolve."[68] The "encounter between God and humanity which has its origin in the movement of God's being is, according to Barth, first and above all the encounter between the electing God and elected humanity, which is an event in Jesus Christ."[69] Thus, Barth sees Christ as the one in whom everything has eternally occurred, who not only responds to the Father's will but fully and actively shares in it from eternity: "As we have to

---

61. McCormack, "Grace and Being," 93. See also Goebel, *Vom freien Wählen Gottes und des Menschen*, 30–44.

62. See Kreck, *Grundentscheidungen in Karl Barths Dogmatik*, 188.

63. See ibid., 188.

64. Nimmo, *Being In Action*, 8. See also McCormack, "Seek God where he may be found," 62–79.

65. Von Balthasar, *The Theology of Karl Barth*, 175.

66. Jüngel, *God's Being is in Becoming*, 14.

67. Ibid., 76.

68. Ibid., 98.

69. Ibid., 11.

do with Jesus Christ, we have to do with the electing God."[70] Barth therefore puts the doctrine of the election that took place in Jesus Christ at the "very beginning, and indeed before the beginning, of what we have to say concerning God's dealings with His creation."[71] For Barth, God is essentially the electing God who "makes the universe in order that it may be the arena on which his gracious purposes may come to pass"[72] and is thus the precondition [*Voraussetzung*] for all of God's works.

The election of grace is therefore the beginning of "all the ways and works of God" and it is here that God sets himself in relation.[73] God's being in relation to humanity is the event of the election in Jesus Christ since "Jesus Christ is the decision of God in favour of [. . .] relation. He is Himself the relation."[74] Election is therefore the beginning of God's *opera ad extra*. However, election is not only an *opus Dei ad extra externum* but at the same time an *opus Dei ad extra internum* since "election as such is not only a decision made by God [but] is equally a decision which affects God himself."[75] Barth says that "God's election of man is a predestination not merely of man but of Himself."[76] It is for this reason that Barth understands the election as "ordination, as God's self-ordaining of Himself. And it is for this reason, then, that we regard the doctrine of election as a constituent part of the doctrine of God."[77] Since the doctrine of election affects not only elected humanity but also God himself, it is understandable that Barth sees the doctrine of election as part of the doctrine of God. Gunton argues that Barth considers himself as the first dogmatician to place the doctrine of election into the doctrine of God.[78] He says that for Barth, "doctrines that are not theologically grounded are not Christian theology."[79] What Barth tries to achieve with his doctrine of election is to "establish a hermeneutical

---

70. CD II/2, 54.
71. CD II/2, 89.
72. Gunton, "Karl Barth's Doctrine Of Election," 384.
73. CD II/2, 3.
74. CD II/2, 7.
75. Jüngel, *God's Being is in Becoming*, 84.
76. CD II/2, 3.
77. CD II/2, 89.
78. See Gunton, "Karl Barth's Doctrine Of Election," 381. See also Pannenberg's comments on Peter Lombard and Aquinas. Both the *Sentences* (1.d.40–41) and the *summas* (ST 1.23) put the doctrine of election at the end of the doctrine of God. Pannenberg, *Systematic Theology Vol. 3*, 441.
79. Gunton, "Karl Barth's Doctrine Of Election," 382.

rule which would allow the Church to speak authoritatively about what God was doing—and indeed, who and what God was/is."[80]

3. The Basis of Barth's Doctrine of Election: God's Self-Revelation

Barth contends that it is impossible to maintain anything about God other than that which God himself has revealed about himself. Therefore, God's self-revelation is for Barth the "criterion of all ontological statements in theology"[81] and, *ipso facto*, election must be measured by the revelation of God. Barth constantly emphasizes in his *CD* that humanity in itself would not be capable of knowing God, if God did not reveal himself to humanity. He states that any analogy between God and the world based on any characteristic of being is insufficient. Divine being cannot be recognized by created being (nature, law, history, or consciousness) and so God cannot be known through any *analogia entis*. Only through *analogia fidei*, an analogy of faith given by God, is it possible for humanity to know God.[82] The initiative is solely and exclusively on God's side. Thus Barth's doctrine of revelation in *CD* II/1, with his famous statement "God is known only by God," is for many the "dominant theme of this theology"[83] and sets the parameters for the exploration of the doctrine of election. He writes:

> No single item of Christian doctrine is legitimately grounded, or rightly developed and expounded, unless it can of itself be understood and explained as part of the responsibility laid upon the hearing and teaching Church towards the self-revelation of God attested in Holy Scripture. Thus the doctrine of election cannot be legitimately understood or represented except in the form of an exposition of what God Himself has said and still says concerning Himself.[84]

The doctrine of revelation in the *CD* forwards Barth's argument that there is no basis for theology other than God's self-revelation as Father, Son and Holy Spirit, the "basic rule of all Church dogmatics."[85] Since "God is

---

80. McCormack, "Grace and Being," 92.
81. Jüngel, *God's Being is in Becoming*, 77.
82. See Williams, "Barth on the Triune God," 148.
83. Gunton, *The Barth Lectures*, 112.
84. *CD* II/2, 35.
85. *CD* II/2, 35.

who He is in the act of revelation,"[86] the event of revelation is always an event of God's self-interpretation as Father, Son, and Holy Spirit, and therefore God's being is thus a "*self-related*" being.[87] God's being as Father, Son, and Spirit, a "unique unity-in-distinction,"[88] is thus a "*being in becoming*."[89] Furthermore, the "doctrines of *perichoresis* and appropriation among the three differentiated modes of God's being united as a trinity specified this knowledge: God's being is in becoming."[90] Barth uses the patristic devices of *perichoresis* and appropriation to highlight the relationship between the doctrine of election and the doctrine of the Trinity.[91] Barth says that the "work of God is the essence of God as the essence of Him who [. . .] is revealer, revelation and being revealed, or Creator, Reconciler and Redeemer."[92] *Perichoresis* works in such a way "that the divine modes of being mutually

---

86. *CD* II/1, 257.

87. Jüngel, *God's Being is in Becoming*, 77.

88. Williams, "Barth on the Triune God," 166

89. Jüngel, *God's Being is in Becoming*, 77.

90. Ibid., 77f.

91. For the relation between the doctrine of the election and the doctrine of the Trinity see Barth's use of *perichoresis* and appropriation in Jüngel, *God's Being is in Becoming*, 42–53. See also Gunton, "Karl Barth's Doctrine Of Election," 389–91. Furthermore, the relationship between election and the Trinity has been a matter of some theological dispute in recent Barth scholarship. I should point out that my interest in exploring the doctrine of election is solely related to the 'dialectical' aspect of God's *Yes* and *No* spoken over Jesus Christ. Hector observes that McCormack and Molnar agree with "Karl Barth's insistence that God's immanent triunity is known only by way of God's economic triunity," in Hector, "God's Triunity and Self-Determination," 246. What they disagree on is "its implications," ibid., 246. I wholeheartedly partake in their agreement. On their disagreement about the implications, all that needs to be said is that this plays no key role in this specific study on Barth. The book does not ask whether God's self-determination in the election of Jesus Christ is logically prior to God's triunity *in se* (McCormack) or whether, as the first of God's works *ad extra*, election is (logically or ontologically) subsequent to God's immanent Triune identity (Molnar). This is not to deny the pressing importance of the issue, but just to say that what concerns this study is whether Barth's account of the cross and the economic Trinity is congruent with the biblical witness. For an introduction to the discussion see Dempsey, *Trinity and Election in Contemporary Theology*, especially essays 2–5 by Molnar ("The Trinity, Election, and God's Ontological Freedom: A Response to Kevin W. Hector," 47–62 and "Can the Electing God Be Without Us? Some Implications of Bruce McCormack's Understanding of Barth's Doctrine of Election for the Doctrine of the Trinity," 63–90), Hunsinger ("Election and the Trinity: Twenty-Five Theses on the Theology of Karl Barth," 91–114) and McCormack ("Election and the Trinity: Theses in Response to George Hunsinger," 115–37).

92. *CD* I/1, 371. Barth writes that "He is always the One, not without the Other, but in and through the Other," in *CD* III/4, 32.

condition and permeate one another so completely that one is always in the other two and the other two in the one."[93] On the other hand, "the doctrine of appropriation, and thus the understanding of the being of God as concrete event, fundamentally determine Barth's whole *Dogmatics*, and in particular his doctrine of election and later his doctrine of reconciliation."[94]

For Barth, there is never an abstract revelation but revelation is always a concrete and personal event. Thus the underlying question of revelation is "how can God make Himself known to human beings without ceasing [. . .] to be the Subject of revelation"—without subjecting himself to the control of human beings.[95] The question is not so much *how* are we to speak about God's revelation but rather "what makes such speech about God's revelation possible."[96] Revelation is first of all the 'Word of God' to a person—the *Deus dixit*—given to us in three ways: in Jesus Christ, in Scripture, and in Church proclamation.[97] Barth argues that we cannot know revelation directly but only indirectly through Scripture and proclamation. The Bible in itself is not seen as the revelation of God; for it to *become* revelation, God must reveal himself in Scripture, through the power of the Holy Spirit; it must become "an event through which, by the act of God, the Word is revealed."[98] The "primary event alone *is* the Word."[99] Firstly "the Word of God must be understood as an event in and to the reality of man. And in the second place it is true that a possibility or capability on man's part must correspond logically and materially to this event."[100] Therefore the question that needs to be asked is not 'How does a person *know* the Word of God?' but 'How *can* people know the Word of God?' For Barth, revelation is "God's self-unveiling, imparted to man, of the God who by nature cannot be unveiled to men"[101]—and this is how Barth abrogates the principle *homo peccator non capax verbi divini*.[102] The *Deus revelatus* is the *Deus absconditus*, who

---

93. *CD* I/1, 370. Barth sees *perichoresis* as "a mutual indwelling and interworking of the three forms of eternity," in *CD* II/1, 640.

94. Jüngel, *God's Being is in Becoming*, 53.

95. McCormack, *Karl Barth's Critically Realistic Dialectical Theology*, 207.

96. Jüngel, *God's Being is in Becoming*, 19.

97. See *CD* I/1, 136.

98. *CD* I/1, 113.

99. Williams, "Barth on the Triune God," 149.

100. *CD* I/1, 193.

101. *CD* I/1, 315.

102. On the question on how sinful humanity is capable for the divine word see Williams, "Barth on the Triune God," 147–52

"graciously honours his creature, in his sacramental being-as-object,"[103] about whom otherwise one would be unable to say anything, if he would not make "the created reality, in whose objectivity he is objective, *speak* for him."[104] For this reason Barth emphasizes that we can know God only where God has made himself known.

Barth gained this insight through reading Anselm, who offered an *a posteriori* proof of God through revelation, which became the exegetical basis for his hermeneutical circle: "God has given the proof of his own existence in his self-expression in history as told in the Bible, and so it is only the biblical stories which render his identity authoritatively."[105] In his doctrine of revelation Barth posits that God is identical with and inseparable from the content of revelation and thus revelation must be understood in terms of its uniqueness, its subject: God himself. Revelation for Barth is *Dei loquentis persona*[106] [the person of God speaking],[107] his own direct speech, the divine 'I' addressing the human 'thou'[108] "communicated in a historical event [. . .] through the biblical account."[109] When Barth talks about revelation attested in Scripture he does not refer just to any kind of revelation but to a unique revelation, alongside which no other exists, the "incarnation of the Word of God,"[110] his self-disclosure in Jesus Christ. It is in the event of God's self-revelation of his being in Jesus Christ that the encounter between God and humanity takes place.[111] It is "Christ, the Word of God, brought to the hearing of man by the outpouring of the Holy Spirit, who is man's possibility of being the recipient of divine revelation."[112]

In Jesus Christ "God reveals Himself as the Lord,"[113] and thus revelation is the annunciation of the βασιλεία τοῦ θεοῦ.[114] As Jüngel writes, "For

---

103. Jüngel, *God's Being is in Becoming*, 65.

104. Ibid., 65.

105. Ford, "Barth's Interpretation of the Bible," 59.

106. See *CD* I/1, 304.

107. See Jüngel, *God's Being is in Becoming*, 27–37.

108. See *CD* I/1, 307.

109. Ford, "Barth's Interpretation of the Bible," 59.

110. *CD* I/1, 168.

111. See Jüngel, *God's Being is in Becoming*, 32.

112. *CD* I/2, 249. For Barth the Holy Spirit is the Spirit of Jesus Christ (see *CD* I/2, 247) and revelation is thus "the outpouring of the Holy Spirit," in *CD* I/2, 203.

113. *CD* I/1, 306. On "man's encounter with the Lord" see Williams, "Barth on the Triune God," 147ff. and 159f.

114. See Gunton, "Karl Barth's Doctrine Of Election," 386. See also Jüngel, *God's Being is in Becoming*, 33 and 62–64.

Barth, the concept of God's lordship of God expresses the capacity for revelation and thus the possibility of revelation, grounded in God's being."[115] Without revelation we are unable to know that we have a Lord, and that this Lord is God. Furthermore, in God's self-revelation we "have to do with the being of God in a *threefold* way":[116] it is *God* himself, who reveals *through* himself, *himself*.[117] "Revelation is that event in which the *being of God* comes to word,"[118] since for Barth "God's Word is identical with God Himself."[119] God is identical with the act and effect of revelation.[120] Thus, in all three modes of being [*Seinsweisen*] it is God himself in unimpaired unity who "according to the biblical understanding of revelation is the revealing God and the event of revelation and its effect on man."[121] Here we see the basic notion that all talk about God in the *CD* is an extended statement of the declaration that 'God is' because, for Barth, the fact that 'God is' is equivalent to saying 'God acts.'

This 'acting' of God has its beginning in his gracious election which is the first of all God's works.[122] For Barth, "God's self-revelation in Jesus Christ is the revelation of the electing God. [. . .] The divine predestination is a revelatory event, it is manifest and not hidden. God's decree is a concrete decree, implemented in Jesus Christ."[123] The aim is the eternal fellowship [*Zusammensein*] of God and humanity through the covenant of grace established in Jesus Christ.[124] Barth links the eternal decree to the historical figure of Jesus, since without the *Gestalt* of Jesus Christ, the Triune God has neither face [*Gesicht*] nor language [*Sprache*] but remains an unknown God for humanity.[125] Through God's revelation in Christ we get a "glimpse into the innermost mystery of God himself: his primal will (6, 175) and decision (4, 53), which are the source and fountain of all the graces that come streaming out of God."[126] Thus without God's self-revelation humanity would neither be able to know anything about its own election in Jesus

115. Jüngel, *God's Being is in Becoming*, 33.
116. Ibid., 28.
117. See *CD* I/1, 295f.
118. Jüngel, *God's Being is in Becoming*, 27.
119. *CD* I/1, 304.
120. See *CD* I/1, 296.
121. *CD* I/1, 299.
122. See *CD* II/2, 3.
123. Gockel, *Barth and Schleiermacher*, 177.
124. See *CD* II/2, 158.
125. See *KD* II/2, 162.
126. Von Balthasar, *The Theology of Karl Barth*, 174f.

Christ nor about the gracious God in Jesus Christ, who is both electing God and elected human.

4. Jesus Christ: the 'Electing God' and the 'Elected Human'

The doctrine of election has been central not only to the Reformed tradition[127] but also in Western Christianity as a whole. Barth's own understanding of the doctrine of God's gracious election [*Gottes Gnadenwahl*][128] is divided more or less into two parts: *CD* II/1 offers an account of God as "the One who loves in freedom," highlighting that God's being is identical with his action,[129] and *CD* II/2 sets out Barth's doctrine of election [*Erwählung*]. Because Barth sees the doctrine of election "within the context of the doctrine of God [. . .] as an integral part of this doctrine" he puts it at the "head of all other doctrines."[130] Together, these two parts "provide something like a 'character sketch' of the biblical God in relation to his human covenant partner."[131] Von Balthasar refers to Barth's architectonics in *CD* II as the "most magnificent, unified and well-grounded section of the whole work,"[132] as the "heartbeat of his whole theology";[133] and for Webster the doctrine of election "forms the centrepiece of the doctrine of God; indeed, it is one of the most crucial chapters in the *Church Dogmatics* as a whole, summing up much of what Barth has had to say so far and pointing forward to essential features of the doctrines of creation and reconciliation."[134]

---

127. For the Reformed tradition on election see Crisp, "The Election of Jesus Christ," 133–36 and 141–47.

128. For an overview of the christological reorientation in *CD* II/2 see McDonald, *Re-Imaging Election*, 42–47.

129. *CD* II/1, 322. Aquinas said that one of the most appropriate ways to talk about God is to say that God is 'He who Is' (Thomas Aquinas, *Summa Theologiae*, I.13.11). However, Barth's talk about God might best be summarized by saying that he defines God as 'the one who chooses or elects in freedom.'

130. *CD* II/2, 91.

131. Mangina, *Theologian of Christian Witness*, 58.

132. Von Balthasar, *The Theology of Karl Barth*, 174. N.B. John Webster points out that von Balthasar's judgment was stated before Barth had published IV, *The Doctrine of Reconciliation*, but that von Balthasar was "not wide of the mark," in Webster, *Barth*, 93. At this point, Barth (now in his mid-fifties) had finished *CD* II/2 and was therefore approximately one third through his *magnum opus*.

133. Von Balthasar, *The Theology of Karl Barth*, 177.

134. Webster, *Barth*, 88.

The opening paragraph of the doctrine of election, §32, *The Problem of a Correct Doctrine of the Election of Grace*, describes what God in his freedom has chosen. Barth opens his analysis of this doctrine with the following statement:

> The doctrine of election is the sum of the Gospel because of all words that can be said or heard it is the best: that God elects man; that God is for man too the One who loves in freedom. It is grounded in the knowledge of Jesus Christ because He is both the electing God and elected man in One. It is part of the doctrine of God because originally God's election of man is a predestination not merely of man but of Himself. Its function is to bear basic testimony to eternal, free and unchanging grace as the beginning of all the ways and works of God.[135]

As stated, Barth's doctrine of election can best be understood by highlighting where and how he differs from and reworks Calvin's doctrine of double predestination. Whereas previously Calvin's doctrine of election was linked with notions of determinism and an arbitrary decree (whereby God had predestined some people to be saved, and others to eternal condemnation—emphasizing the individual aspect of election of a human being),[136] Barth focuses on Christ and places election only on Christ, seeing him as the fulfilment of the eternal covenant of grace.

We saw that, for Barth, election should be seen as "the beginning of all the ways and works of God" which is "grounded in the knowledge of Jesus Christ" who is "both electing God and elected man in one."[137] The significance of Barth's radical transformation of Calvin's doctrine of double predestination and the move of centring both '*Erwählung*' and '*erwählt sein*' on Jesus Christ, making him the subject and object of election at the same time, cannot be overemphasized. Von Balthasar points out that Barth had turned against Calvin's exposition of the doctrine of election as early as the *Römerbrief*.[138] "Barth felt that the whole Augustinian and Reformed approach to this deep mystery was a 'mythologizing' attempt to delimit God's activity,"[139] portraying election as an immutable 'natural law' that bypassed God's role in this decision. It was also in this doctrine, which he saw as so vital because it formed the intersection between soteriology and anthropol-

---

135. *CD* II/2, 3.

136. See *Inst.* III.xxi.5, where Calvin writes that "eternal life is foreordained for some, eternal damnation for others," 926.

137. *CD* II/2, 116.

138. See von Balthasar, *The Theology of Karl Barth*, 174.

139. Ibid., 174. See also Barth, *Der Römerbrief*, 310 and 333f.

ogy, that Barth was painfully aware that he was in dispute with the mainstream orthodox Reformed tradition. Thus he felt "largely alone, lacking in intellectual precedents and at odds even with the Reformed tradition in which the doctrine of election had played such a large role in explicating the soteriological and anthropological consequences of the doctrine of divine sovereignty."[140] Barth himself states the reason for his departure from the traditional understanding of his Reformed background, namely that he sees his own understanding of election as closer to the biblical witness.[141] He writes: "As I let the Bible itself speak to me on these matters, as I meditated on what I seemed to hear, I was driven irresistibly to reconstruction."[142]

The christological revision in *CD* II/2 spells out more clearly the content of God's eternal decision and overcomes an "abstract duality between one eternal decision and many actual decisions."[143] What Barth describes in the doctrine of election of Jesus Christ is an "economic outworking of the identity upon which God eternally decides."[144] "God's decision in time is not different from God's decision 'from all eternity' because it is determined once and for all by the election of Jesus Christ."[145] Therefore, the reconstruction in *CD* II/2 not only "presents a revision of traditional views but also overcomes certain limitations that were inherent in his own earlier positions."[146] Whereas in earlier versions the "*natura humana*"[147] was the object of God's electing, Barth now states that the divine election of grace is an election of Jesus Christ, who is both the 'electing God' and the 'elected human being' (the subject and object of election). Thus the new version talks about God's self-determination, his "gracious choice" or "primal and basic decision"[148] to be the God who determines himself to be gracious towards humanity.

Barth sees the act of divine unconditional self-determination [*unbedingter Selbstbestimmung*] constituting two parts that are related to Christ's divinity and humanity respectively. Thus the doctrine of election must be understood christologically; Jesus is both the subject and object of election,

---

140. Webster, *Barth*, 88.

141. See *CD* II/2, 3f.

142. *CD* II/2, x.

143. Gockel, *Barth and Schleiermacher*, 178.

144. Jones, *The Humanity of Christ*, 80.

145. Gockel, *Barth and Schleiermacher*, 178.

146. Ibid., 3f.

147. Barth, *Gottes Gnadenwahl*, 46. See also Gloege, "Zur Prädestinationslehre Karl Barths," 84.

148. *CD* II/2, 76.

the electing God [*der erwählende Gott*] and elected human [*der erwählte Mensch*]. "It is the name of Jesus Christ which, according to the divine self-revelation, forms the focus at which the two decisive beams of the truth forced upon us converge and unite: on the one hand the electing God and on the other elected man."[149] On the one hand, the Son imparts God's being and act to humanity and in this way Jesus Christ, the divine Son, is the 'electing God.' On the other hand, Barth does not separate God's economic action of the Son from the Son's immanent being. And therefore through the Son's self-determination as the 'electing God' and 'elected human,' his identity becomes "irrevocably bound to the life of the human identifiable as Jesus of Nazareth."[150] This entails an event of determination in which God wills that the life of Jesus Christ "transforms God's life"[151] by drawing the contingent existence of the elected human "into the time and space of God's being."[152] This is the radical newness of Barth's understanding of the overflow of God's love and grace towards humanity.[153]

4.1. *The Electing God: Jesus Christ—the Subject of Election*

Barth's doctrine of the gracious choice, the election of Jesus Christ, is to be understood as the *story* or primal history [*Urgeschichte*] between God and humanity.[154] Election has its beginning in the eternal covenant in Jesus Christ, who is the centre and foundation of the whole doctrine. Jesus Christ is both the subject and object of election,[155] the electing God and the elected human. For Barth, to see Christ as electing God is to see who the subject of that election really is.[156] Election is God's primal decision to be the *Deus pro nobis*. Therefore it is the "redemptive news, that from all eternity God has decided to be God only in this way, and in the movement

149. CD II/2, 59.

150. Jones, *The Humanity of Christ*, 80.

151. Ibid., 80.

152. Ibid., 80.

153. See also Nimmo, who writes that the divine act of election "determines not only the being of God, but also that of humanity itself in Jesus Christ," in Nimmo, *Being in Action*, 93.

154. See Goebel, *Vom freien Wählen Gottes und des Menschen*, 16. For the notion of God's *story* with humanity see Ford, *Barth and God's Story*, 72–93.

155. Brunner cannot accept that the subject of the eternal election is Jesus Christ. He sees only God the Father as the subject and Jesus as the Mediator in whom, through whom and by whom humanity is elect. See Brunner, *The Christian Doctrine of God*, 313f.

156. See CD II/2, 5–7.

towards humanity [...] Jesus Christ Himself [is] [...] the content of this primal decision [*Urentscheidung*] of God, and as such the authentic revelation [*authentische Offenbarung*] of it."[157] Election, as God's 'primal decision,' could be called the *leitmotif* of Barth's doctrine of God;[158] the subject of election is the electing God who decides to elect.

Though Barth looks at election through the lens of the doctrine of God in Jesus Christ, his pastoral concern is still very much present and he "marks sharp disagreement with the characterization of God implied by many Calvinist accounts of predestination."[159] He is worried that some people will be faced by the question of election and salvation by a *Deus absconditus*, and sees this as a problem not properly addressed by theologians in the history of the Church, including Aquinas and the Reformers. Barth rules out this possibility with a pre-emptive strike, identifying Jesus not only as the historical Mediator of the covenant but also actively involved and eternally ordained as the electing God and elected human.[160] This concept, that Christ is the subject of election and inseparably connected to the person Jesus, is the truly new and original idea in Barth's doctrine of election. Thus for Barth, it is the person Jesus Christ who is the subject of election and not an "indeterminate (or 'absolute') *Logos asarkos*."[161]

What lies at the core of Barth's undertaking is to show that the earlier accounts of the doctrine of election distort the basic Christian truth that God loves in freedom and relates graciously to humanity. Something that Barth wants to 'correct' in the traditional Calvinist doctrine of election is the notion of the separateness of God's will from God's love, which Barth sees as a unity. The theological change of Barth's revision consists of the "combination of the doctrine of election, and thus the doctrine of God, with the doctrine of the person and work of Christ."[162] According to Barth, the traditional versions of the doctrine failed in that they did not understand "God's eternal will and decree exclusively in the light of the history of Jesus Christ."[163] The sentence 'Jesus Christ is the electing God' displaces and replaces the idea of a *decretum absolutum* and is substituted by Jesus, the *decretum concretum*.[164] For Barth, the divine predestination is a revelatory

---

157. *CD* II/2, 91.
158. See Jones, *The Humanity of Christ*, 81.
159. Ibid., 78.
160. See Kreck, *Grundentscheidungen in Karl Barths Dogmatik*, 194.
161. McCormack, "Grace and Being," 95.
162. Gockel, *Barth and Schleiermacher*, 170.
163. Ibid., 170.
164. See Gloege, "Zur Prädestinationslehre Karl Barths," 96.

event, not a hidden one. Thus God's decree is a "concrete decree, implemented in Jesus Christ."[165] Its purpose is the covenant of grace, and its goal eternal fellowship between God and humanity.

Therefore, in seeing Jesus as the Mediator of the covenant between God and humanity, Barth sees God's eternal will worked out in history. He understands the gracious God and his self-determination as the beginning of all his works,[166] his primary decision to be the electing God in Jesus Christ: "In so far as God not only is love, but loves, in the act of love which determines His whole being God elects."[167] Barth does not see God's election as referring to a random choice, a hidden decision made by an arbitrary eternal will, dividing humanity into two camps—the elect or reprobate—as described by theologians in the Reformed tradition. What matters for Barth is the specificity of God's will, which he sees in God's self-election and the election of humanity, both actualized in Jesus Christ: "God elected or predestined Himself,"[168] and in this self-election "God elected man, this man,"[169] the person Jesus Christ. Thus first of all, in Jesus Christ we witness divine election as divine self-election. This self-election in Jesus Christ is an election of grace and love, God's eternal decision to be gracious and loving towards humanity. As Webster puts it "God elects to be this God, God in this man, God known in and as Jesus Christ."[170]

One of the ramifications of the above statement, and something that is particular to Barth's thought and crucial for understanding his doctrine of election, is his reoccurring idea that God did not have to enter into a covenant relationship with sinful humanity but chose freely to do so out of his sheer grace. From eternity, God self-determines himself to be in a relationship with humanity and enters as the Son into a covenant relationship with us.[171] Thus, any talk about the humanity of God is based concretely on God's self-determination [*Selbstbestimmung*] which itself is grounded in the person of and "God's *self*-election as Jesus Christ":[172]

> it is in relation to all that follows a necessary witness to the fact that all God's works and ways have their origin in His grace. In

---

165. Gockel, *Barth and Schleiermacher*, 177.

166. See *CD* II/2, 99ff.

167. *CD* II/2, 76. For an account of God's self-determination see Jüngel, *God's Being is in Becoming*, 87.

168. *CD* II/2, 162.

169. *CD* II/2, 162.

170. Webster, *Barth*, 91.

171. See Barth, *The Humanity of God*, 37–65.

172. Jones, *The Humanity of Christ*, 79.

> virtue of this self-determination of His, God is from the very first the gracious God. For this self-determination is identical with the decree of His movement towards man. This movement is always the very best thing that could happen to man. The reality and revelation of this movement is Jesus Christ Himself. This movement is an eternal movement, and therefore one which encloses man in his finitude and temporality. It is free, and therefore it is entirely grounded in the good-pleasure and the will of God.[173]

For Barth, Jesus Christ is God's turning towards humanity and this basic statement becomes the guiding principle for his doctrine of election by grace. Therefore Barth regards Jesus both as "*sowohl Erkenntnisgrund—wie Seinsgrund!*"[174] With this decision to make Jesus the guiding principle of election, Barth challenges and modifies at its root the traditional *Prädestinationslehre*.[175] Barth's rationale behind this is the particularity of God "which is at all costs to be respected in the construction of the doctrine of election."[176] For Barth, the danger to be avoided lies in a wrong starting point, from a "concept of God as omnipotent Will, governing and irresistibly directing each and every creature according to His own law," which will inevitably lead to the error of "supposing that God is irresistibility efficacious *in abstracto*, naked freedom and sovereignty."[177] As Webster highlights, Barth objects not to the concept of the sovereignty of God but to the underlying notion of indeterminateness of deity in such a concept.[178]

4.2. The Elected Human: Jesus Christ—the Object of Election

However this is only half of Barth's doctrine of election—to focus on divinity in election here would be to fail to see the whole picture. For Barth, the election of Jesus Christ also always includes his humanity. The "theme of election is not simply God but also humanity,"[179] the eternal covenant of grace in Jesus Christ played out in history between God and this one human

---

173. *CD* II/2, 91f.

174. Kreck, *Grundentscheidungen in Karl Barths Dogmatik*, 189. See also Jüngel who writes "Das Sein des Menschen Jesus ist der Seins- und Erkenntnisgrund aller Analogie," in Jüngel, "Die Möglichkeit theologischer Anthropologie," 538.

175. See Kreck, *Grundentscheidungen in Karl Barths Dogmatik*, 188.

176. Webster, *Barth*, 89.

177. *CD* II/2, 44.

178. See Webster, *Barth*, 89.

179. Webster, *Barth*, 90.

Election, Rejection, and Exegesis 31

being, Jesus of Nazareth, who is both fully God and fully man.[180] Thus the election of Jesus Christ is an election of humanity. Barth formulates this anthropological aspect of the doctrine of election, the election of humanity, christologically and in close relationship with the incarnation; "Christ's sharing our humanity in the incarnation."[181] As Webster writes:

> The dominance of the notion of the divine decree in parts of the earlier Reformed tradition sometimes gave the impression that the doctrine of election could be expounded largely without reference to the incarnation—as if election concerned a relation between God and humanity to which Jesus Christ was largely incidental, or as if the line from the will of God to the elect did not traverse the history of Jesus.[182]

Barth points out that in the incarnation the *Logos* of God was made flesh, has become a human being, in the elected person Jesus of Nazareth. Jesus Christ alone is the primal object of the Father's election, the cause and beginning of all election. Beside him there is no other and it is in him that God chooses himself in the form of a created human being: "This person, Jesus Christ, was with God in the beginning. And that is just what predestination means."[183] To restate, for Barth election is the "sum of the Gospel" and so it is the confirmation of God's love for us. God in his freedom chose from eternity to love us in Jesus Christ. Since in his freedom God is "God for us,"[184] God's freedom is freedom to love: "That God wills neither to be without the world nor against it can never be stated more clearly than when we speak of His election."[185] Jesus Christ is the Mediator of the new covenant and the Redeemer of all creation from "before the foundation of the world" (Eph 1:4; 1 Pet 1:20), because it is "in him that the family of man is summoned to election."[186]

> From the very beginning (from eternity itself), as elected man He does not stand alongside the rest of the elect, but before and above them as the One who is originally and properly the Elect. [. . .] [T]here are no other elect together with or apart from Him, but, as Eph 1:4 tells us, only "in" Him. "In Him" does not simply

---

180. See *CD* II/2, 8.
181. Webster, *Barth*, 91.
182. Ibid., 91.
183. *CD* II/2, 157.
184. *CD* II/2, 25.
185. *CD* II/2, 26.
186. Von Balthasar, *The Theology of Karl Barth*, 175.

mean with Him, together with Him, in His company. Nor does it mean only through Him, by means of that which He as elected man can be and do for them. "In Him" means in His person, in His will, in His own divine choice, in the basic decision of God which He fulfils over against every man.[187]

Brunner criticizes Barth and contends that in the New Testament the eternal Son *became* a human being and that "[i]f the eternal pre-existence of the God-Man were a fact, then the Incarnation would no longer be an *Event*."[188] Kreck raises the question of whether Barth's view suggests a tearing apart of the 'eternal content' and the 'temporal form' of election,[189] and in this way God's electing action in Jesus Christ is 'torn out of history.'[190] Furthermore, Gloege asks whether Barth makes God's gracious choice in Jesus Christ, his *decretum concretum*, into a principle.[191] The election of Jesus Christ means at the same time the election of humanity "in Him" (Eph 1:4). However, Gloege sees ἐν Χριστῷ as the historical place of humanity's election, where God's will took concrete form as well as the pneumatological place where the individual is incorporated into the Church. He sees this historical aspect as lacking in Barth's understanding, and questions whether any thought of election is evident in the prologue of John.[192] These charges seem to be an overstatement and do not appear to grasp Barth's full intention to consider the pre-temporal decision of the "*logos asarkos* to become and be the *logos ensarkos*."[193] Barth sees the function of the *Logos* in John 1:1 and 1:14 as a "stop-gap" [*Platzhalter*][194] or "preliminary indication" for the name of Je-

187. CD II/2, 116f.
188. Brunner, *The Christian Doctrine of God*, 347.
189. Kreck, *Grundentscheidungen in Karl Barths Dogmatik*, 235.
190. Ibid., 228 and 234.
191. See Gloege, "Zur Prädestinationslehre Karl Barths," 102.
192. See ibid., 100f. Gloege highlights that "Das ,ἐν Χριστῷ' wird so einseitig in die zeitliche Transzendenz transponiert, daß es abstrakt zu werden droht. Das Neue Testament faßt das ,ἐν Χριστῷ' streng geschichtlich. Es denkt nicht von Gott bzw. dem λόγος ἄσαρκος her auf den geschichtlichen Jesus von Nazareth hin, sondern umgekehrt von ihm als dem fleischgewordenen Worte her auf den erwählenden Gott zurück," 100. See also Pannenberg, *Systematic Theology Vol. 3*, who says that Barth "did not link with this verse [Eph 1:4], along the lines of Eph 3:9–11, the thought of a history of the divine electing as a nexus of actions that aims at the summing of all things in Christ," 451.
193. Jones, *The Humanity of Christ*, 94.
194. See ibid., 95. Pannenberg does not seem to grasp Barth's concept of the *Logos* as a 'stop-gap' either. See Pannenberg, *Systematic Theology Vol. 3*, 460 and footnote 71. Barth does not deny that it is the *Logos* that became incarnate, but he avoids speaking

sus.¹⁹⁵ Thus, what Barth observes is that in the Gospel of John the human being Jesus of Nazareth is identified with the eternal, pre-existing *Logos*, and he refuses to "separate the Logos before the incarnation (*logos asarkos*) from the Logos during the incarnation (*logos ensarkos*)."¹⁹⁶ Barth sees election as an event in which God "encloses" the human being.¹⁹⁷ This 'enclosure' does not compromise the integrity of Christ's humanity. Since God draws Christ's concrete person "into the divine life, the eternal event of God includes the spatially and temporally localized event of the *incarnate* Word."¹⁹⁸ In this way, election 'in Christ' is not a static event in history but has to be understood actualistically, as a concrete event of human/divine agency¹⁹⁹ in time and eternity.²⁰⁰

Furthermore, Jüngel acknowledges that Barth does not explicitly use the doctrines,²⁰¹ but that by applying the patristic terminology of *anhypostasia* and *enhypostasia*, the human nature of Jesus with God is not "a projection of a temporal existence into eternity."²⁰² Instead, Jüngel maintains, we "must speak of this temporal existence of Jesus in the sense of the *anhypostasis*."²⁰³ The historical and temporal existence of Jesus of Nazareth would not be what it is if it were not *already* in the "eternal decision of God by which time is founded and governed."²⁰⁴ Therefore, Jüngel continues, "it is precisely in the eternal decision of God in the sense of the *enhypostasis*

---

about an abstract *Logos asarkos*. For Barth, the importance lies in the fact that God became incarnate in this particular person, the man Jesus of Nazareth, and revealed himself to and made his dwelling amongst humanity by coming in the human flesh. For Barth, we can only know God through Jesus Christ.

195. *CD* II/2, 95–99.

196. Gockel, *Barth and Schleiermacher*, 172. See also Kreck, *Grundentscheidungen in Karl Barths Dogmatik*, 226–28.

197. *CD* II/2, 180f.

198. Jones, *The Humanity of Christ*, 91.

199. See Nimmo, *Being In Action*, 92–97, especially 96.

200. Brunner says that the "basis of election never lies in the one who is chosen, but exclusively in the One who chooses," in Brunner, *The Christian Doctrine of God*, 310. However, he does not recognise that when the eternal God chooses, the event of election is not simply an historical event, but one that reaches back to the pre-existing Son of eternity (the Lamb slain before the foundation of the world) and reaches through Jesus Christ into history. For an analysis of the role of time and eternity in election see McDowell, "Contriving Creation Eschatologically under Christological," 123–27.

201. See Greggs, *Barth, Origen, and Universal Salvation*, 42f. and McCormack, *Karl Barth's Critically Realistic Dialectical Theology*, 19.

202. Jüngel, *God's Being is in Becoming*, 96.

203. Ibid., 96.

204. *CD* I/2, 99.

that this existence really is *temporal* existence [. . .] [and] in this way he *corresponds* as elect man to the God who elects in unity with the Son of God"[205] who is "*in concreto* and not *in abstracto*, Jesus Christ."[206]

Jesus Christ is *the* elected human being. The content of God's eternal decision is the existence of Jesus of Nazareth, God's realization of the covenant with humanity in time and history.[207] Thus, for Barth, election and covenant go hand in hand; the election of humanity in Jesus Christ is an election to participate in the covenant established and worked out by him, in order that humanity is "enriched and saved and glorified in the living fellowship of that covenant."[208] This notion of the creature as covenant partner in Barth's theology is clarified in chapter 3, which discusses *CD* III/2, where Barth expounds his theological anthropology. Here Barth states that "the ontological determination of humanity is grounded in the fact that one man among all others is the man Jesus."[209] At the centre of his anthropological exploration is not the being of the Christian as such, but of Jesus Christ as paradigm:

> a decision has been made concerning the being and nature of every man by the mere fact that with him and among all other men He too has become a man. No matter who or what or where he may be, he cannot alter the fact that this One is also man. And because this One is also man, every man in his place and time is changed.[210]

Jesus Christ is the reality behind the *neue Setzung* of humanity because by assuming human nature he has changed every person, since "every man as such is the fellow-man of Jesus."[211] What Barth points out is the derivation of humanity from God, the dual notion of being *from* God and being *with* God. It becomes obvious that this notion of derivation is closely related to that of election: to have one's being from God is to derive from God, and to derive from God is to be rooted in the eternal election "in Christ" (Eph 1:4).[212]

---

205. Jüngel, *God's Being is in Becoming*, 96f.
206. *CD* II/2, 98.
207. See Gockel, *Barth and Schleiermacher*, 173.
208. *CD* II/2, 168.
209. *CD* III/2, 132.
210. *CD* III/2, 133.
211. *CD* III/2, 134.
212. See Gloege, "Zur Prädestinationslehre Karl Barths," 97.

Again, for Barth, predestination is not a doctrine about arbitrary choices or abstract freedom, but finds its concrete and specific content in "the name of Jesus,"[213] which stands at the centre of any discussion of election. It is "in this name [that] we may now confirm the divine decision as an event in human history" and it is under this name that "God Himself became man, that he became this particular man, and as such the Representative of the whole people that hastens towards this man and derives from Him."[214] Barth concludes that "when the bearer of this name becomes the object of our attention and thoughts, when they are directed to Jesus Christ, then we see God, and our thoughts are fixed on Him."[215] In this way, for Barth, the doctrine of election tells us *who* God is (namely the one who has bound himself freely and in an eternal covenant of grace and love with human beings) and, because Christ becomes one with humanity, it also tells us that humanity can share in God's grace and love from the very beginning. Thus Barth states: "As we believe in him and hear his Word and hold fast by his decision, we can know with a certainty which nothing can ever shake that we are the elect of God."[216]

5. *Simul Electus et Reprobatus:* God's Yes and God's No

We have already seen that Barth rejects any 'abstract' division of humanity into two groups, those who are elected and those who are rejected. Instead, for Barth, election includes simultaneously both a *Yes* and a *No*, election and reprobation.[217] However, this raises the question of the nature of reprobation. Barth asks whether Jesus is only the bearer of the divine *Yes* to humankind, without being the bearer of the divine *No* at the same time.[218] He shows that God's self-determination for the covenant of grace "implies a double determination and a double content."[219] Modifying the concept of

---

213. *CD* II/2, 53.
214. *CD* II/2, 53f.
215. *CD* II/2, 53f.
216. *CD* II/2, 115f.

217. Stoevesandt highlights the close relationship between the doctrine of justification and the *simul justus et peccator*, and Barth's doctrine of election and "Personalunion von Sünder und Gerechtem, Erwähltem und Verworfenem," in Stoevesandt, "Karl Barths Erwählungslehre," 109–14. See also Hunsinger, "A Tale of Two Simultaneities," 76–86.

218. See Barth, *Gottes Gnadenwahl*, 19.
219. Gockel, *Barth and Schleiermacher*, 195.

double predestination and relating it to "God's own being,"[220] Barth sees divine reprobation as the reprobation of Jesus Christ who "bears the punishment of the condemned human being 'in our place,' so that the reprobation of humankind is abrogated."[221] Thus Jesus Christ is not only the elect human being but also the bearer of divine reprobation and therefore Jesus Christ is the "only person who can be called the 'elect' and the 'reprobate.' All others are elected in him."[222] He writes:

> In view of His election, there is no other rejected but Himself. It is just for the sake of the election of all the rejected that He stands in solitude over against them all. It is just for them that He is the rejected One (in His rejection making room for them as the elect of God), and therefore the one and only object of the divine election of grace. Thus Jesus Christ is the Lord and Head and Subject of the witness both of 'the elect' and also of 'the rejected.'[223]

The teleological view of the relation between reprobation and election affirms that "although reprobation still occurs for the sake of election, it no longer occurs as the result of God's actual address to individual human beings but has occurred once and for all in the crucifixion of Jesus Christ."[224] This christological simultaneity of the electing God and the elected human in Jesus Christ is seen in the "self-electing of Christ in obedience to the Father's will."[225] However, what does this simultaneity of election and rejection in Jesus Christ look like?

5.1. God's Yes: Jesus Christ—the Elect

In Jesus Christ, God speaks a double *Yes*, to himself as well as to his creature.[226] For Barth, Jesus Christ is the only human being to whom Isa 43:1 applies ("I have called you by name you are mine"), the only human being

---

220. Ibid., 161.

221. Ibid., 161. Maury is given credit by Barth for the insight into the correlation of Jesus' death on the cross and reprobation. Maury sees the cross as 'unjust' but sees this injustice becoming humanity's righteousness. Maury, "Election et foi," 212.

222. Gockel, *Barth and Schleiermacher*, 168.

223. CD II/2, 353.

224. Gockel, *Barth and Schleiermacher*, 196.

225. Greggs, *Barth, Origen, and Universal Salvation*, 23.

226. See Goebel, *Vom freien Wählen Gottes und des Menschen*, 14.

God has called his Son, the only truly elected one.[227] Barth combines the reciprocity in election with the reciprocity he sees in the whole of the biblical *Heilsgeschichte*. He sees election as twofold: (1) God's choosing of one individual always entails not choosing somebody else; (2) the biblical narrative demonstrates that choosing one specific person is always an election for the sake of another, the non-elect—in fact not just on behalf of an individual but invariably for the sake of a whole community.[228] Likewise, Christ is the chosen one for the sake of the non-elect, and in his election and rejection the rejected are in fact elect. Barth highlights the dialectic between election and reprobation in a careful exegesis of Rom 9–11[229] (see the dialectic of Jacob and Esau and of the Church and the Synagogue) and shows how "both groups are bound together in solidarity in Jesus Christ, who is the head of both, the chosen and rejected."[230] Barth argues that both groups bear witness to God's truth and reveal his will—the elect bear witness to what God wills, and the reprobate bear witness to what God does not will. He writes:

> Believers 'are' the elect in this service so far as they bear witness to *the* truth, that is, to the elect man, Jesus Christ, and manifest and reproduce and reflect the life of this one Elect. The godless 'are' the rejected in the same service so far as by their false witness to man's rejection they manifest and reproduce and reflect the death of the *one Rejected*, Jesus Christ. Because this One is *the* Elect and *the* Rejected, He is—attested by both—the Lord and Head both of the elect and also of the rejected. Thus not only the former, but no less indispensably, in their own place

---

227. See *CD* II/2, 351. See also Gignilliat, *Karl Barth and the Fifth Gospel*, 114f.

228. Note here: Barth puts the election of the individual after the election of Jesus Christ and the election of the community. Between II/2 'The election of Jesus Christ' and 'The election of the Individual' von Balthasar rightly highlights another new contrast between Barth's biblical doctrine of election and the traditional view of the dogma—the place of the election of the community, the Church. He writes "For it is for the sake of the Church that Christ is the elect of God (and elected to be rejected). And it is only for the sake of the Church that the individual is chosen to become a member of the Church. The moment of community cannot be removed from the biblical doctrine of election. [. . .] This insertion of the Church as the middle term between the election of Christ and the election of the individual gives unmistakable solidity to the basic thesis of Barth's doctrine of election and makes it seem incontrovertible," in von Balthasar, *The Theology of Karl Barth*, 182f.

229. For a detailed study on Barth's exegesis on Rom 9–11 see Gibson, *Reading the Decree*, 85–153.

230. Von Balthasar, *The Theology of Karl Barth*, 179. Balthasar writes: "By virtue of Christ's death, God elects the unchosen pagans so that the chosen people, the Jews, may come to their definitive election by passing through the experience of rejection," 178.

and after their own totally different fashion, the latter, are His representatives, just as originally and properly He is theirs.[231]

But for what is he chosen? Barth's answer is that he was from eternity chosen to die for us.[232] He writes that Christ is "the Lamb slain, and the Lamb slain from the foundation of the world. For this reason, the *crucified* Jesus is the 'image of the invisible God.'"[233] Jesus takes the place of the sinner not only in history (on the cross) but from all eternity in which God has predestined himself to be the 'slain Lamb' (Rev 13:8). Thus the judgment on the cross, where Barth sees God in Christ taking the rejection for bearing our sins, is the negative counterpart to the positive election of humanity.[234]

> He is the one who has been elected and chosen to lead the as-yet uncreated world back to God. He will stand up for it and plead its case, take its guilt upon his shoulders, atoning for this guilt in place of all those who are to become sinners; and thus he will become in this sense the object of divine 'reprobation' and 'rejection.' And the one who so offers himself to the Father is himself God and therefore the *subject* of election.[235]

Part of the originality in Barth's thought lies in the claim that Christ elects *himself* as both humanity's representative as well as its substitute, and in this way bears the wrath, judgment and damnation that humanity is under and deserves: "The election of the man Jesus means [. . .] that a wrath is kindled, a sentence pronounced and finally executed, a rejection actualized."[236]

5.2. God's No: Jesus Christ—the Rejected

Thus it is clear that Barth agrees with the traditional doctrine of election in that his understanding of double predestination only makes sense if it also includes some aspect of rejection—if there is a *Yes* spoken to something, there needs to be also a *No* spoken to something else. So damnation is not removed from the picture, but remains something that Jesus deals with on the cross: "The rejection which all men incurred, the wrath of God under which all men lie, the death which all men must die, God in his love for men transfers from all eternity to him in whom he loves and elects them, and

---

231. *CD* II/2, 347. Italics added.
232. See *CD* II/2, 122.
233. *CD* II/2, 123.
234. See Maury, *Predestination and Other Papers*, 22.
235. Von Balthasar, *The Theology of Karl Barth*, 175f.
236. *CD* II/2, 122.

Election, Rejection, and Exegesis 39

whom he elects at their head in their place."[237] So election is by "vicarious substitution" and takes place on the cross.[238] In the shortest formula Barth says that "God wills to lose in order that man may gain"[239]—God (who takes condemnation) loses in order that man (who is exalted to fellowship with God) wins. In God's justice and holiness he has to reject the sinner and yet elects his sinless Son for himself. The 'Son of God' takes the judgment upon himself and loses in order that the 'Son of Man' and with him all of humanity can be exalted to the Triune communion of God, God in Christ choosing death for himself and life for humanity. Christ elects suffering and rejection on the cross in order that humanity "may be elect even in its rejection of God."[240] "What is new is that this dialectic is now considered in a wholly christological sense, which brings together the *Yes* and *No* of God in the simultaneously elected and rejected Christ."[241]

Therefore, what is radically new in Barth's doctrine of election is that it is God in his freedom and self-election who chooses an election to the negative side; of rejection, death and exclusion, and the *No* of God,[242] thus to suffer in Jesus Christ all that humanity deserves. In this way, God takes the judgment on himself.[243] For Barth, predestination becomes "*the modus* of the divine work of redemption, indeed of all of God's work *ad extra* (II/2, p. 191)."[244] In Christ's taking rejection on himself, rejection can never befall humanity: "He is the Rejected, as and because He is the Elect. In view of His election, there is no other rejected but Himself."[245] In making Christ simultaneously both the elector and elected, Barth even brings rejection itself under the sovereignty of God, in order that those who reject Christ can be elected in him because he has, in his self-election of being the rejected, elected their rejection for himself.[246] This "pattern of exchange lies at the heart of Barth's doctrine of election" in which God elects rejection so that the rejected might be elect in Christ and receive the benefits of election.[247] In this way Barth radically transforms and goes beyond the binary

237. *CD* II/2, 123.
238. Gunton, *The Barth Lectures*, 115.
239. *CD* II/2, 162.
240. Greggs, *Barth, Origen, and Universal Salvation*, 27.
241. Ibid., 26.
242. See *CD* II/2, 166.
243. See *CD* II/2, 167.
244. Greggs, "Jesus is Victor," 201.
245. *CD* II/2, 353.
246. See Greggs, *Barth, Origen, and Universal Salvation*, 27.
247. McMaken, "Election and the Pattern of Exchange in Karl Barth's Doctrine of

of Calvin's two groups ('elected' and 'rejected') "by positing the integrity of election and rejection and yet uniting these in the person of Jesus Christ in a chiastic move in which the elected of God (Jesus Christ) elects rejection in order that the rejected (sinful humanity) may be elect in His election of rejection."[248]

God's self-offering in Jesus thus incorporates both a *Yes* and a *No*. Yet, Barth argues, we would fail to understand God's mystery if we did not see that the negative component of election is actually designed for the greater positive end. The *No* spoken to sin and death over Jesus Christ is not God's final word, but is incorporated and finally overcome by the *Yes* spoken by God to Jesus Christ in the resurrection, the verdict of the Father. The central statement of the *Stellvertretung* in Jesus' death is thus to be understood christologically and leads directly into a soteriological statement.[249] In fact, the *Yes* and the *No* are two sides of the same coin.[250] Election in Jesus means the 'teleological inclusion' of humanity in the election of the *Stellvertretung* of the Christ-event[251] and the 'exclusion' of humanity in Christ's rejection.[252] In God's election in Jesus Christ we are dealing with a "*Partizipationsgeschehen eines realen Tausches*":[253] God's death for humanity's life. Yet, Barth argues that God wants to give life and that death is not his final word. The *No* on the cross becomes the means to or instrument of the final end of God's *Yes* in the resurrection.[254] Barth writes: "The Yes cannot be heard unless the No is also heard. But the No is said for the sake of the Yes and not for its own sake."[255] Thus the essence of the doctrine of election is that "[o]riginally and finally it is not dialectical but non-dialectical. It does not proclaim in the same breath both good and evil, both help and destruction, both life and

---

Atonement," 209.

248. Greggs, *Barth, Origen, and Universal Salvation*, 27.

249. Neder writes that "Barth does not think of participation and substitution as alternative ways of conceiving of Christ's atoning work. The two are of a piece with one another," in Neder, *Participation in Christ*, 23.

250. See Gloege, "Zur Prädestinationslehre Karl Barths," 116.

251. See Goebel, *Vom freien Wählen Gottes und des Menschen*, 107f.

252. Ibid., 110. Later on Goebel summarises this aspect neatly by saying that "Die Exklusivaussage 'Jesus Christus ist der Erwählte' hat aber einen inklusiven Sinn, sofern die Exklusivaussage 'Jesus Christus ist der Verworfene' einen stellvertretenden Sinn hat," 205.

253. Ibid., 69.

254. Goebel is spot on when he says that "Das Verwerfen bleibt vielmehr dem Erwählen Gottes dienend zugeordnet," ibid., 61f.

255. *CD* II/2, 13.

death. In substance, therefore, the first and last word is Yes and not No."[256] In this way God's *No* is incorporated into the singular *Yes* which God shows towards humanity. For Barth the *No*, the rejection of sin, is spoken for the *Yes*, the raising to new life as the affirmation of the covenantal fellowship of love.

It is from this angle that we must reconsider the destiny of human nature.[257] The soteriological ramifications of this divine-human self-election in Christ, for the individual as well as for the community (in Barth's thought, the individual is always elected for the sake of the community),[258] cannot be overemphasized:

> That which has been eternally determined in Jesus Christ is concretely determined for every individual man to the extent that in the form of the witness of Israel and of the Church it is also addressed to him and applies to him and comes to him, to the extent that in His Word the electing God enters with him into the relationship of Elector and elected, and by His Word makes him an elected man.[259]

Von Balthasar is right in saying that "this binary reciprocity entailed by God's election in Jesus Christ, our brother, is the basic theme and *leitmotif* of the whole of salvation history, indeed is the very watermark of creation itself."[260] Barth posits that in creation there is a binary act of both election and rejection—the choosing of the cosmos and the rejection of the chaos. Barth goes on to say that this decision of election and rejection is derived from the cross, and that it is here that we see the full intensity of rejection. According to Barth, only Jesus has fully experienced the depths of what it means in reality and truth to be abandoned by God. For Barth there is no judgment outside or apart from the cross—"He alone has suffered the eternal death which we have deserved."[261] He writes:

> Only God, our Lord and Creator, could stand surety for us, could take our place, could suffer eternal death in our stead as the consequence of our sin in such a way that it was finally suffered and overcome and therefore did not need to be suffered

---

256. *CD* II/2, 13.
257. See *CD* II/2, 118.
258. See *CD* II/2, 196. See Greggs, "Jesus is Victor," footnote 27.
259. *CD* II/2, 309f.
260. Von Balthasar, *The Theology of Karl Barth*, 177.
261. *CD* II/1, 405.

any more by us. No creature, no other man could do that. But God's own Son could do it.[262]

At this point we have not yet looked in detail at Barth's doctrine of sin and evil. Barth says that from all eternity God has chosen to enter fellowship with sinners, a decision made prior to any human sinful act, even before creation itself; he had decided to be merciful to his creatures in the person of Christ and to rescue them from the bondage of sin through the cross. Here we see the close relationship between divine election and atonement. Election describes the being of God and the eternal covenant of grace and atonement highlights the action of God, that which God is willing to undertake to uphold and fulfil this covenant of grace. We will see when looking at the atonement that, for Barth, reconciliation is the fulfilment of the divine covenant.

Implications and Criticism

Barth's fundamental insight that Jesus is "both the electing God and the elect human being in One," in whom all of humanity exists and thus finds its fulfilment, is his answer to the pastoral questions of personal salvation arising from the traditional Reformed theology of predestination. Barth abrogates any hidden decree of God outside the self-revelation in Jesus Christ. Knowledge of co-election in Jesus enables the believer to see herself as a child of God. This new insight into the doctrine of election as an eternal decision made by God the Father in agreement with the Son, and its centring solely on the person of Jesus Christ, is one of Barth's major contributions to the field of academic theology as well as a key influence on the subsequent preaching of the Church. Challenging both the academic and the believer by overturning expectations of the notion of predestination, Barth's interpretation of the doctrine portrays God as the loving Father who cares for his creation. For Barth, it is not that individuals are either elected or condemned but that election and rejection have their centre in Christ. The election of humanity in Christ is part of God's eternal plan of salvation and thus was decided in eternity before the creation of humankind. Thus, for Barth, humanity belongs eternally to Jesus Christ and is therefore not rejected but elected. This picture of God in election nullifies any concept people might have of God as a tyrant and points the believer towards Jesus Christ as the only way of understanding who God is—love. In the light of

262. *CD* II/1, 401.

Election, Rejection, and Exegesis 43

this it becomes clear why for Barth the doctrine of election is not a doctrine of discomfort but of comfort, indeed, the very essence of the good news.

We saw that the theme of Barth's doctrine of election has both a singular and a double application. The singularity of the *one* divine election that focuses solely on Jesus Christ incorporates a duality: Jesus Christ is "both electing God and elected man in one."[263] He is the God-man to whom both "the active determination of election" as well as "the passive determination of election" are attributed.[264] This duality is accompanied by another duality, that of 'election and reprobation' in Jesus Christ. Yet, Barth goes even further to maintain that Jesus is the single reprobate and that reprobation need not concern humanity any more. In fact, to believe in Jesus' election as well as his rejection means to believe in the non-rejection of humanity. However, as Hays indicates, "even as the heart warms to Karl Barth's doctrine of election, the mind rebels."[265] Barth's dialectical relationship of election and rejection, brought into a synthesis in Jesus Christ, raises several concerns:

1. Brunner rightly points out that Barth's thesis stands in exact opposition to Calvin's double decree. Rather than a particular group being rejected by God, the only person who is rejected is God's own Son. But what does it mean to say that Jesus Christ is the elect reprobate and what is the teleological relationship between reprobation and election? Do these two attributions not conflict with each other? Goebel sees a *"teleologische Ordnung"* in the doctrine of election—the election of humanity for life is the goal of the election of Jesus' death on the cross.[266] However, Brunner asks, "what does this statement, 'that Jesus is the only really rejected man' mean for the situation of Man?"[267] Are hell, condemnation, and judgment eliminated and blotted out? Are people apparently perishing in the stormy sea, but in reality are unable to drown because they are in fact in shallow water, but have yet to realize this?[268] Brunner charges Barth with universalism[269] and calls his understanding of election a "fundamental perversion of the Christian message."[270] Certainly,

263. CD II/2, 3.
264. CD II/2, 103.
265. Hays, "Blessed be Egypt my people," 30.
266. See Ford, *Barth and God's Story*, 30.
267. Brunner, *The Christian Doctrine of God*, 348.
268. See ibid., 351.
269. See also Crisp, "The Universalism of Karl Barth," 305–24.
270. Brunner, *The Christian Doctrine of God*, 349.

Paul writes of the 'double-edgedness' of the "*Wort vom Kreuz*"[271] for those saved and perishing (1 Cor 1:18) and refers to some people perishing in the light of the Gospel (2 Cor 4:3f.). Brunner also accuses Barth of 'objectivism,' arguing that he breaks the relationship between revelation and faith, between the objective Word of God and subjective element of faith.[272] One might say that the distinction in Paul between lost and saved becomes even more apparent in the Gospel of John in relation to faith in the Son, where judgment is inescapable for those who do not believe in the Son (John 3:36).[273]

2. Brunner's concerns will be discussed more fully in chapters 2 and 3. However, he neglects to raise one interesting implication of his own questions: what does it mean for humanity that the *Logos*, who assumed humanity, is rejected by God? Jesus is not only the human elected by God but also the human rejected by God, rejected vicariously for humanity.[274] By taking rejection into the divine Father-Son relationship, what happened in history *ad extra* is also something that corresponds and repeats itself in the 'eternal history' in the Trinity *ad intra*. Thus, in Barth's theology reprobation is of no concern for humanity since it has been dealt with by Jesus on the cross. However, what would happen if reprobation were to be taken outside Christ? Then it would again automatically become a concern for humanity. So this raises a question about the biblical understanding of rejection—what does it mean for a *theologia crucis* that Jesus was sinless and without any guilt, yet died a death on the cross? Is Christ rejected on the cross? This issue is related to the question of how sin is dealt with in the atonement, the question of sin removal. Is it just to transfer all the sins of the world on a sinless Jesus, who is then punished on behalf of others? We have to challenge Barth and ask whether he gives an accurate account of what the Bible says about the solution to sin. Furthermore, Barth sees Jesus' election as an election *for* suffering: "The elect human being

---

271. See Gloege, "Zur Prädestinationslehre Karl Barths," 124.

272. See Brunner, *The Christian Doctrine of God*, 349f. See also Kreck's discussion on 'Erwählung und Glaube,' in Kreck, *Grundentscheidungen in Karl Barths Dogmatik*, 263–83.

273. See Gloege, "Zur Prädestinationslehre Karl Barths," 125.

274. See *CD* II/2, 499ff.

Election, Rejection, and Exegesis 45

Jesus is destined to suffer and to die."[275] However, in which way can we say that Jesus' *suffering* was an integral part of his mission? Is not the biblical testimony instead emphasizing the obedience[276] of the Son of Man rather than his suffering (see Phil 2)?

3. We saw that, for Barth, Jesus Christ is the elected human. Yet in the doctrine of election Barth never defines human nature, leading us to ask, since Jesus is fully God and fully man, how Barth works out this rejection in terms of Jesus' humanity. What are the implications of the negative side of the doctrine of election, reprobation, in relation to Christ's humanity and humanity as a whole? When Barth talks about God and humanity, he can talk about two separate entities— one taking the blame (God) and one taking the bliss (humanity). But when he comes to examine the rejection of Jesus, who is fully God and fully human, this distinction of bliss and blame becomes somewhat blurred. We must challenge Barth and ask whether he takes Jesus' humanity seriously enough, or if instead he makes an exception when it comes to Jesus' humanity. If Christ as representative man is rejected and condemned for the sins of all, are not all of humanity who belong to Christ condemned as well? Barth writes that Jesus Christ elects humanity "in His own humanity."[277] So is Jesus' human nature unique or like the nature of fellow human beings? Or is there a divorce between Christ's human nature and all other humanity, "rendering that election of our humanity meaningless?"[278] These questions will be addressed in chapter 3.

Barth's understanding of election and rejection 'in Christ' and the question about sin removal will be scrutinized in the following section, where we consider Barth's exegetical bedrock to the doctrine of election. The Old Testament sacrifices that have their *Sitz im Leben* in the cultic atonement as described in the book of Leviticus (which is also the basis for Paul's understanding of the death of Christ) talk about sin offerings and purification rites and deal with sin removal and election and rejection. These therefore seem a fitting example to use for any study of the questions raised.

---

275. *CD* II/2, 122.
276. For obedience in relation to election see Neder, *Participation in Christ*, 18–20.
277. *CD* II/2, 117.
278. See Greggs, *Barth, Origen, and Universal Salvation*, 43f.

6. Barth's Typological Exegesis of Leviticus 14 and 16

We have seen that the doctrine of election represents "a new turn in Barth's theology, in which he is most conscious of being original, and therefore must go to great lengths to support his position by Scripture."[279] Barth confirms this in §32.2 (The Foundation of Doctrine) where he says that Scripture is the sole foundation of the dogma. Barth writes in the Preface to *CD* II/2 that the "specific subject-matter of this half-volume made it necessary for me to set out more fully than in previous sections the exegetical background to the dogmatic exposition."[280] It was on this subject of election that Barth says that he would have "preferred to follow Calvin's doctrine of predestination much more closely,"[281] yet had to depart radically from it. Barth sees himself as duty-bound to Scripture as well as to the Reformation theology.[282] Therefore it is appropriate to begin our examination of his ideas by examining Barth's exegesis.

This section focuses on Barth's chapter on election of the individual in §35,[283] II/2, in which he argues that Christ is both the elect and the rejected. Here we unearth the "most important exegeses of biblical narratives in the volume."[284] Barth presents three excursuses, on Lev 14 and 16, on Saul and David, and on 1 Kgs 13.[285] These are part of the line of argument that highlights the biblical pattern of the two sides of election, the elect and the reprobate, starting with Cain and Abel. In all these biblical narratives, Barth sees two lines "running through the biblical history, with the elect and rejected being complementary in a binary structure until finally they meet in one person, Jesus Christ."[286]

---

279. Ford, *Barth and God's Story*, 72.

280. *CD* II/2, ix.

281. *CD* II/2, x.

282. It is a commitment less to the Reformed or Lutheran theology than to the Reformation principle of *sola scriptura*. See Gloege, "Zur Prädestinationslehre Karl Barths," 95.

283. I am aware that for Barth the election of the individual is never seen without the election of the community. My selection of Leviticus 14 and 16 for exegesis is twofold: (1) There already exists a book on Rom 9–11 (Gibson, *Reading the Decree*.) and (2) I am interested in Barth's cultic understanding of the atonement.

284. Ford, *Barth and God's Story*, 79.

285. Hays comments that "[t]hese are rich and significant expositions, and I suspect he purposely avoids the classical loci concerning election and predestination in order to broaden the scope of the debate," in Hays, "Blessed be Egypt my people," 31.

286. Ford, *Barth and God's Story*, 79.

It is in this subsection, *The Elect and the Rejected*, that Barth gives an exegetical explanation and justification of his doctrine of election.[287] He starts his exegesis by looking at Gen 4, which becomes a paradigm for God's election of the individual, and introduces it with the question "why Abel?"[288] or more generally "what makes men elect?"[289] He examines the central biblical enigma that "this individual" is elected whilst "that individual" is not, the "mysterious freedom in which these individuals are present, and complete their course."[290] For Barth, "this mysterious freedom is the most general determination of the election of the individual in the Old Testament."[291] Bächli suggests that we only fully comprehend Barth's biblical exegesis (starting with Gen 4) "*wenn man sie nicht als selbständigen Korpus in den Perikopen wertet, sondern als Exposition zu den folgenden alttestamentlichen Exkursen.*"[292] Besides the story in Gen 4 of Cain and Abel, the archetypal figures of the rejected and innocent sufferer, and the stories of Saul and David and of 1 Kgs 13,[293] Barth provides an intriguing exegesis of Lev 14 and 16 and links the result (his typological-christological exegesis) to the doctrine of the election of the individual. Barth turns to the cultic text of the ritual laws of Leviticus,[294] indicating that we are confronted in Lev 14 and 16 with a restatement and development of the choices found in Genesis—in "two sets of ritual instructions which are very different but obviously related in general structure."[295]

Therefore, the following will be a close reading of Barth's exegesis of Lev 14 and 16. The reason for selecting these particular texts rather than the excursuses on Saul and David or 1 Kgs 13, is that they that have been neglected in Barth scholarship, despite the fact that (as the previous paragraph

---

287. CD II/2, 354–409.

288. CD II/2, 341. See also Bächli, *Das Alte Testament in der Kirchlichen Dogmatik*, 168. In the same question are also included: Cain, Enoch, Noah, Shem, Abraham, Isaac, Jacob, Judah, Benjamin, Joseph and Moses.

289. CD II/2, 342.

290. CD II/2, 342

291. CD II/2, 342. For Barth's use of the Old Testament see Büttner, *Das Alte Testament als erster Teil der christlichen Bibel*, 18–30. On Barth's criticism of von Harnack see also ibid., 51–60.

292. Bächli, *Das Alte Testament in der Kirchlichen Dogmatik*, 169. The excurses Barth looks at are: (1) Lev 14:4–7 and 16:5-6, (2) the story of Saul and David in both books of Sam and (3) 1 Kgs 13.

293. See ibid., 168–184 and Ford, *Barth and God's Story*, 81–84.

294. See CD II/2, 357ff.

295. CD II/2, 357.

48   Election, Atonement, and the Holy Spirit

showed) Barth himself indicates them to be crucial for understanding his doctrine of election and rejection.

6.1. Barth's Exegesis of Leviticus 14 and 16[296]

Barth looks at two ritual instructions found in Lev 14 and 16. The first is the ceremony for cleansing a leper in Lev 14:4–7, the second, the ritual of the great Day of Atonement in Lev 16:5f. In the first ritual of Lev 14, two living birds are brought to the priest together with some cedar wood, scarlet yarn, and hyssop for the one to be cleansed. One bird is killed over fresh water and its blood is caught in a clay pot. The priest then takes the second bird, which is still alive, and dips it together with the cedar wood, scarlet yearn and hyssop into the blood of the first bird that was killed over fresh water. The person who is to be cleansed from leprosy is sprinkled seven times with the blood and the priest pronounces him clean. Finally, the second bird (which was dipped alive in the blood of the first bird) is released to fly away into the open field.

In the second ritual, in Lev 16, the High Priest presents to the Lord two live goats at the entrance to the Tent of Meeting. The Priest draws lots for the two goats—one for the Lord and the other for Azazel.[297] After offering a bull for his own sins and sprinkling its blood on the atonement cover, the High Priest then offers the first goat (upon which the Lord's lot fell) for the purification offering for the people. Taking the blood into the Holy of Holies, he sprinkles it in front and on the ἱλαστήριον, the *kappōret*, the lid of the Ark of the Covenant (Luther's *Gnadenstuhl*, the mercy seat); Barth says that in this way, "expiation, or a covering, is made for the uncleanness and trespasses of the people."[298] After making atonement at the altar and the Holy of Holies, he takes the second goat and confesses over it all the

---

296. Even though Barth does not explicitly mention Kohlbrügge, *Auslegungen zu 3. Mose*, in his exegesis of Lev 14 and 16, I hypothesise that Barth used or at least read and knew his work. This theory was formed on the basis of research undertaken at the Barth-*Archiv* in Basel in December 2011 and I must thank Dr Hans-Anton Drewes for his warm welcome and invaluable assistance. At the archives I had the chance to examine Barth's commentaries on Leviticus in particular his copy of Kohlbrügge's book (KBA H 291:14). I observed substantial underlining, which sparked my suspicion that it had influenced Barth's own work. Though it is impossible to prove conclusively that Barth's exegesis of Lev 14 and 16 was influenced by Kohlbrügge (and this is not the primary contention of this book), I have footnoted parallels between Barth and Kohlbrügge.

297. Azazel is commonly translated from the Hebrew as 'scapegoat,' from 'escapegoat,' but this is based on an inaccurate translation by William Tyndale.

298. *CD* II/2, 357.

wickedness and rebellion of the Israelites. These 'sins' are put on the head of the goat, which is then sent away into the desert, to the realm of Azazel (in some Jewish traditions Azazel is seen as a 'rocky place' or a 'desert demon').[299] In this way the goat carries away all the sins of the Israelites into the desert (according to Jewish tradition, the goat was normally pushed over the edge of a cliff to ensure it wouldn't come back into the camp and contaminate the community).[300] Barth sees these sacrificial rituals as a "sign and testimony" [*Zeichen- und Zeugnischarakter*][301] of God's divine intention.

For Barth, the unifying significance of Lev 14 and 16 is the common form of both rituals: that each time two animals—identical in species and value—undergo completely different treatments. Yet, whereas in Lev 14 the fate of each particular bird appears to be the free choice of the Priest, in Lev 16 it is the Lord's decision—the goats are chosen through the casting of lots. Nevertheless, we see the divine "divisive choice"[302] of 'this' and not 'that' person. Barth concludes, "[w]hat these choices mean, or what it is to which the whole history of Israel points as a history of such choices, is attested by these particular rites, the witness being given a fixed and permanent form by the detailed legal regulations."[303]

This divine decision, Barth explains, becomes even more obvious in the actual treatment of the two animals in Lev 14 and 16, and is an example of the elective principle running through the Old Testament (and is highlighted in his own doctrine of election): one animal is used (it is killed) whilst the other is "not to be used-or only used to the extent that it is, so to speak, solemnly and necessarily not used"[304] (it is released into freedom). At this stage Barth thinks it is too soon to give any further description of *what* is meant by 'using' and 'not using,' 'killing' and 'releasing,' and he also does not elucidate *who* is signified by the first and second animals. What he does is to say that it is almost inevitable that we are reminded here of the Genesis narratives of those like Cain and Abel, Isaac and Ishmael, Jacob and Esau, which parallel the rituals in Leviticus. He states that "the ceremonies are obviously a comment on the history of Israel as a history of the differing

---

299. See Tawil, "Azazel The Prince of the Steepe," 45.

300. See Mishna *Yoma* and Targum *Pseudo-Jonathan*. Grabbe, "The Scapegoat Tradition," 158f. and Helm, "Azazel in Early Jewish Tradition," 225f.

301. *CD* II/2, 357.

302. *CD* II/2, 358.

303. *CD* II/2, 357f.

304. *CD* II/2, 358.

choices, and its character as witness is fixed in the legal instructions which relate to these actions."[305]

Another central similarity to which Barth points is that both ceremonies attest to a purification.[306] In Lev 14 the priest confirms that the person is cured from leprosy and in Lev 16 the High Priest verifies the removal of sin from the entire nation. However, "the rites as such do *not complete but attest* a purification which has already taken place, is still taking place, and takes place again. Neither the priest nor Aaron, but *God, is its author.*"[307] Barth reminds us that God as the author is also to be seen as the underlying rationale in respect to all stories of election. This is seen in the fact that the Israelites were the "object of the purification" and "no more than a spectator," and that these rituals were signs of what God intended for Israel and had already done through his mighty works.[308]

Yet despite all the similarities between the rituals in Lev 14 and 16, Barth also highlights some significant inner differences. He writes that although there is a common theme of 'use' and 'not-use' as well as of 'killing' and 'releasing' of the animals, they nevertheless have different meanings in each ritual.

6.2. *Barth's Explanation of Leviticus 16*[309]

For Barth, to understand the treatment of the animals in Lev 16 for the purification [*Reinigung*] of the nation of Israel is a matter of recognizing that the text talks from a 'standpoint of the presupposition' that what is most important is the way that leads up to the killing, *why* it is necessary and *what* medium is being used. As Barth points out, what is important is "not so much the nation's new status of reconciliation to God as the fact that a reconciliation is necessary if the nation is to be transferred to this new status, and that there is in fact this reconciliation."[310] The purpose and use of the death and blood of the first goat are primary for Barth, and the '*for what*' that they serve is secondary, because the emphasis is on the fact that

---

305. *CD* II/2, 358.

306. See Ford who comments that the "common aim of the chapters is purification," in Ford, *Barth and God's Story*, 79.

307. *CD* II/2, 358. italics mine. As Calvin confirms, "*Solius Dei est peccata remittere.*"

308. *CD* II/2, 358.

309. See Kohlbrügge, *Auslegungen zu 3. Mose*, 316–29.

310. *CD* II/2, 358f.

they are indeed actually used.[311] The 'presupposition' of the whole ritual is therefore God's willingness to be merciful towards the sinner, the fact that he, as the wise and omnipotent Judge, has provided the means and medium for dealing with the impurities of Israel, the object of his wrath.

> It is this redemptive endurance of death as such, ordained and accomplished by God in His love for him, which is brought before his eyes in the slaughtering of the different animals on the Day of Atonement, and therefore in the slaying of the first goat, and then in the blood-sprinkling of the ark of the covenant and the tabernacle, in the sanctification of the first goat, and then in the blood-sprinkling of the ark of the covenant and the tabernacle, in the sanctification of the sanctuary by the slaying of the first goat, by the total outpouring of its life as accomplished in the shedding of its blood. Man is chosen for the Lord, and not for Azazel, not for the wilderness; and God has made it His own concern that there should be visited on him the redemptive suffering and death by which the presupposition of his purification and renewed life is secured. He may—and this is God's great love—totally surrender his blood, that is, his impure life. The redemptive method by which God leads him is that he is placed under the utter graciousness and terror of this law of death.[312]

In the ritual Israel should see that it is God who is dealing with her impurities, and she is invited to recognise herself in the first goat as the chosen nation, elected by and for God and not for Azazel.

The question that Barth then addresses is how it is possible that Israel, lost and in the realm of Azazel, can be elect. How can God still accept the offering, despite Israel's impurities and transgressions against God, her forfeit of her relationship with God through sin? Barth sees the power of God's grace in the fact that Israel is placed first under God's judgment and through this on the way to life, and it is this divine mercy that provides for Barth the answer to his question. However, in some sense this picture of two animals fails to express fully what is being communicated in the ritual, that in fact the two animals represent *one and the same identity*. The picture uses two animals to show the duality of the event but in fact they are intended to represent the one thing at the Day of Atonement. Alongside the first animal, 'used,' slain for the sins of the nation, we see the second animal; "the death of the one, which is, in fact, full of grace and salvation, is accompanied by

---

311. See *CD* II/2, 359.
312. *CD* II/2, 359.

the life of the other, which is, in fact, the essence of desolation, indeed of death itself."[313] All that is revealed in the second animal is that Israel (in fact all of humanity) in itself is unfit, unworthy to do God's service; that the blood of a human being is of no value; that humanity has no capacity to make good what is evil; and that no judgment placed on her, not even death, can turn her evil status into one that is deemed good. This is what the second goat represents—not a freeing of the animal into liberty but rather a chasing away "into the realm of Azazel, the demon of the wilderness; his surrender to an utterly distressful non-existence, to a life which is as such no life."[314] What the treatment of the second goat symbolizes to Israel through the picture is a proclamation that the place where they really belong is in the wilderness:

> It is from thence that you have been taken and called, and apart from the grace of God you could never find yourself elsewhere, nor know any other life than this life in the shadow of death. But the grace of God has now led you forth from that place. That which was promised you in your elect ancestors, and is now revealed in the picture of the first goat used for sacrifice, is that God leads from darkness into light, from the wilderness into the land of promise.[315]

It is in this way that the non-elect do not simply testify to their own hopeless existence but are in fact representatives of all humanity, her sins and her punishment, a life in the wilderness away from the community, lacking any chance of purification, a redemptive sacrificial death and hence a life beyond reconciliation and new life.[316] The second goat is the "image of the non-elect as they (Cain, Ishmael, Esau) stand apart from the elect,"[317] the embodiment of a human being as he is without the divine grace of God.

Barth ends his examination of Lev 16 with the observation that even the second goat is being 'placed before God,' and that his tragic treatment is also a part of the ritual and thus a sign and testimony that plays an integral part in the Day of Atonement:

> Cain is just as indispensable as Abel, and Ishmael as Isaac. For the grace which makes an elect man of the first can be seen only from the second, because the first, the elect, must see in

---

313. *CD* II/2, 359.
314. *CD* II/2, 359.
315. *CD* II/2, 359.
316. See *CD* II/2, 360.
317. *CD* II/2, 360.

the second, the non-elect, as in a mirror, that from which he was taken, and who and what the God is who has delivered him from it. It is only as one who properly belongs to that place that God has transferred him from it. Because election is grace, the unused belongs to the used, the sacrificed goat to the goat driven into the wilderness, the non-elect to the elect.[318]

6.3. Barth's Explanation of Leviticus 14[319]

In Lev 14, however, the ceremony of the ritual described runs in exactly the opposite direction to the ritual in Lev 16. The purification based on the divine election "is not manifested here in the first bird which is slain but in the second which is released."[320] So what we see in Lev 14 is a witness to the fact that the human being with leprosy has to die in order to be freed from life under the wrath of God, a life limited in existence as a result of his disease, and to be accepted again by God by his grace descending on him. Barth interprets the shedding of the blood as the only way for the person to receive grace and be welcomed back into the community, the only possible way—radical as it sounds—that renewal of life can take place: "His pure new life can be born only through such a total surrender of his previous impure life. The treatment of the first bird speaks of this necessary presupposition of his purification."[321] After the blood is shed, what follows is parallel to the ritual in Lev 16. However, what follows, Barth points out, is in sharp contrast to Lev 16 where it was not so much the status of reconciliation that was of importance but the fact that reconciliation was necessary as well as available at all. In Lev 14 we need to establish the essential part of the ritual, since everything depends on the purpose, on the 'for what.' What is the purpose of the death of the bird and the shedding of its blood? For what purpose is the blood used? We read in verse 6 that the living bird is dipped into the blood, together with the other material, of the first bird. After that, two events happen simultaneously: (1) the healed leper is sprinkled seven times with the blood, whilst (2) the second bird is released to fly away into the open field, into freedom. Barth states that it is the fact that

> the first bird has yielded its life and blood for the purification
> of the second bird, the latter is actually pure, and freedom may

---

318. CD II/2, 360.
319. See Kohlbrügge, *Auslegungen zu 3. Mose*, 234–37.
320. CD II/2, 360. See also Kohlbrügge, *Auslegungen zu 3. Mose*, 234.
321. CD II/2, 360.

and must be given it—and when the healed leper is sprinkled with the same blood, he is told that he is now removed from the realm of the divine wrath, and is once more a free member of the congregation.[322]

6.4. Linking the Exegesis back to the Doctrine of Election

What does the second bird mean? For Barth, the bird undoubtedly signifies the resurrection,[323] God's grace towards Israel. It is a sign of the freedom that God bestows as well as of the restoration and renewal of life that God brings about. Yet it is also a witness to the fact that freedom, restoration, and renewal of life cannot happen without the other bird first having to die.[324]

What remains is the key question 'who do the birds in Lev 14 represent?' because throughout the entire history of Israel, the Bible contains no analogy or picture to identify the slain and living birds.[325] The same question should be attached to the ritual in Lev 16, for the identification of the sacrificed goat and the unusable non-sacrificial one. What we see in the texts is that there have to be two animals involved (and therefore two human beings) which, despite being ostensibly separate, both point to and represent the 'one thing.' It is this duality that we observe in the texts—"the use which is made of the death of the one; and the purpose for which it is used—the life of the other. The one has necessarily to die in order that the other may live."[326] For Barth, the fact that one has to die in order that the other may live is the crux of all differentiation that occurs in election. Barth sees this as a consolation for all those who are separated and non-elect because "according to Lev 14, it is to the second bird, which has no part in the accomplishment of the decisive action, and which is unusable in the sense of Lev 16, that the benefit of the sacrifice of the first and usable bird accrues."[327]

What occurs to the first animal is to the advantage of the second one. The second bird remains unhurt by partaking of the salvation, which was accomplished by the death of the first bird by being dipped in its blood. It is released into freedom as a sign for the previously diseased and outcast person that he can go back into the community, because his purification has

---

322. *CD* II/2, 360.
323. See Kohlbrügge, *Auslegungen zu 3. Mose*, 236f.
324. See *CD* II/2, 361.
325. See Staubli, "Die Symbolik des Vogelrituals," 230–37.
326. *CD* II/2, 361.
327. *CD* II/2, 361.

been achieved and his new life—as a part of the community—has begun.[328] The unusable one benefits from the use of the other. Election is not simply for the benefit of the one being elected to be used, but also for the one non-elected, for the unused. Barth concludes:

> The recipient of the fruit of election is obviously the non-elect. How can we fail to see that Cain and Ishmael and Esau are now given yet another right than that which is remotely visible in Lev. 16? They are witnesses to the resurrection reflected in Lev. 14. The promise addressed to the men on the right hand is manifestly fulfilled in those on the left. The one exalted by God through his election is humbled unto death in order that the one humbled by God through his rejection may be exalted.[329]

Barth warns the reader to see the humbled simply as a 'dark shadow,' as a contrast to the light of the exalted one. So what is the benefit to the one exalted by his election, what are his riches? The simple answer is that the only benefit is one of being used by God—his becoming poor by pouring out his life and blood unto death, by giving away his riches in order that the poor become rich.[330] This is the purpose of his election—he is elected to be used for the benefit of others. In the Old Testament, "individuals are chosen or called to serve the people."[331] For Barth this reality displays the glory and grace of God's election. In light of the Lev 14 picture Barth boldly asks whether any trace of God's unrighteousness is left towards the non-elect. He concludes his analysis of the texts and their differences by saying that Israel

---

328. See Kohlbrügge, *Auslegungen zu 3. Mose*, 234.

329. *CD* II/2, 361.

330. See 2 Cor 8:9.

331. Pannenberg, *Systematic Theology III*, 455. This is particularly true of the kings in relation to the people. Like Barth, Pannenberg understands the Old Testament notion of the election of the individual to occur in order that the individual can serve the people at large, and sees it as a key issue in Israel's election traditions, see Barth's excursuses on 1 Kings 13 and Saul and David. Pannenberg also highlights that the election of people cannot be fully comprehended if viewed only from the "standpoint of service to others," 456. He provides an example from Deuteronomy, which emphasizes YHWH's "possession." It is not until Deutero-Isaiah, however, that Israel is depicted as God's servant, elected and given the Spirit to "take justice to the peoples (42:1) and bring them to know the deity of Yahweh (43:10). Thus Israel is the light to the people (Is 42:6; 49:6)." This notion of Deutero-Isaiah of the servant, to bring justice and be a light to the nations will be picked up in chapter 5 (in the conclusion of section 3) of this book. Furthermore, "in the NT, too, the electing will of God aims at the community and beyond it at all humanity," 457. Schleiermacher sought to shatter the "individualism in the doctrine of election that we may trace back to Augustine," and Ritschl related the doctrine of election to Jesus himself, 458.

needs to recognise herself in both pictures of Lev 14 and 16: (1) in Lev 16 as the elected goat, grateful to be accepted and used for God's purposes; and (2) in the same way as the non-elect in the picture of the second bird of Lev 14, grateful for the new life given by God's mercy. Barth writes:

> If, according to Lev. 16, the non-elect, those who are separated and rejected, stand in the shadows in order that the grace of God may illumine and continue to illumine the elect, we are also taught by Lev. 14 that it is into the realm of Azazel that the light of God's grace is poured and streams abroad.[332]

6.5. *Commonalities and the Meaning of Death and Life in the Cultic Rituals*

Now Barth turns to the examination of the texts and their commonalities. Most broadly, these cultic texts demonstrate God's interaction with humanity's sin (new life being possible only through death). Both death and life are essential parts of *one* whole being and refer to the relationship of all creaturely beings and their Creator. For Barth, "death is the saving judgment of God, which is necessary in the operation of His grace towards man and therefore exhibits His love for him, and through which he is cleansed and led into life."[333] Barth points out that death in a cultic setting has to be seen from God's perspective and to be understood with reference to God's merciful will and action. Our human and limited view of death distorts the true picture of the purifying and salvation-bringing sacrifice that we read about in these texts and means that we find it difficult to harmonize death with the love of God. Death in a cultic setting utterly transcends our human understanding; we can only start to comprehend death fully when it is seen in its relationship to the new and better life that it brings about:

> Death is the sacrifice willed and ordained and accepted by God in His goodness to man. The life of which these two passages speak has two possible meanings in contrast to the unequivocal meaning of death. It may be the wretched life of man that does not deserve this death and does not partake of the salvation secured by it. But it may also be the new liberated life of the man who has merited this death, and by means of it passed through to his salvation.[334]

332. *CD* II/2, 361.
333. *CD* II/2, 362.
334. *CD* II/2, 362.

Election, Rejection, and Exegesis 57

Barth calls death in the context of these rituals a transcending reality. This can also be said when talking about new life. The life known by humanity is a limited life, a limited reality, and just as we neither know life in the 'realm of Azazel' nor life of 'real freedom,' the Israelites were also unable to recognise themselves directly in the sacrifice of the first animal and in the casting out of the second; both pictures transcend the human reality.[335]

Barth concludes that the events described cannot be allowed to occur to a person in reality because "this death and life are too superhumanly great to be exhibited to the Israelites otherwise than in the picture of this sacrificial ritual. They are too great to be expected of the Israelites themselves or enjoined on them."[336] Therefore, the reality of the rituals described in the texts can only be attested to Israel in pictures of these ceremonies, spoken to her as a word of truth, as a revelation of a hidden and deeper reality. Similarly, the biblical stories of election and rejection of individuals point to truths far more significant than is apparent on a superficial reading—their fate transcends and points beyond their reality to a deeper truth. What Barth is aiming to communicate from the beginning is that it is a matter of faith[337]—a question of whether one believes in the Word of God spoken in these texts, whether one trusts in what is said and believes in it by faith. Only then can the death and life described in the texts become a person's own experience.[338]

Another point highlighted by Barth is that of the unity of the events. Even if one could recognise the 'realm of Azazel' and the 'realm of true freedom,' how could one see oneself simultaneously in both?

> What Israelite could think of the ritual of the purification of the leper at the very moment when the atonement ritual was administered, or *vice versa*? Obviously the fact that we have here a single reality, the one grace of God which has decreed life and death for man, is no less hidden than the grace of the death and life themselves and as such. This shows us again how the matter attested transcends the reality known to us.[339]

What follows is that it is necessary that this unity be attested to in a duality, in two pictures, or rather (to be precise) in four (death and life in both Lev

---

335. See *CD* II/2, 362.

336. *CD* II/2, 362.

337. On the matter of faith Ford writes that "the logic of the story converges uniquely with the necessity for faith," in Ford, "Barth's Interpretation of the Bible," 82.

338. See *CD* II/2, 362.

339. *CD* II/2, 362.

14 and 16).³⁴⁰ Death and life cannot be seen in only one picture—they are mirror images and yet also part of one event. The salvific death that is common to both texts can be seen as the axis around which the different aspects of the event rotate: (1) Lev 16 looks back from the standpoint of death to the old life which is annulled by death, and (2) Lev 14 looks forward from the salvific death towards the new life that has been won. Yet it is the one event, the one salvific death, which stands at the centre of both, one event that is portrayed from two different perspectives, backward and forward looking. Furthermore, Barth draws a parallel to the elected and the rejected individuals in the biblical narratives and contends that these stories do not escape the same duality described in the ritual texts. Yet with regard to the rejected and unusable he leaves us with the following note:

> But then there are, of course, the intersections, in virtue of which the relationship seems suddenly to be reversed, and suddenly and in spite of everything God reveals Himself to the rejected and unused. This shows how inherently fluid are the testimonies of these stories, so that we are prohibited from too hastily identifying the elect with certain persons, or too hastily identifying the rejected with other persons in the stories.³⁴¹

However, what all these texts hold in common is that, first, they are witnesses to a higher reality and thus point beyond themselves and, secondly, they all have the same provisional character "and in this way the Old Testament as a whole, in this matter at least, is determined as the witness to a reality of which, even in the Old Testament itself, we can only say positively that it is that which it attests, its true and proper subject."³⁴²

6.6. *The Mysterious Subject of the Cultic Texts*

Barth's analysis at this point hits an *impasse*, with one question remaining: 'What is the subject of the Old Testament witnesses?' Barth maintains that we are confronted with a choice here, that either (1) the "subject of the Old Testament witness may be regarded as an unknown quantity. This might mean that for some reason it is not yet known to us. [. . .] But it might also mean that the Old Testament has no subject at all, that its testimony points into the void" or (2) that the "subject of the Old Testament witness may be

---

340. On the duality and relationality of the animals see Kohlbrügge, *Auslegungen zu 3. Mose*, 321.
341. *CD* II/2, 363.
342. *CD* II/2, 363.

Election, Rejection, and Exegesis 59

accepted as identical with the person of Jesus Christ as it is seen and interpreted and proclaimed by the apostles because He had Himself revealed and represented Himself to them in this way."[343] These two options hinge, Barth asserts, not so much on an exegetical question—even though exegesis is ultimately forced to speak a final word—but once again on a question of faith.[344]

To summarize Barth's argument, he sees Lev 14 and 16 (alongside the stories and pictures in Genesis) as prophecies of and witnesses to Jesus Christ.[345] Indeed, Barth shows that the Church Fathers' exegesis also read Scripture typologically, looking at pictures that appeared to point towards Christ and be fulfilled in him. Here Barth stresses his own "originality in relation to 'the older exegesis' which came to the same conclusion, but by a different method."[346] For Barth "only the positive decision of faith in Jesus Christ (as the only way really to know Him as the One He is) can vindicate the older Christian exegesis of these texts as prophecies of Christ."[347] He continues to contend that if this is the case then "this exegesis is rendered not merely possible but even necessary. How can we believe in Jesus Christ and not of necessity recognise Him in these passages?"[348] This decision made by faith allows Barth finally to uncover the mystery of the subject in these ritual texts, and to conclude that the solution to the enigma is faith in Jesus Christ. Ford highlights the "lack of any systematic connection between the literary analysis and the judgment of faith. The analysis is admitted to be inconclusive, and there is no attempt by exegesis to prove anything more than the possibility of a christological interpretation."[349]

With regard to the election of the individual, Barth sees Jesus Christ as the presupposition and the underlying subject of any further talk of election. He sees the elected individuals in the Old Testament stories as witnesses to and types of Christ himself, because "it is He, Jesus Christ, who is originally and properly the elect individual. All others can be this only as types of Him, only as His prototypes or copies, only as those who belong to Him."[350] So Barth, who identifies Jesus Christ as the revealed secret of the transcend-

---

343. *CD* II/2, 363.

344. See *CD* II/2, 364.

345. See Ford, *Barth and God's Story*, 81.

346. Ford explains that Barth sees "their exegesis is explicitly looked to Christ from the start, whereas he claims that he begins by letting the text 'speak by and for itself,'" ibid., 81.

347. *CD* II/2, 364.

348. *CD* II/2, 364.

349. Ford, *Barth and God's Story*, 81.

350. *CD* II/2, 364.

ing reality of the slain and living person in the Old Testament, sees each of the four animals in Lev 14 and 16 as representing Christ, being a type of him.[351] It is only the New Testament texts that attest to the fulfilment of the prophecies of the Old Testament—whilst the Old Testament texts point beyond their own reality to another, the New Testament witnesses to this reality in the person and life of Jesus Christ.

6.7. Jesus Christ: Vere Deus et Vere Homo

In a final step Barth turns to Calvin's exegesis of Lev 16 and agrees with it.[352] He links his exegesis of the Levitical texts, that Jesus Christ is the meaning and purpose as well as the hidden subject of the texts, to his doctrine of election, in which Jesus Christ is the one elect individual. Here in the doctrine of election,

> according to His divine nature, Jesus Christ is the eternal Son [...] who coming thence took our flesh upon Him to be and to offer this sacrifice, for the glory of God and for our salvation, and by taking our place to accomplish our reconciliation to God.[353]

And in the same way that he came in honor and glory as the blameless and sinless lamb, he is also the second goat, the rejected one, the Son of David who suffers, allowing

> the sin of many to be laid upon Him (and it is the faith of His Church that it can and should lay all its sin upon Him), in order that He may bear it away: out from the camp into the greatest shame (Heb 13:12); out into the darkness, the nothingness from which it came and to which alone it belongs; and just as radically away from the many, that it may no longer and never again be to them a burden. For this, in our flesh, according to His human nature, as the Son of David, He must be the Rejected.[354]

Barth asks how one person might simultaneously partake of both the glory of the lamb and the shame of the second goat. He continues that only in

---

351. See *CD* II/2, 365.

352. See also Kohlbrügge, *Auslegungen zu 3. Mose*, 322.

353. *CD* II/2, 365. It is interesting that here Barth forgoes even mentioning the election, whereas later he writes about rejection (the rejected God).

354. *CD* II/2, 365.

Christ, who was "very God and very man, in perfect unity, the glory and the shame and abandonment were reality, one reality."³⁵⁵

Romans 4:25 has the last word: "He was delivered over to death for our sins and was raised to life for our justification." Barth sees this verse as the fulfilment of the prophetic picture of Lev 14. He links the "delivered" [παραδίδωμι]³⁵⁶ to the first bird in the ritual, which is a picture for or type of Christ, not because he is impure, but because he became a pure sacrifice for our sake. Through his obedience and sinless humanity Jesus steps into the place of the leper and dies the death without which the leper would not be made pure again. Yet, the second bird that is released into freedom is also a picture of Christ, of his resurrection. Its overcoming death is a picture of the new life in Christ that he brings about through his death and resurrection (Rom 6:4). Jesus Christ was unique in representing both the spotless lamb and the sin-laden animal at the same time, both the humiliated and exalted one. Only in Jesus Christ, both very God and very human, can the humiliation and the exaltation be one simultaneous reality.

> If, according to this commentary, the stories deal with a reality, and indeed a single reality, then the man who in these stories is inscrutable, who transcends all humanity as we know it, who is beyond the always twofold form in which he is revealed in them, is the one man Jesus Christ, who as such is the Son of God.³⁵⁷

If it is the case that Jesus Christ is at one time God's elect and God's rejected, then the election stories in the Old Testament—which we have seen can be read as foreshadowing Christ—have to be read in the same light. Then, Barth continues, it is not only Abel who is a type of Christ but also Cain; not only Isaac, but also Ishmael (the rejected one, who was sent away into the desert).³⁵⁸ Then we see not only Israel as the elected nation belonging to God, but also the excluded heathen nations as a part of God's salvation plan, not utterly excluded after all. Barth maintains that this becomes the case if the final word of one's exegesis of these texts in Leviticus is the name Jesus Christ, "if He is understood as the individual in whom we recover both the

---

355. *CD* II/2, 365.

356. See *CD* II/2, 365. See also Barth's excursus on Judas where his typological exegesis "reaches its greatest concentration," in Ford, *Barth and God's Story*, 85, and where the "divine παραδοῦναι coincides with its antitype, Judas' παραδοῦναι," ibid., 86. Here Jesus and Judas stand opposite each other.

357. *CD* II/2, 365.

358. See *CD* II/2, 366.

unity of that which they all commonly attest, and that which is the peculiar individuality of each."[359]

Barth's last comment regarding the exegesis of Lev 14 and 16 is a challenge to his reader:

> Those who think they must reject this as the final word in exegesis of Lev. 14 and 16 must either undertake to prove another and better final word in explanation of these passages, or they must admit that they do not know of any, and therefore that ultimately they do not know to what or to whom these passages refer. The same has necessarily to be said about the election stories on which these passages are simply a commentary.[360]

Conclusion

We have seen that one of the most interesting and perceptive features in Barth's doctrine of election is the way he uses Scripture to support his systematic theological reflection. What is his hermeneutical way of reading Scripture? And what are we to make of the exegesis in the small-print on Lev 14 and 16 in relation to his systematic-theological reflection and in relation to Scripture? Barth insists that the only way to do biblical exegesis is by "listening to what Scripture is saying and [. . .] repeating what is heard."[361] Ford shows that Barth's lecture in 1916, *Die neue Welt der Bibel*, set the scene for seeing the role of Scripture as witness to the divine revelation,[362] and its "insistence that the Bible interprets itself."[363] Barth's theological approach can be called 'holistic' in the sense that he incorporates both the Old and the New Testament texts. His exegesis shows how he sees the stories of both the Old and New Testaments as intertwined and coming to fulfilment in Jesus Christ. The method of relating the two testaments is that of typology, in which the "literal meaning or historical reality *both* is itself *and* at the same time points to another event or person of fuller meaning."[364] Barth's understanding accords with the "older"[365] biblical interpretation that sees

---

359. *CD* II/2, 365.

360. *CD* II/2, 366.

361. Sykes, "The Study of Barth," 13. See also Ford, "Barth's Interpretation of the Bible," 55.

362. *CD* I/2, 462.

363. Ford, "Barth's Interpretation of the Bible," 57.

364. Ibid., 65.

365. *CD* II/2, 365.

Lev 14 and 16 as prophecies of Jesus Christ. Indeed, the Church Fathers' exegesis also reads Scripture typologically, looking at pictures that appear to point towards Christ and are fulfilled in him. Barth's approach was to leave the name Jesus Christ out of the picture—since the texts at the time could not utter Jesus' name—and to let the texts speak for themselves. However, by leaving Jesus in the background, Barth admits, we are presented with yet another enigma. The question of the subject remains a mystery, because the subject to which the rituals testify cannot be identified through any of the Old Testament texts and, indeed, transcends all human reality.[366] For Barth, the 'easy way out' would be to say that because we arrive at an exegetical 'dead end' and since the New Testament points to Jesus Christ as a perfect solution to the Old Testament exegetical puzzle, these texts are therefore prophecies of and witnesses to Jesus Christ. However, Barth believes "only the positive decision of faith in Jesus Christ (as the only way really to know Him as the One He is) can vindicate the older Christian exegesis of these texts as prophecies of Christ."[367] Hence according to Barth, it was a decision made by *faith* that allowed him finally to uncover the mystery of the subject in these ritual texts, and to conclude that the solution to the enigma is faith in Jesus Christ.

Barth sees the two doves and two goats as types pointing towards Christ. He sees the Old Testament bearing witness to Christ and this makes Jesus Christ the *key* to unlocking the Old Testament narrative. Christ is the one who gives meaning to the whole narrative of God and Israel, the content, centre, and fulfilment of the Hebrew Scriptures. Thus Barth sees Jesus Christ as the "biblical hero"[368] of both testaments in whom God has fully revealed himself. Ford's thesis is that Barth in his doctrine of election uses "one dominant approach"[369] that provides structure for his entire theology. Barth offers a literary analysis of biblical stories "in such a way as to find the will of God making sense of the interweaving of good and evil, by creating the master pattern, Jesus' death and resurrection, in which the relation of evil to good is finally defined."[370] His hermeneutical circle focuses on two events, the crucifixion and resurrection (God's *No* and God's *Yes*), which become his exegetical foundation.[371] We see this dialectic between *Yes* and *No* as early as the first edition to the *Römerbrief*, and Barth's whole theology,

366. See *CD* II/2, 364.
367. *CD* II/2, 364.
368. Wallace, "Karl Barth's Hermeneutic," 406.
369. Ford, "Barth's Interpretation of the Bible," 56.
370. Ibid., 67.
371. See ibid., 58.

what came to be known as 'dialectical theology' actually "pivots around two events in one man's life-story, the crucifixion and resurrection."[372] On the one hand, Jesus' crucifixion is understood as the only rejection (he is the single reprobate); on the other hand, his resurrection shows God's election of humanity. Election is thus understood as Christ suffering "rejection on the cross and elect[ing] this in order that humanity may be elect even in its rejection of God."[373]

We have seen this dialectical aspect of the "pattern of exchange"[374] exemplified in the exegesis of Lev 14 where the first bird that died, who represented death and the cross, was brought into relationship *with* and was 'used' *for* the sake of the second bird who was released into freedom, signifying life and the resurrection. This is also reflected in the large print section of the *CD*, where Barth depicts Christ as simultaneously elected to both cross and resurrection. There Jesus' crucifixion is understood as the only rejection, and the resurrection shows God's election and in this way the binary of "Yes and No (ultimate and penultimate) must stand in the present in perfect but ordered simultaneity."[375] We can conclude that Barth's exegesis and systematic-theological reflection are in harmony with each other and form a unity, which has to be seen together in order to grasp his understanding of God's story of election with humanity, which unfolds and comes to fulfilment in Jesus Christ.

But a number of questions remain. Is Barth's intoxicating Old Testament exegesis "*zu schön*" [too neat]?[376] Can the binary of election and rejection in the biblical stories—beginning with Cain and Abel—be resolved and brought into a synthesis in Jesus Christ, or is Barth in danger of fabricating a biblical system and hermeneutical method that is not in line *with* and faithful *to* the biblical witness? Does he press the typology for a positive verdict to which the texts do not witness, and in doing so is it not the case that he "not only tries to know more of God's purposes than can be elicited

---

372. Ibid., 70.

373. Greggs, *Barth, Origen, and Universal Salvation*, 27.

374. See McMaken, "Election and the Pattern of Exchange in Karl Barth's Doctrine of Atonement," 209. What McMaken calls the 'pattern of exchange' is the 'one dominant approach' Ford highlights, the underlying dialectical relationship between God's *Yes* and *No* in the doctrine of election. For the relationship between election and the pattern of exchange see ibid., 215–17.

375. Greggs, *Barth, Origen, and Universal Salvation*, 51.

376. Stoevesandt, "Karl Barths Erwählungslehre," 99.

from the story but also does violence to its realism?"[377] Is the charge that he "uses typology in a way that obscures the literal, realistic sense"[378] justified?

In the next chapter we will pick up Barth's challenge to his reader and provide an alternative exegesis for the cultic texts in Leviticus. For now, our interim conclusion is that Barth's exegesis links up with his systematic-theological reflection in a harmonic hermeneutical circle, though we have raised some serious questions in relation to his doctrine of election in the large print which were confirmed in his exegesis in the small print. Here, all four animals were seen as a type pointing towards Christ's election and rejection; God's *Yes* and God's *No* were brought into a synthesis in Jesus Christ. However, the question remains: how can Jesus simultaneously fulfil the role of both goats, that of the sin offering as well as the goat sent to Azazel, two animals that serve completely different functions and have different fates?

---

377. Ford, "Barth's Interpretation of the Bible," 85.
378. Ibid., 86.

2

Jesus Christ the Elect
Through and Beyond Barth

Aaron shall cast lots on the two goats, one lot for the LORD and the other lot for Azazel. Aaron shall present the goat on which the lot fell for the LORD, and offer it as a sin offering; but the goat on which the lot fell for Azazel shall be presented alive before the LORD to make atonement over it, that it may be sent away into the wilderness to Azazel.
    (Lev 16:8–9)

Introduction

THIS CHAPTER WILL PICK UP BARTH'S CHALLENGE TO HIS READER (FOUND in the small print of §35.2) to surpass his argument and give a better interpretation of these cultic texts.[1] Despite partly agreeing with Barth's methodology and exegesis, I cannot reach the same conclusion. Instead, I shall argue that Jesus should *only* be seen as the elect and not the rejected. This chapter will investigate whether or not Barth does justice to the biblical texts by giving an alternative exegesis. Here I shall outline the concept of *Existenzstellvertretung*—a notion that I see as vital in understanding the Old Testament concept of atonement—and show that it is partly contained in Barth's thinking, though not fully developed or explicitly mentioned. The last step will be to focus on Barth's typological interpretation and outline some of the implications that my new alternative exegesis together with the concept of *Existenzstellvertretung* might have for Barth's doctrine of election.

---

1. See *CD* II/2, 366.

1. An Exegetical Challenge to Barth's Doctrine of Election

The aim of this section is to give an alternative exegesis of the texts and answer the questions addressed in chapter 1 before 'implanting' this exegesis back into Barth's own interpretative approach. The method I want to follow is Barth's own. First, I shall conduct an outer examination of the texts, but with a more exegetical approach (paying more attention to the texts). Secondly, I shall take a closer and more detailed look at the texts, particularly highlighting the media through and ways in which the individual comes into contact with the animals and vice versa. Thus, besides exegesis of the text and interpretation of the rituals the analysis will also include an examination of the ritualistic use of blood and the *sĕmîkâ*, the ritual of laying on hand(s).

Furthermore, though this section gives an alternative exegesis to the cultic texts of Lev 14 and 16, chapter 1 of this book, where Barth's understanding of the atonement was highlighted, will continue as the background to the discussion and will be occasionally drawn into the argument, especially when it comes to the concept of sin and sin bearing or, more generally, of sin removal. Here Barth's understanding in relation to election will be scrutinized.

However, before taking up this challenge, Bächli asks two questions in relation to Barth's exegesis of Lev 14 and 16, to which I would like to add two more followed by an attempt to answer them. The first of Bächli's questions relates to Barth's exegesis and the second to his conclusion linking his exegesis to his doctrine of election.[2] (1) Does Barth do justice to the texts in Leviticus? Has he portrayed the rituals accurately and interpreted them correctly? (2) Has Barth discovered a new exegesis, a new dimension to the hitherto accepted exegesis? (3) What is the role and function of blood as well as that of the human being in the ritual events? (4) In what way can we say that Jesus is a type of all four animals in Lev 14 and 16? This raises the question of the removal of sin in the atonement. Thus, we need to ask more precisely: can (and does) Jesus simultaneously fulfil the role of both goats of Lev 16, the sin-laden Azazel-goat as well as the sinless sin offering, two goats which are entirely separate, serving different functions and experiencing different fates (the Azazel-goat released into the desert bearing away the sins, the sin offering slain in a salvation-bringing and purifying death)? This is the underlying question of this book, whether Jesus is the elect as well as the rejected.

2. See Bächli, *Das Alte Testament in der Kirchlichen Dogmatik*, 173.

The questions addressed and the aspects of Barth's exegesis that are highlighted and given an alternative exegesis will vary in length. I will look at two significant questions: (1) exegetical questions—apparent 'errors' in the immediate context of these ritual portraits, and (2) questions of omissions in Barth's approach (asked in light of his own thought and approach). What aspects does he exclude and why, and what significance might these excluded aspects carry in the bigger picture of Barth's typological-exegetical approach?

1.1. *The Cultic Atonement in Leviticus: An Exegesis*

The book of Leviticus, and in particular chapter 16, summarizes the theology of the atonement cult. The following study neither asks whether or not the complex ritual of *Yom Kippur* ever actually happened in the way described in Leviticus, nor does it examine its redaction history. It will simply analyze the cultic atonement texts as described in Leviticus and compare them to Barth's reading. After an outline of the concept of *Existenzstellvertretung* as a paradigm used to describe the cultic atonement, my first step will be to look at the verb *kipper* (to atone), before considering the sin offering, the *ḥaṭṭā't*. What will follow is an analysis of the role of the blood and the purpose of the rite of laying the hand upon the animal's head, followed by an examination of the implications of the *Yom Kippur* and finishing with an exploration of the concept of sin bearing.

(A) THE CONCEPT OF *EXISTENZSTELLVERTRETUNG*[3]

Existenzstellvertretung is understood to be an atoning death, a vicarious offering of one's life as an equivalent substitution for the forfeited life of another. *Existenzstellvertretung* should be seen as a concept making sense of the theology of cultic atonement and events in the Old Testament, in particular in Leviticus. To contend that atonement is *Existenzstellvertretung* is to argue that the ungodly are redeemed from their sinful nature by participating in the death of the sacrifice through which they come into contact with the transcendent and holy God. The slaying of the sacrificial animal

---

3. For the concept of *Existenzstellvertretung* see Gese, "Die Sühne," 85–106; Janowski, *Sühne als Heilsgeschehen*; Stuhlmacher, "Existenzstellvertretung für die Vielen," 27–42; Hofius, "Sühne und Versöhnung," 33–49; Hofius, "Sühne IV," 342–477; Janowski and Stuhlmacher, *The Suffering Servant*; Graf, *Unterwegs zu einer Biblischen Theologie*, 174–77. For engagement within the English-speaking world see Bailey, "Concepts of Stellvertretung in the Interpretation of Isaiah 53," 223–59; Bell, "Sacrifice and Christology in Paul," and Bell, *Deliver Us from Evil*, 190–92.

should not be seen as a punishment of the animal, nor should the priestly offering of the blood be seen as a human work to appease an angry deity. Instead the sin offering and the sprinkling of the blood should be seen as a salvific act (restoring the covenantal fellowship previously breached by sin) enabled by God himself.[4]

(B) The Hebrew word Kipper—כִּפֶּר

Scholars have arrived at two possible derivations for the *piʿel* verb כִּפֶּר (*kipper*—to atone) from other Semitic languages: the Akkadian *kuppuru* 'to uproot,' 'wipe away,' and 'cleanse or purify' (cultically) or the Arabian *kaffara* 'to cover, hide.' However, Janowski[5] and Levine[6] point to a historical relationship between the Akkadian *kuppuru* and the Hebrew *kipper*, at least in Old Testament cultic contexts. Additionally, it should be observed that in its *piʿel* form *kipper* means 'to atone' and in the Old Testament the focus is on the result achieved rather than the process by which the result is reached.[7] In an interpersonal context the verb כִּפֶּר presupposes an act of legal-social, religious, or moral breach, due to which the existence of a person or community is forfeited.[8] The *kipper* texts describe situations in which a person's guilt thrusts him between the spheres of life and death, his situation being irreparable from the human side. Atonement, requested by a person and accomplished by God, "makes possible a restitution that affects one's very own being [. . .] in which a substitution is made or atonement accomplished symbolically."[9] The redemption price for the individual life is paid by a *kōper*, כֹּפֶר, a ransom, which should be understood as "a substitution for one's existence" פִּדְיוֹן נַפְשׁוֹ (see Exod 21:30).[10] The ransom 'takes the place,' תַּחַת, of a forfeited life, and rescues the individual from the sphere of death. Thus, *kōper* is understood as *Existenzstellvertretung*,[11] and the atonement act, "a saving of life, for which the person strives and which God accomplishes,"[12] enabling the continuation of life for the person.

---

4. See Janowski, "Atonement," 152f.
5. Janowski, *Sühne als Heilsgeschehen*, 15–102 passim.
6. Levine, *In the Presence of the Lord*, 56–63 and 121–27.
7. See Maass, "כפר," 626.
8. See Janowski, *Sühne als Heilsgeschehen*, 115.
9. Gese, "The Atonement," 95.
10. Ibid., 95.
11. See Janowski, *Sühne als Heilsgeschehen*, 174.
12. Gese, "The Atonement," 96.

So far, we may note two ways in which this exegesis differs from that of Barth. The first point, which in Barth's exegesis plays a relatively minor role but is nevertheless worth mentioning, is that Barth sees expiation as a 'covering' up of sin, whereas we did not follow the Arabian *kaffara* but the Akkadian *kuppuru*, to 'wipe away' and 'cleanse and purify.' The other more important aspect is the meaning of the verb *kipper*, to atone. Barth writes from a particular presupposition—his emphasis is on the *necessity* of the process of atonement in the light of humanity's sinful *status* rather than the resulting covenantal fellowship. Barth's primary focus is therefore not the new status of reconciliation—rather he simply understands reconciliation as 'necessary and available.' He focuses not on the result of the event (restoration of covenantal fellowship) but instead on the current state of Israel's sinfulness, where the reconciliation comes from and the way leading up to it.[13] In contrast, we have seen that the focus of the verb *kipper* is on the *result* rather than the process by which the result is achieved; what is important is the sinner's final reconciliation and his or her new status. In chapter 4 we will hear that for Barth, the removal or rather the "battle against sin"[14] is the main purpose of the atonement. He writes: "The very heart of the atonement is the overcoming of sin."[15] We will return to this important aspect later, having looked at the rituals.

(c) The *Ḥaṭṭā't* —חַטָּאת

The goat sacrificed in the ritual of Lev 16 is called the חַטָּאת (*ḥaṭṭā't*). The *ḥaṭṭā't* can be regarded as the primary expiatory offering in the Levitical system of offerings.[16] In the Leviticus texts the "priest is always the subject of the action denoted by *kipper*"[17] and God's response is indicated by the recurring phrase "the priest effects atonement [*wĕkipper*] for him" along with the phrase "so he will be forgiven [by God]," which is the basis of the *ḥaṭṭā't* ritual.[18] Thus the priest is the Mediator; he acts not only on his own behalf, but more importantly on behalf of others, removing the tension between the sinner (both individuals and community) and the deity through a sacrifice,

---

13. See Barth, who writes "[w]hat is important is not so much the nation's new status of reconciliation to God," in *CD* II/2, 358f.

14. *CD* IV/1, 254.

15. *CD* IV/1, 253.

16. See Averbeck, "Sacrifices and Offerings," 720.

17. See Lang, "כפר," 294.

18. See Lev 4:26, 31, 35; 5:6, 10, 13, 18, 26; 14:18, 20; 15:15; 19:22 and Rendtorff, *Studien zur Geschichte des Opfers im alten Israel*, 230.

a *kōper* (Exod 21:30; Lev 16:18; Lev 17:11) provided by the guilty party.[19] The emphasis is not on God's anger (and the notion of an angry God who must be appeased is not expressed)[20] but instead on the tension that previously existed between humans or between a human being and God due to sin, which has now been neutralized.[21] Thus the "verb *kipper* never refers to a 'propitiation' of God."[22] This "classic Priestly *kipper* ritual"[23] included the purification, atoning, laying of hands on the sacrificial animals and application of blood on the horns of the altar, the so-called blood rite (Lev 4:25, 30, 34).[24]

The steps of the *ḥaṭṭā't* (which also occurs on *Yom Kippur*, examined below) were the following: the animal was forth (הִקְרִיב and הֵבִיא), the hand was laid upon the head of the sacrificial animal (סָמַךְ יָדוֹ עַל רֹאשׁ), the animal was slaughtered (שָׁחַט), the priest announced the declaration formula (חַטָּאת הוּא) that it be a sin offering,[25] the blood was manipulated (שָׁפַךְ) and finally the last parts of the animal were removed (שָׂרַף and הִקְטִיר). However, the focal point of the *ḥaṭṭā't* was the blood manipulation (and the laying of hands upon the head of the animal, which will be explained later).[26] The sinner who provided the sacrifice also laid a hand upon the animal, identifying with it and symbolizing the offering of his or her own life.[27] Then the blood of the animal was applied to the altar by the priest. For the minor blood-rite, the blood was only applied on the horns of the altar of burnt offering—the rest was poured out at the base of the altar (Lev 4:25ff). On special occasions, such as *Yom Kippur*, the blood was carried into the Holy of Holies.

Koch, in agreement with Milgrom,[28] observes that the translation of *ḥaṭṭā't* as 'sin offering' appears to be a serious blunder, "dating to a time when every non-Christian ritual act was conceived of in the sense of the

---

19. See Lang, "כפר," 293.
20. Besides special cases such as Num 16:46; 25:11, 13.
21. See Lang, "כפר," 292.
22. Ibid., 294.
23. Ibid., 294f.
24. See Janowski, "Atonement," 153.
25. See Rendtorff, *Studien zur Geschichte des Opfers im alten Israel*, 256.
26. Space limitations prevent my providing a detailed analysis of the minor blood-rite and the differences of the *ḥaṭṭā't* for a leader and a common person, or a priest and the congregation.
27. See Lang, "כפר," 295.
28. Milgrom translates the *ḥaṭṭā't* as "purification offering," in Milgrom, *Leviticus 1–16*, 232.

Latin *do ut des* as a sacrifice of the deity."[29] YHWH does not receive the sacrifice, but rather it is he who makes it possible—"he is not the object but the subject of an act that is performed in his name by the priest."[30] Also, the term 'sin offering' might lead to the conclusion that it was just intended for moral sin when in fact it was also intended for physical impurities (Lev 5:2–3) which on many occasions had nothing to do with moral failure. 'Purification offering' might be a better translation as this simply signifies that it was required before an *unclean* person could be brought back into the community as a ritually *clean* person (Lev 12:6–8; 14:18–20).[31] The understanding of *ḥaṭṭāʾt* is made more problematic because in the LXX it can mean both 'sin' and 'sin offering' (see Lev 4:3). This can cause confusion in New Testament contexts such as Rom 8:3 or 2 Cor 5:21.

At this stage the overall notion of our exegesis agrees with Barth, who also emphasizes that God is the sole author of the atonement. Furthermore, for Barth, the aspect of purification is also very important. He sees the death as God's saving act, which is necessary for the sinner since it is through death that he is cleansed from sinful existence and led into life.[32] Death, which Barth sees as "full of grace and salvation,"[33] is God's remedy, his *Heilmittel*, against sin and a forfeited life, effecting God's love and mercy towards sinful humanity. It is his means for salvation and not, therefore, a punishment but a loving act towards the sinner that allows the continuation of life, indeed, a new and better life.

Yet, whilst Barth briefly mentions the role of blood in Lev 14 (in the context of the second bird being dipped into the blood as a sign of purification), he does not provide the rationale behind Lev 16 (the blood-sprinkling on the Ark of the Covenant and tabernacle). Nor does he give an explanation of the function and use of blood in these rituals, other than stating that it has a purifying and sanctifying function. But the 'why,' the reason behind it, remains unexplained. So our next step is to look at the cultic role of blood in the rituals.

(d) The Role of the Blood—דָּם

We have seen that blood, דָּם, played a significant role in the offerings and was applied by the priest on the horns of the altar at the blood-rite, sprinkled on

---

29. Koch, "חטאת," 316.
30. Ibid., 316.
31. See Milgrom, *Studies in Cultic Theology and Terminology*, 67–69.
32. See *CD* II/2, 362.
33. See *CD* II/2, 362.

the leper, and always handled with great care. Besides the gesture of laying the hand upon the head of the animal, the execution of a blood-rite was a constitutive element of the *ḥaṭṭāʾt*-ritual. The two forms of the blood manipulation were the minor (Lev 4:25, 30, 34) and the major (Lev 4:5–7, 16, 18) blood-rites; besides them there was the blood-rite at the *yôm kippūrîm*, to be examined later. In the *ḥaṭṭāʾt*-tradition the blood was used to atone for humanity—for Israel, her representatives, and the common person.[34] Leviticus 17:11 provides an explanation of why blood was significant for the atonement: "For the life of a creature is in the blood, and I have given it to you to make atonement for yourselves on the altar; it is the blood that makes atonement for one's life." Both in Exod 30:11–16, where a 'ransom' was used to make atonement, and Lev 17:11, where the blood of the slaughtered animal is used to make atonement, we find the identical expression: "to make atonement for our lives" (lit. soul) לְכַפֵּר עַל־נַפְשֹׁתֵיכֶם. Comparing the two texts, we see that the blood of the animal, the locus of life/soul, becomes the ransom for the person who offers the blood, which again is paralleled with the ransom money in Exod 30:11–16. Through the use of the preposition b^e the blood becomes the instrument of atonement.[35] The blood was a symbol of the surrender of the worshipper's own life to the sanctuary and thus to YHWH himself.[36]

Leviticus 17:10–14 describes the prohibition of the consumption of blood and why it was handled with so much care—namely because contained in the blood is the life of the animal. The reason for draining the blood from the animal (and covering it with earth—Lev 17:13) before eating the meat was to ensure that it was only the meat that was eaten and not the blood. Blood contained the *nepeš*, נֶפֶשׁ (see Deut 12:23), which was the substance of life and reserved for God alone (Gen 9:3–5). If in a cultic ritual the blood was released—and only in a ritual slaughter was human interference with life allowed—that individual life, *nepeš*, was freed.[37] Blood was sacred and given by God for the purpose of atonement alone (Lev 17:11, 14).[38] It was not that blood acted by means of inherent expiatory power, "but because Yahweh had designated it as a means of atonement" (see Lev 17:11)[39] and thus the blood manipulation, regulated by YHWH, depended on his

---

34. See Knöppler, *Sühne im Neuen Testament*, 16.
35. See Janowski, *Sühne als Heilsgeschehen*, 244ff. and Averbeck, "כפר," 688.
36. See Lang, "כפר," 295.
37. See Gese, "The Atonement," 107.
38. See Trebilco, "דם," 965.
39. Gerleman, "דם," 338.

sovereign will.⁴⁰ This is a key point—blood was the agent of atonement, not from its substantial nature but from its appointment by God as the carrier of life.⁴¹ Thus the life-containing blood (see Gen 9:6; Deut 12:23) was the basis of the cultic atonement and should be seen as a gift from God. So if a person offered up a sacrificial animal, he or she did so on the presupposition that God had created the possibility for the blood to atone. Therefore, the sacrifice in the Old Testament was not a human payment in order to appease God; rather the priestly atonement took place only because God had made it possible. This concept of atonement therefore annuls the common sacrifice logic of *do ut des*.⁴²

In conclusion it might be said that the blood in Lev 17:11 finds its rationale in the belief that YHWH himself gave it to Israel to make atonement possible. YHWH inaugurated the possibility that the blood could be used as an atoning instrument for the cult, because it was the "bearer of life."⁴³

As previously indicated, Barth states that blood has a purifying function but does not give an explanation for the 'why.' For him it is by God's grace and love that the sinner is allowed to surrender his blood, his impure life.⁴⁴ Yet, we saw the rationale behind the blood in our analysis. In the same way that the offering is not an offering *to* God but an agent given *from* God to Israel to make atonement (Lev 10:17), so also God has ordained the blood for Israel to be used to make atonement (Lev 17:11). Barth is partly right in writing that the blood symbolizes the total surrender of life to God, and yet this is not all—it has to be seen in relation to the ransom motif. It is not simply that the sinner's impure life is eliminated and poured out; rather, that the blood of the animal represents the *kōper*, the ransom-substitution, thus pointing beyond and transcending the sinner, towards the need of something/somebody else, a blameless and sinless sacrifice, without which the sinner would be lost. Barth talks about the hidden subject in the rituals but does not explicitly make the link to the blood. He states that the "renewal can take place no less radically—that man should die, that his blood should be shed to the last drop. His pure new life can be born only through such a total surrender of his previous impure life."⁴⁵ But what Barth neglects to see is the *meaning* of blood as the *kōper* in relation to the hidden subject; he sees in the rituals the hidden subject, who dies as a substitute for the sinner,

40. See Kedar-Kopfstein "דם," 248.
41. See Knöppler, *Sühne im Neuen Testament*, 18.
42. See Janowski, *Sühne als Heilsgeschehen*, 247.
43. See ibid., 246.
44. See *CD* II/2, 359.
45. *CD* II/2, 360.

but does not sufficiently emphasise that it dies 'in-place' in order to give its blood (which contains the *nepeš*) as a *kōper*. This offering of blood is not simply an act of deity-appeasement through the paying of a price, but an act of reconciliation between the transcendent God and Israel and a restoration of the covenantal fellowship. This will be examined in the section on the *kappōret*-rite below.

(E) THE SĔMÎKÂ—סְמִיכָה

Having undertaken a detailed study of the verb *kipper* and considered the offering of the *ḥaṭṭā't* and the role of the blood in the cult, what remains is an examination of the rite of 'laying the hand upon' the animal, סְמִיכָה, the *sĕmîkâ*-rite. This is something that Barth completely overlooks in his study. After this we can move on to *Yom Kippur* itself, at which all the rites converge.

The ritual of laying of hands becomes pivotal here. Whereas it is explicitly mentioned that during the *sĕmîkâ* the High Priest confessed all the iniquities over the goat for Azazel, this is not the case with the *sĕmîkâ* of the sacrificial *ḥaṭṭā't*. Here no confession or transferal of transgression is mentioned. What then is the meaning of the *sĕmîkâ* in the *ḥaṭṭā't*? The *sĕmîkâ* should be seen in the same context as the appointment of a successor (Num 27:18.23; Deut 34:9) or the consecration of the Levites (Num 8:10)—an 'authorization' or 'ordination,' a dedication to YHWH. It should not be regarded as a transferal of sin material, but rather as "an identification between the offerer and animal,"[46] "a continuation of the subject in a delegated succession" [*Subjektübertragung*].[47] A simple transferal of sin by the consecutive killing of the sin-laden animal would only amount to an exclusive *Stellvertretung* (a substitution happening 'outside' or without the sinner's existence involved). However, the significance of the atonement is the identification of the one bringing the sacrifice by his laying his hand upon the head of the animal. The person bringing the animal "affirmed that it was he who was offering the animal and that he was offering himself" through the sacrifice as a gift or dedication to God.[48] It is not a passing on of *materia peccans* to the animal, as in the Azazel-rite, but through the gesture of the *sĕmîkâ*, an identification of the *homo peccator* with the dying animal occurs and the person 'participates' in the animal's death[49] in a

---

46. Wright, "The Gesture of Hand Placement," 434.
47. Gese, "The Atonement," 105.
48. Wright, "The Gesture of Hand Placement," 434.
49. See Janowski, *Sühne als Heilsgeschehen*, 220f.

symbolically-real manner.⁵⁰ This presupposes an identification, through the *sĕmîkâ*, of the offerer's *nepeš* with the *nepeš* of the animal.

Thus the gesture expresses a "*Subjektübertragung, aber keine Objektabladung*"⁵¹—a symbolic offering up [*zeichenhaft*]⁵² of the person's life through the shedding of the animal's blood. The animal's death becomes the sinner's own death [*real*], taken over by the sacrificial animal in substitution.⁵³ Finally, through the blood-rite the *nepeš* is dedicated and incorporated into the holy.⁵⁴ Thus, the cultic atonement is a surrender, a "total substitutionary commitment of a life"⁵⁵ in which the sacrifice of the animal's life is a "substitution that *includes* the one bringing the sacrifice."⁵⁶ The sacrifice of the animal and the blood ritual should be seen as a holy rite in which the animal is not punished for the guilty, but brought into the sanctuary "where it comes into contact with what is holy."⁵⁷ It is not merely a death and a removal of sin that accomplishes the atonement but an inclusive *Stellvertretung* and the commitment of life to what is holy—this "ritual brings Israel into contact with God."⁵⁸ We can conclude that it is the inclusive *Existenzstellvertretung* occurring through the *sĕmîkâ* that has the atoning function in the blood-rites.⁵⁹ It is the covenantal fellowship, and its restoration, that stands at the centre of these rituals.

Barth does not mention the *sĕmîkâ* in his analysis of the sin offering. He sees "the Israelite who as an individual or as the whole nation is the particular object of the purification in question [is] both here and according to the whole sacrificial legislation no more than a *spectator*, as it were, of the actions which represent this purification."⁶⁰ However, as Bächli notes, the individual or the collective group were not simply spectators in the ritual events but were actually part of and involved in the rituals, since they were dependent upon them in their everyday life.⁶¹

---

50. See Hofius, "Sühne und Versöhnung," 36–37.
51. Gese, "Die Sühne," 97.
52. See Gese, "The Atonement," 107.
53. See Janowski, *Sühne als Heilsgeschehen*, 359.
54. See Gese, "The Atonement," 108.
55. Ibid., 106.
56. Ibid.
57. Ibid.
58. Ibid.
59. See Janowski, *Sühne als Heilsgeschehen*, 218.
60. CD II/2, 358.
61. See Bächli, *Das Alte Testament in der Kirchlichen Dogmatik*, 173.

Through the offering of a sacrifice, which first had to be brought to the priest by the individual and which then included the specific ritual of the sĕmîkâ with the consecutive slaying of the animal, every Israelite was brought not only into close contact with cultic rituals, but also to an understanding of the seriousness of sin. The people were therefore not simply passive bystanders. Furthermore, we saw that the sacrifice of the animal was not only a sign [*Zeichen*] for Israel, demonstrating to her the treatment that she deserves and otherwise would be destined for because of her sinfulness (i.e., death or banishment from the presence of God).[62] Rather, the Old Testament sacrifice holds a meaning that is more than a mere "sign and testimony" [*Zeichen- und Zeugnischarakter*][63]; it has real inherent value. The bird that was previously in captivity stands for the life of the leper who was cast out of the community, and the ritual of releasing the bird in freedom stands for the leper's life brought back into the communal fellowship.[64] As Hofius concludes, by identifying with the animal through the sĕmîkâ, the sinner's death happens "*zeichenhaft-real*"[65] in the substitutionary death of the sacrificed animal, where "*mit seiner Sünder-Existenz Schluß gemacht wird*,"[66] and "*die Heraufführung eines, neuen, weil in seinem Sein neu gewordenen Menschen*"[67] occurs. Through the offering of the נֶפֶשׁ of the person "*wird eine zeichenhaft-reale Lebenhingabe des Opfernden an das Heiligtum Gottes vollzogen.*"[68]

(f) The Ritual on The Day of Atonement —Yom Kippur—יוֹם הַכִּפֻּרִים

At the centre of Leviticus, and thus at the centre of the Pentateuch, is *Yom Kippur*—יוֹם הַכִּפֻּרִים. It was a day of holiness for both the tabernacle and the nation, and observance of it laid the foundation for YHWH to forgive the people their sins in order that he could continue to bless them and have a covenantal relationship with Israel.[69]

---

62. See *CD* II/2, 358.
63. *CD* II/2, 357.
64. Staubli, "Die Symbolik des Vogelrituals," passim.
65. Hofius, "Sühne und Versöhnung," 43, and Janowski, *Sühne als Heilsgeschehen*, 247.
66. Hofius, "Sühne und Versöhnung," 42.
67. Ibid., 43.
68. Janowski, *Sühne als Heilsgeschehen*, 241.
69. See Hartley, "Day of Atonement," 55.

According to the biblical description,[70] on the tenth of Tishrei (i.e., in September or October) two goats were presented to the High Priest who would draw lots for them, symbolizing a transfer of ownership.[71] One animal would be assigned for the Lord, "for YHWH" (לַיהוָה), to be slain and offered as a חַטָּאת (*ḥaṭṭā't*), a sin offering. Some of the blood was carried into the Holy of Holies (הַקֹּדֶשׁ) and sprinkled seven times on the *kappōret*, כַּפֹּרֶת (Lev 16:14f). The other animal, "for Azazel" (לַעֲזָאזֵל), was to be sent away alive into the wilderness as an elimination rite. The priest laid his hands on the head of a ram, confessed the Israelites' sins, and sent the animal away into the desert.

(G) The *Kappōret*-rite—כַּפֹּרֶת

We saw that in the minor blood-rite the blood was applied only on the horns of the burnt offering altar, but that in the major blood-rite the blood was brought further inside the sanctuary, right up to the edge of the Holy of Holies, sprinkled against the veil and applied on the incense altar. However, the most central event of *Yom Kippur* was the *kappōret*-rite (Lev 16:14f.). In this blood-rite, the blood was sprinkled on the כַּפֹּרֶת or ἱλαστήριον, the mercy seat over the cover of the ark where the divine שכינה [*Shekinah*] rested (Lev 16:14f.).

On *Yom Kippur*, the presence of YHWH above the *kappōret* declared to the congregation YHWH's willingness to atone for their sins,[72] as the High Priest entered the Holy of Holies to make atonement for the whole nation. He had to cover the *kappōret*, the place where YHWH was present (Exod 25:22), with a cloud of incense before sprinkling blood on it, in order not to die by the divine *doxa* of YHWH (Lev 16:13). According to Lev 16, the High Priest, the representative of Israel, applied the *Yom Kippur* blood on the *kappōret* twice: the blood of the bull for the priest's transgressions (Lev 16:14) and the blood of the goat for the transgressions of the people (Lev 16:15).[73]

---

70. The biblical description of *Yom Kippur* is rather brief and a more detailed explanation is found in the Rabbinic literature—see the rabbinic tractates *Yoma*, the day, in the Mishnah.

71. See Gane, *Cult and Character*, 250.

72. See Janowski, *Sühne als Heilsgeschehen*, 266.

73. Furthermore, the blood of the *ḥaṭṭā't* animals, some of which is applied on the *kappōret*, was also used to make atonement for the burnt offering altar (Lev 16:18–19).

The climax of the atonement process was reached at the priest's sprinkling of the blood of both sin offerings seven times on the *kappōret*.[74] The animal's blood stood for the life of the Israelites and in being sprinkled on the *kappōret*, their lives were offered to God.[75] Through the blood-rite the נֶפֶשׁ (*nepeš*) was dedicated and incorporated into the holy.[76] There on the *kappōret* the guilty nation, otherwise doomed to death, met the transcendent God and in this atonement act, YHWH bestowed his salvific presence onto Israel.

(h) The Azazel-rite and Sin Removal

The Azazel-rite should be seen as separate from the offering rites of *Yom Kippur*. In Lev 16:7 the lot-rite of the two goats for the people is a transfer of ownership, one for a sin offering for YHWH and the other one for Azazel, sent away into the desert[77] as a rite of elimination.[78] Gane argues that the goat for Azazel was not a sacrifice, explaining that it was not the lack of slaughter which excluded the Azazel-rite from the category of sacrifice (see grain offering Lev 5:11–13) but rather the fact that neither the animal, nor any part of it, was given over to YHWH as a gift.[79] Rather the goat for Azazel should be seen as an elimination, as Janowski highlights, with its origin in the ancient Mediterranean region.[80] The rite "represents a struggle against chaos, against transgression and disorder, which threaten the harmony and safety of man, and [. . .] expels them to the desolation to which they pertain."[81] Milgrom highlights that demonic impurities were often exorcised through banishment to their place of origin.[82] This was the role and function of the Azazel-goat which—by bearing the iniquities of the people, evil spirits,[83] and the demonic impurities transferred onto him—became "a symbol of evil."[84] One might even go so far as to say that the rite did not simply send away a goat *to* Azazel, but rather identified the goat with all

---

74. See Maass, "כפר," 630.
75. See Hübner, "Sühne und Versöhnung," 289.
76. See Gese, "The Atonement," 108.
77. See Gane, *Cult and Character*, 250.
78. See Maass, "כפר," 629.
79. See Gane, *Cult and Character*, 251f.
80. See Janowski, *Sühne als Heilsgeschehen*, 211f.
81. Zatelli, "The Origin of the Biblical Scapegoat Ritual," 263.
82. See Milgrom, *Leviticus 1–16*, 1042 and 1072.
83. Tawil, "Azazel The Prince of the Steepe," 59.
84. De Roo, "The Goat for Azazel," 238.

the iniquities *as* Azazel itself, and we know from rabbinic sources that in practice, the goat was pushed over a cliff in order that it would not return to the camp of the people.[85]

The cleansing rite of the leper with two birds in Lev 14 is generally seen as an elimination rite in the same sense as the Azazel-rite, the live bird taking away the ṣāraʿat impurity.[86] However, we might question whether the live bird, which is dipped into the sanctifying blood, does in fact 'bear' the disease of the leper or whether the ritual is actually a symbolic exchange. In this case the release of the bird into its natural habitat[87] and into freedom would be seen to correspond to the 'new life' of the leper and his being brought back into the community from the sphere of death.[88]

(1) The Two Goats

Thus we must distinguish between the elimination-rite (for the spatial removal of the substance of evil, the *materia peccans*) and the substitution rite of the ḥaṭṭāʾt, an inclusive *Existenzstellvertretung*. In the sĕmîkâ-rite at the ḥaṭṭāʾt the person lays "his hand" (see Lev 4:4, or 4:15 as a collective group) on the animal's head, whilst in the Azazel-rite the priest (Aaron) lays "both his hands" on the animal's head and confesses over it "all the iniquities of the

---

85. See Mishna *Yoma* and Targum *Pseudo-Jonathan*, Grabbe, "The Scapegoat Tradition," 158f., and Helm, "Azazel in Early Jewish Tradition," 225f.

86. See Wright, *The Disposal of Impurity*, 75–80. See also Milgrom, *Leviticus 1–16*, 833.

87. Milgrom points out that "the bird had to be wild, else there would remain the ever-present fear that the live bird dispatched to the open country would return to the settlement. [. . .] A ḥaṭṭāʾt bird, or for that matter any sacrificial animal, perforce had to be domesticated," in Milgrom, *Leviticus 1–16*, 833. The fact that the birds were wild animals serves to strengthen our argument of exchange. The same way that the wild bird is released into freedom from its captivity, so too is the leper, brought out of the sphere of death and back into the community.

88. See Staubli, "Die Symbolik des Vogelrituals," passim. He writes in his abstract that "the bird ritual for the purification of the leper is usually interpreted as an elimination rite in analogy to the scapegoat rite at Yom Kippur. However, all constitutive elements of an elimination rite are missing: an evil is not mentioned, nor a demonic place for the evil nor a beast, sympathetic with the demon. On the contrary birds in the Bible and elsewhere in the Ancient Near East symbolise in many ways human vitality, just as the other ingredients of the ritual do. So the article argues, that the ritual symbolises the return of the healed leper from social death to life, as the first act of a threefold ritual for the reintegration of a person into human society." See also Jenson, who calls the live bird rite an "unusual" elimination rite, in Jenson, *Graded Holiness*, 170. Jenson also highlights the social reintegration of the leper back into the camp.

people of Israel, and all their transgressions, all their sins, putting them on the head of the goat" (Lev 16:21).

Daly highlights another important difference between the Azazel and the *ḥaṭṭāʾt*: whilst the "scapegoat was considered unclean after the imposition of hands on it, the flesh of the hattat [was considered] most holy."[89] The Azazel became ritually unclean after the transference of Israel's impurities on its head while the priests in Leviticus were allowed to eat the flesh of the *ḥaṭṭāʾt* because it was holy (see Lev 10:17).[90] Moreover, neither is it a purification rite like the *ḥaṭṭāʾt*, with the aim of coming into close and healing contact with God.

The tabernacle/temple was the meeting place of heaven and earth and the *kappōret* in the Holy of Holies was the throne of the Lord, which was simultaneously heaven and earth. The Holy of Holies, where the blood of the *ḥaṭṭāʾt* was sprinkled and atonement was effected, stands in contrast to the desert, the place of the Azazel-goat. On the Day of Atonement, when God came down into the tabernacle in his *doxa*, the Holy of Holies can be regarded as a "microcosm of creation,"[91] standing in polar opposite to the desert, the "home of chaos"[92] and habitat of demons into which the 'scapegoat' was sent. If the rituals of the temple are understood in this way, as creation rituals, then the Azazel-rite removes impurities and sin (understood as chaos) "not just outside the camp, but outside creation itself into the chaotic area of the wilderness."[93] Therefore the *kappōret*-rite and the Azazel-rite should be seen not as occurring successively, but together performing one mirror-inverted act.[94] Whilst the purpose of the *kappōret*-rite was to meet God, that of the Azazel-rite was to go into the desert, as far away from the sanctuary as possible. Thus the movements of the two rites are extreme opposites—the *kappōret*-rite faces towards the Holy of Holies and the Azazel-rite faces far away into the wilderness. This ritual should be seen in a similar light to Barth's understanding of God's *Yes* and *No* spoken in creation, which we will hear about in chapter 3.

The *Yom Kippur* ritual became the annually-repeated image of the Sinaitic covenant[95] between YHWH and Israel (see Exod 24:15f.), through

---

89. Daly, *Christian Sacrifice*, 104.

90. Though this did not occur on *Yom Kippur*, when it was burned outside the camp (Lev 16:27).

91. Rudman, "A Note on the Azazel-goat Ritual," 398.

92. See ibid., 399.

93. Ibid., 400.

94. See Jenson, *Graded Holiness*, 203.

95. See Janowski, *Sühne als Heilsgeschehen*, 349.

which the guilty nation was brought into contact with YHWH. For Israel as the receiver of YHWH's willingness to reconcile, the only appropriate response was to perform the blood-rites, through the High Priest as Israel's representative. Therefore, the sacrifice of the animal and the blood ritual should be seen as a holy rite, in which the animal is not punished for the one who is guilty of sin, but a rite of sanctification in which (1)[96] the sanctuary was cleansed with blood[97] so that God could dwell amongst Israel, and (2) a rite through which Israel was brought into the sanctuary where it came into contact with holiness.

Hence the ritual performed stood for the "commitment of life to what is holy,"[98] and the sacrifice brought Israel back into contact with her holy God and restored the covenantal relationship. Nehemia Polen points out that the essential purpose of the offerings and sacrifices was to "cultivate and maintain the relationship between God and Israel, to assure the continuity of the Divine Presence"[99] with Israel "so that God might abide with (לְשָׁכְנִי)" Israel."[100] He explains that we have to understand the cultic atonement from a theocentric perspective, a perspective of God's wanting to have fellowship with Israel.[101]

In the inclusive *Existenzstellvertretung*, the Israelites participated in the death of the substitutionary sacrifice of the animal; through the priest's sprinkling the animal's blood (which stood for the life of the Israelites) on the *kappōret*, their lives were offered to God.[102] Thus new life was possible. This atonement was not simply a negative act removing sin, but a sanctifying act—"*ein Zu-Gott-Kommen durch das Todesgericht hindurch.*"[103]

(J) THE CONCEPT OF SIN BEARING—נָשָׂא עָוֺן

We have yet to consider how sin is actually dealt with in the atonement and what is really meant by 'bearing iniquities.' It is this that we will scrutinize in this final step.

---

96. Milgrom explains this urgency to purge the sanctuary: "the God of Israel will not abide in a polluted sanctuary," in Milgrom, *Leviticus 1–16*, 258.

97. The *ḥaṭṭāʾt* blood was the purging element—see Milgrom, *Leviticus 1–16*, 254.

98. See Gese, "The Atonement," 106.

99. Polen, "Leviticus and Hebrews . . . and Leviticus," 216.

100. Ibid., 216.

101. See ibid., 216.

102. See Hübner, "Sühne und Versöhnung," 289.

103. Gese, "Die Sühne," 104.

The root נשא (nāśāʿ) in Lev 16, which describes the sin bearing aspect of the Azazel-goat, literally means 'to lift, raise high, pardon, take away, bear, carry'—referring to a physical movement.[104] In the "Old Testament this notion has been expanded to include the principle of forgiveness, and forgiveness is itself associated with the idea of lifting away or taking away guilt, sin, and punishment" and therefore "forgiveness is frequently understood as 'to bear, carry away, settle etc."[105] Moreover, the expression נשא עון (nāśāʿ ʾāwôn) in the sense of 'to forgive' is synonymous with the verb *kipper*, 'to atone',[106] and when it is God who bears the guilt of others by removing the iniquity "the reference is to divine forgiveness."[107]

Furthermore, Baruch Schwartz argues for two *uses* of the term nāśāʿ with only *one* meaning.[108] He argues that when the sinner himself 'bears' his sin, he suffers its consequences—this is to say that "the sinner deserves punishment."[109] However, when God "'bears' the sinner's burden, it no longer rests on the shoulder of the wrongdoer; the latter is relieved of his load and of its consequences."[110] However, Schwartz goes on to say that the sinner has nevertheless not 'transferred' his burden to somebody else, meaning that the bearer is not "'weighed down by the sin of the sinner,' but rather the burden does 'no longer weigh upon anyone. It has disappeared.'"[111] The question remains—how? He answers this by saying that in both cases the primary meaning of nāśāʿ is to 'bear,' yet whilst in the first case it means to bear in the sense of 'to be laden with,' in the second, "when the sinner is relieved of his burden, it means not 'to carry' but 'carry off, take away, remove.'"[112] So when it is God who is said to 'bear sin,' what he actually does is to 'remove *sins*,' namely by forgiving them. Sin thus disappears.

Furthermore, Polen points out that the animal is "not dying in place of, for the sins of, the human [. . .] if there is any suffering, it plays no role in the ritual per se."[113] Thus the taking of the animal's life for sacrifice is not

---

104. See Freedman, "נשא," 24. See also Stolz, "נשא," 770.

105. See Freedman, "נשא," 25. Stolz explains that "the nuance 'to carry away' can be understood against the meaning 'to bear,'" in "נשא," 770.

106. See Freedman, "נשא," 27f. See also Stolz, "נשא," 772.

107. See Freedman, "נשא," 34.

108. See Schwartz, "The Bearing of Sin in the Prieslty Literature," 9. I am indebted to Mark Scarlata for directing me towards this article.

109. Ibid., 9.

110. Ibid., 9.

111. Ibid., 10.

112. Ibid., 10.

113. Polen, "Leviticus and Hebrews . . . and Leviticus," 218f.

murder but a "making sacred."[114] The blood—the fluid of life itself—was the sign of the bond between Israel and God, and should be seen as a "gift of the self, applied to the divine table,"[115] the altar which represents God. The blood intimates for the Israelites "contact with God Himself whose Presence hovers over the ark-cover."[116] Therefore the *ḥaṭṭā't* sacrifice effects a "renewal of right relationship"[117] between God and the person bringing the offering, enacting and maintaining the relationship between God and Israel, Creator and creature, heaven and earth.

Implications and Criticism

We saw that the cultic atonement was an event that must be understood as an inclusive *Existenzstellvertretung*. It was not so much a division of the sinner from his sin—a transferal of sin onto a vicarious or substitutionary object and an annihilation of sin with the animal's death—but rather an inclusive identification. When the person making the offering laid his hand upon the animal in the *sĕmîkâ*, the person's *nepeš* was identified with that of the animal, the person participated in the *stellvertretenden* death of the animal and the person's life was symbolically offered up. It was an inclusive act signifying a life surrendered to God, and through the blood-rite at the *kappōret*, the place of God's presence (Exod 25:17), the sinner again came into contact with God. Atonement therefore must be seen as a coming-to-God through the death, out of which a new creation is born.[118] We explained that the sacrificial *ḥaṭṭā't* did not bear sin—in fact it was just the goat for Azazel that carried away the iniquities of the people. Instead, the *ḥaṭṭā't* performed a rite that brought the people back into contact with their holy and transcendent God through the blood-rite performed by the High Priest on the *kappōret*.

We have already identified similarities between the concept of *Existenzstellvertretung* and Barth's thought, especially in his exegesis of Lev 14. Barth affirms more than once that the second bird partakes in the salvation accomplished by the death of the first bird by being dipped into its blood, a sign that the human being is freed from her limited existence and transferred to freedom as a new human being.[119] Barth also states that Lev 16

114. Ibid., 219.
115. Ibid.
116. Ibid., 222.
117. Kiuchi, *The Purification Offering in the Priestly Literature*, 15.
118. See Hofius, "Sühne IV," 343.
119. See *CD* II/2, 360f.

Jesus Christ the Elect

attends to the same purification when it highlights the fate of the first animal. We saw that for Barth the similarity in the rituals of Lev 14 and 16 is found in the death of the first animals. Yet whereas the first animals highlight the redemptive endurance of death (ordained and accomplished by God)[120] and the redemptive suffering and death (the presupposition of purification and renewed life),[121] the second animals highlight completely opposite aspects from one another. The focus in Lev 14 is the new life accomplished by this redemptive death and in Lev 16 it is the life in sin before the redemptive death:

> Death is the saving judgment of God, which is necessary in the operation of His grace towards man and therefore exhibits His love for him, and through which he is cleansed and led into life. Death is the sacrifice willed and ordained and accepted by God in His goodness to man. The life of which these two passages speak has two possible meanings in contrast to the unequivocal meaning of death. It may be the wretched life of man that does not deserve this death and does not partake of the salvation secured by it. But it may also be the new liberated life of the man who has merited this death, and by means of it passed through to his salvation.[122]

Yet, there are also fundamental differences between Barth's thinking and the concept of *Existenzstellvertretung*. First, because in Lev 16 Barth looks backwards from the cultic death and in Lev 14 he looks forward, he comes to the conclusion that the rituals of Lev 14 and 16 look in opposite directions. But our exegesis shows that in fact both rituals are forward-looking, with their focus on the result achieved, towards meeting YHWH in the act of atonement and reconciliation.

Secondly, Barth sees all four animals as relating to each other as types of Christ. However, we saw that the Azazel-goat was seen as separate to the rites of the cultic atonement and the *ḥaṭṭā't* sacrifice. In contrast, in the bird ritual in Lev 14, the two parts of the ritual are connected through the blood.[123] The shedding of the blood of the first bird into which the second bird is dipped unites both parts of the ritual. In Lev 16 it was Israel that was united to the *ḥaṭṭā't* sacrifice through her representative the High Priest, in his performing the *sĕmîkâ* on behalf of all of Israel. So whereas the goat for Azazel

---

120. See *CD* II/2, 359.
121. See *CD* II/2, 359.
122. *CD* II/2, 362.
123. See Staubli, "Die Symbolik des Vogelrituals," 232.

does not come into contact with blood or anything holy, the second bird is dipped into the blood, the same blood that is also applied to the person.

Thirdly, Barth sees the purification as founded in total surrender, by the outpouring of the impure life of the first goat.[124] However, we have seen in our analysis of the role of the blood that the cultic use of blood must be seen in a different way, not as *impure* but as a *kōper*, a ransom, holding a vital role. It is not simply that the blood is surrendered to God and eliminated but rather that it (and through it life itself) is offered up to God, that it is the means through which Israel meets her transcendent God. Israel transcends her own state of sinfulness and offers her soul afresh to YHWH, who meets her in his transcendent *Shekinah*. This happens through the *sĕmîkâ*-rite at the *ḥaṭṭā't*, where the blood (containing the *nepeš*) was offered. Thus the sinner participates in the death of the animal. By and through the blood being sprinkled at the *kappōret*-rite on *Yom Kippur*, the sinner is also brought into contact with YHWH. Furthermore, it is not a surrendering of *impure* blood but in fact it is the blood of the *sinless* animal that is poured out as a *kōper* for the benefit of the sinner. Thus, the shedding of the blood should be seen as an act of *Existenzstellvertretung* in which one offers their life vicariously for another. Barth sees this in Lev 14 when he says that "the one has necessarily to die in order that the other may live"[125] yet never explains why (and this notion of the use of blood as a *kōper* is entirely absent in Barth's commentary on Lev 16).

Fourthly, Barth's view is that the individual is only a passive bystander observing the cultic act, which is a sign for what should actually happen to the person. However, we saw that in this act of *Existenzstellvertretung* the person's death happens *zeichenhaft-real*, by participating in the animal's death. Thus, the person is far from being a spectator—instead he is actively involved in the ritual and changed from within.

After concluding our examination in this section, we can state as an interim evaluation that we can answer questions 1[126] and 3[127] and have highlighted various aspects of questions 2[128] and 4.[129] So in the next section of

124. See *CD* II/2, 359.

125. *CD* II/2, 361.

126. Does Barth do justice to the texts in Leviticus? Has he portrayed the rituals accurately and interpreted them correctly?

127. What is the role and function of blood as well as that of the human being in the ritual events?

128. Has Barth discovered a new exegesis, a new dimension to the hitherto known exegesis?

129. In what way can we say that Jesus is a type of all four animals in Lev 14 and 16?

this chapter we want to tackle these remaining issues and highlight possible implications of our own exegesis for Barth's doctrine of election.

2. Barth's Typological Interpretation Revisited

We saw that Barth sees all four animals as a type of Christ. In the final step of Barth's exegesis he looks at the Church Fathers' typological approach to exegesis and compares his understanding of Leviticus to that of Calvin. He comes to the conclusion that he is in line with the Church Fathers' older Christian investigation of the Bible and states that Jesus Christ is both the blameless and sinless lamb as well as the second goat, the rejected one, who suffers. Therefore, he concludes, Jesus Christ must be seen as simultaneously God's elect, according to his divine nature, and God's rejected, according to his human nature.[130]

It is this typological approach of the older Christian investigation of the Bible to which we now turn, before we give in our final section an alternative typological interpretation. At the forefront is question 4: how can Jesus simultaneously fulfil the role of both goats of Lev 16, the sin-laden 'Azazel' as well as the sinless sin offering, two goats which are entirely separate, serving different functions and experiencing different fates (the Azazel is released into the desert, the sin offering is killed)?

2.1. A Typological Exegesis

Even though Barth sees himself in line with the Church Fathers in his typological exegesis, it is actually only Calvin whom he mentions. In fact, long before Calvin, many Church Fathers read the Old Testament passage of Lev 16 typologically, finding its true meaning and fulfilment in Christ. Justin in his *Dialogue with Trypho* refers to both animals as prophecies for the two appearances of Christ.[131] Tertullian in *Against Marcion* seeks to prove that Jesus is the Messiah of the Old Testament and gives an interpretation of the two goats as both prefiguring Christ.[132] The scapegoat represents the passion of Christ, the human nature which is passible, and the paschal lamb symbolizes the Eucharist, the divine nature which is impassible. Hippolytus sees the 'sacrificial goat' and 'the goat leading the flock' both as types of Christ. In mentioning only a few patristic examples, we have seen that Jesus Christ was regarded as fulfilling both types of goats in the Old Testament.

130. See *CD* II/2, 365.
131. See Stökl Ben Ezra, *The Impact of Yom Kippur on Early Christianity*, 155f.
132. Ibid., 156–58.

The early Church "saw Christological imagery throughout the Old Testament."[133] Whereas in Christian theology there was clear consensus from the beginning that the sacrificial ḥaṭṭā't of Yom Kippur was a type for the final once-and-for-all sacrifice of Christ on the cross for the sins of the world,[134] the Azazel-goat proved to be more difficult to allocate typologically. This might be because the Christian canon does not explicitly refer to Jesus as scapegoat,[135] whereas it does make reference to Jesus as a sacrifice in the letter to the Hebrews (Heb 9:26; 10:10).[136] This therefore became "*the hermeneutical key for the sacrificial understanding of Christ's death*"[137] of the early Church. Furthermore, Jewish interpreters saw the goat for Azazel carrying away the iniquities of Israel, "bringing them back to their author, the demon Azazel."[138] Thus the "Jewish authors of the New Testament refrained from using the scapegoat as a type of Christ because it was identified or connected with a demon. Early Christian authors, however, did develop a range of various typologies of the scapegoat as part of the Christianisation of the Old Testament."[139]

Jesus was regarded as a vehicle bearing away evil, somewhat similar to the Greek Φαρμακός (*pharmakos*) ritual,[140] as a spacial distancing of *miasma*, evil substance.[141] According to Stökl, the "rise of the scapegoat-typology

---

133. Grabbe, "The Scapegoat Tradition," 161.

134. Stökl, "The Christian Exegesis of the Scapegoat between Jews and Pagans," 212 and 223.

135. See ibid., 208. However, the Epistle of Barnabas, in which the first explicit scapegoat typology appeared, had major significance and was one of the reasons why the scapegoat was often interpreted in a christological typology by the early Church.

136. Paul also refers to Jesus as the Passover lamb (1 Cor 5:7). Frances Young writes: "Only two of the Jewish feasts are of special importance as background to Christian thought, the Day of Atonement ritual and the Passover," in Young, *The Use of Sacrifical Ideas in Greek Christian Writers*, 43.

137. Stökl, "The Biblical Yom Kippur," 497.

138. De Roo, "The Goat for Azazel," 239. See also Grabbe, "The Scapegoat Tradition," 156.

139. Stökl, "The Christian Exegesis of the Scapegoat between Jews and Pagans," 226f. Grabbe writes: "It should not really be surprising that the goat of Azazel was associated with Christ since the Greek translation—which constituted the Bible of the early Christian writers—does not render 'Azazel' in a way to suggest the figure of Satan," in Grabbe, "The Scapegoat Tradition," 162.

140. See Westbrook and Lewis, "The Scapegoat in Leviticus," 419. Stökl, "The Christian Exegesis of the Scapegoat between Jews and Pagans," 224.

141. See Janowski and Wilhelm, "Der Bock, der die Sünden hinausträgt," 129–132 and Janowski, *Sühne als Heilsgeschehen*, 209–15. See also Bremmer, "Scapegoat Rituals in Ancient Greece," passim.

was probably fostered by the fact that its rationale was easily understandable to non-Jewish converts [. . .] [and] because of its comparability to their own cultural institution of *pharmakos* rituals."[142] For some of the early Christian (often non-Jewish) authors therefore, both the sacrificial goat and scapegoat simultaneously became symbols for or types of Christ (here we particularly think of the *Epistle of Barnabas*[143]).

The scapegoat motif had "tremendous impact on the development of the early narratives and interpretation of Jesus' death."[144] From the perspective of 'Penal Substitution,' Jesus Christ is often understood as something of a cosmic scapegoat who bears the sin of the entire world on the cross, a type of the Old Testament Azazel-goat. One such New Testament passage influenced by scapegoat typology is John 1:29, the "Lamb of God." Furthermore the notion of 'bearing' enters New Testament thought from citations of Isa 53 in the Septuagint, and from the translation of נשׂא with ἀναφέρω—Christ bore our sins (Heb 9:28, 1 Pet 2:24).[145] Thus both of these Old Testament concepts of sin bearing—that of the Azazel-goat in Lev 16 and the Suffering Servant in Isa 53—are paradigmatic in interpreting the way Jesus deals with sin on the cross, namely by 'bearing' it.

Yet whereas Jesus is explicitly mentioned as the paschal lamb (1 Cor 5:7) or as a sin offering (*ḥaṭṭā't*) in texts such as Hebrews or 2 Cor 5:21, he is *never* referred to anywhere in the New Testament as the Azazel-goat. The letter to the Hebrews clearly shows Jesus to be both High Priest and self-sacrifice, offering his own blood through the eternal Spirit, representing the one-way movement of the sacrificial *ḥaṭṭā't* into the Holy of Holies. But there is no mention of Jesus also acting as a type for the Azazel-goat, by going away into the wilderness, the place of chaos and destruction, with the iniquities of the people.

Again, 'does Jesus fulfil the role of the Azazel-goat, and if so, how?' Are we provided with any further explanation as to how Jesus 'bore' our infirmities, diseases and sin? A brief look into the Gospels seems to open up an entirely new view of Jesus' act of 'bearing.' In the Gospel of Mark the first signs of Jesus' messianic ministry are the casting out of a demon, healing Peter's mother-in-law, cleansing the leper, and forgiving the sins of the paralytic (as well as healing him). These are all signs of his messianic authority. Chapter

---

142. Stökl, "The Christian Exegesis of the Scapegoat between Jews and Pagans," 225.

143. See chapter 7 in Barnabas, "The Epistle Of Barnabas," 141f.

144. Stökl Ben Ezra, *The Impact of Yom Kippur on Early Christianity*, 147. See also the Epistle of Barnabas.

145. See Janowski and Stuhlmacher, *The Suffering Servant*, 184.

8 of Matthew's Gospel also narrates the story of Peter's mother-in-law and only here do we find a full citation of Isa 53:4, after Jesus drove out many evil spirits with a word and healed all the sick. It says in verse 17 that "this was to fulfil what was spoken through the prophet Isaiah: 'He took up our infirmities and carried our diseases.'"

In quoting Isa 53 "Matthew does associate the prophet and his book with Jesus as the bringer of salvation,"[146] the Servant or Messiah of whom it was said "that he would take and bear the sickness of the people."[147] Yet Matthew does not follow the LXX—he translates the text independently, highlighting and emphasizing the physical aspect of the sicknesses that Jesus healed.[148] Whereas the LXX translated *nāśā'* with φέρω, which might be seen to imply that Jesus became sick, Matthew chooses to use λαμβάνω.[149] In this way he "eliminates the possibility that Jesus himself was sick"[150] and instead states that he removed sicknesses. So according to Matthew, Jesus bears our iniquities and diseases *by removing them*, namely by driving out the evil spirits from the possessed, healing the sick, cleansing the leper, and forgiving the sins of the sinners.[151]

3. An Alternative Typology

It was Origen who first maintained that it is only the sin offering that is a type of Christ and not the Azazel-goat. In homily 10:2:2 of his *Homilies on Leviticus* he interprets the Barabbas episode in Matt 27:15-23 against the background of the scapegoat-rite. Origen writes:

> Let us also now attempt to add something to what was said long ago to the best of our ability, that we may show how 'as a type

---

146. Davies and Allison, *Matthew*, 37.

147. Hagner, *Matthew 1-13*, 210.

148. See Gundry, *Matthew*, 150.

149. The *LXX* in Lev 16:22 also uses λαμβάνω to describe that the goat carried away the iniquities of the people.

150. Davies and Allison, *Matthew*, 37.

151. See Turner, *Matthew*, 236. Turner points out that "Matthew 8:17 connects Isa. 53:4 to Jesus' earthly ministry, not to his atoning death." Whilst there is some truth to this, I would emphasise that Jesus' entire life amounts to the act of atonement, and his life and death cannot be separated when it comes to his salvific work. Nevertheless, Turner's view provides something of a useful counterbalance to other commentators who see Matthew's use of Isa 53 as 1) failing to capture the "true sense of the Old Testament text" (Davies and Allison, *Matthew*, 38); or else 2) "'ignoring' the element in the Isaiah text" (Nolland, *The Gospel of Matthew*, 361), and linking the bearing only as a proleptic act to his death on the cross.

of things to come' (1 Cor 10:11; Heb 10:1) this one he-goat was sacrificed to the Lord as an offering and the other one was sent away 'living.' Hear in the Gospel what Pilate said to the priests and the Jewish people: 'Which of these two do you want me to send out to you, Jesus, who is called the Christ, or Barabbas?' (Matt 27:17) Then all the people cried out to release Barabbas but to hand Jesus over to be killed (v.21f.). Behold, you have a he-goat who was sent 'living into the wilderness,' bearing with him the sins of the people who cried out and said. 'Crucify, crucify.' (Luke 23:21) Therefore, the former is a he-goat sent 'living into the wilderness' and the latter is the he-goat which was offered to God as an offering to atone for sins.[152]

He sees Barabbas as fulfilling the type of the scapegoat in Lev 16. The episode of Barabbas in the Matthean version gains depth when read in the light of the lottery of the two goats in the *Yom Kippur* ritual. In Matt 27:11ff. we see Jesus before Pilate. It was customary at the Passover Feast to release a prisoner. At that time there was a notorious prisoner called Jesus Barabbas ('son of the father'!), whom Luke tells us in chapter 23 had been thrown into prison for insurrection in the city and for murder.[153] Pilate asks the crowd which of the two Jesuses he should release and the chief priests and elders stir up the crowd to demand that Barabbas should live, and Jesus should be crucified. In verse 26 Barabbas is released and Jesus is flogged and handed over to be crucified. Luke tells us that Pilate finds no charges against Jesus and has him punished—Luke 23:16, but the crowd cries 'Give us Barabbas!' Pilate argues with them, saying that he found no grounds for the death penalty, but eventually he grants their demand to have Jesus crucified.

The following four significant characteristics are similar in both events: (1) the 'victims' are presented; (2) they both have the first name Jesus;[154] (3) they symbolize opposed powers (peaceful Messiah *versus* murderer); (4) there is a lottery/election happening as to which of the two is to be released or killed.

So, at first glance the similarities between the ritual of *Yom Kippur* and the Barabbas narrative are obvious. Furthermore, Stökl Ben Ezra shows that the description of the selection of Jesus and Barabbas, who are very similar in name but not in character, agrees with the halakhic ruling regarding the

---

152. Origen, *Homilies on Leviticus: 1–16*, Homily 10:2:2, 204f.
153. From now on I shall use the names Barabbas and Jesus.
154. See the textual apparatus in Aland and Aland, *Novum Testamentum Graece*, on Matt 27:16.

two goats in *Yom Kippur*.[155] The significance of these connections would be more obvious were it not for the assumption, in accordance with long-standing Christian tradition, that Jesus was the scapegoat.

However, the release and person of Barabbas has troubled many exegetes and historians, and some have labelled Jesus Christ and Jesus Barabbas as two aspects of the one historical Jesus. Maccoby writes that "Jesus of Nazareth and Jesus Barabbas were the same man."[156] Some scholars contend that the scarcity of information about Barabbas makes it unlikely that he was a historical figure. Nevertheless, Maclean also reads Matt 27 as the back-drop of Lev 16 and points out that "the story of Barabbas's release by Pilate appears in all four canonical Gospels (Mark 15:6–15; Matt 27:15–26; Luke 23:18–25; John 18:39–40)" in a fairly consistent plot.[157]

It might therefore be suggested that the only thing that these texts have in common is that Jesus is more strongly identified with the sin offering than the Azazel-goat due to his death on the cross and Barabbas' release. To focus on just one of the accounts, John's Gospel connects several events in Jesus' ministry and passion with the Passover Feast in Jerusalem. Pilate's release of Barabbas to the crowd (John 18:39–40) again echoes the scapegoat ritual of Lev 16:6–10, which involved the sacrifice of one goat to YHWH and the release of another into the wilderness. Also, when Pilate hands Jesus over to be crucified, the narrative informs us that "it was the day of Preparation of the Passover" (John 19:14), the day on which the paschal lambs would have been sacrificed. From these examples and others, it is clear that John's Gospel interprets Jesus' death on the cross at least partly in terms of a sacrifice offered to atone for sins.

What can we conclude from all this? *Prime facie* it appears simply as though Barabbas is fortunate and Jesus is unlucky. Jesus seems to be treated like the Azazel-goat. Jewish tradition tells us that the goat was driven out of the city, spat upon, and beaten. Furthermore, the fact that Jesus is given a scarlet coat, which resembles the scarlet wool placed on the head of the Azazel-goat in order to identify it from the other goat, prompted early Christians to believe that Jesus is a clear 'type' of the Azazel-goat from Lev 16. However, even though Jesus appears to be treated as such, he is *not* a type of the Azazel-goat; rather it seems clear that Barabbas' release is the release of the 'living goat into the wilderness.' What it significant is the fact

---

155. See Stökl Ben Ezra, *The Impact of Yom Kippur on Early Christianity*, 169.

156. Maccoby, *Revolution in Judea*, 164. In an earlier article, Maccoby suggests that Barabbas was a title by which Jesus was known to his followers, see Maccoby, "Jesus and Barabbas."

157. Maclean, "Barabbas, the Scapegoat Ritual, and the Development of the Passion Narrative," 309.

Jesus Christ the Elect 93

that Barabbas—the murderer—was released as a sinner, and Jesus—the sinless one—was crucified, becoming a *ḥaṭṭā't*. So again we have the mirror-inverted act of one released and one sacrificed as seen in Lev 16—but this time the procedure is reversed. Whereas normally the Azazel-goat was driven out into the wilderness into order to take the contamination away as far as possible, now it is released in the midst of the people. Conversely, the spotless sin offering whose blood would normally be taken into the Holy of Holies is driven out like the Azazel-goat, outside the city gates, spat upon, severely beaten and finally crucified, becoming a *ḥaṭṭā't* for the sins of the world, as well as the new *kappōret*, the place where we can again be at one with God. The *kappōret* was the place where God himself dwelled (1 Sam 4:2), the place of meeting with YHWH's presence (Exod 25:22) of his self-disclosure, where God spoke to Moses and the place where on *Yom Kippur* atonement was made (Lev 16)[158] and "the people were reconciled to God by the sprinkling of blood."[159] In the performed *Existenzstellvertretung* of his Son, the saving presence of God is present and thus atonement occurs.[160] Stuhlmacher thus sees Jesus in the context of the Day of Atonement, being installed by God as a reconciler:

> God publicly made Jesus the place of meeting with God, of his revelation of reconciliation that has been brought about by virtue of the atonement effected in Jesus' sacrifice of his life, in his blood. So God himself has in the death and resurrection of Jesus made himself known as the one who meets humanity and makes atonement.[161]

The *kappōret*, the place of atonement in the Holy of Holies, is no longer locked away but now openly displayed at Golgotha in the form of Christ on the cross. Jesus becomes the כַּפֹּרֶת of the new covenant,[162] and the main implication of this is that the kingdom of God is sufficiently close that his coming and redeeming power are recognized.[163] God speaks to his people in the way he previously spoke with Moses from the *kappōret* (see Exod 25:22) and thus there is now "no longer any need for a priestly mediation between the God who is encountered in secret and the people of God who

---

158. See Stuhlmacher, "Recent Exegesis on Romans 3:24–26," 100.
159. Barth, *The Epistle to the Romans*, 105.
160. See Knöppler, *Sühne im Neuen Testament*, 117.
161. Stuhlmacher, "Recent Exegesis on Romans 3:24–26," 100.
162. See Knöppler, *Sühne im Neuen Testament*, 116.
163. See Barth, *The Epistle to the Romans*, 105.

exist outside in front of the temple."[164] Thus the cross where Jesus died becomes the new meeting place of God; the cross becomes the *kappōret*.[165] The temple is no longer the place to meet God and to make atonement—Jesus himself becomes the place where the presence of God dwells, and chose the cross as the throne where humanity can meet him. This is how God chooses to reveal himself, in Jesus Christ on the cross, God's self-unveiling, symbolized by the temple curtain being torn in two.

Conclusion

In the light of our own exegesis of Lev 14 and in particular Lev 16, it is difficult to agree with Barth's exegetical conclusion, that Jesus is both the elect and the rejected. Our exegesis shows that applying Barth's typological approach in the way that he does to support his doctrine of election, Jesus Christ should only be seen as the sacrificial animal, giving his life for the sinner in an act of *Existenzstellvertretung*. This would result in the conclusion that Jesus Christ, with *both* his divine *and* his human nature, is only the elect of God. This result is in accord with Luther and the Formula of Concord where the parallel structuring of election and reprobation is given up and election is based "solely of God's gracious will to save as it is revealed in Jesus Christ."[166]

Barth's typological exegesis is, as he says, in line with that of the Church Fathers. Linking the typological exegesis to the doctrine of election is new, though somewhat problematic, since it does not harmonize entirely with his systematic-theological reflection. The two elements (the systematic part and the exegetical part) sometimes do not seem to match entirely. The 'God-human' pair in his systematic part is arranged differently to the 'God-human' pair in his exegetical part and thus the two do not tessellate. Whereas in the large text section, when talking about God and humanity, Barth can sum up his ideas in the phrase "God wills to lose in order that man may gain,"[167] seeing God as the one taking reprobation in order that humanity is elected; when talking about the God-man Jesus, Barth's argumentation is somewhat unsatisfactory. At times Barth says that the "Son of Man was from all eternity the object of the election of the Father"[168] and thus sees the

---

164. Stuhlmacher, *Paul's Letter to the Romans*, 60.
165. See Bailey, "Jesus as the Mercy Seat."
166. Pannenberg, *Systematic Theology Vol. 3*, 446.
167. CD II/2, 162.
168. CD II/2, 158.

"Son of God in His whole giving of Himself to the Son of Man,"[169] committing himself from all eternity to "unite Himself with the lost Son of Man."[170] He also sees the dialectic that is between God and humanity reflected in a dialectic between the 'Son of God' (taking rejection) and the 'Son of Man' (being elected): "The exchange which took place on Golgotha, when God chose as His throne the malefactor's cross, when the Son of God bore what the son of man ought to have borne."[171]

However, in his exegetical section it is the human nature of Jesus (Son of Man) who bears the punishment as pictured by the Azazel-goat and it is the divine nature (eternal Son) who is brought into contact with God through the sin offering. This seems to contradict Barth's explanation in his systematic section. Furthermore, we will see in chapter 4 that the dialectic in his exegesis in *CD* II/2 also does not fit with Barth's doctrine of reconciliation in *CD* IV, where the Son of God is the one who humbles himself in order that the Son of Man is lifted up into the divine Triune fellowship (a notion that we also see in the large text section in *CD* II/2 where Barth writes about "the humiliation which the Son of God accepted on behalf of the lost son of man").[172] Therefore we have to reiterate our question from chapter 1 and ask 'How does Barth see Jesus' humanity in relation to the humanity of all others in reference to rejection and reprobation?'[173] Can Jesus Christ really be divided up into his divine and human nature in the act of election and atonement, fulfilling two completely different functions? And if Jesus is, according to the doctrines of the *enhypostatic* and *anhypostatic* union, fully man but also simultaneously incorporates all of humanity, would it not be fatal for humanity that the human nature of Christ be cast out?

We must now return to the nature of Barth's dialectic. One useful approach is that of Welker, who shows that there is an affinity in method between Barth and Hegel.[174] In 1953, Barth said to a group of pastors "*Ich*

169. *CD* II/2, 157.
170. *CD* II/2, 158.
171. *CD* II/2, 167.
172. *CD* II/2, 173.

173. The English translation seems to have identified this problem of how to allocate rejection and election to the different natures of the God-man Jesus, as well as the fact that Barth is inconsistent in this. The translation appears to solve this by capitalizing 'Son of Man' when talking about the object of election and using lower case for 'son of man' when talking about the cross. However, in the German version of the *KD* no distinction is made when talking about the 'Menschensohn.'

174. On Barth's affinity to Hegel's method see Welker, "Barth und Hegel." Welker highlights that after 1929, when Barth read several hundred pages of Hegel, he never engaged intensively with Hegel (309). I am grateful to Robert Leigh for directing me

selbst habe eine gewisse Schwäche für Hegel und tue gern immer wieder einmal etwas 'hegeln.'"[175] This method is for Barth the 'dialectical method' of "*Thesis, Antithesis und Synthesis.*"[176] In the Tambach lecture of 1919 we see that, like Hegel, Barth sees the divine as something that humanity perceives as "wholly other,"[177] "complete in itself [*in sich Geschlossenes*], something new and different in contrast to the world [*Verschiedenes gegenüber der Welt*]."[178] Barth explains that the "synthesis we seek is in *God* alone, and in God alone can we find it. [. . .] The synthesis which is *meant* in the thesis and *sought* in the antithesis."[179] It is the binary structure of thesis and antithesis, of a "critical No and a creative Yes"[180] that is brought into a synthesis in Jesus Christ, God incarnate.

Welker explains that Barth uses this Hegelian method primarily, but not exclusively, to bridge the gap and make a smooth transition between his systematic-theological reflection and his exegesis.[181] We have seen that this dialectical method permeates Barth's doctrine of election, and is in fact the backbone to his entire theological structure. It is seen in the thesis of God's *No* in rejection (the cross) and the antithesis of God's *Yes* in election (the resurrection), which were brought into synthesis in Jesus Christ. Barth is correct in saying that it is not simply that the "antithesis is more than mere reaction to the thesis; it issues from the synthesis in its own original strength, it apprehends theirs and puts an end to it."[182] However, in light of our exegesis, we realize that election and rejection cannot be synthesized in the way Barth attempts.

Barth accuses Hegel of having identified "God with the dialectical method" and of "making the dialectical method of logic the essential nature of God."[183] Barth says that in this way Hegel was a prisoner of his own method and also blocked access to the free and concrete God for humanity. With regard to his own dogmatic (dialectical) method, Barth emphasizes, in opposition to Hegel, that the only justification for using his method (which

---

towards this article.

175. Busch, *Karl Barth: His Life from Letters and Autobiographical Texts*, 402.

176. Welker, "Barth und Hegel," 315. See also Ward, "Barth, Hegel, and the Possibility for Christian Apologetics," 63.

177. Barth, "The Christian's Place in Society," 288.

178. Ibid., 277.

179. Ibid., 322.

180. Ibid., 274.

181. See Welker, "Barth und Hegel," 321.

182. Barth, "The Christian's Place in Society," 311.

183. Barth, "Hegel," 304.

is Hegel's as well) is by being constantly in the process of listening *to* and waiting *for* answers from the living Word of God. As soon as the concentration shifts to the method instead of the focus being on the Word of God, the method loses its function (which is to support theological enquiry) and it hinders the theological work. It moves from supporting to hindering. Thus it is only a renewed centring on the Word of God that justifies for Barth in using the dialectical method in theology.[184]

Although Barth's method is in itself coherent,[185] following our exegesis and a fresh engagement with Scripture, we have to challenge Barth and ask whether he has fallen victim to his own method and "misuses the method in the service of a system."[186] The exegetical conclusion of Barth's method becomes even more apparent in the light of our exegesis. Highlighting the axiomatic relationship between Old Testament and New Testament, Barth highlights the problematic tension of his doctrine of election by comparing David and Saul: "David is no more unambiguously a figure of light than Saul is unambiguously the offspring of darkness. There is something of Saul in David, just as there is something of David in Saul. We must undoubtedly see both in each."[187] Just as in the cultic text of Leviticus where Barth sees all four animals as types of Christ, so too does he see the two sides of the two persons David and Saul representing one "total picture."[188] His conclusion is that the elected as well as the rejected have traces of characteristics of the other and *vice versa*. Saul belongs to David, "as does the shadow to light."[189]

The climax of his typological exegesis is finally reached in the story of Judas' rejection,[190] where Barth fades Jesus and Judas into one, Jesus himself becoming Judas, the *Urbild* of rejection.[191] The pattern of exchange is seen by Jesus the sinless one dying for Judas, full of guilt for betraying Jesus [παραδίδωμι]. The rejection of Christ at Golgotha becomes the election of

---

184. See Welker, "Barth und Hegel," 327. On 'Hearing and Obeying the Word of God' see Wood, *Barth's Theology of Interpretation*, 136–74. See also Bächli, *Das Alte Testament in der Kirchlichen Dogmatik*, 96–113 and 134–41, who considers what it means to let Scripture talk to oneself, Barth's understanding of exegesis and the relationship between dogmatics and exegesis.

185. See Stoevesandt, "Karl Barths Erwählungslehre," 114.

186. Ford, *Barth and God's Story*, 93.

187. *CD* II/2, 372. See also Bächli, *Das Alte Testament in der Kirchlichen Dogmatik*, 174–180.

188. *CD* II/2, 372.

189. See Kreck, *Grundentscheidungen in Karl Barths Dogmatik*, 266.

190. See Ford, "Barth's Interpretation of the Bible," 66.

191. See Ford, *Barth and God's Story*, 85.

Judas, making his "ultimate rejection inconceivable."[192] For Barth, this exegesis is an "answer to the problem of divine providence and evil"[193] (namely how evil and God's will can be reconciled—"sin is made righteousness, and evil good").[194] We will address this in detail in chapter 3. For now, we have to interrogate Barth's provocative typology. Scripture emphasizes that "God is light; in him there is no darkness at all" (1 John 1:5). We must ask whether Barth in his provocative typology has genuinely seen "an aspect of 'what is there' in the New Testament texts no one had noticed before him? [. . .]. Is Barth's reading original in the sense of genuinely shedding light on a mainly neglected aspect of the texts, or is he imposing a predetermined theological schema?"[195]

The conclusion in Barth's typology suggests that all—Cain, the goat sent to Azazel, and Judas—are finally elected and the sting of finality is removed. Yet for Ford, there seems to be a "misuse of typology which spoils the realism of the literal story for the sake of trying to know more of God's purpose than can properly be elicited. [. . .] [Barth is pressing] his method to the point of producing contradictions."[196] The New Testament gives "little indication that Judas was anything other than lost, even if it is not entirely conclusive in this issue."[197] What we see in Barth is that he has a tendency to synthesize contradictions or antitheses in Scripture that the texts themselves either do not try to resolve, or which they purposefully leave ambiguous. Either way, Barth seems to "peep over God's shoulder,"[198] giving us an answer that the Bible might not want to give. What these apparent contradictions of the text might intend is to provoke in the reader a "humble *Nachdenken* of the story,"[199] and reflect on the question of personal salvation (maybe in the way that the words of the prophets in the Old Testament sought to stir the reader to repentance). And so, in Barth's synthesizing the tensions of the text he in fact is in danger of undermining their own intention.

By using Barth's own typological method we have stayed faithful to his undertaking, while identifying several contradictions in his exegesis. We then offered an alternative exegesis and gave an alternative interpretation that concluded that, according to our understanding of Scripture, Jesus

192. Ford, "Barth's Interpretation of the Bible," 66.
193. Ford, *Barth and God's Story*, 86.
194. CD II/2, 503.
195. Cane, *The Place of Judas Iscariot in Christology*, 65f.
196. Ford, *Barth and God's Story*, 91.
197. Cane, *The Place of Judas Iscariot in Christology*, 64.
198. Ford, "Barth's Interpretation of the Bible," 86.
199. Ibid., 86.

Jesus Christ the Elect 99

Christ is only the elect and not the rejected. In this way we have attempted to correct Barth with Barth, "from within by using his own method."[200] Instead, Barth has produced a construct of "*Inklusivverhältnissen*" that is justified from neither the Old nor the New Testament.[201] Through Barth's typological exegesis and employment of *Aufhebung*, the symmetrical contradictions in election and rejection are resolved universally in their synthesis, Jesus Christ. Yet shifting rejection onto Christ still does not solve the dogmatic problem of whether or not the rejected are included in the elect; instead, Barth has only shifted it with the help of newly created symmetries and analogies.[202]

In conclusion, Cain (*et al.*) who bears his own sin (*nāśā' 'āwôn*) becomes a picture of the rejected and unredeemed.[203] He is a type of the Azazel-goat and, like the goat, is trapped in sin and sent away from the presence of God, becoming a restless wanderer. This notion is undergirded by the New Testament references to Cain as an example of how not to be (1 John 3:12) and whose footsteps one should avoid at all costs (Jude 11). Furthermore, in the New Testament, texts like Matt 25 that talk about the division between the sheep and the goats, again present us with a binary of elected and rejected as that seen in the Old Testament, and this seems to indicate that the writers of the Gospels had no intention, even in the light of the death of Christ, of smoothing out the tensions.

---

200. Ford, *Barth and God's Story*, 93.
201. Gloege, "Zur Prädestinationslehre Karl Barths," 126.
202. See ibid., 127.
203. On the topic of Cain and sin bearing see Scarlata, *Outside of Eden*, 157–59.

3

The Covenant, Humanity, and *das Nichtige*

But this is the covenant that I will make with the house of Israel after those days, says the LORD: I will put my law within them, and I will write it on their hearts; and I will be their God, and they shall be my people.

(Jer 31:33)

Introduction

THIS CHAPTER LOOKS AT THE DOCTRINES OF THE COVENANT, HUMANITY and *das Nichtige*—three aspects that stand in close relation to the doctrines of election and atonement. For Barth, election in eternity is the ontological ground of the covenant and atonement is the historical event of the restoration of this eternal covenant which was previously jeopardized by sin. Thus, in order to understand election and atonement, we also need to understand Barth's view of the covenant, humanity, and sin. For it is sin that is the cause of the broken covenant between God and humanity and it is the atonement which deals with the removal of sin and thus brings about the restoration of the covenantal fellowship. Barth links the importance of the doctrine of the covenant in relation to the doctrine of election and atonement to various other themes, such as creation, 'the real man,' and sin and nothingness, which we will also look at in detail in this chapter (Barth discusses this in detail in *CD* III). In light of the previous two chapters, we now have to ask ourselves whether the anthropological account of humanity that Barth develops in *CD* III (especially III/2 and 3) is in harmony with his view of humanity with regard to election as expressed earlier in the *CD*. We must also ask whether his account contradicts or undergirds other doctrines found previously and subsequently in the *CD*, especially those of election and atonement. In other words, is Barth's theology internally coherent? We will also consider the charges that were brought against Barth in chapter 1 relating to Jesus' and humanity's human natures and the relationship between the two, as well as the charge of 'objectivism' and humanity's 'subjective element of faith' brought by Brunner. By highlighting these various aspects of Barth this chapter functions to present various different lenses, providing different perspectives on the atonement, which will be the focus of chapter 4.

1. The Covenant

By now we have come to understand that Barth's message and concern is to "hold fast at all costs and at every point to the Christological thread."[1] This christological concern, to hold fast to the supremacy of Christ, is the underlying method in all his systematic undertaking, and this is no different in *CD* III, where he talks about creation and the covenant between God and humanity. It is through God's self-revelation and through faith in Jesus Christ[2] that humanity can know and does know God as her Creator. Barth goes on to say that this self-revelation is based on the revelation of Jesus Christ as the Word through which all things were created: "The whole Bible speaks figuratively and prophetically of [God], in Jesus Christ, when it speaks of creation, the Creator and creature."[3]

1.1. The Covenant and Creation

The covenant of grace in Jesus Christ might be seen as bringing all the different strands of the *CD* together in one uniting and overarching thread. It is God's calling of all humanity, in fact the whole cosmos, heaven and earth, into redeeming fellowship with him, which is the essence of the cross. Robert Jenson in *Alpha and Omega* highlights Barth's question 'Why did God create the world?' and answers it by saying that the Bible bears witness to the 'why': it was created in order that God, in Christ, can shower his grace upon

---

1. *CD* III/3, xi.

2. Barth states that it is an "appeal to faith" to see God as the Creator of heaven and earth, in *CD* III/1, 11.

3. *CD* III/1, 23.

the creatures he loves.[4] In the creation "saga"[5] of Gen 1–2 Barth explains the covenant of grace:[6] "Creation sets the stage for the story of the covenant of grace."[7] For Barth, "Creation is the outward basis of the covenant (Gen 1) and the covenant the inward basis of creation (Gen 2)."[8] Thus creation itself is the unique sign of the covenant.[9] In the doctrine of creation Barth reports that God created a world and creatures distinct from himself, yet he created them with the purpose of being in covenantal relationship with him, a free responsive life and partnership with the divine.[10] God brings into being a reality different from himself and establishes a covenant relationship with that which he has created. Creation for Barth is not a theological "reflection on how the world came into existence, but a witness to God as Creator who in his eternal purpose in love elected a people for a covenant in which the creation of the world provided the stage for this history of redemption."[11]

Barth sees creation as—to use Webster's words—"that reality which God destines for fellowship with Jesus Christ," and thus he concludes that 'creation' and 'covenant' are "correlative terms."[12] Though creation is a gift of God, it never exists without the consummation in Christ, without God's self-giving promise through Christ to be the loving *Deus pro nobis*. Thus the covenant is first of all God's act of faithfulness towards himself.[13] It is here in *CD* III/1 that we read that God chooses to call humanity into fellowship with himself, the goal and purpose of God's work of creation, which finds its finality of fellowship in the saving and redeeming work of Christ. In Christ, God has bound himself in an eternal covenant of fellowship with humanity. Thus Barth can say that the covenant of grace has its ontological foundation

---

4. See Jenson, *Alpha and Omega*, 22f. See also Käfer who says that "[d]ie Schöpfung ist nach Barth das Mittel, durch das Gott seine Gnadenzuwendung verwirklichen und seinen Bund realisieren könne," in Käfer, *Inkarnation und Schöpfung*, 264.

5. N.B: When Barth uses the word 'saga' he does not mean 'myth.' He sees "saga [...] as an intuitive and poetic picture of a prehistoric reality of history which is enacted once and for all within the confines of time and space," in *CD* III/1, 81.

6. For Barth, 'creation' and 'covenant' are two interwoven and correlative themes. He explains with an extensive exegesis of Gen 1 in §41 that creation is the *external* basis of the covenant. In §42 with the help of Gen 2 he deepens his understanding of the covenant as the *internal* basis of creation.

7. *CD* III/1, 44.

8. *CD* IV/1, 27.

9. See von Balthasar, *The Theology of Karl Barth*, 124.

10. See *CD* III/1, 5.

11. Webster, *Barth*, 110.

12. Ibid., 98.

13. See Härle, *Sein und Gnade*, 77.

in Jesus Christ.[14] Furthermore, Barth's doctrine of creation is bound to his doctrine of the Trinity.[15] It is the Triune God—Father, Son, and Spirit—who is the Creator of the world and who brings the world into being out of "the good-pleasure of the free omnipotence of the divine love."[16] This divine love is the foundation of the covenant of grace, the basis for God's relationship with the creatures of this world.

1.2. The Covenant, Election, and Providence

There is a close association between Barth's concept of derivation and the doctrine of election: "To be with God is to derive from God, and to derive from God is to rest upon God's election."[17] As we have already come to know from chapters 1 and 2, Barth's doctrine of election is not interested in dividing humanity into two groups, of chosen or reprobate, since the election of all is secured in Jesus Christ, but is concerned with the *Yes* of God to creation. In election we learn about the will of God to preserve estranged humanity and in the atonement we see how God works his will out. Both times it is Jesus who is the "spearhead" and executor of God's will and the divine purpose through which humanity has its being.[18] He is the only true elect human being, who was chosen before the foundation of the world and chose himself to be the Savior of humankind, from whom humanity derivers her existence.

Furthermore, creation for Barth, following Calvin, becomes the "*theatrum gloriae Dei*"[19] the stage on which God acts out his gracious election in history and brings about the fulfilment of the salvation bringing covenant in Jesus Christ. For Barth creation is always an action of divine grace, a protecting from the *tohu wa-bohu* as well as an act of sustaining creation in spite of chaos and evil, in which we see a witness to the triumphant *Yes* spoken on the cross. Whereas creation and providence are secondary elements in Barth's theology and stay separate from one another (the election of grace must be understood as the "root"[20] of the doctrines of providence and creation), together they build the external basis of the covenant. Yet

---

14. See *CD* IV/1, 47. See also Härle, *Sein und Gnade*, 76 and 100.
15. See the discussion on the creation, the Trinity and the Spirit in Webster, *Barth*, 110f.
16. *CD* III/1, 15.
17. Webster, *Barth*, 102.
18. See *CD* III/2, 144 and Webster, *Barth*, 102.
19. *CD*, III/3, 47.
20. *CD* III/3, 6.

creation and providence are not identical for Barth. While creation highlights the 'beginning' as well as the "ontic chasm"[21] that exists as the gulf between Creator and creature, providence on the other hand demonstrates the 'continuation' of this story made manifest in God's longing and desire in history to dwell amongst his people.

Thus both creation and providence highlight the one will of God to have relationship with his creatures and in both cases have their "meaning in the divine election and covenant as its final secret and basis."[22] Barth writes: "He wholly identifies Himself with the world and man, willing to be fully immanent even in His transcendence."[23] McCormack has argued that Barth's doctrine of election (or rather the revision of the doctrine in 1936) has led to his view on creation and providence.[24] For Barth there could be "no independent doctrine of creation and providence."[25] He saw the fatal traditional error of the doctrine stemming from an understanding "without reference to the covenantal purposes of God which ground God's creative activity."[26] The "covenant is the meaning, basis and goal of this act [creation] [. . . ,] the execution of the eternal decree of God's eternal election of grace"[27] and "providence guarantees and confirms the work of creation."[28] For Barth it is important always to bear in mind that the God of the Bible is not the god of the philosophers or a 'mere manufacturer' and therefore the theological concept of Creator, creature, and of creation should always be kept in view.[29] We might sum up the doctrine of providence with Barth's own words:

> in the act of creation God the Creator as such has associated Himself with His creature as such as the Lord of its history, and is faithful to it as such. God the Creator co-exists with His creature, and so His creature exists under the presupposition, and its implied conditions, of the co-existence of its Creator.[30]

Though, for Barth, God's sovereignty, grace, and predestination remain crucial, Calvin's doctrine of election and its relation to the doctrine of

---

21. Kennedy, "A Personalist Doctrine of Providence," 146.
22. CD III/3, 8.
23. CD III/3, 8.
24. McCormack, *Karl Barth's Critically Realistic Dialectical Theology*, 453–63.
25. Ibid., 454.
26. Ibid., 454.
27. CD III/3, 6.
28. CD III/3, 6.
29. CD III/3, 9.
30. CD III/3, 12.

providence—election falling into the sphere of providence—are from Barth's point of view "unbiblical and therefore unacceptable."[31] Barth critiques many others who follow Calvin, who understood election as a subset of the doctrine of providence.[32] Bruce McCormack points out that Barth's aim in the doctrine of providence is to safeguard the 'theological values' of the Reformed orthodox tradition, whilst liberating it from abstract philosophical and non-christological thought.[33] Even though both doctrines, election and providence, deal with God's lordship over the creature, Barth argues that election is rooted and is part of the inner-being of the triune God, whilst providence is contingent upon creation. The eternal election of grace is thus "a matter primarily and properly of the eternal election of the Son of God,"[34] an *opus Dei internum* and thus "belongs to the being of God and is identical with it";[35] whereas the doctrine of providence on the other hand is an *opus ad extra* and "describes an outer and not an inner work of God."[36] Furthermore providence, which Barth sees as "the execution of this decree" and "grounded in this decree" (the decree of election), presupposes creation and the existence of a creature to act upon, but the eternal decision does not presuppose the *act* of creation or the creature.[37] Barth sums up:

> The root of the doctrine of predestination is to be found in the being of God. But the doctrine of providence has no corresponding root of which this may be said. On the presupposition of the finished work of creation and the given existence of the creature we can certainly say that as Creator God would be untrue to Himself in His relationship with His creature without the knowing, willing and acting described in the doctrine of providence. But He would be no less God even if the work of creation had never been done, if there were no creatures, and if the whole doctrine of providence were therefore irrelevant.[38]

31. Kennedy, "A Personalist Doctrine of Providence," 145.

32. Wendel argues that "Predestination can in fact be regarded as in some respects a particular application of the more general notion of Providence," in Wendel, *Calvin: Origins and Development of His Religious Thought*, 178. Furthermore, Dowey shows that "Providence is a description of God's universally although personally active will in creation, while predestination specifically concerns the redemption and condemnation of men," in Dowey, *The Knowledge of God in Calvin's Theology*, 239.

33. See McCormack, "The Actuality of God," 223–31.

34. CD III/3, 4.

35. CD III/3, 6.

36. CD III/3, 6.

37. CD III/3, 6.

38. CD, III/3, 5.

This identification of election with divine being separates Barth's theology significantly from that of Calvin's, which sees "election as a subset of providence."[39] Much of the rest of *CD* III/3 is spent by Barth expounding the implications of this statement. However, "Barth's removal of election from within the larger sphere of providence indicates a strong formal break with the theological tradition."[40] Yet, Barth's doctrine of providence, like so many other doctrines, must be understood christologically and finds its meaning in God's fatherly and caring being as revealed in the incarnation in Jesus Christ. Thus all world events stand under the lordship of the living and personal God and are either acts of obedience or disobedience in regard to his gracious election. Therefore, the "myth of neutrality evaporates in the face of the personal God with whom all creatures have to do."[41]

Kennedy has shown that Barth shifts away from a rather mechanical understanding of providence towards a personal one. Election, we have seen, is the foundation and basis of providence and creation as it proceeds both of them. Barth argues that, before the foundation of the world, God had made the decision to elect creatures into covenant fellowship with himself, and thus election "reflects the nature and intent of the Creator towards the creature."[42] Furthermore, Barth claims that in this covenant relationship, the creature is most free and therefore real human freedom can only be understood in the light of the proper relationship to God. By equating the will of God with the election and incarnation of Jesus Christ, Barth takes away the veil of any mystery or hiddenness of God as well as of his will and providence. It is not that God wills this or that event in abstraction from history but that God is sovereign and so all events are 'determined' according God's singular will in Jesus Christ. By situating the covenant between Creator and creature and *Heilsgeschichte* in world history, history becomes entangled and intersects with the story of God's salvation of the world in and through Jesus Christ,[43] yet without becoming identical with it. Barth uses the Chalcedonian christological formula, the mystery of the relationship between the two natures of Christ—divine and human which remain together without confusion or separation—as an analogy to describe the two realities of covenantal history, or *Heilsgeschichte*, and world history with its occurrences.

---

39. Kennedy, "A Personalist Doctrine of Providence," 146.
40. Ibid., 145.
41. Ibid., 147.
42. Ibid., 151.
43. See Ford, *Barth and God's Story*, passim.

Jesus Christ as very God and very man, the basis and fulfilment of the history of the covenant, is certainly not to be found again in general creaturely occurrence. [. . .] The contrast and connexion of heaven and earth, of the inconceivable and conceivable world, is not the same as that of God and man in Jesus Christ; but it is similar.[44]

Thus for Barth, divine election of grace becomes the basis and hermeneutical key for understanding and interpreting world events as well as human action.

1.3. *The Covenant and Salvation*

We saw that Barth sees creation as the 'stage of redemption' where, in Jesus Christ, God undertakes divine acts of pure grace for the salvation of humanity. Jesus re-establishes the covenant of grace, which is the fulfilment of the purpose and "essential nature as established by the Creator."[45] Barth writes that, like a temple built for the purpose of worshipping God, so too does creation find its purpose in the saving events of Christ. To summarize, "creation is in no sense *necessary*; it exists *only* for the sake of God's overflowing grace."[46] In his section on the covenant Barth uses the dogma of the two natures (*vere Deus et vere homo*) of Christ and combines them with the teaching of the two states (*status exinanitionis et status exaltationis*).[47] This has to be seen in relation to the doctrine of election where Jesus is both electing God and elected human. Thus both in Christology and soteriology we have to understand Christ's two natures and see him as very God and very human in one person, in the mystery of that duality in unity. God's downward movement (see also CD IV/1) towards humanity and the exaltation of humanity (see also CD IV/2) is one single act in Jesus Christ.[48] These two dialectical movements of humiliation and exaltation take place in the incarnation, life, death, resurrection and ascension of Christ.[49] In the downward movement where the *Logos* became incarnate, when the Word

---

44. CD III/3, 49.
45. Webster, *Barth*, 98.
46. Mangina, *Theologian of Christian Witness*, 91.
47. See Mikkelsen, *Reconciled Humanity*, 165. See also Jones, *The Humanity of Christ*, 183–86.
48. See Hunsinger, *Disruptive Grace*, 141. On Barth's combination of humiliation and exaltation see Prenter, "Karl Barths Umbildung der traditionellen Zweinaturlehre in lutherischer Beleuchtung."
49. See Mikkelsen, *Reconciled Humanity*, 168.

of God was made flesh, humanity encounters the eternal in time. In Christ we are "confronted with the eternal Word of God which has assumed our human nature and existence into oneness with God."[50] God in time, God as man, God active in history: everything centres on the event of the Word becoming flesh (John 1:1f.), the incarnation of the Son of God.[51]

Torrance sees the Word of God as penetrating into the innermost existence of Israel, into its mind and flesh, assuming all humanity into itself; "gathering it into covenant relation with God, it is here above all that we see the Word made flesh in unity of person and word, truth and life, word and deed in Jesus Christ" that fulfils and completes the covenant.[52] Jesus' life from start to finish is in perfect union with God. Thus in the incarnation we see the union of God and man, eternity and time, the eternal decision that nothing can undo. Here "God and man meet in Jesus Christ and a new covenant is eternally established and fulfilled."[53] The linking of the incarnation with the covenant enables Barth to "interpret the incarnation as the ultimate manifestation of God's eternal mercy toward all human beings."[54]

Thus, the core of the Christian message is summarized by Barth with one word—*Immanuel*.[55] Barth uses the words of the prophet Isaiah (Isa 7:14) as "the description of an act of God, or better, of God Himself in the act of His" which has to be seen as an event [*Ereignis*].[56] 'God with us' is an event which means both the unity of God's being and his act—God as the one who "lives as what He is, in that He does what He does."[57] For Barth, the 'God with us' means that God has intended salvation for humanity, that humanity is not only created or preserved for salvation but ordained [*bestimmt*] for salvation.[58] Thus salvation is participation in the divine being of God, the fulfilment of being, an eternal being hidden in God, a being clothed with eternal life.[59] Salvation is ordained for humanity through the eternal grace of God and reveals the original and basic will [*Ur- und Grund-*

---

50. Torrance, *Incarnation*, 8.

51. Barth sees the incarnate Word as "der echte Realgrund der Schöpfung," *KD* III/1, 54.

52. Torrance, *Incarnation*, 107.

53. Ibid., 106.

54. Mikkelsen, *Reconciled Humanity*, 171.

55. *CD* IV/3, 2.

56. *CD* IV/1, 6.

57. *CD* IV/1, 6.

58. See Härle, *Sein und Gnade*, 78. He writes "die Versöhnung (als der in Jesus Christus erfüllte Bund) ist der innere Grund der Schöpfung."

59. See *CD* IV/1, 8 and 116.

wille] and salvation-plan of God, which is grounded in the eternal covenant of grace. 'God with us' is a *Heilsgeschehen* that means the "revelation and confirmation of the most primitive relationship between God and man, that which was freely determined in eternity by God Himself before there was any created being."[60] So in God's coming to *us* he himself becomes, at his own cost and initiative, the executor of his own will. For Barth, this event is not simply a restoration of the *status quo ante*, the *restitutio ad integrum*— rather, God's participation in humanity's being means the "coming of salvation itself [. . .] the man in whom God Himself intervenes for us, suffers and acts for us, closes the gap between Himself and us."[61]

So Barth can say that *Jesus Christus ist die Versöhnung*, the "accomplishing and fulfilling of the divine covenant as executed by God Himself. He is the eschatological realisation of the will of God for Israel and therefore for the whole race."[62] Jesus Christ, the Word of God, makes known that this covenant with Israel is made for the salvation of the whole world. He is the Mediator of the covenant, the revelation of the *Urwille* of God. Jesus reveals that God is for humanity, the *Deus pro nobis*, the covenant God. In God's act of atonement that took place in Jesus Christ, the basic determination [*Grundbestimmung*] of the relationship between God and humanity is revealed as applicable to all of humanity and attains the goal of the covenant history with Israel. The covenant was given its fullest manifestation at Sinai. The promise and command of the covenant (God's promise to 'walk among you and be your God'—Lev 26:12), and his command to the people to 'be holy' (Lev 11:44) rested on the "twin foundations of the Sinaitic Law and Levitical liturgy."[63] Throughout the history of God's interactions with Israel it became clear that "the covenant did not depend on Israel's worth, but on the contrary, was conditioned by the pure unstinted outflowing love of God in the continuous act of grace, of grace for grace," as Torrance writes.[64] Thus in Jesus Christ we can "look into the heart of God—for in Him He has revealed to us: 'I will be your God'—we are permitted, indeed we are constrained, to look at ourselves that what is proper to and is required of us is: 'Ye shall be my people.'"[65] This is so because Jesus Christ is both fully divine and fully human, both God of the covenant and man of the covenant simultaneously; thus in him, the 'I will be your God and you shall be my

---

60. *CD* IV/1, 10.
61. *CD* IV/1, 13.
62. *CD* IV/1, 34.
63. Torrance, *Incarnation*, 46.
64. Ibid., 46.
65. *CD* IV/1, 43.

people' has come to fulfilment. In Christ, God's promise and command are a unity and are eternally grounded in him, the eternal Word of God at the beginning of all things.[66]

1.4. The Covenant and Sin

Since for Barth 'being human' becomes equivalent to 'being elect,' he sees both from a covenantal point of view—humanity is chosen to live in the covenant communion of the mercy and grace bestowed by Christ, who has made this covenant a reality when dying on the cross for the sins of all humanity. As said above, the *Yes* or call of God is spoken to all human beings and, since all of humanity derives from God, the incarnation of the *Logos* alters and affects the state of entire humanity before God. Hence, for Barth unbelief (sin and evil) takes on the nature of something paradoxical, something that contradicts human existence, a state of 'nothingness' (see §50) from which God has preserved humanity when Jesus exposed himself to nothingness in the incarnation and conquered it on the cross once and for all.[67] Therefore, Barth's concept of sin is summed up as 'an impossible possibility' (as we will see in the second part of chapter 3) since to be human is to be united to God in Christ, and Christ has defeated and conquered sin on the cross. Thus, for Barth, sin can no longer be a reality that can alter and/or affect the 'being' of humanity so not to answer to God's call or to remain in a state of ungodliness is for Barth "an ontological impossibility."[68]

Having said that, it does not mean that Barth ignores sin or thinks of it as unreal or illusory but, rather, he sees sin as a "contradiction of the very constitution of human being."[69] For a human being to live a life of sin and not to obey the call and command of God is more than simply to disobey God. To be called by God is to be summoned by God, and this address of God to a person means it is directed to a being called into communion and fellowship with God who upholds humanity's being, and therefore it is a being called into being itself.[70] Hence, a life of sin is counter to a person's being and thus is a negation of the entire purpose of one's existence. And even

66. See *CD* IV/1, 48f.
67. See *CD* III/3, 311.
68. *CD*, III/2, 146.
69. Webster, *Barth*, 102.
70. For Barth the word "real" must be equated to the word "summoned" (*CD* III/2, 150). Thus the question of humanity's condition before they receive the call of God is intensely problematic, since even to ask such a question appears to Barth to deny the divine act of *creatio ex nihilo*.

The Covenant, Humanity, and das Nichtige 111

though a life of sin happens, it does so not as an ultimate or final fact, but rather as penultimate, as something that is not fully 'real' yet. The ultimate and final *Yes* of God spoken over Christ is the last and final word, that which brings everything ultimately into fulfilment. (We will come back to this notion of penultimacy and ultimacy at the beginning of chapter 5.)

But how do we make sense of the incarnation as the fulfilment of the covenant between God and humanity and the cross where the human being, Jesus of Nazareth, is condemned, rejected and abandoned? In §42 Barth argues that "God the Creator did not say No, nor Yes and No, but Yes to what he had created."[71] Yet how does this relate to Barth's doctrine of election where he clearly argues in a dialectical way when explaining the election and reprobation of Christ? Surely the human Jesus, who lived in Nazareth and who died on the cross on Golgotha, is also God's creation. Is there also a *No* spoken in the covenant? And if so, what does this reprobation in the covenant look like? This question will be fully addressed in the next part of this chapter. For now, we will try to give a provisional answer.

For Barth, the event of salvation occurred in Jesus Christ on the cross by virtue of his true humanity and true deity, as the Mediator of the covenant. Hunsinger writes:

> In his true humanity Jesus Christ was at once the embodiment of grace and the victim of human enmity toward grace. He embodied grace as the true human covenant partner which God had always intended and sought, but which human beings in their sin had failed miserably to become. In his role as the true covenant partner, Jesus Christ took the place of humankind before God in a positive sense, enacting obedience and service to God on humankind's behalf. Yet in the course of fulfilling this role, Jesus Christ was at the same time rejected and slain, becoming the victim of humankind's enmity toward the very grace which he embodied. In his true deity, furthermore, Jesus Christ made himself to be the embodiment of the very sin by which he was victimized, and of God's righteous enmity toward sin. Although sinless in himself, he bore the consequences of sin in humankind's place and on its behalf. By his suffering and death he thereby also took humankind's place before God in a negative sense, assuming to himself the accusation, judgment, and punishment that were rightfully humankind's.[72]

---

71. *CD* III/1, 330.
72. Hunsinger, *How To Read Karl Barth*, 116.

As has already been stated, one of the pivotal matters is how sin is dealt with in the atonement. If Jesus bore the sins of all of humanity *to* the cross and was furthermore substitutionally punished for them *on* the cross—his death being a judgment of sin inflicted upon Jesus by God's wrath—then the consequence of this sin bearing and the pouring out of the judgment of wrath over him results in the separation of God and Jesus, of Father and Son, made manifest by Jesus' cry of dereliction and abandonment. However, the implications of this position are that, if Jesus is the bearer of sin and punishment, then not only is there a separation between the Father and the Son, but the covenant between God and humanity (planned before the foundation of the world) would also be broken, even if this were just for three days. Would this make Jesus a covenant-breaker? And if so, how are we to make sense of this abandonment in Trinitarian terms? If Jesus takes the sins of all of humanity upon himself, becoming "the one great sinner" (Luther),[73] it would raise questions not only about sin removal and its condemnation but also about the firmness and consistency of the covenant between God and humanity established in Jesus Christ. We will revisit the topic of sin in our last section of this chapter (3. *Das Nichtige*). However, before we do so, we will first discuss Barth's theological anthropology.

2. Humanity

Barth's consideration of the covenant led him to ask questions about a sound understanding of humanity's existence in relation to God. Barth sets the scene in §43, *Man as a Problem of Dogmatics*, and begins expounding his doctrine of 'The Creature' with the following christological premise: "As the man Jesus is Himself the revealing Word of God, He is the source of our knowledge of the nature of man as created by God."[74] He sums up his christological anthropology as "expound[ing] the knowledge of man which is made possible by the fact that man stands in the light of the Word of God. The Word of God is thus its foundation."[75] The doctrine of human beings has its reality in Jesus Christ, who destines and establishes humanity for fellowship with God, as covenant partner.[76]

---

73. *CD* IV/1, 239.
74. *CD* III/2, 1.
75. *CD* III/2, 20.
76. For more on the theme of 'God's partner' see von Balthasar, *The Theology of Karl Barth*, 125–36.

2.1. Humanity as Covenant Partner

For Barth, the key to understanding humanity as a covenant partner is not to look at humanity itself, as an objective anthropology.[77] Instead he challenges modern theology by stating that it is only through Jesus Christ, the Word made flesh, that we can understand humanity. "He [Jesus] is the source of our knowledge of the nature of man created by God,"[78] because it is only he alone who is "primarily and properly man,"[79] and who "reveals and explains human nature with all its possibilities."[80] For Barth, the *Yes* spoken to humanity in the self-revelation of God in Jesus Christ is the only foundation for a true anthropology and the basis for humanity's existence before and in fellowship with God as a covenant partner.

Human beings are created for the purpose of being drawn into a relationship with the transcendent God in heaven. In *Dogmatics in Outline* this becomes very apparent: "Heaven is the creation inconceivable to man, earth the creation conceivable to him. He himself is the creature on the boundary between heaven and earth."[81] Human beings are dynamic in their existence as creatures living on earth, yet bound for heaven. The temptation in theology to make a choice between two mutually exclusive alternatives—either to concentrate on earth and thus neglect heaven, or *vice versa*—is countered by Barth with his doctrine of Jesus Christ. Barth sees Jesus as the human made in the image of God who (and thus in whom also humanity) "inhabits the boundary between heaven and earth."[82] Mangina points out that Barth's view of what it means to be a human being is an 'eccentric' understanding. He explains that "ek-centric literally means being off-centre, having one's centre located outside a given boundary. Barth thinks about human identity in ek-centric terms, referring it to the particular life of the man Jesus."[83]

The only proper response to an understanding of God's free grace in the *Yes* spoken towards humanity and the realization of what God has done through Christ is gratitude, since "gratitude is the precise creaturely counterpart to the grace of God."[84] Moreover, this attitude of gratitude

---

77. See Krötke, "The Humanity of the Human Person in Karl Barth's Anthropology," 163–66.
78. *CD* III/2, 41.
79. *CD* III/2, 43.
80. *CD* III/2, 59.
81. Barth, *Dogmatics in Outline*, 59.
82. Mangina, *Theologian of Christian Witness*, 97.
83. Ibid., 95.
84. *CD* III/2, 166.

and thanksgiving encapsulates for Barth the right existence as a covenant partner before God, the true essence of what it means to be truly human, to be a 'real man' (see §44), since "to be human is to act out of gratitude for grace."[85]

2.2. Jesus' Covenantal Humanity as 'Real Man'

We have seen that creation and the creature have to be understood and interpreted through the lens of the covenant.[86] This is the same with Barth's ontology of the person in his *"theologische Anthropologie."*[87] Barth differentiates between 'man as such' or *'in abstracto'* as the 'man of sin' on one side, and the 'real man' who stands in covenant relationship with God on the other side.[88] According to Barth's anthropology the threat of nothingness is only an *irrealis* for the 'real man,' since it is the 'man *in abstracto*' who is threatened and not the 'real man' who is in covenant relationship with God.[89] Here we need to understand Barth's anthropology and his logic behind the Christ-Adam antithesis.[90] In the light of Jesus Christ, sin is an "ontological impossibility" which means that "our being does not include but excludes sin."[91] For Barth, though sin and nothingness are an "ontological impossibility"[92] for the 'real man,' for the 'man *in abstracto*'—here Barth finishes this thought logically—the fall and sin are an "ontological necessity."[93] Barth draws a sharp dialectical antithesis and we need to bear this in mind when we come to his doctrine of sin and nothingness.

The key sentence of Barth's anthropology is: "The ontological determination of humanity is grounded in the fact that one man among all others is the man Jesus."[94] Here we see that Barth's anthropology rests on the basis

---

85. Webster, *Barth*, 95.

86. See Härle, *Sein und Gnade*, 99.

87. See *KD* III/2, 20ff.

88. For an excellent treatment of 'Der wirkliche Mensch' see Härle, *Sein und Gnade*, 99–130. See also Mikkelsen, *Reconciled Humanity*, 121–24 and Neder, *Participation in Christ*, 31.

89. See Krötke, "The Humanity of the Human Person in Karl Barth's Anthropology," 159–63.

90. *CD* III/2, 46 and *CD* IV/1, 509–13.

91. *CD* III/2, 136.

92. *CD* III/2, 146.

93. *CD* III/2, 146.

94. *CD* III/2, 132.

of Christology and soteriology.[95] Thus "Christian anthropology will make constant reference to Jesus as 'true man,' in whom human existence has been faithfully actualized once and for all."[96] Barth does not say that only Jesus is the 'real man' but he does say that Jesus is first and foremost the 'real man,' excluding any possibility of deriving a concept of what it means to be human detached from Jesus. Barth frequently uses the formula of the New Testament 'in him' to highlight the inclusiveness of Jesus' humanity.[97] He defines 'in him' as "like Him, to be His brothers, to have a share in that in which He is quite unlike us, in His fellowship with God, in God's pleasure in Him, but also in His obedience to God, in His movement towards Him."[98]

However, what does Barth mean by to 'have a share' [*Anteil haben*]? We get the answer by reconsidering God's election and incarnation.[99] In the doctrine of election we have already spoken about God's free choice to be the *Deus pro nobis* which we saw was the basis and source from which humanity derived its nature—to be elect means to be human. The covenant is the historical outworking of this choice, fulfilled in the incarnation of the *Logos*, God's *Yes* spoken to all of humanity, and further affirmed and worked out through the atoning sacrifice of the cross. Therefore the foundation of Barth's christological anthropology is to comprehend the far-reaching significance of the incarnation: the fact that the Word became flesh has all-encompassing consequences for all of humanity, irrespective of whether one is aware of it or not. In the incarnation of the *Logos* the covenant of God and man was established in the person of Jesus of Nazareth. Barth's understanding of the incarnation of the *Logos* becomes paramount for his existential picture of human beings with a transcendent nature who are "self-transcending" subjects.[100] As we saw in our section on the covenant, God has united himself with human nature in Jesus Christ and in this way God's decision [*Bestimmung*] over every person is made. Therefore Barth can say: "To be a man is to be with Jesus [. . .] to be with the One who is true and primary elect of God."[101] Thus, any understanding of what it means to be human is grounded in Jesus Christ.[102] This, for Barth, alters the entire

---

95. See Härle, *Sein und Gnade*, 100.
96. Mangina, *Theologian of Christian Witness*, 95.
97. See Härle, *Sein und Gnade*, 101.
98. *CD* IV/2, 270.
99. See Härle, *Sein und Gnade*, 102.
100. Mangina, *Theologian of Christian Witness*, 97.
101. *CD* III/2, 145.
102. See Härle, *Sein und Gnade*, 101.

human reality and makes every person a "fellow-man of Jesus."[103] Thus, in Barth's view what makes us 'human' is nothing intrinsic to ourselves but our relationship with God as a covenant partner. For Barth to say 'covenant' or 'grace' is equivalent to saying Jesus Christ, because Barth always has the person of Jesus of Nazareth in mind who is God's grace for humanity, the image of God, that which makes humanity truly human. Furthermore, Barth does not speak about the individual when he talks about anthropology, but the collective. He states that because Jesus Christ has assumed human nature "a decision has been made concerning the being and nature of every man" and "every man in his place or time is changed."[104]

Barth's doctrine of humanity, which can only be conceived of in relational terms,[105] starts from the concrete particular person Jesus and then moves to universal humanity. Barth sees Gen 1:26—human beings created in the image of God—in the context of his theological anthropology and explains the *imago Dei* christologically with the help of Col 1:15: "He [Jesus] is the image of the invisible God, the firstborn over all creation."[106] The man Jesus of Nazareth is the image of God, and in this man all of humanity's destiny, in fact all of creation, is fulfilled. Barth does not see the *imago* as some sort of attribute or something intrinsic to a human being, something a person can possess, but sees the *imago* relationally, as the relationship a person has to the 'true man' Jesus Christ. Barth is making the relational assertion that because Christ is our brother, neighbor, and counterpart, we are constituted human 'beings.'[107] For him to speak ontologically and noetically about human beings is based on the fact that "man is with God because he is with Jesus."[108] Barth's argument continues by saying that "to be man is to be with God. What a man is in the Counterpart is obviously the basic and comprehensive determination of his true being. Whatever else he is, he is on the basis of the fact that he is with Jesus and therefore with God."[109] Here we encounter Barth's twin concepts of 'being with Jesus' and thus 'being with

---

103. *CD* III/2, 134.

104. *CD* III/2, 133.

105. On *Mitmenschlichkeit* ('co-humanity'—Barth's understanding of humanity is that it has a fundamentally relational character) see §44 'Man as the Creature of God' which explores humanity in the light of Jesus as a creature made for fellowship with God, as 'man for God' as well as §45 'Man in His Determination as the Covenant Partner of God' which highlights the aspect of human existence as "man for others."

106. On the human as the image of God see Krötke, "The Humanity of the Human Person in Karl Barth's Anthropology," 166–69.

107. See *CD* III/2, 134.

108. *CD* III/2, 136.

109. *CD* III/2, 135.

God.' He sums up the concept of being with the statement that a person is a "being which derives from God."[110] The derivation from God means that human beings are both *from* God as well as *with* God, on one hand totally distinct from God yet on the other hand "absolutely grounded" in God.[111]

However, Barth insists that humanity's being is different from that of God and emphasises that even though God took on flesh, God still remains sovereign, even in Jesus Christ. Through the covenant of God and man in the God-man Jesus Christ, who is fully God and fully man, in tune with Chalcedonian orthodoxy,[112] man is a free, autonomous and separate partner of God, qualities which again are derived from God's free grace. To understand that God and humanity are "neither identical nor absolutely unrelated" is to understand a key concept in Barth's anthropology, namely that God and humanity are two "realities which exist in an ordered relation of giver and recipient of life and grace."[113] God confronts humanity in the person Jesus—"God *comes* to man"[114]—and this constitutes a genuine union of being with God. In this union or covenant it is the 'being' of humanity "which is acted upon in this action of God."[115] In a nutshell—for Barth, humanity exists and has her being because she is "with Jesus and therefore with God."[116] This is the essence of human existence before God, because humanity exists through Christ or, to use Barth's terminology, 'derives' from the divine *Logos*.

2.3. *The Summoning of Humanity*

We saw that this relational concept of God and humanity, and man and fellow man, has been actualized in Christ in the incarnation where God bound himself to the Jew Jesus of Nazareth and through him to all humankind.[117]

---

110. *CD* III/2, 140.

111. See *CD* III/2, 140.

112. See Hunsinger, *How To Read Karl Barth*, 185–88. See also Mikkelsen, *Reconciled Humanity*, 145–64.

113. Webster, *Barth*, 101.

114. *CD* III/2, 141.

115. *CD* III/2, 141.

116. *CD* III/2, 135.

117. Barth makes use of the patristic doctrine of anhypostatic and enhypostatic union: "*anhypostasis* refers to the fact that the humanity of Jesus had no independent reality of its own apart from the incarnation of the Son, while *enhypostasis* refers to the fact that the humanity of Jesus did have real personal being *in* the person of the Son as a result of the incarnation," Torrance, *Atonement*, 452.

This demonstrates that the being of humanity is different from the being of the human Jesus.[118] Whereas Jesus is in direct contact with God, the rest of humanity has a mediated and indirect contact with God. In view of this, Barth develops two related primary statements: "the being of man as a being with Jesus rests upon the election of God; and that it consists in the hearing of the Word of God."[119] With regard to election, we have already seen that Barth sees humanity as destined ontologically in Jesus Christ to participate in the victory of Christ over nothingness. With regard to hearing the Word of God, Barth says that "man is the creaturely being which is addressed, called and summoned by God."[120] A person "is summoned by the Word of God. [. . .] Summoned because chosen—here we have a first definition of real man. When the reality of human nature is in question, the word 'real' is simply equivalent to 'summoned.'"[121] Barth makes a pre-emptive strike and says that questions like 'Who is summoned?' and 'What was the person before she was summoned?' have to be dropped immediately, because

> what precedes human being as a being summoned by the Word of God is simply God and His Word; God in the existence of the man Jesus. On the level of our own being, of human being as such and in general, if we see and understand it in terms of summons we are on an extreme edge beyond which we cannot look, at a beginning which on the creaturely level has no basis other than the sure basis which the Creator has ordained in the existence of that one man.[122]

He goes on to say that the question of "anything preceding our being apart from the divine summons can arise only if we try to explain ourselves by ourselves instead of by our concrete confrontation with God."[123] For Barth, to be summoned means "to have heard, to have been awakened, to have to arouse oneself, to be claimed."[124] This is what it means, according to Barth, to be human in its entirety. When one asks 'Who am I really?' the only answer that can be made in the light of God and his Word is that "I am

---

118. See Härle, *Sein und Gnade*, 105.
119. *CD* III/2, 142.
120. *CD* III/2, 149. See Neder, *Participation in Christ*, 31f.
121. *CD* III/2, 150.
122. *CD* III/2, 151.
123. *CD* III/2, 151.
124. *CD* III/2, 150.

The Covenant, Humanity, and das Nichtige 119

summoned by this Word, and to that extent I am in this Word."[125] Thus, for Barth "men are those who are summoned by this Word."[126]

It is important to remember that Barth is writing dogmatics for the *Church*.[127] He writes from a Church perspective for believers. He sees the *CD* as instructions and theological reflections about Scripture that can be used by the preacher. The preacher's sermon is not (always) concerned with the mechanics of a person's coming to faith or whether this is even possible; preaching is concerned with the Word of God summoning, calling and awakening to faith. Furthermore, we need to remember that Barth addresses the Church, the *ek*-klesia, those who have already been *called out* by the Word. So when Barth talks about humanity or a human being, this is from the perspective of the 'real man' Jesus Christ. Therefore Barth refuses to consider the 'ifs,' 'whats' and 'hows' of abstract human existence outside of God, but instead focuses on the concrete basis and reality for humanity, Jesus Christ, the one in whom humanity has her existence. For Barth,

> the fundamental mistake in all erroneous thinking of man about himself is that he tries to equate himself with God and therefore to proceed on the assumption that he can regard himself as the presupposition of his own being. [. . .] Thus it is only in a denial of man corresponding to the denial of God that we can appeal beyond this summons to another being, asking concerning the man who is not yet summoned.[128]

As we have shown, to be called by God is to be summoned by God, and for Barth, God's address to a person means calling them into communion and fellowship; Barth sees it as a process that involves humanity being called into being itself.[129] However, for Barth, to answer the grace of God in his call necessarily initiates two human responses, that of gratitude or thanksgiving as well as that of responsibility. Barth writes that "thanksgiving for the grace of God, this is the act in which he accepts the validity of the act which not he but God has wrought. [. . .] It calls for gratitude."[130]

Therefore, had he been presented with it, Barth would probably have simply ignored the accusation made by Brunner that we highlighted in

125. *CD* III/2, 150.
126. *CD* III/2, 150.
127. See Buckley, "Christian Community, Baptism, and Lord's Supper," 195.
128. *CD* III/2, 151.
129. See also Chapter 5, section 3.3. and 3.4., in which Jesus' call to fellowship— 'Follow Me'—is further expounded in relation to the work of the Spirit and humanity's being.
130. *CD* III/2, 168.

chapter 1, where he charged Barth with 'objectivism,' arguing that Barth breaks the relationship between the objective Word of God and the subjective element of faith.[131] To say that Barth is not interested in these matters would be to miss the point; Barth simply does not speculate about these sorts of questions and instead grounds his theology in the concrete reality of Jesus Christ as revealed in Scripture.

2.4. Humanity as Soul and Body

For Barth, the humanity of Jesus, his existence [*Daseins*] and nature [*Soseins*], consists of both 'soul' [ψυχή] and 'body' [σῶμά] in unity.[132] He says that this unity of soul and body is the simplest description of the being of humankind.[133] Furthermore, for Barth man *is* or *exists* [*ist*] because he has '*Geist*.' This is Barth's shortest formula representing his theological anthropology. Of course, the fact that man has '*Geist*' does not mean that he is God, though God is the Creator of man[134] and man cannot exist without God. This means that man's being is "grounded, constituted and maintained by God as the soul and his body."[135] Humanity is "ontically and therefore noetically dependent on the fact that she is not without God"[136] and this means that "man without God is not; he has neither being [*Wesen*] nor existence [*Existenz*]."[137] Barth sees Jesus' humanity as the paradigm for what it means to be human as it is here that "we find our bearings and our instruction" for a "theological doctrine of man's nature."[138] To be human always means "being with God and therefore being with fellow-men":[139] and thus the human Jesus, as encountered in the New Testament as the 'true man' who is born, lives, suffers, dies and is resurrected, is a man in this union of these two parts, the "one whole man, embodied soul [*leibhafte Seele*] and besouled

---

131. See Brunner, *The Christian Doctrine of God*, 349f. See also Kreck's discussion on 'Erwählung und Glaube,' in Kreck, *Grundentscheidungen in Karl Barths Dogmatik*, 263–83.

132. For a thorough treatment of *CD* III/2 on the human person as the soul of the body, see also Cortez, *Embodied Souls, Ensouled Bodies*. See also Krötke, "The Humanity of the Human Person in Karl Barth's Anthropology," 169–71.

133. See *CD* III/2, 325.

134. See *CD* III/2, 344.

135. *CD* III/2, 344.

136. *CD* III/2, 345.

137. *CD* III/2, 345.

138. *CD* III/2, 327.

139. *CD* III/2, 325.

body [*beseelter Leib*]."[140] Barth emphasizes that this does not change in his death or resurrection but even though there is a 'transformation' happening it is not an "alteration, division or least of all subtraction" of the unity of soul and body.[141] In the death and resurrection of Jesus, he maintains that "[t]he body does not remain behind, nor does the soul depart. As the same whole man, soul and body. He rises as He died, and sits at the right hand of God, and will come again."[142] Therefore we need to safeguard this "oneness and wholeness" when we consider the human nature of Jesus in his work on the cross because "the interconnexion of the soul and body and Word and act of Jesus is not a chaos but a cosmos, a formed and ordered totality."[143]

Barth goes on to say that "*Der Mensch ist, indem er Geist hat.*"[144] Thus we see that the '*Geist*' is always something that humanity encounters, something that comes towards her and can only be received. It is a person existing as a soul of her body that has '*Geist.*' To be more precise a person exists "*indem der Geist ihn hat.*"[145] Through this expression Barth again highlights that humanity has her existence through her being grounded in God; she is God's possession and without God she would cease to exist. This we also see reflected in the concept of *Existenzstellvertretung* where humanity is also grounded in Jesus' death and given a new existence in him.

Again, humanity cannot simply be called '*Geist*' as it was in the school of Hegel. Although she achieves existence through it, it is always characterized by the soul and body. But Barth does affirm that humanity is '*Geist*' insofar as she is soul and body in virtue of the '*Geist*',[146] making her a "spiritual soul" [*geistige Seele*] and also a "spiritual body" [*geistiger Leib*].[147] One might argue that *geisthaftige Seele* [spiritually enclosed soul] and *geisthaftiger Leib* [spiritually enclosed body] would harmonize better with Barth's terminology of the 'embodied soul' and 'ensouled body.' The German verb *haften* expresses the clinginess and encompassing power of the '*Geist*' which, for Barth is *immortal* and does not belong to the creaturely realm, in contrast to the human soul and body.[148]

---

140. *CD* III/2, 327.
141. *CD* III/2, 327.
142. *CD* III/2, 327.
143. *CD* III/2, 331f.
144. *KD* III/2, 425.
145. *KD* III/2, 426.
146. See *CD* III/2, 354.
147. *CD* III/2, 354.
148. See *CD* III/2, 355.

We conclude by saying that '*Geist*' is the *conditio sine qua non* of being, the principle of renewal without which the person cannot live. The Spirit is the "transcendental determination"[149] of, and has the "preserving role in human ontology."[150] Only with the Spirit is a person alive and "becomes and is soul [. . . and] becomes and is physical body."[151] Without the Spirit, there would be no soul and no body.[152]

Therefore even without explicitly stating it, Barth does not have a concept of an immortal soul.[153] He states that only the '*Geist*' is *unsterblich* and says that both soul and body without the Spirit would be dead. However, he indicates the mortality of the soul when he writes in §47 *Man in His Time* that "humanity is temporality"[154]—to be human means to be temporal. Thus this temporality and mortality "belongs to human nature, and is determined and ordered by God's good creation and to that extent right and good, that man's being in time should be finite and man himself mortal."[155] Furthermore, temporality necessarily indicates finitude, and "finitude means mortality [. . . and] mortality means subjection to death, and death means the radical negation of life and therefore of human existence."[156] Thus we see that Barth "strongly opposes any move to understand some portion of the human person to be inherently immortal."[157] Krötke emphasizes that death for Barth should not be seen as the result of original sin. Humanity's

---

149. *CD* III/2, 348.

150. Cortez, "Body, Soul, and (Holy) Spirit," 337.

151. *CD* III/2, 359.

152. See also chapter 5 section 2.2 (a) and (b), where this particular notion of the Spirit is confirmed in the discussion of Spirit as 'Creator and Sustainer' and as 'Reconciler and Redeemer.'

153. Barth says that "even Mt. 10:28 does not say that the soul cannot be killed, but only that no man can kill it, while God has the power to cause both soul and body to pass away and be destroyed in the nether world. Hence we do not have here a doctrine of the immortality of the soul," in *CD* III/2, 379. He denies the immortality of the soul and with it any Greek tendencies of dualism between body and soul, and states that "[w]e necessarily contradict the abstractly dualistic conception which so far we have summarily called Greek, but which unfortunately must also be described as the traditional Christian view. According to this view, soul and body are indeed connected, even essentially and necessarily united, but only as two 'parts' of human nature. Of these, each is to be understood as a special substance, self-contained and qualitatively different in relation to the other. The soul is spiritual, non-spatial, indissoluble, and immortal; the body material, spatial, dissoluble and mortal," in *CD* III/2, 380.

154. *CD* III/2, 522.

155. *CD* III/2, 632.

156. *CD* III/2, 625.

157. Cortez, "Body, Soul, and (Holy) Spirit," 344.

finitude and limited time show that humanity is mortal and should not be understood "to be an evil or negative fate which the Creator imposed upon us as a result of our sin."[158] In fact, finitude is part of being a creature and therefore for Barth "eternal life did not mean the negation of the mortality of the human, but rather the redemption of his this-sided, finite and mortal being by the eternal and gracious God."[159]

Barth's view appears to be in line with what is called the doctrine of the 'conditional immortality' of the soul.[160] It is not only the body, but also the soul that is conditioned by the life-giving Spirit in order to have life and thus only in relation to the Spirit is a person given immortality. The Pastoral Epistles talk about God's immortality—the New Testament says that Christians are partakers in the imperishable and the immortal, by being in relationship with God. The Church Fathers saw the atonement in terms of regaining or rather gaining immortality, which is nothing other than eternal fellowship with God. The Eucharist was seen as 'the medicine of immortality' (Ignatius of Antioch) and as 'spiritual food and drink and eternal life' (Didache) giving the body incorruptibility and 'the hope of Resurrection' (Irenaeus). From this angle the doctrine of the atonement becomes less about the removal of sin, instead centering itself upon covenantal fellowship with the triune God.

3. *Das Nichtige*

In our section on the covenant we already heard about God's *Yes* and God's *No*. We have seen that this dialectical structure is what permeates all of the *CD* and, as Ford has argued, is Barth's "one dominant approach" and basic structure to theology.[161] In §50 Barth discusses 'God and Nothingness' and shows how God in Christ has reconciled the "inner antithesis in His own person."[162] The term '*Nichtiges*' does not belong to the terminology

---

158. Krötke, "The Humanity of the Human Person in Karl Barth's Anthropology," 171.

159. Ibid., 172.

160. For an overview on conditional immortality, see Wenham, "The Case for Conditional Immortality," 161–91.

161. Ford, "Barth's Interpretation of the Bible," 56.

162. *CD* III/3, 296. Since God has reconciled this inner antithesis, for Barth the creature is no longer in danger of nothingness as she partakes in the divine antithesis. However, to question this antithesis and highlight the notion of the antithesis in Jesus Christ, and to point out the problems in Barth's thought is the undertaking of this book. Our contention is that the dialectic in Barth's theology that was apparent from the beginning was confirmed and deepened in 1936 when Barth tackled the doctrine

that ecclesiastical tradition has used to describe the concept of standing in opposition to God, as depicted in Scripture,[163] but is Barth's own coinage.[164] From the beginning, Barth rules out the absurdity of calling God the 'author of sins.' According to Barth's own definition, *'das Nichtige'* is

> the 'reality' on whose account (i.e., against which) God Himself willed to become a creature in the creaturely world, yielding and subjecting Himself to it in Jesus Christ in order to overcome it. Nothingness is thus the 'reality' which opposes and resists God, which is itself subjected to and overcome by His opposition and resistance, and which in this twofold determination as the reality that negates and is negated by Him, is totally distinct from Him.[165]

3.1. Knowledge of das Nichtige

For Barth all theological knowledge is christological knowledge. Thus we have to ask whether it is possible to deduce nothingness from our knowledge in Jesus Christ. Barth affirms this and says that though humanity can see the "deficiency" [*Mangelhaftigkeit*] of her own existence (which is not true sin),[166] real knowledge of sin and nothingness can only be known through Jesus Christ, the objective "ground of knowledge"[167] [*Erkenntnisgrund*].[168] It is only in Jesus Christ, who has defeated and conquered nothingness on the cross, that we can truly know *das Nichtige*. Thus, for Barth, the real knowledge of 'nothingness' as the alien factor [*Fremdkörper*],[169] one that is not just simply misunderstood with the negative side of creation, comes through the

---

of election. Here he brought this dialectic into the *CD* to explain the two sides of predestination, election and reprobation, which are brought into a synthesis in Jesus Christ.

163. See Krötke, *Sünde und Nichtiges bei Karl Barth*, 23.

164. See *CD* IV/3, 177f.

165. *CD* III/3, 305.

166. *CD* III/3, 306.

167. *CD* III/3, 306–313 passim.

168. Barth writes: "Yet it is only in Jesus Christ and not in an abstract divine law, however founded and formulated, that we have a revelation of real sin, of its nature as real enmity against the grace of God, and of man's refusal of the gratitude natural to him," *CD* III/3, 309.

169. The English translation 'alien factor' for the German '*Fremdkörper*' does not capture the relation to sin as '*das Nichtige*' as that which God does not will and yet exists. A better English translation than 'alien factor' would be 'foreign body.'

The Covenant, Humanity, and das Nichtige

revelation of the mighty act of salvation achieved in Jesus Christ. Nothingness is neither God nor creature, yet "nothingness is not nothing."[170] God takes it seriously and acts upon it in Jesus Christ. Creature and nothingness do not stand in a dialectical relationship that can be brought into a synthesis but stand in a diastatical antithesis.[171] Barth explains that it is the "antithesis which is only comprehensible in correlation with creation not as an equilibrating but an absolute and uncompromising No."[172] This *No* is first and foremost in opposition to God himself, and thus also to his work of creation. He says that nothingness is the

> negative which is more than the mere complement of an antithetical positive, the left which is not counterpoised by any right, the antithesis which is not merely within creation and therefore

---

170. *CD* III/3, 349. In his work *On Nature* Parmenides highlights the revelatory character of his ontology in poetic form. Parmenides outlines his ontology and describes it as 'truth' [*aliteia*] coming directly from the mouth of the Goddess Dike. The underlying basis of Parmenides' logical insight that that which *is* cannot simultaneously also *not be*. And because 'becoming' and 'passing away' presuppose non-being, the terms 'becoming' and 'passing away' are excluded from the concept of being. Parmenides writes: οὐδέ ποτ' ἦν οὐδ' ἔσται, (now it is, all at once, a continuous one.) For Parmenides there are only two ways to talk about being, ἡ μὲν ὅπως ἔστιν τε καὶ ὡς οὐκ ἔστι μὴ εἶναι, (The first, namely, that *It is*, and that it is impossible for anything not to be, [not possible not to be]) and ἡ δ' ὡς οὐκ ἔστιν τε καὶ ὡς χρεών ἐστι μὴ εἶναι, (The other, namely, that *It is not*, and that something must needs not be, [it is necessary not to be]). What Parmenides is interested in is the question of 'truth.' He highlights two kinds of negation and differentiates them linguistically: the *ouk on* and *me on*. Whereas the *ouk on* can be seen as a simply negation, like the *nihil*, as something that does not exist in a specific context, the *me on* stands for the impossible, for the non-being *per se*—that which threatens all order. Thus the *me on* is characterized by Parmenides not simply as something that is not but also as something that should not be. The *me on* is the embodiment of that which is not supposed to be, that which should-not-be, which stands in opposition to the *on*, being, in its perfection and timelessness, and threatens it. Just as for Barth, for whom nothingness has no being in itself, so too for Parmenides the 'non-being [*me on*] is not [*ouk estin*].' However, Barth further explains that 'nothingness is not nothing' and here follows the parmenidian basic statement of being, which expresses that the *me on* is not simply nothing (which is the *ouk on*) but that it is that which should-not-be, the impossible, or in Barth's term, the 'impossible possibility.' Though I am not arguing that Barth uses Parmenides as the basis for his doctrine of nothingness, we cannot deny the proximity in their basic ontological arguments. It might be argued that a reading of Barth's doctrine of nothingness through the lens of Parmenides ontology sheds new light on Barth's own thought and helps to de-code Barth's understanding of nothingness as the 'impossible possibility.'

171. See Härle, *Sein und Gnade*, 246f.

172. *CD* III/3, 302.

dialectical but which is primarily and supremely to God Himself and therefore to the totality of the created world.[173]

Yet God has mastered this negative antithesis in Jesus Christ, which is the "negative content and significance of His saving decree [*Heilsratschlusses*],"[174] the negative side where a *No* is spoken in election. He does this by giving his only Son, becoming a creature and "taking on Himself the sin, guilt and misery of the creature [. . . ;] in the person of the man Jesus He becomes the bearer [*Träger*] of the creature's guilt and shame, and [. . .] what befalls this man God pronounces His No to the bitter end."[175] He is the one who has fought and conquered 'nothingness' on the cross and he is the one who exposed and destroyed it. "Because Jesus is Victor, nothingness is routed and extirpated."[176] This rejected and abandoned nothingness is the chaos we read about in the creation story of Gen 1. From the beginning, God as Creator has negated nothingness before he even speaks his first creative Word.[177] However, he does so not *without* the creature by his side, without allowing the creature to have a share [*Anteil*] in the fight against *das Nichtige*. It takes place in Jesus Christ, a creature, though "only in the strength of the work of the Creator."[178] However, this makes the creature not simply a spectator but a "co-belligerent"[179] [*Mitstreiter*] in the struggle against nothingness: "It is that which in this One who was both very God and very man has been absolutely set behind, not only by God, but in unity with Him by man and therefore the creature."[180]

Barth explains that the only valid examination of nothingness must start from a look backwards, only from the other side of the cross, from the resurrection side where the Christian gets a glimpse of what Christ has achieved on the cross, as a "retrospect [*Rückblick*] of the fact that it has already been judged, refuted and done away by the mercy of God revealed and active in Jesus Christ";[181] as well as a look forwards, "in prospect"

---

173. *CD*, III/3, 302.
174. *CD* III/3, 302.
175. *CD* III/3, 362.
176. *CD* III/3, 363.
177. See *CD* III/3, 352.
178. *CD* III/3, 355.
179. *CD* III/3, 355.
180. *CD* III/3, 363.
181. *CD* III/3, 366.

The Covenant, Humanity, and das Nichtige 127

[*Ausblick*]¹⁸² to Christ's coming in glory.¹⁸³ Thus, the last word about nothingness must always be the first word—*Jesus is Victor* and "nothingness has no perpetuity."¹⁸⁴ On the cross it is revealed that nothingness is really past and finally overcome. Thus for Barth *das Nichtige* is

> the past, the ancient menace, danger and destruction, the ancient non-being which obscured and defaced the divine creation of God but which is consigned to the past in Jesus Christ, in whose death it has received its deserts, being destroyed with this consummation of the positive will of God which is as such the end of His non-willing.¹⁸⁵

Barth warns fervently that one must avoid a twofold problem—not to stray on one side or the other, either to argue that therefore nothingness derives from God's good will and work, or to say that it only derives from the actions of the creature under God's lordship and his passive permission and observation.¹⁸⁶ Barth goes on to say that one might go astray on yet another path, forgetting that nothingness has already been judged in Jesus Christ (and can therefore no longer kill and destroy) and giving the power of sin more attention than the Easter joy. This would lead either to a pessimism and overestimation of its power or an optimism in humanity's power and underestimation of her in relation to it. Barth's answer is that the required confidence [*Zuversicht*] and humility [*Demut*] come from a sober recognition that all theological thought and utterance is *theologia viatorum* and thus 'broken' [*gebrochen*] and 'piece-work' [*Stückwerk*]. The reason for this is evident and obvious since the "existence, presence and operation of nothingness [. . .] are also objectively the break in the relationship between Creator and creature."¹⁸⁷ All theology wears the mark of this 'break' [*Bruch*], which runs counter to the nature of God's intention for his creature. The story of this break is the object of theological thought, and theology is the record [*Bericht*] of this 'story' [*Geschichte*], its aim being to report [*erzählen*] God's story of liberation.¹⁸⁸

---

182. *CD* III/3, 366.

183. Barth writes: "Indeed, we may say that if nothingness is not viewed in retrospect of God's finished act of conquest and destruction, it is not seen at all. It is confounded with the negative side of God's creation, and viewed only in its negative and not in its privative character," *CD* III/3, 366.

184. *CD* III/3, 364.

185. *CD* III/3, 363.

186. See *CD* III/3, 292.

187. *CD* III/3, 294.

188. See *CD* III/3, 295. I use 'story' rather than 'history' since the context shows

3.2. *The Origin of* das Nichtige *and its relation to God*

Barth sees nothingness not as a serious counterpart [*Widerpart*] of God but rather as a "fleeting shadow"[189] which both "arises and is at once dispelled by His wrath."[190] However, this raises a question about the "*unde malum*,"[191] the origin of nothingness. For Barth, though nothingness exists, it has no independent ground of existence. It is that which God "does not and cannot will," and because of this, still lives on and is potent; it is in pure negative relation to God and has the "essence only of non-essence."[192] Furthermore, Barth also denies that nothingness is derived solely from human activity and this eventually leaves us to derive the existence of nothingness from God. However, can this—which God did and does not want—have its origin in God? Barth denies this and says that we stray "if we argue that this element of nothingness derives from the positive will and work of God."[193]

Härle highlights a difficult and problematic issue—the relation between the will of God and God's knowledge. We have already said that "what God positively wills" is the "action of His mercy."[194] Hence nothingness, which is merciless [*gnadenlos*], cannot have its origin in God's positive will.[195] We have to ask Barth whether he knows a 'negative will' of God which might be the origin of nothingness. Barth does not use this particular term, but the term that he does use is "non-willing"[196] [*Unwillen*] in order to describe that which God does not will and therefore negates and rejects.

In order to grasp fully Barth's doctrine of nothingness, Härle suggests returning to one of Barth's theses in his doctrine of God: "God's knowledge is God Himself, and again God's will is God Himself."[197] For Barth, God's knowledge does not come about in a 'special capacity' or through a 'special act' but "by the very fact that He is God, God knows [. . .] His

---

that Barth sees the whole biblical narrative in the sense of a story rather than as recorded history that has been written by a scribe. The Bible is God's story of salvation of the world through and in Jesus Christ. See Ford, *Barth and God's Story*, passim.

189. *CD* III/3, 352 and 361.

190. *CD* III/3, 77. See again Parmenides' view of being, which he understands to be imperishable and everlasting, as opposed to *doxa*, shadow.

191. See also McDowell, "Mend your speech a little," 158.

192. *CD* III/3, 352.

193. *CD* III/3, 292.

194. See *CD* III/3, 358f.

195. See *CD* III/3, 353.

196. See *CD* III/3, 353, 355, 360, 361, 363.

197. *CD* II/1, 549.

being is itself also His knowledge."[198] What Barth describes with these two statements, that 'God knows' and 'God wills,' is "one total essence of God."[199] Therefore Barth concludes (rightly according to the rules of logic) that "[w]hat God knows He wills, and what He wills He does."[200] From this deduction Barth arrives at his insightful ontological statement: "the sphere of the will of God is the sphere of being itself."[201] Since God is omniscience, for Barth God's knowledge (and therefore also his will) not only "embraces" [*umfaßt*] all things but also "defines" [*bezeichnet*] the limits of being [*Grenze des Seienden*].[202] Again, it is critical here to understand that "these aspects of the nature of God are interchangeable in that what God knows He wills and what He wills He knows."[203] Therefore there is nothing which is hidden from God's will and knowledge, because that would "not be something but nothing. It would not simply be without being like sin or death. It would be *nihil pure negativum*."[204] For Barth this means that God's will can sometimes be expressed by what he confirms or rejects, by his love or hate. However, in this sphere of God's will (which we said is nothing other than the sphere of being) God wills everything, and thus being as well as non-being must therefore logically be subject to God's will. Therefore, "the Yes and No of the divine will are absolutely and definitely the true circumscription of the area of being."[205]

What logical consequences result from this with regard to the relationships between God and nothingness, and humanity and nothingness? If God knows nothingness, does this mean that he also wills it, and that it belongs to the sphere of his will? Furthermore, does nothingness therefore belong to the sphere of being? We have to answer in the affirmative and say that even *das Nichtige* belongs to the sphere of God's will. This however

---

198. *CD* II/1, 549.

199. *CD* II/1, 549.

200. *CD* III/3, 120f. See also *CD* II/1, 551: "God's knowledge is His will and God's will His knowledge."

201. See *CD* II/1, 556, translation—author's own. Here I use my own translation due to the fact that the translation gives a misleading rendering of Barth's ontology: "The sphere of His will is as such the sphere of spheres." In contrast, the original German makes an ontological statement: "Der Bereich des Willens Gottes ist als solcher der Bereich des Seienden," in *KD* II/1, 625.

202. *CD*, II/1, 553.

203. Rodin, *Evil and Theodicy in the Theology of Karl Barth*, 91.

204. *CD* II/1, 566.

205. *CD* II/1, 557. For more on God's *Yes* and *No* see Krötke, *Sin and Nothingness in the Theology of Karl Barth*, 26–29.

leads to following dilemma:[206] either nothingness is *not* by the will of God (in which case God is not really Lord over all) or nothingness *is* by God's will (which would make God the author of it). Yet Barth denies that God is the author of nothingness:

> He [God] wills it in so far as He gives it this space, position and function. He does not do so as its author, recognising it as His creature, approving and confirming and vindicating it. On the contrary, He wills it as He denies it His authorship, as He refuses it any standing before Him or right or blessing or promise, as He places it under His prohibition and curse and treats it as that from which He wishes to redeem and liberate His creation. In this way, then, in His turning away from it. He wills what He disavows. It cannot exist without Him. It, too, is by Him, and is under His control and government.[207]

Barth's solution is that the impossible and non-existent is *only* by God's "refusing and rejecting will."[208] It is that which God does not will and is therefore not God's creation; it does not stand in any relation with God.

In retrospect Barth argues that though nothingness (encompassing evil, sin, wickedness, the devil, death and non-being) exists and has a reality, "it does so in its own way by the will of God and not without it,"[209] yet is not created by God. Only that which God created and brings forth is that which he positively affirms. Barth arrives at this point of view through his understanding of God's positive and negative will, his "*voluntas efficiens* and His *voluntas permittens*,"[210] equating God's *voluntas efficiens* with his positive will as Creator [*Schöpferwille*]. His permissive will on the other hand is that which judges, negates and overcomes nothingness.[211]

To the question of why God wants *das Nichtige*, even within his permissive will, Barth answers:

> It is the very essence of our reconciliation as grace to depend on the existence of a divine *voluntas permittens*, and in virtue of this on the reality of disgrace, damnation and hell. If God is greater in the very fact that He is the God who forgives sins and saves from death, we have no right to complain but must praise

---

206. Härle, *Sein und Gnade*, 236. Härle points out the dilemma and highlights how Barth solves it, see 236–42.

207. *CD* II/1, 556f.

208. *CD* II/1, 556.

209. *CD* II/1, 594.

210. *CD* II/1, 594.

211. See *CD* II/1, 595.

> Him that His will also includes a permitting of sin and death. God is not less but greater—He does not come under suspicion, but shows Himself to be holy and righteous, in the fact that He not only *efficit*, but also *permittit*. For in this way His will appears as the will of the gracious God who in His grace is the glorious God.[212]

So Barth does not deny the reality of nothingness as such but affirms it as a reality *sui generis*, meaning as a reality that it is of a different nature from the reality of God and created beings.[213] However, this does not answer the question about Barth's explanation for the origin of this 'reality.' Does the statement that everything, even nothingness, is *under* the will of God, not imply the conclusion that at the same time nothingness is *through* the will of God? Is it not rather the case that the former [under] enables the latter [through]?

Barth does not shy away from the consequence and confesses the fact that even nothingness is 'through God';[214] to be precise, through the negative will of God, "for not only what God wills, but what He does not will, is potent, and must have a real correspondence."[215] "Since God's omnipotence is that of His will, God has the power according to His will also to not-will, and God's non-willing is effectual!"[216] Barth concludes that "[e]ven on His left hand the activity of God is not in vain. He does not act for nothing. His rejection, opposition, negation and dismissal are powerful and effective like all His works because they, too, are grounded in Himself, in the freedom and wisdom of His election."[217] God's negating "*Willensakt*" [act of will or will-act] therefore also has for Barth "*realitätssetzenden Charakter*"[218] and

---

212. *CD* II/1, 595.
213. See Härle, *Sein und Gnade*, 237.
214. See Käfer who writes: "Weil das Nichtige zwar kein Teil der (gewollten) Schöpfung Gottes sei, jedoch abgesehen von der schöpferischen Macht Gottes nicht wirklich geworden wäre, muß nach Barth zumindest angenommen werden, daß Gott selbst das Nichtige, indem er es verwarf, ‚wirklich' werden ließ," in Käfer, *Inkarnation und Schöpfung*, 236.
215. *CD* III/3, 352.
216. Rodin, *Evil and Theodicy in the Theology of Karl Barth*, 91.
217. *CD* III/3, 351f. Rodin explains that the "'Yes'–'No' dichotomy (which is the same as the 'Right Hand'–'Left-Hand' dichotomy) is a description of the very essence of God in Barth's discussion of God's perfections," in Rodin, *Evil and Theodicy in the Theology of Karl Barth*, 95.
218. Härle, *Sein und Gnade*, 238.

has to be understood as a divine 'will-act.' Thus that which "corresponds to that which God does not will is nothingness."[219]

Again, God's negative 'will-act' is in line with what has already been said: there is nothing that is not under the will of God, or to express this in positive terms, everything is under God's will and lordship. Barth therefore concludes that God is the "*Grund und Herr*"[220] even of *das Nichtige*:

> He says Yes, and therefore says No to that to which He has not said Yes. He works according to His purpose, and in so doing rejects and dismisses all that gainsays it. Both of these activities, grounded in His election and decision, are necessary elements in His sovereign action. He is Lord both on the right hand and on the left. It is only on this basis that nothingness 'is,' but on this basis it really 'is.' As God is Lord on the left hand as well, He is the basis and Lord of nothingness too.[221]

Though Barth avoids saying that God is the cause and author of nothingness he concludes that it has its ground, basis, and origin of existence in God's negating will. So we should perhaps push Barth a bit further and ask what is the distinction between describing God's will as the '*Grund und Herr*' of nothingness and to call God's will the author and cause of it. Furthermore, when Barth says that nothingness is 'through' God's will is this not essentially asserting that God is the author of *das Nichtige*?[222]

Barth has argued that God could not be the author of nothingness because there is no correspondence between him and nothingness. However, this thesis is refuted by Barth's own thought when he highlights that there is in fact a correspondence between nothingness and the negating will of God. Furthermore, since nothingness gets its reality from God, it is under his lordship, is willed by God (though negatively) and God knows about it (otherwise, if he did not know about it, how could he defeat it in Jesus Christ?). Thus, the fact that nothingness finds a correspondence in God, and God knows and wills it, leads to the conclusion that God wills nothingness, as well as to the contradictory statement that "*Gott will auch dasjenige, was er nicht will und nicht einmal wollen kann.*"[223]

Is this conclusion guilty of ignoring Barth's own theological method and his warning that theology should not turn into a 'system,' a theology that

---

219. *CD* III/3, 352.
220. *CD* III/3, 405.
221. *CD* III/3, 351.
222. See footnote 73 in Härle, *Sein und Gnade*, 240.
223. Ibid., 242.

can only be comprehended as an "object in broken thoughts and utterance?"[224] Is Barth intentionally illogical when he deals with the doctrine of nothingness, because the nature of nothingness is a contradiction in terms? In *Credo* Barth writes that theology has to be "*logisch inkonsequent*" on this matter.[225] Since nothingness is just a fleeting shadow, all theological thought about nothingness takes place under this shadow, and is thus 'broken' and 'piecework,' reflecting the break caused by nothingness between Creator and creature.[226] Therefore, according to Barth, it should play no proper role in any systematic theology, in order that nothingness is denied a positive function in theological thought in relation to God and the world. This is in order that nothingness is not trivialized as something that can be 'explained' and made 'comprehensible.' Barth avoids this danger by being '*logisch inkonsequent*' on the matter of *das Nichtige*.[227]

3.3. Election and the Ontology of das Nichtige

Härle points out that nothingness is part of Barth's ontology, not because it is diametrically opposed to 'being' (which would be 'nothing'), but because it has the character of a 'reality.' In this way '*das Nichtige*' is a component (a 'cog') in Barth's ontology and should be treated as such.[228] For Barth, nothingness is not equivalent to sin. Human sin, according to Barth is the 'most important of all its forms' (that is, the most important of all the forms of nothingness)[229]—but not the only form. Barth talks about sin specifically in his doctrine of reconciliation, naming it pride, sloth, and falsehood[230] in relation to the cross and its achievements.[231] Nothingness on the other hand is not "exhausted" in sin but also takes the form of "evil and death."[232] In

224. *CD* III/3, 294.

225. Barth, "4. Vorlesung: *Creatorem coeli et terrae*," 36.

226. See *CD* III/3, 293f.

227. See Härle, *Sein und Gnade*, 243–46, who highlights that Barth is in fact contradicting himself.

228. See ibid., 227f.

229. *CD* III/3, 305.

230. For an exposition on pride, sloth and falsehood see Jenson, *The Gravity of Sin*, 155–82. See also Krötke, *Sin and Nothingness in the Theology of Karl Barth*, 61–65, and McFayden, *Bound to Sin*, 134–54.

231. The limitations of space preclude a fuller discussion on the different kinds of sin. This book looks at the 'dialectics' of the doctrines of election and atonement and chooses to focus on §50, a paragraph often neglected yet one in which Barth expounds his ideas about ontology and the dialectic between God's *Yes* and *No*.

232. *CD* III/3, 310.

this way Barth avoids a one-sided understanding of nothingness as merely a moral failure or a human lapse (missing the target) and brings in the physical aspect of nothingness as a power of destruction that stands in opposition to God as well as to his creatures.[233]

The place of nothingness in Barth's ontology is founded in his doctrine of providence. Election on the other hand is the 'inner ground' of providence.[234] Barth explains the ontic reality of 'nothingness' in relation to God's activity in election and the covenant between him and humanity, which is the goal of creation. He sees God's dealing with nothingness and its 'ontic context' simultaneously occurring with creation both grounded in God's primordial election as well as rejection.[235] The ontic correlation in which *das Nichtige* is a reality, occurs in the rejecting will of God and is grounded in election.[236]

For Barth, election is always the election of *something* and thus automatically is also the *rejection* of something else. By God electing something, he rejects that which he does not elect, and in this way rejection is the inverse of election: "Nothingness is the negative consequence of election, as it expresses what is not elected."[237] On the one hand, God's *Yes* in election determines and precedes election, highlighting God's positive will; and on the other hand, God's rejection, highlighting the *No* of God, determines and precedes nothingness.[238] Barth says that "nothingness is that from which God separates Himself and in face of which He asserts Himself and exerts His positive will."[239] "*Das Nichtige, ist das was Gott nicht will*" is a recurring theme that is characteristic of nothingness in Barth[240] and might be called the *Kernsatz*[241] of Barth's doctrine of *das Nichtige*. Thus rejection for Barth becomes a necessary (and negative) corollary of election; or to put it differently, God's positive electing will necessarily includes his active non-willing of rejection.[242] We therefore conclude that the reality of nothingness is a

---

233. See *CD* III/3, 310f and Härle, *Sein und Gnade*, 228.

234. See ibid., 256. See Sung Min Jeong, who writes that "[s]ince nothingness is an alien element among the objects of God's providence, nothingness is neither God nor His creature," Jeong, *Nothingness in the Theology of Paul Tillich and Karl Barth*, 69.

235. See *CD* III/3, 351.

236. See Härle, *Sein und Gnade*, 257.

237. Mikkelsen, *Reconciled Humanity*, 135.

238. Kennedy, "A Personalist Doctrine of Providence," 196.

239. *CD* III/3, 351.

240. Härle, *Sein und Gnade*, 231.

241. Ibid., 232.

242. See Kennedy, "A Personalist Doctrine of Providence," 202.

consequence of divine rejection, since rejection is the counterpart to divine election. It is first and foremost "God's own affair"[243] [*Gottes eigene Sache*], the problem that God deals with himself. Barth writes:

> God elects, and therefore rejects what He does not elect. [. . .] He says Yes, and therefore says No to that which He has not said Yes. [. . .] Both of these activities, grounded in His election and decision, are necessary elements in His sovereign action. He is Lord both on the right hand and on the left.[244]

Barth uses Luther's picture of the left and right hand of God, claiming that in one way or the other all of humanity is continually determined by God.[245] In this way God demonstrates his work of grace in election, his *opus proprium*, and his *opus alienum*,[246] the "obverse of divine election" [*Kehrseite des göttlichen Erwählens*],[247] his work of divine negation and rejection, of wrath, jealousy and judgment, the two representing the *Yes* and *No* of God.[248] Barth writes:

> What God positively wills and performs in the *opus proprium* of His election, of His creation, of His preservation and overruling rule of the creature revealed in the history of His covenant with man, is His grace—the free goodness of His condescension in which He wills, identifying Himself with the creature, to accept solidarity and to be present with it, to be Himself its Guarantor, Helper and King, and therefore to do the best possible for it. What God does not will and therefore negates and rejects, what can thus be only the object of His *opus alienum*, of His

---

243. *CD* III/3, 354. On the theme of 'nothingness as God's own problem' see Krötke, *Sin and Nothingness in the Theology of Karl Barth*, 21–25.

244. *CD* III/3, 351.

245. Rodin comments that here we have an "internal war of sorts between the two hands of God; the right hand in wrath and judgment separating itself from and finally annihilating the work of the left hand," in Rodin, *Evil and Theodicy in the Theology of Karl Barth*, 187.

246. See also McDowell, "Mend your speech a little," 159.

247. *CD* III/3, 361.

248. Barth does not see the *opus alienum* in the same light as the *opus proprium*. The former is secondary and transitory, see *CD* III/3, 361. See also Klappert, *Die Auferweckung des Gekreuzigten*, who writes that "das Nein des Gerichtes Gottes is Funktion seines Ja, Gottes Nein steht functional im Dienst seines Ja, sein opus alienum vollzieht sich im Dienst des opus proprium," 245f. See also Thomas, "Der für uns gerichtete Richter," footnote 14.

jealousy, wrath and judgment, is a being that refuses and resists and therefore lacks His grace.[249]

Kennedy points out that it is crucial to understand that "Barth grounds God's election in God's being *ad intra*, but not the resulting creation or nothingness itself. While creation is God's work *ad extra* in its positive connection to God's willing, nothingness is not."[250] In this way Barth precludes a place for nothingness and sin in creation, which has its limits of reality in God's *No*; it exists only as a converse to his grace in election.[251] In his primal election of grace, God chose to be the *Deus pro nobis* in Jesus Christ. Creation in its totality is in Barth's view perfect and we see that every aspect of creaturely existence stands under and in relation to the positive will of God, his *Yes ad extra*.

Barth sums up that this *Yes* and *No* "has taken place in Jesus Christ."[252] But how are we to understand this in relation to God's double election in and of Jesus Christ, both as the positively elected one as well as the negatively rejected one? How can God simultaneously say both *Yes* and *No* to Jesus Christ? How can both the *opus proprium* and the *opus alienum* be executed over Christ? How can Jesus stand under both the right and the left hand of God? Barth said that God elects what he wills and rejects what he opposes (that which he does not will). So how can Jesus be both that which God wills and that which God does not will? Is it possible that Christ incorporates both, or is it that God elects Jesus Christ and rejects that which is 'outside' Christ? Rather than talking about God's *No* spoken against Christ, can we not talk about a *No* spoken by God through Christ against sin? If so, Jesus would not be 'The Judge Judged in Our Place,' but 'the Judge who judges on our behalf.' Then the *Yes* spoken over Jesus Christ and God's holiness would automatically presuppose the *No* over everything else that is not Jesus Christ and not in line with God's positive will. This will be discussed further in chapter 4.

3.4. *Creation and* das Nichtige

Yet, we need to dig a bit deeper and come to the core understanding of Barth's doctrine of nothingness, sin, and evil to how he sees it in relation to the negative side of creation. As we have already seen, Barth starts off with

---

249. *CD* III/3, 353.
250. Kennedy, " A Personalist Doctrine of Providence," 197.
251. See *CD* III/3, 355.
252. *CD* III/3, 355.

the premise that "God has judged nothingness by His mercy as revealed and effective in Jesus Christ."[253] In view of God's providence, Barth acknowledges in world-occurrence a "sinister system of elements" which is not governed and preserved by God with his fatherly care and lordship in the same way as the creaturely events.[254] Barth points out an 'alien factor' [*Fremdkörper*] which resists and is in opposition to God's will. This stubborn element Barth calls '*das Nichtige*'—nothingness—that which is inherent in contradiction to God's positive will and therefore the "impossible possibility."[255] It exists only because in the sense that it is that which God does not will for "not only what God wills, but what He does not will is potent, and must have a real correspondence."[256] However, God's will for his creatures is the continuation and thus preservation [*Bewahrung*] of the creatures from being "overthrown by the greater force of nothingness"[257] and liberation in order to live a life in covenantal fellowship with him and each other. For this to happen, Barth explains, God himself became a creature in Jesus Christ, in whom he has "set Himself in opposition to nothingness, and in this opposition was and is the Victor."[258] He warded off nothingness by his divine preservation so that the creatures, though constantly threatened and corrupted by it, will never be overwhelmed and destroyed.

(a) The shadow side of *Das Nichtige*

However, we need to address the question of how humanity in first place could become sinful and how is it possible for God's creatures to sin at all. In the same way that nothingness stands in opposition to God, this is also true for the relationship of nothingness and creature. Nothingness affects both Creator and creatures as well as their relationship. Humanity is destined to be God's covenant-partner; her ontological existence is threatened by the non-being of nothingness which stands in opposition to the creaturely realm. We have said that creatures and nothingness do not stand in a dialectical relationship which can be brought into a synthesis but stand in a diastatical antithesis.[259] But because nothingness has been "attacked and

---

253. CD, III/3, 289.
254. See CD, III/3, 289–95.
255. CD, III/3, 351.
256. CD, III/3, 352.
257. CD, III/3, 290.
258. CD, III/3, 290.
259. See Härle, *Sein und* Gnade, 246f.

routed"[260] as the adversary [*Feind*] of God, as "His own enemy,"[261] what the creatures experience of their actuality and potentiality in the present, is only the broken power of "fragmentary existence," which according to Barth, is only an "echo" and a "shadow" of what it once was yet is no longer.[262] Barth explains that nothingness may still have "standing and assume significance to the extent that the final revelation of its destruction has not yet taken place and all creation must still await and expect it. But its dominion, even though it was only the semblance of dominion, is now objectively defeated as such in Jesus Christ."[263] Nothingness in its "concrete form is human sin, although Barth issues the caution that one cannot know it directly from knowledge of our own sin."[264] The outward sign of sin is disobedience to and repudiation of the will and command of God and a person's own guilt by the refusal to accept God's mercy and grace in Jesus Christ and thus a breaking off [*Herausbrechen*] from a gratitude and praise towards God.[265] This notion reveals the seriousness of sin that humanity rejects God's goodness which creates a "rupture"[266] in relationships with God and neighbor. Instead humanity wants to be her own master and in this way condemns herself, becoming simultaneously not only an offender of the law or an agent [*Täter*] for sin but also its victim [*Opfer*],[267] "sharing its nature and producing and extending it."[268]

Barth sees sin not as an "attribute or defect"[269] of the creature, but rather as an insult towards the Creator and therefore as the creature's guilt. Here Barth seems to contradict himself again when he says later that humanity is responsible for her own sin, by surrendering to the alien power, but is not merely a doer of sin but becomes its victim which "disturbs, injures and destroys the creature and its nature."[270]

Though Barth acknowledges that the *non posse peccare* and the reality of sin in the world are in tension, he nevertheless sees it as something that he does not even try to solve logically. He calls nothingness and sin the

260. CD III/3, 366.
261. CD III/3, 366.
262. See *CD*, III/3, 367.
263. CD III/3, 367.
264. Bromiley, *An Introduction to the Theology of Karl Barth*, 149.
265. See CD III/3, 305, 308.
266. CD III/3, 308.
267. See *CD* III/3, 352.
268. CD III/3, 306.
269. CD III/3, 307.
270. CD III/3, 308.

"impossible possibility" or the "absurd" and comments that it is not possible to describe the "intrinsically absurd" other than with an absurd logic.[271] The fall occurred as an act against the will of God and therefore *without* the will of God.

Yet as Härle indicates, for Barth, the relationship between God and *das Nichtige* does not suggest that the '*contra Dei voluntatem*' means the '*praeter voluntatem Dei*'; rather, nothingness can be understood simultaneously as both "against the will of God" as well as "through the will of God."[272] Barth is very reluctant to draw any conclusions which could be seen to be logically derived from the above statement. What he does assert is that "the fall of man, while it formed no part of [God's] intention, was not outside His foresight and plan."[273] Elsewhere Barth speaks of God's "permitting of the fall"[274] and goes as far as to assert that nobody can escape the sphere of God's will; even in disobeying God "we merely fulfil God's decision."[275]

We have already shown that Barth understands humanity's sin as a reality *against* God and *through* God. Furthermore, Härle emphasizes, Barth speaks of human sin as a necessity[276]—Barth states that "man is necessarily a sinner"[277] or, as the original German text suggests,[278] has to be a sinner! Barth goes on to explain that "on the basis of the covenant Jesus Christ had to be crucified."[279] According to Barth, humanity has to be sinful in order for reconciliation to take place, for grace to be revealed and for Jesus Christ to triumph. It is necessary for humanity to be sinful in order that the Son "in His person [. . .] should bear and bear away the curse of sin for all men."[280] The positive converse of this remark is that because of the Son's obedience, he is also exalted (and with him humanity), becoming "in His person, the Bearer of the divine image for all men."[281] For Barth, although they stand in opposition, nothingness is the presupposition for grace in the same way

---

271. *CD* IV/1, 410.

272. See Härle, *Sein und Gnade*, 253.

273. *CD* III/2, 144.

274. *CD* II/2, 165.

275. *CD* II/2, 557.

276. See Härle, *Sein und Gnade*, 254.

277. *CD* I/1, 91.

278. See *CD* I/2, 100, where Barth writes: "der im Bunde mit Gottstehende, von Gott in den Bund mit ihm versetzte Mensch muß ein Sünder sein."

279. *CD* I/2, 92.

280. *CD* III/1, 50.

281. *CD* III/1, 50.

that illness is the presupposition for healing, and death is for resurrection.[282] Grace defeats and negates nothingness.

(B) The shadow side of Creation

When Barth turns to the misconception of nothingness in order to rule out what nothingness is and is not, he goes on to say that there are two sides in creaturely occurrence, a positive side and a negative side, light as well as shadow. Barth sees this twofold character as biblical and identifies it in the first biblical narrative, the creation story, where God distinguishes night and day, darkness from light.[283] Thus, on the positive aspect of election we also encounter a shadowy negative aspect [*Schattenseite*][284] which

> belongs to the essence of creaturely nature, and is indeed a mark of its perfection, that it has in fact this negative side, that it inclines not only to the right hand but also to the left, that it is thus simultaneously worthy of its Creator and yet dependent on Him, that it is not 'nothing' but 'something,' yet 'something' on the very frontier of nothingness, secure, and yet in jeopardy.[285]

This is particularly interesting for our understanding of sin's relationship to the atonement (particularly how sin is dealt with) as well as its relationship to the two sides of election (particularly reprobation). The negative aspect of creation is not identical with 'nothingness' but they are coterminous.

For Barth, this negative *Schattenseite* represents a danger only in the sense that it stands on the "frontier" [*benachbart*] of nothingness, and because it is "orientated towards it" [*zugewendet ist*].[286] Therefore it is "continually confronted by this menace."[287] God's No, which stands in opposition to the will of God does not belong to the essence of created nature and order in the way that the negative aspect of creation does (the shadow side *is* part of God's perfection).[288] Barth explains that the positive and negative sides of cre-

---

282. See Härle, *Sein und Gnade*, 264.

283. See *CD*, III/1 § 42.3.

284. Barth directs his readers to his discussion of this twofold character in *CD* III/1, §42.3.

285. *CD* III/3, 296.

286. *CD* III/3, 296.

287. *CD* III/3, 296.

288. See Käfer who writes that "die Verwirklichung der menschlichen Disposition, Gottes Bundesgenosse wahrhaft zu werden und zu sein, ist nach Barth dadurch gefährdet, daß das menschliche Geschöpf mit einer Licht- und einer Schattenseite geschaffen sei. Eigentlich sei das menschliche Geschöpf gerade mit diesen beiden Seiten

ation do not oppose the creative will of God but do in fact reveal creation's goodness, as seen in the incarnation. He sees these two sides, the negative and positive aspects, the left and right hands of creation, as corresponding to Christ's humiliation and exaltation in his reconciling work, for "in Him God has made Himself the Subject of both aspects of creaturely existence."[289] Barth explains that the inner antithesis between the negative and positive sides (Christ's humiliation and exaltation) is relative and provisional and in fact salutary with regard to Jesus Christ who has reconciled this antithesis in his own person.[290] Again, there is no common ground between the negative aspect of creation and nothingness. Nothingness is a constant reminder of threat and corruption but because in creation both a *Yes* and a *No* were spoken,[291] creation has its own shadow side (though this does not belong to nothingness—it has its place in the covenant).[292]

Barth finishes his argument by saying that if one confuses the negative aspect of creation with nothingness and sees them as identical, one has fallen into its trap of concealment and this is a triumph of nothingness. Because if nothingness is seen as something created, it takes on the alibi of creation. This covers it so it cannot be identified as nothingness and, unhampered, it can then pursue its destructive course, its mayhem, even more freely.[293] If one mistakes the negative aspect of creation for nothingness, one fails to recognise true nothingness, and ends up justifying nothingness as just another part of creation. Then nothingness, understood as the negative side of creation, would be brought into a "positive relationship with God's will and work"[294] and the enemy would therefore go unrecognized.[295] The two aspect of creation (nothingness and the negative) must be discerned and differentiated.

---

vollkommen geschaffen und Gottes sehr gute Schöpfung," in Käfer, *Inkarnation und Schöpfung*, 220. See also *KD* III/3, where Barth writes: "Es gehört allerdings zum Wesen des [d.h. eines jeden menschlichen] Geschöpfes, und es ist in der Tat ein Merkmal seiner Vollkommenheit, auch jene Schattenseite zu haben," 335.

289. *CD* III/3, 296.

290. See *CD* III/3, 296.

291. Barth highlights that there are always two sides to creation, which include, growth and decay, beginning and end, success and failure, laughter and tears, birth and death.

292. Barth explains this fact with Mozart and says that nobody else apart from him (Mozart) has understood it and heard it so beautifully. "He [Mozart] heard the negative only in and with the positive," in *CD* III/3, 298.

293. See *CD* III/3, 299.

294. *CD* III/3, 301.

295. See *CD* III/3, 299.

Furthermore, one fails to see that this antithesis is part of God's good creation which is always created towards Christ, and therefore is an antithesis which is not only temporal and provisional but also salvific in regard to Jesus Christ. In Jesus Christ as the *Logos* incarnate, God brought himself under the two aspects of creation with its *Yes* and *No* and has revealed the twofold form of creation and its goodness. Barth sums up: "In the knowledge of Jesus Christ we must abandon the obvious prejudice against the negative aspect of creation and confess that God has planned and made all things well, even on the negative side."[296] In the incarnation God showed his faithfulness and goodness towards his creatures by exposing himself to real nothingness and in his condemned death destroyed nothingness and liberated and reconciled humanity to God once and for all. This is summed up in the resurrection where it is revealed that *Jesus is Victor*.

In the end, nothingness for Barth is nothing other than a shadow, and does not have the final power of destruction; the destruction power that it appears to have is illusory and in fact is conquered and defeated on the cross. Thus, in this defeated and 'harnessed' shadow-existence nothingness is allowed to have its existence or rather non-existence apart from God. Kennedy sums up: "Affirming the positive and negative aspects of creation as good, Barth leaves no room for evil in either Creator or creature."[297]

We have to question whether or not Barth leaves room for any real rejection and how this *Yes* and *No* relate to Jesus Christ. When Barth talks about God's *Yes* and *No* in Jesus Christ and relates them to God's election (his positive will) and rejection (his negative will), we see the two sides of predestination that are both encompassed in Jesus Christ. As we have seen, when it comes to creation Barth talks about a shadow side that is still part of God's positive will and which should not be confused with *das Nichtige*, which has no relation to God's positive will. When it comes to the cross we need to ask Barth whether he means that the cross is part of the shadow side of creation or whether the cross deals with the 'left hand' of God (*das Nichtige*). If the 'Son of God' deals with the 'left hand' of God and the 'Son of Man' is also involved in the fight against 'nothingness' then humanity, which participates in Jesus, is also involved and affected by nothingness. However if the cross is just part of the shadow side of creation, we also need to question Barth's theology when it comes to the reality of Christ's dealing with nothingness and its rejection. If the cross is not part of the 'left hand' of God, then it does not affect nothingness, since they do not stand in any relationship, rendering the cross meaningless with regard to sin. If however

---

296. *CD*, III/3, 301.
297. Kennedy, "A Personalist Doctrine of Providence," 199.

it is part of God's 'left hand,' then humanity is also affected by nothingness and thus the clear line Barth draws between nothingness and the shadow side of creation is not an uncrossable line but does not in fact exist in reality. Either way, it seems that one of Barth's conclusions is wrong and contradicts the other. Either Jesus does not properly deal with nothingness on the cross or humanity is affected by and is a victim of nothingness.

Conclusion

A closer look at Barth's doctrine of nothingness and sin has highlighted not only the interrelation of the doctrines of election and atonement, but also sheds new light on both doctrines, thus bringing the reader deeper into Barth's understanding of the Christ event.

How are we to understand God's *Yes* and *No* in election in relation to nothingness and what has that to do with the negative aspect—the shadow side—of creation? Barth says that God has spoken a *Yes* over creation and a *No* over nothingness. Furthermore, as stated in chapter 1, Jesus is both the elect as well as the rejected over whom a *Yes* (the resurrection) and a *No* (the cross) is spoken. How are we to understand this? Barth appears to describe two distinctive yet related negative concepts when he talks about the divine *No*'s in §50. It seems as though one is always an ultimate and distinct *No*, whereas the other is a penultimate *No*, a *No* which stands in antithetical relationship to and can thus be brought into a dialectical relationship with and can be overcome [*Aufhebung*] in a synthesis in Christ. God and nothingness cannot be synthesized in Christ. God speaks an absolute *No* over nothingness and rejects it utterly. Yet sometimes Barth calls it a 'semblance' [*Schein*] whereas at other times he calls it a 'reality' [*Wirklichkeit*]. What are we to believe and which should we take as Barth's final word?

The two apparently contradictory statements must be viewed from two different angles.[298] Sometimes Barth talks from the perspective of the 'sinner' and at other times (indeed, most of the time) he analyses from the perspective of the risen Christ; one is penultimate whereas the other is ultimate.[299] So we have already answered the question as to which statements should be given more weight. It is obvious that the christological statements that speak from the retrospective angle, from the other side of the cross, through the achieved and finished work of Christ, should be given ultimate

---

298. See also Mikkelsen who shows the relationship between God's perspective and the human perspective, in Mikkelsen, *Reconciled Humanity*, 124.

299. See 'I.1. Der wirkliche Mensch,' 218–23 and 'I.2. Der Mensch der Sünde—der „unmögliche" Mensch,' 224–27 in Käfer, *Inkarnation und Schöpfung*.

preference. When Barth talks about the sinner, he talks about nothingness as a reality, which makes the human being a victim of sin. And so over both nothingness as well the creature, God's total rejection is spoken in his *No*. The death of Christ on the cross is the shadow side of creation. And since ultimately Christ's death is salvific, Barth sees the cross as part of God's perfect creation, always in this transitory sense. However, when Barth talks about Jesus Christ, the 'real man,' he speaks in terms of the total defeat of nothingness, a conquered force that has no more power. Then, the shadow becomes that which is no longer a reality, but simply a semblance, a passing shadow or echo of nothingness. Thus the shadow is not negative but highlights something that has no tangible reality.

Here we have to make a decision, either to affirm Barth's position or to part company with Barth and propose our own position. To help us decide this the main question that needs to be addressed is whether or not Barth is in line with the biblical witness. We will look at this in the following chapter.

4

Jesus Christ the Judge
Through and Beyond Barth

How much more, then, will the blood of Christ, who through the eternal Spirit offered himself unblemished to God, cleanse our consciences from acts that lead to death, so that we may serve the living God! For this reason Christ is the mediator of a new covenant, that those who are called may receive the promised eternal inheritance.
   (Hebrews 9:14–15)

Introduction

THE DOCTRINE OF THE ATONEMENT IS CONCERNED WITH THE NATURE OF the death of Christ. This chapter will look afresh at how, according to Barth, the death of Christ atoned for the sins of humanity, in light of what we unearthed in the exegesis offered in chapters 1 and 2, and the questions raised in chapter 3. Our exegesis concluded that Jesus Christ with his natures—both divine and human—is only the elect of God (and not the reprobate). But how are we to see these two natures in the hypostatic union in relation to the work of Christ? And what does God's *Yes* look like? More significantly, if God only speaks a *Yes* over Jesus, how is his *No* over sin executed? This raises the further question of 'Who is the reprobate?' If Jesus is not condemned on the cross by bearing sin and being judged for it, how is sin dealt with on the cross?

Before we look at Barth and God's *No*, let us first begin with a look at some patristic understandings of the atonement. Barth stands in a tradition of theologians who have attended to the Anselmian question *Cur Deus*

Homo? For Barth, 'Why did God become man?'—or rather 'Why the God-Man?'—is the core question of the doctrine of the atonement. Any study of Barth's views on the atonement must take into account (1) what tradition Barth stands in and (2) what Barth is reacting against, or rather what errors is he trying to avoid and correct. So we shall look at some of the Fathers and their understanding of the atonement and the two natures of Christ; then revisit Calvin; and finally recollect some of the exegetical outcomes from the Old Testament texts and review their relationship with New Testament ideas about Jesus' death. Here we will look at Barth's cultic *pro nobis*, revisit the concept of sin bearing and conclude by contrasting Barth's view on the atonement with the paradigm of *Existenzstellvertretung*.

1. Atonement in the Early Church

Despite the all-encompassing biblical significance of the atonement (or perhaps *because* of it), a further explanation of the doctrine's logical implications for the Church is necessary.[1] Traditionally, many images, explanations descriptions and metaphors have been proposed to explain the doctrine's practical consequences, yet as Frances Young highlights, the parameters of the atonement have never officially been defined: "For the early Church, sacrificial imagery was powerful and inevitable. For us, it is by no means inevitable, and far from powerful—indeed, it is more often an offence and a stumbling-block."[2] The fact that Christ died on the cross played such an unquestionably fundamental role in the early Church and the immediate post-apostolic period that the Church never found it necessary to provide an elaborated doctrine of the atonement and therefore failed to construct any sort of special theory to explain it.[3] For the early Church, the "experience of Redemption through Christ was far richer than its attempting formulations of this experience."[4] As so often is the case in the history of the Church, the Christian principle *lex orandi* was placed prior to the *lex credendi*.[5] The reasons for the *lex orandi* to be expressed and formulated in a theological and intellectual form might be said to be twofold: the early Church (1) needed to defend her beliefs against rival religions and philosophical systems, and

---

1. See Blocher, "Atonement," 73f.
2. Young, *Sacrifice and the Death of Christ*, 103.
3. McDonald, *The Atonement of the Death of Christ*, 115.
4. Turner, *The Patristic Doctrine of Redemption*, 13.
5. On the development of the *lex orandi* in relation to the Spirit and the Trinity see Coakley, "Why Three? Some Further Reflections on the Origins of the Trinity," 39–49.

(2) needed to formulate doctrine to mediate rivalries within the Church herself. Thus, whilst the "*via crucis* [was] followed religiously, the *theologia crucis* lagged somewhat until other elements in Christian Theology were set in a clearer light."[6]

Though some of the Church's early theology represented an act of self-expression motivated by the formation of Christian orthodoxy, nevertheless much of it was a reaction against outside polemics and internal heresies. Many important Christian works "up to the time of Origen's *De Principiis* take the form of treatises directed to pagan, Jewish, or heretical opponents of the Church,"[7] showing that most theology was produced 'under fire.' Attention was given by theologians to the "problems which were of greatest relevance"[8] at the time. The apologists raised their arguments to a "more philosophical level,"[9] by presenting Christianity as a new philosophy, but by doing so they could be said to have laid "too little stress on the elements in Christianity which could not readily afford bridgeheads into paganism."[10] What these apologists—who were in fact the "first Christian philosophers [rather] than the first Christian theologians"[11]—were attempting to do, was to make Christianity "intellectually respectable in a thought-climate largely alien to that in which it was born."[12] The outcome of this, however, was that what was unique in Christianity tended to be "passed over in preference to what could more readily be understood by those to whom their treatises were principally directed."[13]

The formulation of a common understanding of the doctrine of Redemption was further complicated by questions like 'What constitutes a human being?' and 'What was lost during the fall?' Consequently the doctrine of the person of Christ had an enormous impact upon the doctrine of Christ's death. Was redemption an *act* of the incarnate Lord or was it a rescue mission from sin *effected* by the *Logos*?[14] The early Church emphasized

6. Turner, *The Patristic Doctrine of Redemption*, 18.
7. Ibid., 16f.
8. Ibid., 17.
9. Ibid., 44.
10. Ibid., 44.
11. Ibid., 44.
12. Ibid., 45.
13. Ibid., 44.
14. See ibid., 20. Turner highlights that one of the main competitors was Greek philosophy, upon which "much of the religion of the Graeco-Roman world had come to base itself," (ibid., 15). The Church had to defend itself against accusations aimed at ideas that appeared to those outside the Church to be contradictory. These included polytheism: how could the Church claim to be the heir of monotheistic Judaism whilst

the mediation of the death of Christ through the sacraments, and the Eucharist was described by Ignatius as *pharmakon athanasias*, "the medicine of immortality, and the antidote which wards off death but yields continuous life in union with Jesus Christ."[15] It might be said that the early fathers' theories on redemption highlighted the restoration of "incorruption" and "immortality"[16] (Rom 2:7; 1 Cor 15:53f.; 2 Tim 1:10), which had been lost through the fall, and they saw the atonement as being made through the "whole Incarnation."[17] It was not just the dying or rising of Christ, but the 'Total Christ' in life, death, and resurrection that constituted atonement for them. Aulén also highlights this view and again calls attention to the idea that the victory of Christ in the atonement involved every aspect of Jesus' human life—his incarnation and life, his dying and rising again.[18] The Fathers saw the person and work of Christ as two sides of the same coin and their understanding of the hypostatic union in Christ prompted them to examine Christ's incarnation as something never removed from his death, which was itself examined as something never removed from his resurrection—they were all constituent parts of the one atonement achieved by the one divine and human Jesus.

The question *Cur Deus Homo?* was first posed as early as the time of the Church Fathers (notably by Irenaeus and Athanasius), though the circumstances of the early Church were such that no satisfactory answer was ever reached. Irenaeus' principal answer to the *Cur Deus Homo?* question was "that He might kill sin, deprive death of its power, and vivify man."[19] He expresses his understanding of the atonement in a similar way elsewhere, maintaining that "the Word of God was made flesh [. . .] in order that he might destroy death and bring us to life, for we were tied and bound in

---

insisting upon the full divinity of Jesus? The Church also struggled with interior tensions such as the Arian controversy, which revolved around the divergent christological understandings of Arius and Athanasius, leaders in the early Church, and which divided the Church. It was out of these sorts of polemical attacks that the early Church's 'apologetic' emphasis arose, leading to the establishment of various Church councils. The Council of Nicaea eventually formulated the unity of the Godhead, which reached "doctrinal maturity by the time of the Council of Constantinople" and "received credal expression at the Council of Chalcedon," (ibid., 15).

15. Ignatius, "The Letters of Ignatius: Ephesians," Eph 20:2, 93.
16. See Athanasius, "On The Incarnation of the Word," §9, 40f. and §20, 46f.
17. See here Torrance, *Incarnation*, passim.
18. See Aulén, *Christus Victor*, 48.
19. Irenaeus, "Against Heresies," III.18.7, 448. 'Ut occideret quidem peccatum, evacuaret autem mortem, et vivificaret hominem,' in Irenäus von Lyon, *Gegen die Häresien*, III:236.

sin, we were born in sin and lived under the dominion of death."[20] Rather than being regarded as a legal/forensic breach of God's law, sin is seen as a power that enslaves humanity. It is something that entraps, which requires freedom from and redemption in a way that can only be achieved in the death of Christ. As Irenaeus puts it: Christ began to "destroy sin, and redeem man under the power of death [. . .] so that sin should be destroyed by man, and man should go forth from death."[21] Similarly, Origen also sees the death of Christ as "the beginning and progress of the destruction of the Evil One."[22] He states that in Christ's visible crucifixion, where he overthrew the "power of that evil spirit the devil, who had obtained dominion over the whole world,"[23] the "devil and all his princes and powers were invisibly crucified" (see Col 2:11ff.).[24]

The Fathers related the thoughts of the *Christus Victor* very closely to the doctrine of recapitulation—the summation of all things in Christ[25]— and to the underlying notion of restoration. This is also represented strongly in Barth's theology; the movement of the Son of God into the far country and the return of the Son of Man. The *Christus Victor* theory places strong emphasis on the incarnation and the new life brought about in Christ. Another strength of the *Christus Victor* model is that it takes both natures of Christ seriously, the human as well as the divine, representing both God's act on humanity's behalf and an act before God himself. Barth shares the patristic doctrine[26] of recapitulation with Irenaeus, seeing Jesus as the second Adam fulfilling the promises of the first and understanding the "whole of the events that form the life, death, and resurrection of Jesus as the way by which salvation is achieved."[27] In Christ, through whom all things were made, and through his resurrection, the new creation is coming forth, and what humanity had lost in Adam's disobedience is restored and re-created by the obedience of the Son of Man. This parallelism in the Adam-Christ antithesis (see Rom 5:12ff.) is especially apparent in the cross and we could argue that all of *Heilsgeschichte* hangs between these two trees—the tree of

20. Irenäus von Lyon, *Gegen die Häresien*, I.Epideixis:37, 58.
21. Irenaeus, "Against Heresies," III.18.7, 448.
22. Turner, *The Patristic Doctrine of Redemption*, 53.
23. Origen, "Origen Against Celsus," XVII, 617.
24. Turner, *The Patristic Doctrine of Redemption*, 53.
25. See ibid., 62f.
26. On Barth's patristic theology see Torrance, *Karl Barth: Biblical and Evangelical Theologian*, 182–212, especially 198–201.
27. Gunton, "Salvation," 146. For more on the doctrine of *anakephalaiosis* see Torrance, *Worship, Community and the Triune God of Grace*, 52.

the knowledge of good and evil and the tree where Jesus himself hangs, the cross. Indeed, Irenaeus writes that Jesus' death rectifies "that disobedience which had occurred by reason of a tree, through that obedience which was [wrought out] upon the tree [of the cross]."[28]

However, the atonement model that became dominant in the West was the 'Victim' model—Christ our Victim. It is again Aulén who highlights that the idea of 'satisfaction' was part of the earliest Western theory as well as the practice of penance.[29] He shows the essential two-sidedness in the *Christus Victor* theory as an act done by God and towards God, and shows that the 'Victim' theory reduces the two-sidedness to only one aspect.[30] According to the 'Victim' theory, what is achieved in the atonement is a work of man directed towards God and thus *Cur Deus Homo?* could be answered with a short '*Mori missus*.' Turner points out that the "simplification was almost imperative if the Western passion for clarity were to be saved."[31] Christ is then only seen in penal and substitutionary terms, only acting on behalf of humanity; the act of God on behalf of man is forgotten. Thus from the beginning the doctrine of the Christ Victim is at constant risk of—or might even be said to have fallen victim to—becoming a theological *pars pro toto*. Augustine, who affords a link between the earliest fathers and the scholastics, sees the purpose of the incarnation only in relation to sin and its cure, contending that "if Man had not sinned the Son of God would not have come."[32] He sees Christ as "both victor and victim."[33] The logic of Penal Substitution can already be clearly seen in Augustine's work: (1) death is the penalty of sin; (2) Jesus Christ died, hence he took the penalty and became the victim of sin; (3) he bore ours sins and thus he took the punishment of sin, that is, he assumed the wrath of God upon himself. The crux for Augustine (as well as for proponents of Penal Substitution) lies in what he sees in the Pauline letters, that Christ carried the burden of sin and was subsequently punished for it. Augustine writes: "Christ [. . .] submitted as man, and for man, to bear the curse which accompanies death. And as He died in the flesh which He took in bearing our punishment [. . .] He was cursed for our offences, in the death which He suffered in bearing our punishment."[34]

28. Irenaeus, "Against Heresies," V.16.3.
29. See Aulén, *Christus Victor*, 128.
30. See ibid,. 55–60.
31. Turner, *The Patristic Doctrine of Redemption*, 99.
32. Augustine, *Ser. clxxiv.*2. "Si homo non perisset. Filius hominis non venisset." Quoted in ibid., 108.
33. Augustine, "Confessions," X.43.69, 162.
34. Augustine, "Reply To Faustus The Manichaean," 14.6, 209.

However, the 'Victim' theory fails to grasp the breadth of the atonement, especially the second aspect of Christ's death bringing humanity back to God. This in itself is problematic and thus led to a legal/forensic and practical as well as a transactional understanding of the atonement in much Western thought, emphasizing the human act of Jesus' appeasement of the Father's wrath. There is no doubt that the New Testament presents the death of Christ as a sacrifice (an idea based on the Old Testament cult), but the idea of appeasement rests upon an interpretation of the Old Testament cult in chiefly transactional terms. In contrast, for much Eastern scholarship the "cultus is much less a matter of sacrificial transaction than of mystical transplantation,"[35] highlighting the death of Christ as the rescue and the cure from sin and the conclusion in the filial fellowship with God. Thus the answer to *Cur Deus Homo?* is therefore not only '*mori missus*,' but also involves Christ's entire life, death, resurrection and the ascension of humanity to the right hand of God, as well as the sending of the Spirit at Pentecost (which we will examine in chapter 5). We will argue in this chapter that the atonement is not simply a dealing *with* something or rescuing *from* something, but a bringing *into* something. The New Testament testifies to the fact that we are not only brought out of darkness into light but are made sons and co-heirs of Christ and thus partakers of the divine communion (see Rom 8:17; Gal 4:7; Titus 3:7).

2. The Reformed Backdrop of Barth's Theology of Atonement

In *For Us and Our Salvation*[36] McCormack highlights the sixteenth-century christological controversy over the "proper understanding of the hypostatic union and the *communicatio idiomatum*"[37] and the solidification of the doctrines of incarnation and atonement in the Reformed tradition. He argues that in the 1560s a "more positive treatment of Christology began to emerge, through its reappropriation of the ancient anhypostatic-enhypostatic Christology of the post-Chalcedonian period."[38] McCormack shows that Calvin's theology lacks a proper understanding of the hypostatic union, which might be because he never set forth a "careful investigation into the ontological constitution of the Mediator";[39] and also because Calvin regards

35. Turner, *The Patristic Doctrine of Redemption*, 116.
36. McCormack, *For Us and Our Salvation*.
37. Ibid., 3.
38. Ibid., 1.
39. Ibid., 6.

exposition of Scripture in his *Institutes* as the main authority and sees the Councils as subordinate to Scripture.[40]

McCormack highlights another aspect of seventeenth-century Reformed theology of the *communicatio* that is of immediate interest to this chapter in the way it sheds new light on soteriology: the concept of the *communicatio operationum* or *apotelesmatum*.[41] After the Reformed theologians had safeguarded the orthodox teaching of the union of the two natures (simultaneously distinct and unimpaired in their properties) they deepened the understanding of the *communicatio* and its ramifications for the saving work of Christ. McCormack shows that whilst they said that even though the work of the "God-man is single as regards its result, it is dual as regards its origination in the natures. In every action of the God-man, the two natures work together."[42] This means that though the redemptive work of the God-man Jesus was produced by two natures, the effect and result is still a unity since the two natures work together in harmony in one and the same person.[43] To the question of humanity's salvation, we have to say in accord with the *communicatio apotelesmatum* that it was neither God alone nor man, but the God-man Jesus Christ, in the unity of his divine and human nature. The human nature is neither an 'object' or an 'instrument' for the divine nature (Docetism), nor is it only the *man* Jesus of Nazareth; instead it is the God-man, or as Torrance neatly phrases it, "God *as* man,"[44] who brings about the redemption of the entire cosmos. Following the Chalcedonian formula, the subject[45] of humanity's redemption is God in his divine-human unity, and this redemption is therefore worked out by *one* united person, both fully divine and fully human—*vere Deus et vere homo*.

Calvin's forgoing of anhypostasia, due to his primary concern to maintain the distinction between the divine and human nature, led him to miss the insight that it is the one person in the unity of the two natures who accomplishes the work on the cross. As McCormack points out: "Because he [Calvin] had not reflected deeply enough on the anhypostasia of the human nature assumed in the incarnation, he was not able to see clearly that what

---

40. See Ibid.. 6.
41. Ibid.,14f.
42. Ibid., 15.
43. See ibid., 15.
44. Torrance, *The Trinitarian Faith*, 150.
45. McCormack stresses that in talking about 'subject' he does not mean *hypostasis* as such—instead, the subject is the *hypostasis* together with the two natures.

is accomplished in and through the human nature has to be attributed to the Logos as the Person of the union."[46]

Calvin sees original sin as "hereditary depravity and corruption of our nature, diffused into all parts of the soul, which first makes us liable to God's wrath."[47] He maintains that sinful humanity is guilty in a legal or forensic sense and for that reason is liable to be subjected to God's wrath and judgment. One of the passages in the New Testament that Calvin uses to link Christ's death with sin is 2 Cor 5:21: "He who had no sin became sin on our behalf." Calvin understands this passage as making use of the Suffering Servant of Isa 53, which he sees as a picture of Christ. He sees the sins that Christ bore on the cross as the guilt of humanity; these sins were made Christ's by "transferred imputation,"[48] just as the Lord laid the iniquity of Israel on the Servant of Isa 53:6. Thus, for Calvin, to be 'made sin' means that the "guilt that held us liable for punishment has been *transferred* to the head of the Son of God [Isa. 53:12]."[49] Calvin sees a divine verdict behind this transferal of sin and interprets being 'made sin' as a "judicial act of God in which the God-man is made liable for our sins and judged in our place."[50]

Furthermore, the sixteenth- and seventeenth-century Reformed understanding of the atonement was a "modified Anselmianism of Thomas Aquinas."[51] What this means is that the so-called 'satisfaction-theory' as advocated by Anselm underwent a very important modification under Aquinas. The theory is founded on the idea that through sin God's honor is offended and this demands satisfaction. Whereas Anselm had propagated a mutually exclusive 'either-or' theory between either satisfaction of this demand or punishment as an alternative, Aquinas picked up the two concepts and united them in his theory of satisfaction through punishment. Aquinas' view of the atonement can be regarded as Penal Substitutionary atonement: Christ offered himself to take the punishment (penal) and die the death that humanity deserves, by taking her place (substitution) by dying on the cross, freeing humanity from her sin. This death was understood in terms of 'punishment of sin' and 'satisfaction of the wrath of God' in response to humanity's sin.

This view of a Penal Substitutionary atonement might be seen as the linchpin of the Reformed understanding of the atonement to this day.

46. McCormack, *For Us and Our Salvation*, 32.
47. *Inst.* II.i.8, 251.
48. *Inst.* II.xvi.5, 510.
49. *Inst.* II.xvi.5, 509f. Italics mine.
50. McCormack, *For Us and Our Salvation*, 20.
51. Ibid., 25.

However, this view brings about one major error, which as McCormack has pointed out, has huge ramifications. The Penal Substitution idea propounds the idea that God the Father is appeased by the death of God the Son. In other words, the Reformed theologians endorsed a view of the atonement that might be seen as contradictory in that it posits a loving God who nevertheless is angry and wrathful towards humanity and must be 'turned back' to her through appeasement of his Son's death. Though Calvin is aware of the problem he leaves this contradiction to stand, regarding it as "accommodated to our capacity" something that we cannot fully comprehend with our limited understanding.[52] However, this view implies a change of heart in God's being. First, this is in itself is a contradiction in terms; secondly this view must assume that God's being and God's saving action are not in harmony. McCormack asks: "If God were not graciously and mercifully inclined toward the human race from the outset, why would He have sent His Son to redeem us?"[53]

In this way, Calvin's view makes God's mercy a 'prisoner' of God's righteousness, only capable of turning to the sinner when his righteous demands are fulfilled. The underlying understanding of the atonement is that "God revealed his love for us when he was reconciled to us by Christ's blood."[54] Thus, this interpretation is contingent upon the assumption that, because all humans are sinners and under judgment, God can neither ignore sin nor simply forgive repentant sinners, as his righteousness demands a penalty (since sin dishonors God, the only treatment the sinner deserves is death). Thus the only way salvation can be possible for a sinner is within the context of God gaining justice. The implication of this, however, is that God can only turn to the sinful person in mercy when his righteousness has been justified.[55] But since no human can achieve this perfection, the sinless Son of God himself becomes the instrument by giving himself as the sacrifice. With his bloody death on the cross the 'wrath of God' is stilled and only then can God show mercy to the sinner and be reconciled to humankind. This appears to resemble the heathen principle of *do ut des*: I (human) give, that you (God) give to me. It also appears to assume that the sinful person would offer the deity a sacrifice in order to effect a change of mood—from anger to mercy. The primary reasoning behind this argument is its separation of

52. *Inst.* II.xvii.2, 504. As Peterson, *Calvin and the Atonement*, points out, "[t]he relationship between God's love and his wrath makes a worthwhile study in Calvin's theology. Time and again in both the *Institutes* and the commentaries, Calvin refers to 'some sort of contradiction,' or 'inconsistency' between the love and wrath of God," 20.

53. McCormack, *For Us and Our Salvation*, 27.

54. Peterson, *Calvin and the Atonement*, 23.

55. See Hofius, "Sühne und Versöhnung," 34.

Jesus Christ the Judge 155

God's righteousness from God's mercy—to argue that God's righteousness punishes the sinful person and God's mercy comes only when the sinfulness of men has been punished—and this is to argue that the two aspects of God are fundamentally discrete. What is troubling with this theory is that it suggests God having two wills towards humanity.[56]

McCormack sees the notion of original sin as being conceived of as *inherited* depravity as a "fundamental flaw" in Calvin's theology.[57] He gives an alternative interpretation in which he grounds sin in Adam's primal decision to disobey God in which "each individual participates through his/her *own* primal decision to affirm the disordered relationship with God,"[58] making every person responsible for their own sin towards God. If this is the case, then Christ's life stands out as a life of entire obedience to the will of God, a life that stands firm against the primal decision of Adam from birth to death. This explanation opens the way to argue that Christ, though coming in human flesh, did not sin and thus did not have a sinful nature. This contrasts with the rest of humanity which, by making the primal decision to sin her own, shares in Adam's broken relationship with God. Christ achieves this life of obedience through the hypostatic union, which is the "work of the Spirit who brought together divine and human nature [...] who continually empowered the God-man in His life of obedience."[59] The

---

56. Calvin's theory of the atonement, in which God appears to have two wills towards humanity, reflects (and informs) that of many Christians. In his article, "Do We Believe in Penal Substitution?," Lewis highlights what he perceives as a myopic view of justice when it comes to the death of Christ, and though some of his presuppositions are questionable, he nevertheless provides a persuasive explanation for what he sees as the two-mindedness of Christians when it comes to justice in the context of Penal Substitution. Lewis highlights that it would be unheard of in any legal system for a murderer to go free because his friend offers to serve the death sentence for him (308f.). He also queries the function of the punishment of an innocent substitute and asks whether this would be just, concluding that "the substitutionary punishment of the innocent friend is never any reason to leave the offender unpunished," 310. In this way, Lewis concludes that Christians who have a penal understanding of the atonement are of two minds since "[a]lthough these Christian do believe in Penal Substitution in the context of theology, they do not seem to believe anything out of the ordinary in the context of the mundane criminal justice," 310. Crucially, "the heart of the rebuke against those Christians who explain the Atonement as a case of Penal Substitution is not that they are out of date and disagree with our 'intuitions.' Rather, it is that they disagree with what they themselves think the rest of the time," 310.

57. See McCormack, *For Us and Our Salvation*, 20f.

58. Ibid., 20. Italics mine.

59. Ibid., 21. The important point here is not simply that Christ suffered but that he was obedient despite suffering. Suffering thus becomes not an end in itself but rather a means to an end, obedience to the will of God.

Reformed theologians of the sixteenth and seventeenth century were unable to recognise their dilemma, arising from their view of original sin as hereditary. It was Barth's "'actualistic' ontology that enabled him to finally overcome this inconsistency and to integrate the God-man's life of obedience into the judicial framework within which he also interpreted the significance of the cross."[60] Barth does not see human nature in substantialist terms but understands nature to be a function of "decision and act."[61] What Barth means by the *assumptio carnis* is the self-election of the *Logos* from eternity to deal with human sin. Yet Barth had to face his own difficulties in shaping his doctrine of the atonement.

3. Barth on *Cur Deus Homo?*

Anselm's classic question *Cur Deus Homo?* forms the background to *CD* IV and Barth's excavation of the reconciling work of Christ.[62] Barth's description of the fourfold *pro nobis* provides an answer to Anselm's question. In §59, *The Obedience of the Son of God*, Barth discusses God's self-revelation in Jesus Christ coming to its fulfilment in the humiliation of the Son of God; he is the God, *Qui propter nos homines et propter nostram salutem descendit de cœlis*. For Barth it is not only that God descends from heaven to us, taking on sinful flesh, but also that he is willing to be 'The Judge Judged in Our Place.' Christ is obedient in going to the cross and becoming "our Representative and Substitute,"[63] taking upon himself our sins, judgment and condemnation. In this way, God's inner generosity is turned outwards and bestowed upon humanity. Whereas the Church has clearly defined the person of Christ in his divinity and humanity as one undivided person consisting of both the divine *Logos* and the human Jesus of Nazareth, no council has ever clearly defined the work of Christ—the atonement and his death on the cross. Theologians through the centuries have thus had the freedom to develop different concepts of the atonement, highlighting the atoning work of Christ from different biblical angles, themes, and historical circumstances.

---

60. Ibid., 22.
61. Ibid., 21.
62. See Klappert, *Die Auferweckung des Gekreuzigten*, 241.
63. *CD* IV/1, 230.

3.1. Die Sache Gottes and the Munus Triplex of Christ

Barth's objective in *CD* IV/1 is the revelation of *"Die Sache Gottes"*[64]—how he is known. This includes both God's being and his act; who he is and what he does. The message of reconciliation lies at the heart of theological undertaking itself and also of Barth's *CD*. It is here that we read that God takes the lost cause of humanity into himself and makes it *"zu seiner eigenen Sache"* in Jesus Christ.[65] In this way sin and human separation from God become primarily 'God's own business'; that is to say the business that he himself does, namely by dealing with sin on the cross where he has once and for all negated the problem of sin and humanity's rebellion and separation from him.[66] For Barth, "to say atonement is to say Jesus Christ."[67] Since the work of reconciliation is nothing less than the fulfilment of the covenant of grace from eternity between God and humanity, it is in this way that reconciliation becomes the centerpiece of God's work and thus the heart of the Christian faith.[68] He writes that "we enter that sphere of Christian knowledge in which we have to do with the heart of the message received by and laid upon the Christian community and therefore with the heart of the Church's dogmatics: that is to say, with the heart of its subject-matter," Jesus Christ.[69] Thus, in the preface Barth writes that "to fail here is to fail everywhere."[70] This sets the challenge of the task ahead not only for Barth but also for anyone who seeks to understand the full meaning of the Christian faith.

In *CD* IV we encounter Barth's most mature thought. For Webster it is "one of the incontestably great pieces of Christian literature of the century."[71] Topics that Barth dealt with in previous chapters such as revelation, the Trinity, incarnation, election, and Christology are woven together in one

---

64. See *KD* IV/1, 103.

65. *KD* IV/1, 1.

66. Barth deals with sin after dealing with reconciliation since "die Rede von der Versöhnung die Voraussetzung der Rede von der Sünde ist." See also Ruddies, "der Erniedrigung des Gottessohnes entspricht negativ der Hochmut des Sünders; der Erhöhung des Menschensohnes entspricht negativ die Trägheit des Sünders; dem wahrhaften Zeugnis des Gottmenschen entspricht negativ die Verlogenheit des in sich verkehrten Sünders," in Ruddies, "Christologie und Versöhnungslehre bei Karl Barth," 179.

67. *CD* IV/1, 157f.

68. See *CD* IV/1, 3.

69. *CD* IV/1, 3.

70. *CD* IV/1, ix.

71. Webster, *Barth*, 113.

multifaceted pattern resulting in his seminal work on reconciliation.[72] This, according to T. F. Torrance, "constitutes the most powerful work on the doctrine of atoning reconciliation ever written, in which Barth interweaves Patristic and Reformation insights into a single fabric."[73] *CD* IV—which is in one sense "nothing more than an extended paraphrase of the name of Jesus"[74] and God's work through him—centres around the God-man Jesus Christ (*CD* IV/3) as the divine-human agent of reconciliation. Barth harmonizes the unity of Christ's two natures and two states in a twofold parallel movement, "*die Doppelbewegung von versöhnendem Gott und versöhntem Menschen.*"[75] On the one hand, Barth posits Christ's humble deity and sacrificial condescension (*CD* IV/1) into alien territory of human sinfulness, into the far country to reconcile all things to himself (Col 1:20).[76] He writes: "In being gracious to man in Jesus Christ, he also goes into that far country, into the evil society of this being which is not God and against God."[77] On the other hand, Barth describes the victorious exaltation (*CD* IV/2) and homecoming of the Saviour's humanity in the ascension of the Son of Man.

Whereas theology had traditionally identified Christ's humanity with humiliation and his glorious ascension with his deity, Barth reverses this and "ties together the deity of Christ and his obedience, thereby pushing the lowliness of the incarnate one back into the being of God himself."[78] For Barth, it is the being of the Trinitarian God who chose to be *pro nobis*, for humanity, and thus it is Christ's deity that is humbled (rather than his humanity) and it is the humanity of Christ that is exalted in victory and triumph. He writes: "God is not proud. In his high majesty he is humble."[79] In his shortest formula Barth writes, "It was God who went into the far

---

72. See Webster, who writes that "the intellectual structure of the doctrine of reconciliation is complex: no section of the argument is discrete, each part simultaneously building upon and expanding the other (this is one reason why *Church Dogmatics* IV needs to be read as a whole). Moreover, far from offering simply a treatment of the doctrine of salvation, the treatise interweaves Christology, soteriology, harmatiology (the doctrine of sin), pneumatology, ecclesiology and a theology of the Christian life," in Webster, *Barth*. 114f.

73. Torrance, *Karl Barth: Biblical and Evangelical Theologian*, 133.

74. Webster, *Barth*, 116.

75. Klappert, "Gott in Christus—Versöhner der Welt," 143.

76. Here Barth follows a narrative approach using the Christ-hymn of Phil 2:6ff. and the story of the Prodigal Son of Luke 15.

77. *CD* IV/1, 158.

78. Webster, *Barth*, 115.

79. *CD* IV/1, 159.

country, and it was man who returns home."⁸⁰ This statement should be read in the light of the pattern of exchange we encountered in the doctrine of election where Barth's short formula was "God wills to lose in order that man may gain."⁸¹

Barth divides his systematic outworking of the doctrine of reconciliation and atonement, his soteriology (*De applicatione salutis*), into three parts.⁸² The underlying notion of this scheme is that God is the subject of the whole event, both the *auctor* and *applicator salutis*. When he elaborates on the work and person of Christ, he follows Calvin's Reformed tradition in referring to the *munus triplex*, the threefold office of Christ as prophet, priest, and king—*munus propheticum, munus sacerdotale,* and *munus regium*. However, he changes the sequence: (1) the 'Son of God' as the 'Lord as Servant' (*CD* IV/1) fulfils the priestly work in his condescension, self-emptying and taking the judgment upon himself in obedience to the Father's will which led him to the cross; (2) the 'Son of Man' as the 'Servant as Lord' (*CD* IV/2) fulfils the kingly work in his exaltation of man; and (3) the 'God-Man' as the 'true Witness' (*CD* IV/3) fulfils the prophetic work as Mediator between God and man.⁸³ However, Barth emphasizes that in the same way that Christ's person and work should not to be seen separately, neither should his offices be seen separately and studied in isolation from each other. They all should be seen as three aspects of the same life and work of Christ and must be seen as one holistic picture. To split them up into three offices in the first place is only done by Barth to explain the redemptive work of Christ in its full scope and to highlight and illuminate different aspects of Christ's saving act. But in the end they are all aspects of the same event, and have to be seen as a whole.

---

80. *CD* IV/2, 21. However, God's 'humiliation' is suddenly identified much more with the incarnation than the cross. In *CD* IV Barth is influenced by patristic thought and is moving away from the seventeenth-century theology of an atonement of punishment as witnessed in *CD* II/2. It is God's humiliation (Phil 2:6ff), his sacrificial condescension, that brings about humanity's salvation.

81. *CD* II/2, 162.

82. For the threefold office of Christ in the *CD* see Butin, "Two Early Reformed Catechisms, The Threefold Office, and the Shape of Karl Barth's Christology," 200–205.

83. For the structure of the *CD* see Jüngel, "Einführung in Leben und Werk Karl Barths," 55.

3.2. 'The Judge Judged in Our Place'

In §59, *The Obedience of the Son of God*, Barth lays the christological groundwork for his doctrine of reconciliation,[84] which centres on the incarnation and the atonement of Christ.[85] Here we read about the divinity of the Son of God, the subject of reconciliation, who goes into the far country. Barth highlights the "manner in which his elect path of humiliation and death is the manifestation of the true majesty of God."[86] The underlying notion is the 'high humility' of Christ in the condescension of grace.[87] This is the hermeneutical key for §59—Jesus' willingness, humility and obedience to go into the far country in order to reconcile a lost world to God (2 Cor 5:19).[88] But how is it possible for God to assume the form of a servant [*forma servi*]? Barth explains this with a Trinitarian theology of incarnation and atonement. Barth sees Christ's humility in the incarnation as grounded in the very being of God, who is free and able to act in this way. Barth's way of dealing with this is to "trace the work of God in the economy of salvation back into the immanent being of God and, correspondingly, to determine the nature of that immanent being from God's works in salvation."[89] God is what he does; his works point to his being and highlight his very essence. The significance of this is that the work of reconciliation manifests "a movement or relation within God himself."[90] God chose condescension in Jesus Christ and therefore "we can speak of an obedience of the one true God Himself in His proper being."[91] Thus in his humiliation God does not cease to be God: "God is always God even in His humiliation."[92] It is this humility that embodies God's sovereignty, which is nothing else than God's self-emptying (Phil 2:6ff.). God humbled himself and became incarnate in the flesh, and "to be flesh is to be in a state of perishing before God."[93]

---

84. Zum Aufbau der Versöhnungslehre Barths see Ruddies, "Christologie und Versöhnungslehre bei Karl Barth," 179–86.

85. See Webster, *Barth*, 120.

86. Webster, *Barth*, 120.

87. See *CD* IV/1, 159. It is with this 'high humility' that he speaks and acts as the God who reconciles the world to himself.

88. For more on the theme of Jesus' divine/human obedience see Jones, *The Humanity of Christ*, 203–29.

89. Webster, *Barth*, 121f.

90. Ibid., 121.

91. *CD* IV/1, 200.

92. *CD* IV/1, 179.

93. *CD* IV/1, 175.

In the presentation of Jesus' atoning work in §59, Barth follows three phases depicted in the Gospel narratives, moving from (1) the *subject* of reconciliation in his life, to (2) the *object* of God's wrath on the cross, and finally to (3) the vindication by the Father.[94] The three interrelated themes are as follows: 'The Way of the Son of God into the Far Country' deals with Christ's condescension and coming among sinful humanity; in 'The Judge Judged in Our Place' Barth expounds Christ's taking the sins of humanity and thus judgment upon himself and dying vicariously on the cross;[95] and in 'The Verdict of the Father' he talks about Jesus' vindication through the resurrection from the dead on Easter morning.[96]

Our focus here is on the question of atonement and we will therefore look at the second section, where Barth concentrates on Jesus as the judged Judge.[97] Here we see Barth's reconceptualization of the high priestly office of Christ. In explaining the 'Judge Judged,' Barth uses a juridical model and mixes the cultic concept of the atonement with a forensic one when he goes on to say that Christ dies *pro nobis*, 'in our place.' Barth writes: "*Es hängt alle weitere Theologie—es hing ja auch schon die ganze, der Versöhnungslehre vorangehende Theologie an dieser, der theologia crucis, in dem besonderen Licht, in dem sie als Lehre der Stellvertretung [. . .] zu entfalten war.*"[98] He illustrates this from four angles, the fourfold "in our place" (*vierfache Stellvertretung*):[99]

94. *CD* IV/1, 224-28. Here Barth highlights Jesus' atoning work life, death and resurrection. On this point see also Jones, *The Humanity of Christ*, 155.

95. See Webster who writes: "What Barth is doing here is pulling into one complex arrangement blocks of dogmatic material from the Christian tradition: the Chalcedonian notion of Jesus Christ as 'true God,' and two themes from older Protestant dogmatics, that of the 'state of humiliation' of the incarnate one and that of the priestly office of Christ in which he effects reconciliation between God and sinners," in Webster, *Barth*, 115.

96. Here Barth argues against Bultmann that the resurrection does not belong to an ahistorical realm but is an historical fact. He writes: "It has happened in the same sense as his crucifixion and his death, in the human sphere and human time, as an actual event within the world with an objective content," in *CD* IV/1, 333.

97. Klappert says that "der Richter als der an unserer Stelle Gerichtete [. . .] ist in nuce der Inhalt des §52,2 der Versöhnungslehre," in also Klappert, *Die Auferweckung des Gekreuzigten*, 194. See 4.Kapitel: Der Tataspekt der Versöhnung im Kreuz, 194-225.

98. *KD* IV/1, 300. Note here that the German word *Stellvertretung* has both meanings—that of substitution as well as representation. See Janowski, "He Bore Our Sins: Isaiah 53 and the Drama of Taking Another's Place," 52-54.

99. *CD* IV/1, 273. See Bakker, "Jesus als Stellvertreter für unsere Sünden und sein Verhältnis zu Israel bei Karl Barth," 39f., who writes "dass wir uns mit der Lehre über die vierfache Stellvertretung im Zentrum der Barthschen Theologie befinden," 40. Furthermore, Bakker highlights that the temptation narratives in the desert already

"He took our place as Judge. He took our place as the judged. He was judged in our place. And He acted justly in our place."[100] This for Barth, is the *"enge Pforte"* around which there is no way. If the fourfold 'for us' does not stand firm, he says, then everything else, including the salvation of humanity, will sooner or later break and fall to the ground.[101] What becomes immediately apparent in Barth's understanding of Jesus' *Stellvertretung* is that he identifies Jesus as judged, convicted and condemned instead of humanity, and dying in humanity's place as the one great sinner who made repentance.[102]

(A) Jesus' Stellvertretung Pro Nobis

Jesus' *Stellvertretung pro nobis* is what Barth means when he identifies Jesus as "the first and greatest sinner"[103] who stands in solidarity with sinful humanity and stands against God on the cross. This is the way he sees John 1, the Word became flesh: "To be flesh means to exist with the 'children' of Israel under the wrath and judgment of the electing and loving God. To be flesh is to be in a state of perishing before this God."[104] Barth sees Jesus as taking the place of the disobedient son described in the Old Testament.[105] Yet he does not end here; he goes on to say that "in the one Israelite Jesus it was God Himself who as the Son of the Father made Himself the object of this accusation and willed to confess Himself a sinner, and to be regarded and dealt with as such [. . .] in the person of the one Israelite in whom God Himself has come amongst sinners in the form of a sinner."[106] We see that for Barth the baptism of Jesus in the River Jordan is of significance and stands in close relationship to the cross as well as identifying Jesus as the disobedient son of the Old Testament. At his baptism, Jesus not only shows his solidarity with sinful humanity but, according to Barth, goes even further. Jesus, who

---

mirror and precede the *vierfache Stellvertretung*. See also Maurer, "'Für uns': An unserer Stelle hingerichtet. Die Herausforderung der Versöhnungslehre." As well as Webster, *Barth*, 121f. and Klappert, *Die Auferweckung des Gekreuzigten*, 198–223.

100. *CD* IV/1, 273.

101. See *CD* IV/1, 273.

102. See Bakker, "Jesus als Stellvertreter für unsere Sünden und sein Verhältnis zu Israel bei Karl Barth," 40.

103. *CD* IV/3, 653.

104. *CD* IV/1, 174f.

105. See *CD* IV/1, 171.

106. *CD* IV/1, 172.

himself is without sin, decides to step into our place as a sinner. This, Barth explains, is the relationship between Jordan, Gethsemane and the cross:

> It was a matter of the obedience and penitence in which Jesus had persisted coming to fruition in His own rejection and condemnation—not by chance, but according to the plan of God Himself, not superficially, but in serious earnest. That was what came upon Him in His suffering and dying, as God's answer to His appeal.[107]

"*Es ging um das Trinken des Kelches des göttlichen Zornes.*"[108] Here Barth is in line with the *Heidelberger Katechismus*[109] where it says that "during the whole time of His life on earth Jesus [...] bore the wrath of God against the sin of the whole human race";[110] he is "the judge who 'has represented me before the judgment of God, and has taken away all cursing from me.'"[111] Barth concludes that "*He* stands under the wrath and judgment of God, *He* is broken and destroyed on God. It cannot be otherwise. It has to be like this."[112] For Barth, the removal or rather the "battle against sin"[113] is the main purpose, the heart of the atonement and the passion, "the radical divine action which attacks and destroys at its very root the primary evil in the world."[114] Thus the cross shows the *Gottesferne*, the separation of God and humanity:

> The very heart of the atonement is the overcoming of sin: sin in its character as the rebellion of man against God, and in its character as the ground of man's hopeless destiny in death. It was to fulfil this judgment on sin that the Son of God as man took our place as sinners. He fulfils it—as man in our place—by

---

107. *CD* IV/1, 271.

108. *KD* IV/1, 298. The English translation omits this sentence: "Es ging darum, daß die Frucht des Gehorsams und der Buße, in der Jesus verharrt hatte—nicht von ungefähr, sondern nach Gottes eigenem Plan, nicht nur auf der Oberfläche, sondern in letztem Ernst—seine eigene Verwerfung und Verdammnis sein sollte. Es ging um das Trinken des Kelches des göttlichen Zornes. Das war es, was in seinem Leiden und Sterben auf ihn zukam: als Gottes Antwort auf die Anrede seines Gebetes!" See also Bakker, "Jesus als Stellvertreter für unsere Sünden und sein Verhältnis zu Israel bei Karl Barth," 50.

109. See questions 14, 17 and 37.

110. See *CD* IV/1, 165.

111. See *CD* IV/1, 211.

112. *CD* IV/1, 175.

113. *CD* IV/1, 254.

114. *CD* IV/1, 254.

> completing our work in the omnipotence of the divine Son, by treading the way of sinners to its bitter end in death, in destruction, in the limitless anguish of separation from God, by delivering up sinful man and sin in His own person to the nonbeing which is properly theirs, the nonbeing, the nothingness to which man has fallen victim as a sinner and towards which he relentlessly hastens. We can say indeed that He fulfils this judgment by suffering the punishment which we have all brought on ourselves.[115]

Maurer highlights the way that Barth describes the destruction of sin, specifically as the destruction of sin from within:[116] "Jesus Christ tore up this tissue once and for all and disclosed the real truth of sin by confessing Himself one with sinners, by making their situation His own, by declaring and creating His own solidarity with them, by undertaking to represent their case before God—the case of sinners."[117] Maurer writes: "*Der Sünder muss aufs Kreuz gelegt werden.*"[118] At the cross, in the

> death of Jesus Christ it has come to pass that in His own person He has made an end of us as sinners and therefore of sin itself by going to death as the One who took our place as sinners. In His person He has delivered up us sinners and sin itself to destruction. He has removed us sinners and sin, negated us, cancelled us out: ourselves, our sin, and the accusation, condemnation and perdition which had overtaken us.[119]

Thus for Barth, the cross is the sign of an enactment of God's judgment, his *No* to the sinful creature. The *Deus pro nobis* means that "God in Jesus Christ has taken our place when we become sinners, when we become His enemies, when we stand as such under His accusation and curse, and bring upon ourselves our own destruction."[120] For Barth "the passion of Jesus

---

115. *CD* IV/1, 253.

116. Maurer, "'Für uns': An unserer Stelle hingerichtet. Die Herausforderung der Versöhnungslehre," 192. "Die Struktur wird nicht etwa aufgehoben, sondern *von innen* gesprengt." Maurer has highlighted that Barth thinks that "all sin has its being and origin in the fact that man wants to be his own judge. And in wanting to be that, and thinking and acting accordingly, he and his whole world is in conflict with God. It is an unreconciled world, and therefore a suffering world, a world given up to destruction," in *CD* IV/1, 220.

117. *CD* IV/1, 404.

118. Maurer, "'Für uns': An unserer Stelle hingerichtet. Die Herausforderung der Versöhnungslehre," 192.

119. *CD* IV/1, 253f.

120. *CD* IV/1, 216.

Christ is the judgment of God in which the Judge Himself was the judged. And as such it is at its heart and centre the victory which has been won for us, in our place, in the battle against sin."[121] This reconciliation occurs in Jesus Christ and Barth even goes so far as to say that "*Jesus Christus ist die Versöhnung*," because he is all three, the agent of reconciliation and the one who carries it out as well as the one who mediates its effects.

We will see that Barth's second point, that Jesus makes an end by delivering up the sinner and dying on the cross, stands in close proximity to the concept of *Existenzstellvertretung*. Barth says that the "cross is teleologically ordered to the resurrection"[122] and warns against an abstract preaching of the cross without the resurrection, saying that the *No* of God spoken against Jesus on the cross is not an end in itself but is spoken only in service of God's *Yes* in the resurrection. This *Yes* is eventually spoken to all of humanity and to the "community [that] lives by the fact that the first and final Word of God is this Yes."[123] However, we have to disagree with Barth's first point where he talks about God's *No*, Jesus standing *under* the wrath and destruction of God. Pannenberg points out that the Son's offering himself up on the cross is not "identical with his rejection by the Father."[124] In fact, Jesus was rejected by others and "precisely herein he was not rejected by this Father. Instead he was obedient to the mission he had received from the Father."[125] It is this obedience to the will of the Father that is confirmed in the resurrection. As we have already seen, the heart of the atonement is not simply the overcoming of sin, but also the reconciliation achieved—the renewed covenantal fellowship between God and humanity.

(b) Christology and Gethsemane

Barth's mature Christology in *CD* IV has its foundation in and derives its framework from the doctrine of election of grace that he expounded in *CD* II/2.[126] In *CD* II/2 we read about the covenant of grace from all eternity and in *CD* IV we read about what God in Christ was willing to do to uphold this covenant. We have seen that, for Barth, Jesus Christ is "both electing God and elected man in one,"[127] the God-man to whom both "the active

---

121. *CD* IV/1, 254.
122. Mangina, *Theologian of Christian Witness*, 128.
123. *CD* IV/1, 347.
124. Pannenberg, *Systematic Theology Vol. 3*, 452.
125. Ibid., 452.
126. See Jones, "Karl Barth on Gethsemane," 154.
127. *CD* II/2, 3.

determination of electing" as well as "the passive determination of election" are attributed.[128] Furthermore we saw that this duality is accompanied by another duality—that of 'election and reprobation' in Jesus Christ. These two sides of the doctrine of election, of 'election and reprobation' that we see in CD II/2 correspond to and are closely linked with (one might say are the counterparts of) God's condescension and humility in going to the cross that we see in CD IV/1; as well as humanity's exaltation and ascension into the Triune life of the Godhead that we see in CD IV/2. In this way, election is linked with humanity's exaltation and reprobation is linked to God's condescension.

Many commentators have criticized Barth for not saying enough about Christ's humanity, arguing that his Christology seems unbalanced, or worse, even tends towards a mild form of Docetism.[129] In considering Barth's view of the role of Christ's human identity and agency in the atonement, we must also take into account his treatment of the Gethsemane story (Mark 14:32–42). Jones gives an account of Barth's understanding of Christ's humanity and agony in light of Gethsemane and the cross in §59,[130] contending that "Barth views Jesus' humanity as a history in motion, propelled towards crisis; an event of justificatory responsibility; a struggle that marks both the life of God and the life of all human beings; and finally, a key moment in a covenantal relationship that rejects sin and evil."[131]

The passage referring to Gethsemane in §59.2 is short yet, like the Leviticus passages in CD II/2, it plays a vital part in understanding Barth's view of Christ's humanity in the atonement. Jones summarizes the events and the significance of Gethsemane: "Jesus confronts what it means for him to be 'flesh,' and therefore subject to judgment. [. . .] Jesus realizes that his life constitutes the exclusive point of conflict between what humankind intends for itself (sin and the propagation of evil) and what God intends for humanity (freedom in companionship with God)."[132] Barth portrays Jesus

---

128. CD II/2, 103.

129. See Jones, "Karl Barth on Gethsemane," footnote 2. See also Jones, *The Humanity of Christ*, which comprehensively redresses the complaint.

130. See Jones, "Karl Barth on Gethsemane," passim. Paul Dafydd Jones has done an excellent job in analyzing these fourteen pages and my interpretation builds heavily upon his work. I am indebted to Ashley Cocksworth for directing me to this article. See also Bakker, "Jesus als Stellvertreter für unsere Sünden und sein Verhältnis zu Israel bei Karl Barth," who highlights that the temptation narratives in the desert are the key to understanding Gethsemane and the death on the cross, as well as Jones, *The Humanity of Christ*, 229–42 (much of what Jones writes here parallels his article).

131. Jones, "Karl Barth on Gethsemane," 149.

132. Ibid., 157.

in Gethsemane as coming to terms with the fact that he has been assigned an exclusive role in God's salvific work, distinct from that of anyone else, but one that also requires him to bear the burden of a dark and negative side—the judgment and condemnation of the sins of humanity in his own body on the cross. He must offer himself so that divine justice can be executed upon him. Barth asserts that Jesus willingly and freely agrees to "bear shame and curse in the place of all."[133] By putting the old nature to death a new creation, a new human being, can come forth through Christ's resurrection. Barth writes that in his election as the one 'elected human' and in his identification in the incarnation with the σάρξ (flesh) Christ ends his earthly life in death, judgment, and rejection.[134] In the garden pericope, he comes to the realization that "his identity as the 'elected human,' assumed by the 'electing God,' must ultimately result in his demise as the 'rejected human,' assumed by the 'rejected God.'"[135] Similarly, Barth writes:

> Taking our place, bearing the judgment of our sin, undertaking our case, He gave Himself to the depth of the most utter helplessness in which He could not and would not dispose even of the help of God, the depth in which He had nothing but nothingness under and behind and beside Him, and nothing but God before and above Him—nothingness in all its unsearchableness and power, and God as the One into whose Hands He was delivered up without reservation and without claim—He the man who was Himself also the Son of God. He did this for us. This is—in its sharpest form—the humility of the act of God which took place for us in Jesus Christ.[136]

In Gethsemane we are confronted with Jesus' struggle to understand God's mysterious means of reconciliation; Barth says that for all Jesus knows at that stage, the work of reconciliation might not only incorporate his death, but might terminate altogether with his death on the cross. So the question that Jesus brings before God in his petition of prayer is whether it really has to happen. Is his death on the cross really the only way to judge sin? And is the cross really the place where God's love for humanity will be revealed? The riddle posited by Barth sits right at the centre of this study:

> that of the impending *unity* between *the will of God* on the one hand, that will which He had hitherto obeyed, and which He

---

133. *CD* IV/1, 59.
134. See Jones, *The Humanity of Christ*, 43.
135. Jones, "Karl Barth on Gethsemane," 158.
136. *CD* IV/1, 458.

> willed to obey in all circumstances and whatever it was, that will which He was quite ready should be done—and, on the other hand, *the power of evil* which He had withstood, and which He willed to withstand in all circumstances and in whatever form He might encounter it, which He could not allow to be done.[137]

Furthermore, Gethsemane plays an integral part in Barth's understanding of both the working out of the covenant in history and his understanding of God's rejection of sin and evil. Barth asserts that the reconciliation between God and humanity hinges upon Jesus' free choice and obedience to the will of the Father to take the punishment of the cross upon himself for the salvation of the world. At the end of this struggle, he acts according to and in line with the Father's will—"a radiant *Yes* to the actual will of God"—and thus "stands upright with a supreme pride"[138] "(this pride undermining and replacing the sinful pride that §60 describes) setting out to crucify himself."[139] This '*strahlende Ja*' "uttered in the face of the worst of all possible ends, the terror of rejection by God, anchors the covenant as a deliberate and agential relationship between God and humankind."[140]

But what is the answer Jesus receives from his petitions from his Father? Barth writes the following words:

> The answer which Jesus receives is in itself this and no other, this answer which was no answer, to which His prayer itself alluded. Note that it came in the same language in which Satan now spoke with Him as the prince of this aeon, triumphantly avenging His contradiction and opposition in the wilderness. *The will of God was done as the will of Satan was done. The answer of God was identical with the action of Satan.* That was the frightful thing. The coincidence of the divine and the satanic will and work and word was the problem of this hour, the darkness in which Jesus addressed God in Gethsemane.[141]

So what Barth does is to juxtapose the will of God and the will of evil and bring them together in a synthesis on the cross.[142] The way God deals with sin on the cross, according to Barth, is to judge sin in the Son. For Barth,

---

137. *CD* IV/1, 269, italics mine

138. *CD* IV/1, 270, italics mine.

139. Jones, "Karl Barth on Gethsemane," 162f. See also, John 10:17–18.

140. Ibid., 163.

141. *CD* IV/1, 268. Italics mine.

142. See Maurer, "'Für uns': An unserer Stelle hingerichtet. Die Herausforderung der Versöhnungslehre," on Gethsemane: "Hier kommt es zur Kongruenz von Sünde und Gottes Willen [. . .] Gottes Wille geschieht, indem Satans Wille geschieht," 208.

das Nichtige, which threatens not only humanity but also the whole world, is therefore being punished in the Son. In this way, God's action against *das Nichtige* is the identical action he operates against his Son—punishment and reprobation. On the cross, the Son and sin are seen as identical and thus the Son on the cross becomes the symbol of rejection. Jones highlights that, for Barth, the key point is that in "Gethsemane, Jesus discerns that God intends to *utilize evil* to effect both the abolition of evil and God's punishment of sin."[143] We have seen through the Gethsemane pericope that Barth links the wrath of God and Jesus' death on the cross directly with the will of God. For Barth the key point is that Jesus realizes at Gethsemane that God is willing to utilize evil to fight evil. The reason to link the will of the devil so closely with the will of God, indeed to make them identical on the cross, is to safeguard the sovereignty of God and to close any door which might lead to the portrayal of the cross as a victory of the evil one, as something that happens against the will of God. In this way, the sovereignty of God is safeguarded and the devil and the powers of evil simply become "involuntary instruments" in the hand of God.[144]

Yet we have to ask Barth whether this is the only way to talk about the cross and whether we can say that the will of the devil is in line with the will of God. If the devil becomes the instrument of God, does this not mean that God indirectly does evil? We have already heard in Barth's doctrine of nothingness about God's 'non-willing.' However, what Barth seems to imply is that God is not only the 'author' of the passion but wills and thus utilizes evil to fight evil.[145] So we have to ask whether the relationship Barth draws between the cross and the will of God provides a false synthesis and whether it is congruent with the biblical witness.

(c) THE QUESTION *CUR DEUS HOMO?*

When looking at the concept of election it was interesting to look at how Barth differs from Calvin. When considering the atonement, however, it is Anselm who is Barth's main interlocutor. So how does Barth answer the

---

143. Jones, "Karl Barth on Gethsemane," 166f. Italics added.

144. CD IV/1, 272. Bakker, "Jesus als Stellvertreter für unsere Sünden und sein Verhältnis zu Israel bei Karl Barth," 50. Bakker asks a valid question: "Denn was hat es noch für eine Bedeutung, dass Jesus, stellvertretend für Israel, den Zorn Gottes auf sich genommen hat, wenn auch danach noch das jüdische Volk ein Zeichen für den Zorn Gottes in der Welt ist?," in ibid., 51.

145. "Die Passion is Aktion Gottes, weil Gott seinen eigenen Zorn in kreativer Weise erträgt," in Maurer, "'Für uns': An unserer Stelle hingerichtet. Die Herausforderung der Versöhnungslehre," 194.

Anselmian question? Barth's interpretation of Jesus' death on the cross appears *prima facie* to be very similar to Anselm's teaching of satisfaction. Anselm's question *Cur Deus Homo?* finds resonance in and is repeated by Barth, becoming his own question.

> Jesus Christ has to be the Judge, the judged and in His own person the fulfilment of the judgment; His decisive work and word has to be His suffering and dying. [. . .] The suffering and death of Jesus Christ are the No of God in and with which He again takes up and asserts in man's space and time the Yes to man which He has determined and pronounced in eternity. [. . .] *Cur Deus homo?* Because God, who became man in His Son, willed in this His Yes to do this work of His, [. . .] this work for the reconciliation of the world.[146]

However, it would be false to assume that Barth's approach is identical to Anselm's. Barth differentiates his view of Christ's death from Anselm's by critiquing his theory of satisfaction, saying that it is not simply a 'theory.' Indeed, Barth explicitly rejects any theory that contends that Jesus makes 'satisfaction' to the Father, even though he says that Jesus '*satis fecit*' over against the wrath of God.[147] Furthermore, for Barth it is not the 'satisfaction' of an offended God that is at the heart of Christ's reconciling work but the *Stellvertretung pro nobis*. The aim of Christ's death on the cross is not the punishment of a crime, a *quid pro quo*, but the destruction of the 'old man.' On the cross the old sinful human being is sacrificed and eliminated.[148] Therefore, Barth says that the "man of sin, the first Adam, the cosmos alienated from God [. . .] was taken and killed and buried in and with Him on the cross."[149]

Though Barth explicitly states that his atonement theology is different from that of Anselm, we have to probe this further and ask whether this is actually the case. McMaken highlights the "pattern of exchange"[150] in Barth's forensic treatment of atonement and argues that though God's righteous judgment is in the service of God's mercy (God's No serving God's Yes), Barth's understanding of the atonement in *CD* II/1 retains the character of

---

146. *CD* IV/1, 257.

147. See *CD* IV/1, 276.

148. See Bakker, "Jesus als Stellvertreter für unsere Sünden und sein Verhältnis zu Israel bei Karl Barth," 44.

149. *CD* IV/1, 254.

150. McMaken explores 'the pattern of exchange' in Barth's exposition of the doctrine of atonement and the forensic decision of election, in "Election and the Pattern of Exchange in Karl Barth's Doctrine of Atonement," passim.

"Penal Substitution,"[151] because it is still the "wrath of God that is satisfied in Christ's death."[152] Thus we have to ask who the first Adam is, this 'old man' to which Barth is referring. Barth's answer is that it is Jesus Christ in the *Stellvertretung pro nobis*, for sinners. In the process of Christ's *Stellvertretung*, humanity's sin becomes his and he takes her place as a sinner. "Our sin is no longer our own. It is His sin, the sin of Jesus Christ."[153] Barth specifically says that the suffering and death of Christ are not a substitutionary punishment in order to bring about God's satisfaction, yet the death of Christ is the consequence of humanity's transferred sin. In this way, Barth argues, Jesus died in our place and took the punishment of sin upon himself, enduring the wrath of God that was due to each sinner and rescuing humanity from eternal death.

> That is what happened when Jesus Christ, who willed to make Himself the bearer and Representative of sin, caused sin to be taken and killed on the cross in His own person (as that of the one great sinner). And in that way, not by suffering our punishment as such, but in the deliverance of sinful man and sin itself to destruction, which He accomplished when He suffered our punishment, He has on the other side blocked the source of our destruction; He has seen to it that we do not have to suffer what we ought to suffer; He has removed the accusation and condemnation and perdition which had passed upon us; He has cancelled their relevance to us; He has saved us from destruction and rescued us from eternal death.[154]

Therefore for Barth, God executes a punishing *iustitia distributiva* on Jesus and sees the passion of Jesus resulting in his death as "the judgment of God in which the Judge Himself was the judged."[155] And because the wrath of God is executed upon Jesus and the judgment substituted as a penalty by him, God does not need to exact it directly upon the sinner.[156] Thomas highlights that Barth argues for a model of "*exklusiver Stellvertretung*" and how this makes it possible for Barth to hold up divine justice and to link it

---

151. Ibid., 206.
152. Ibid., 206.
153. *CD* IV/1, 238.
154. *CD* IV/1, 254.
155. *CD* IV/1, 254.
156. See Thomas, "Der für uns gerichtete Richter," who says that "[i]n diesem Sinne ermöglicht die Stellvertretung des Sohnes es Gott, die distributive orientierte Rechtsordnung aufrecht zu erhalten und *zugleich* gegenüber den Sündern barmherzig zu sein," 212.

with divine love.[157] He says that Anselm had argued that either "*necesse est ut omne peccatum satisfactione aut poena sequatur*"[158] and that Barth has chosen, within the alternative given by Anselm, *punishment*.[159]

Thomas is right to question Barth about his conception of divine righteousness, which seems to divide into destructive righteousness when it comes to Jesus and a saving righteousness when it comes to the sinful creature.[160] He further asks whether this conception of justice—that of the deadly judgment of wrath of the Father against the Son—drives a wedge between Father and Son and breaks the *vinculum amoris*. How does the destruction of the Son on the cross correspond with Barth's statement in *CD* II/2 where he says that "*Gott ist in seiner überströmenden Herrlichkeit ganz und gar schenkende Liebe: Liebe, die nicht das Ihre sucht, sondern das, was des Andern ist?*"[161] Can God as the Father be so different in his Father-relation towards his Son, who is also the person Jesus of Nazareth, than the Son is in relation to humanity?[162]

Furthermore, does this not raise additional questions, both about Barth's portrayal of the immanent Trinity as a "determination of the love of the Father and the Son in the fellowship of the Holy Ghost,"[163] and also about the economic Trinity and whether they are congruent in their being and act? Barth writes:

> In Him it comes to pass for the first time that God wills and posits another being different from Himself, His creature. Be it noted that this determination of the will of God, this content of predestination, is already grace, for God did not stand in need of any particular ways or works *ad extra*. He had no need of a creation. He might well have been satisfied with the inner glory of His threefold being.[164]

---

157. Ibid., 212. Thomas is right that Barth argues a case for '*exklusive Stellvertretung*' when talking about Christ's work *pro nobis*. However it is also the case that at different places he argues for a concept of '*inklusive Stellvertretung*.' For the two concepts of '*exkludierende*' and '*inkludierende*' Stellvertretung see Hofius, "Sühne und Versöhnung," 41.

158. Anselm von Canterbury, *Cur Deus Homo*, 50.

159. See Thomas, "Der für uns gerichtete Richter," 212 as well as footnote 5 for Barth's understanding of God's honour.

160. See ibid., 213.

161. *KD* II/2, 190. The English translation does not entirely convey the point here.

162. See Thomas, "Der für uns gerichtete Richter," footnote 7.

163. *CD* II/2, 169.

164. *CD* II/2, 121.

Before we give answers to the questions raised in section 3, we need to look once more at Barth's understanding of the fourfold *pro nobis*.

4. Jesus the High Priest

At the end of what are probably *the* most important sections in the *CD* dealing with reconciliation and Anselm's question *Cur Deus Homo?* (Barth's forensic discussion of the atonement in §59.2 and the fourfold *pro nobis* of what Jesus Christ was and has done for us as 'The Judge Judged in Our Place') we encounter Barth's discussion of cultic sacrifice and Christ's role as High Priest in IV/1 of the *CD* in an excursus.[165] At the end of his discussion about this juridical framework, Barth says that everything else he asserts "depends upon the fact that [...] the Judge [was] judged in our place. All theology, both that which follows and indeed that which precedes the doctrine of reconciliation, depends upon this *theologica crucis*,"[166] and the doctrine of *Stellvertretung*.[167] He goes on to say that nothing other than "Amen" can be added to this statement and that he needs to come to a "full-stop" because the above "statement is complete in itself" and can "stand alone."[168] However, in some ways Barth ignores his own statement and immediately launches into an excursus about the cultic language of sacrifice in the New Testament. He explains his reason for doing this as follows:

> When we spoke of Jesus Christ as Judge and judged, and of His judgment and justice, we were adopting a definite standpoint and terminology as the framework in which to present our view of the *pro nobis*. In order to speak with dogmatic clarity and distinctness we had to decide on a framework of this kind. And the actual importance of this way of thinking and its particularly good basis in the Bible were a sufficient reason for choosing this one.[169]

So his reasons for presenting a second framework to describe the meaning of Christ's death is that "exegesis reminds us that in the New Testament there are other standpoints and terminologies which might equally be considered as guiding principles for dogmatics" and as guiding principles for

---

165. *CD* IV/1, 273–83.
166. *CD* IV/1, 273f.
167. See *KD* IV/1, 300.
168. *CD* IV/1, 273.
169. *CD* IV/1, 273.

"systematic reflection on the *pro nobis*."[170] In particular, what Barth wants to do is to test such cultic language against the fourfold juridical framework that he has just proposed and prove that everything he has said through forensic terminology could also be stated through cultic language. He explains the reasons for his using forensic rather than cultic language,[171] arguing that he first refrained from it because "material which is already difficult would have been made even more difficult by trying to understand it in a form which is now rather remote from us"; and second, that one can see the matter "better and more distinctly and more comprehensively [...] from the forensic area [...] than would have been possible [through the] cultic view."[172] This notion, of the forensic priority over the cultic, will be challenged in this chapter.

4.1. The Cultic Pro Nobis

In the excursus on the cultic atonement, Barth's main focus with sacrifice is *reconciliation*. He uses the cultic terminology of sacrifice in the Bible to support his juridical framework of the doctrine of reconciliation which he has established in *CD* IV/1, to describe what God has done '*pro nobis*' in Jesus Christ. He recapitulates his forensic description point-by-point in cultic terms. Just as Jesus Christ is the sole agent of atonement under Barth's juridical framework ('The Judge Judged in Our Place'), Jesus Christ is also the sole agent in the cultic framework (both the bringer of the sacrifice, the High Priest, as well as the sacrifice itself, simultaneously, "*Opfer und Opfernder*").[173]

At the beginning of the excursus, Barth reminds us that the New Testament speaks of the atonement in different ways; the language of the Bible is not just limited to juridical imagery. For example, the New Testament uses financial language (ransom in Mark 10:45) to explain Christ's self-offering [*Selbst- und Lebenshingabe*] of life. It also portrays a military view of overcoming the devil and death (*Christus Victor*) to describe what Christ has done 'for us.' However, Barth argues that there is one language in particular—namely the cultic language of sacrifice—which stands apart from the forensic one in terms of "sufficient distinctness and importance to

---

170. *CD* IV/1, 273f.

171. See also Jüngel, "Das Opfer Jesu Christi als Sacramentum et Exemplum," 263.

172. *CD* IV/1, 275.

173. Söding, "Sühne durch Stellvertretung: Zur zentralen Deutung des Todes Jesu im Römerbrief," 392.

merit a special appraisal."¹⁷⁴ This he sees as being the predominant use of language in, for example, the Letter to the Hebrews, as well as presupposed in the Johannine writings and in Paul. He goes on to explain that anywhere where Christ's self-offering is mentioned in relation to his shedding of his blood, the New Testament uses cultic language and imagery, which stands in close proximity to the Old Testament images and categories.¹⁷⁵

1. Accordingly, Barth restates his fourfold juridical framework in cultic terms. First, in the same way in which Jesus takes our place as Judge, Jesus Christ is the Priest who represents humanity (weighed down by sin) before God and achieves *Sühnung* [translated 'propitiation']. As Barth correctly observes, it is humanity—not God—that needs *Sühnung*. The English translation of the German word *Sühnung* as 'propitiation' is misleading on two accounts. First, whereas the German word *Sühnung* has its focus on humanity's need, in the English propitiation the focus is on the deity that is in need of being propitiated and not on humanity; in fact the emphasis is on humanity effecting propitiation. Secondly, the language of propitiation is completely absent in the cultic language in the New Testament (as well as the Old Testament) and it is therefore misleading to use this term in this context. However, what Barth says is that Christ as priest is the Mediator (μεσίτης—1 Tim 2:5) and representative who, by virtue of his office, "*den Zugang des Volkes zu seinem Gott faktisch möglich macht und eröffnet.*"¹⁷⁶ Thus Barth rightly emphasizes the notion of effecting access [*Zugang*] to God achieved by Jesus' self-offering, which approach to sacrifice stands at the centre of the cultic atonement in Leviticus as well as in Hebrews. This highlights the one-way movement towards God in the atonement,¹⁷⁷ resulting in the restoration of the covenantal fellowship with God, previously destroyed by sin. Therefore, a better translation that captures the full meaning of *Sühnung*, which is etymologically related to the German word *Versöhnung* [reconciliation], would be atonement—'at-one-ment,' being at one.

The New Testament makes clear that, unlike the high priests of the Old Testament or any other human priest, Jesus Christ does not need to atone for any of his own sins, nor does he require the benefits of a sacrifice for himself; instead, he "acts exclusively on behalf of the people and not for Himself."¹⁷⁸ Therefore he is the "true, and essential and original Priest, the

---

174. *CD* IV/1, 274.
175. See *CD* IV/1, 274.
176. *KD* IV/1, 303.
177. Heb 4:16; 6:20; 9:24; 10:20.
178. *CD* IV/1, 275.

'great high-Priest,'"[179] as we read in Heb 4:14, who is "a priest forever after the order of Melchizedek" (Ps 110:4 as referenced in Heb 5:6); one who "entered once for all into the holy place, not by means of the blood of goats and calves but by means of his own blood, thus securing an eternal redemption" (Heb 9:12). The Aaronic priesthood served as a sanctuary which was only a "type and shadow" of the true sanctuary in heaven (Heb 8:5) and therefore Barth identifies the role of the priesthood as one of "symbolising and attesting of the atonement which will be made by God *Himself*."[180] In this way, Barth describes the work of Christ as the "essence [*Wesen*] and fulfillment [*Erfüllung*] of all other priestly work," replacing [*Aufhebung*] it and making it "superfluous" [*Erledigung*].[181] Barth maintains that in the work of Christ we encounter the "real and sufficient"[182] priestly work, the true *sacra dans* who *satis facere* through his sacrifice.[183] This Barth sees as achieving the same "as those justified by Him as Judge,"[184] that is peace and access to God. Therefore Barth concludes that one can equally

> describe the work of Jesus Christ as His highpriestly work as His judicial work, and we shall mean and say exactly the same thing. In both cases He takes the place of man, and takes from man an office which has to be filled but which man himself cannot fill. In both cases a new order comes into force to establish a new covenant, which is really the genuine fulfilment of the old.[185]

2. Secondly, Barth combines the second and third points of his main discussion of the juridical framework into one element of the cultic framework, arguing that in the same way that Jesus takes our place *as* the accused, condemned and judged and is judged *in* our place in the event of judgment (the second and third points of the juridical framework), likewise Jesus Christ takes the place of the cultic sacrifice which is offered up.[186] As we read in the epistle to the Hebrews, the main function of the priest was to offer sacrifices. However, according to Barth, the priest imagery here—even the parallel with Melchizedek—breaks down, because Jesus "is not only the

179. *CD* IV/1/, 275.
180. *CD* IV/1, 276. Italics mine.
181. *CD* IV/1, 276.
182. *CD* IV/1, 276.
183. *Sacrificium*, from the Latin *sacer*, 'holy' and *facere*, 'to make.' This is the act of making something holy by transforming it or setting it apart for God's use.
184. *CD* IV/1, 276.
185. *CD* IV/1, 277.
186. See *CD* IV/1, 277.

One who offers sacrifices but also the sacrifice which is offered"—both the bringer of the sacrifice, the High Priest, as well as sacrifice itself. Jesus is simultaneously "*der Opfernde [...] [und] auch das von ihm dargebrachte Opfer*,"[187] just as he is also both "the Judge and the judged."[188] Jesus as High Priest "simply offers Himself"[189] without blemish to God through the eternal Spirit (Heb 9:14); the Lamb of God that takes away the sin of the world (John 1:29), our paschal lamb (1 Cor 5:7), whose blood, which is sprinkled on the *hilasterion* (Rom 3:25), establishes the new covenant. In this way, Barth says, Jesus is the fulfilment and end of all the Old Testament sacrifices.[190]

Barth asks the question: 'What does *sacrifice* mean?' We have to follow his line of enquiry here and highlight another interesting linguistic point in the translation of the German term '*Opfer*.' Barth points out that according to the Old Testament it was God himself who instituted the sacrifices to "order the encounter of a sinful people with God" to bring about the "possibility and actuality of communication and communion of Israel [...] with God."[191] The priest took the mediating role of the covenant between Israel and God previously threatened by sin and the sacrifice he offered bridged this gulf of discord. Through the sacrifice, sinful and unfaithful Israel "is summoned to bow beneath the divine judgment, but also to hold fast to the divine grace" of God's mercy.[192] These sacrifices did not follow the simple principle of *do ut des* but were genuine elements of the covenantal relationship and of the "*Bundes- und Heilsgeschichte*."[193] Yet, the sacrifice of the animal could restore the relationship between God and Israel only temporarily and made the "broken relationship between the two [...] at least bearable and possible."[194] It was a promise and not yet the fulfilment itself, only a shadow of things to come (Heb 10:1). As Barth explains: "Israel [only] *signifies* man judged by God and judged therefore to his salvation, man brought to actual conversion by the judgment of God, man passing through death to life. But Israel is *not* that man."[195] However, unlike the sacrificial system of the Old Testament, in which the priest (who is also a member of the covenant and thus himself needs atonement) only restores the discord to

187. *KD* IV/1, 305.
188. *CD* IV/1, 277.
189. *CD* IV/1, 277.
190. See *CD* IV/1, 277.
191. *CD* IV/1, 277f.
192. *CD* IV/1, 278.
193. *KD* IV/1, 306.
194. *CD* IV/1, 278.
195. *CD* IV/1, 279. Italics mine.

order temporarily, Jesus Christ the High Priest is the final and real sacrifice. He effects and proclaims "complete forgiveness" for humanity once and for all and brings about the "just man" before God.[196] Jesus' sacrifice is thus not simply a further image symbolizing reconciled humanity but the actual "fulfilment of the reconciliation of man with God."[197] The crux lies in the understanding that Christ is not simply another human who dies and whose death would amount to no more than "an improper and provisional" act; Christ's death *is* a human one, but "in and with the human action [. . .] is also a divine action"[198] [*Tun Gottes selbst*]. As Barth writes:

> Our whole understanding depends upon our recognising that God's own activity and being, His presence and activity in the One who is His own Son, very and eternal God with the Father and the Holy Spirit, is the truth and power of that which takes place here as a history of human sacrificing and sacrifice.[199]

In Jesus Christ God not only wills and demands the bridging of the gulf but fulfils the discord in the covenant. In Christ he

> wills and demands the sacrifice of the old man (who can never be this man, who can only die). He wills and demands the setting aside of this man, his giving up to death, which is not fulfilled merely by giving up this or that, even the best he has. God wills and demands the man himself, to make an end of him, so that the new man may have air and space for a new life. He wills and demands that he should go through death to life.[200]

In Christ, God himself "acted in place of the human race, Himself making the real sacrifice which radically alters the situation between Himself and man."[201] God thereby brings about the fulfilment of his covenantal will (Lev 11:44 and Lev 26:12)[202] and a new beginning. In this sacrifice it is God himself who not only demands the sacrifice but makes it himself.[203] He does so in the person of Jesus, in becoming one with the sinner and taking our

196. *CD* IV/1, 279.
197. *CD* IV/1, 279.
198. *CD* IV/1, 280.
199. *CD* IV/1, 280.
200. *CD* IV/1, 280.
201. *CD* IV/1, 280.

202. Lev 11:44: "I am the Lord your God; consecrate yourselves and be holy, because I am holy." As well as Lev 26:12: "I will walk among you and be your God, and you will be my people."

203. See *CD* IV/1, 280.

place as sinner, and in dying our death, the death of the old man, in order to do the will of God, killing our sin in his death.[204] By becoming "the greatest of all sinners"[205] he achieves the penitence and conversion demanded by God of the sinner and experiences the bitter reality of being "the accused and condemned and judged and executed man of sin."[206] He does so not for himself but for the sake of all humanity, "in order that when He Himself has been this man no other man can or need be, in order that in place of this man another man who is pleasing to God, the man of obedience may have space and air and be able to live."[207]

There is another unfortunate mistranslation of a term used by Barth which unhelpfully obscures his meaning in this section of the *CD*. The German term *Opfer* is sometimes translated in the English version of the *CD* as 'victim,' emphasizing that Christ became a victim on the cross when he carried humanity's sin and died a God-forsaken death. However, in a cultic setting the German word *Opfer* never implies that the sacrifice or offering should be seen as a victim. Therefore, the reader of the *CD* should take Barth's small print section on Christ the High Priest as the key to understanding how Barth uses the term *Opfer* in the juridical framework. I would argue that Barth never sees Jesus as a victim, neither in the cultic setting (in which the translators interestingly never translate *Opfer* as 'victim') nor in the juridical setting (where the translation 'victim' frequently occurs).

3. Thirdly, in the same way in which he *is* just and *acts* justly in our place in the juridical framework, Jesus Christ has also made a perfect sacrifice in our place in the cultic setting. In other words, as the perfect High Priest offering himself as a sacrifice for all human priests, he has "substituted a perfect sacrifice for all the sacrifices offered by men."[208] As we have seen, this means that in giving himself as an offering to God, Jesus Christ has fulfilled the will of God (Heb 10:8f. and Ps 40:7) and has offered a sacrifice for the sanctification of humanity that was proper and pleasing to God and thus acceptable. John's Gospel makes clear that on the cross, Jesus knew ὅτι ἤδη πάντα τετέλεσται (John 19:28) and in this way said what God said:

> that what took place was not something provisional, but that which suffices to fulfil the divine will, that which is entire and perfect, that which cannot and need not be continued or repeated or added to or superseded, the new thing which was the

204. See *CD* IV/1, 280.
205. *CD* IV/1, 281.
206. *CD* IV/1, 281.
207. *CD* IV/1, 281.
208. *CD* IV/1, 281.

end of the old but which will itself never become old, which can only be there and continue and shine out and have force and power as that which is new and eternal.[209]

Everything that was demanded by God was done in the person of Jesus Christ because in Christ everything that was given was "accomplished by God Himself."[210] According to Barth, in Jesus the "work which was necessary on man's side for the making of atonement"[211] [*Versöhnung notwendige Werk*] was achieved. By God affirming his own perfect sacrifice in Jesus he proclaimed a *Yes* not only to himself but also to his Son, this man Jesus, and therefore to all of humanity in Christ, because Jesus' sacrifice fulfilled the will of God and "took place in our stead and for us."[212] It was *for humanity* that Jesus became the Mediator of the covenant—this mediation was not for God's benefit but for humanity's. As Barth sums it up: "The will of God towards us is the purpose of this sacrifice, and His good pleasure towards us is its end."[213] To express this differently, what God achieved in Jesus Christ is what humanity needs but cannot do or bring about on her own. Christ's achievement is humanity's peace with God, her freedom for, her reconciliation with and access to God and therefore the "alteration of our human situation" and the "taking away of that which separates us from Him."[214] Sinful humanity's death results in life as obedient covenant partners. And finally, in this perfection of sacrifice we see the "love with which God has loved us,"[215] through which his work of reconciliation was achieved for us. Furthermore, according to Barth, this work of reconciliation [*Versöhnung*] through Christ's sacrifice, resulting as it does in righteousness [*Rechtstat*], becomes not simply a benefit for humanity (in that humanity becomes righteous before God). Rather, by accepting the sacrifice of Christ, righteousness is attributed to humanity as if she has achieved it herself. It becomes her *own* act of righteousness, the work and sacrifice she has done herself.[216] Thus the righteousness of Christ becomes humanity's own righteousness, not as an alien righteousness as the Reformers called it. Barth goes further and contends that humanity will experience God's perfect love in the fact that Christ's perfect sacrifice was done for her. In this way, this becomes

209. *CD* IV/1, 281.
210. *CD* IV/1, 282.
211. *CD* IV/1, 282.
212. *CD* IV/1, 282.
213. *CD* IV/1, 282.
214. *CD* IV/1, 282.
215. *CD* IV/1, 282.
216. See *CD* IV/1, 283.

humanity's *own* sacrifice and through this she receives the forgiveness of sins and access to God as his children.[217]

Implications and Criticism

Does Barth's restatement of the forensic fourfold *pro nobis* with cultic terminology work and do both accounts match? Can we agree with Barth that ultimately it does not matter whether the atonement is stated in forensic terms or cultic ones? Is the interpretation of the text flexible when it comes to forensic and cultic views and is this verified in the exegesis? Furthermore, does Barth's use of the cultic imagery work with the cultic imagery of the Letter to the Hebrews in relation to the cross? And is his claim—that prioritizing the forensic framework over the cultic one—valid and faithful to the context? Can we say that the forensic terminology and metaphors are the clearest way to express what God has done in Christ?

Both the juridical and cultic frameworks make the same point: God in Christ has brought about humanity's salvation. This is done "without any merit of ours, indeed in the face of our resistance."[218] Whether it is Jesus Christ as (a) the *Judge* who was (b) the *judged* (c) *in our place*, and who (d) *acted justly*; or whether it is Jesus Christ as (a) the *Priest* who (b) offered himself up as (c) a *sacrifice* which is (d) *perfect* before God; in either case God has met our sinful defiance with divine defiance and turned towards humanity in love. Through Christ's sacrifice, his righteousness becomes humanity's own righteousness, not as an alien one but as a righteousness that is properly her own. According to Barth, in a nutshell, what God has done through Christ's sacrifice has enabled humanity to become the children of God, resulting in the forgiveness of sins, peace with God and her access *to* and freedom *for* God. Barth's restatement of the cultic does parallel his forensic view, though it deepens, broadens and brings about new insight into the subject.

Drury rightly highlights two aspects from the Letter to the Hebrews for which Barth does not account. He observes the emphasis that Hebrews gives to Christ, the High Priest's exaltation, and that "in contrast to its forensic counterpart, the cultic narration of the work of Christ assigns great significance to the *location* of its execution."[219] The High Priest sacrifices in the true tabernacle and enacts an eternal sacrifice once and for all, entering

---

217. See *CD* IV/1, 283.

218. *CD* IV/1, 282.

219. Drury, "The Priest Sacrificed in Our Place: Barth's Use of the Cultic Imagery of Hebrews in Church Dogmatics IV/1, §59.2," 7.

into the heavenly tabernacle by the use of his own blood (Heb 9:11–12). Though this raises a number of questions which cannot all be addressed here we need to ask how the historical event of the cross can simultaneously be seen as also taking place in heaven. We also need to ask about the function of the Spirit in the atonement through whom Jesus offered himself to God (as stated in Heb 9:14). Does, as Drury suggests, the Spirit function as the "point of connection"[220] between the cross on Golgotha and the heavenly tabernacle? This raises questions about the relationship between heaven and earth, the relationship between God and humanity in the atonement, and the way earthly sin affects the heavenly tabernacle. Furthermore, how does Barth's statement *"Er [Jesus] wählt das Kreuz von Golgatha zu seinem Königsthron,"*[221] relate to all of this?

5. *Jesus is Victor*: The Conquering of Sin

The removal of sin plays a pivotal part in the atonement, though it is not the heart of it. The heart of it is the reconciliation achieved. Nevertheless, it is important to consider *how* sin is dealt with and this will be discussed in this section.

5.1. *A Challenge to the Common View of Sin*

Sin is often viewed as a defilement, something that must be removed. It is also seen as a barrier preventing fellowship with God. This idea, that sin is the reason that someone is unable to commune with God, is also often linked to the atonement in terms of Jesus taking the sins of all humanity away and bearing them on the cross. Both Calvin and Barth asserted that sins were transferred onto the sinless Christ who died in place of humanity and was punished in God's wrath, a form of divine judgment for the sins of humanity, so that humanity could go unpunished. As we stated in the previous section, this not only raises a question of justice—whether or not it is just to punish a sinless person and let the guilty go free—but also challenges Trinitarian theology by 'dividing' the persons of the Trinity at the cross-event. Of course, neither Calvin nor Barth actively thought in terms of a 'divided' Trinity. However, the implications of their position point in this direction. It has to be said that this inconsistency is something that does not seem to have occurred to either Calvin or Barth. The corollary of Calvin and Barth's view that Jesus' death on the cross was a judgment of sin, afflicted

220. Ibid., 7.
221. *KD* II/2, 180.

upon him by the Father's wrath, is the separation of the human Jesus from God—the abandonment of one person of the Trinity by another.

We have seen that it is correct to regard sin as the cause of the broken relationship with God from humanity's point of view. However, to say that sin 'prevents' a person being 'at-one' with God might be seen as rather misleading. To say as Barth does, that the atonement is all about the removal of sin makes sin an object that can be dealt with, and a reality that Jesus deals with on the cross. In this understanding, reconciliation simply requires the removal of a blockage. The Penal Substitutionary picture of Jesus dying on the cross, bearing all humanity's sins and being punished by God on her behalf is consistent with this view—that sin is an object that can be taken away. However, if this is not an accurate understanding of sin and the way God deals with it in Christ, then we must consider alternatives to the Penal Substitution model. This prompts us to conceive of sin not as something that can be taken away from a person—by analogy, similar to, for example, a heavy bag—and not as something that stands between God and a person like a wall or some sort of barrier. Instead, it is something that resides within the person; so it is not simply an object that needs to be dealt with. Rather, the sinful nature is intimately bound up with the entire person and it is therefore the person, as opposed to simply the sin, that is sinful and constitutes the problem. And thus, as Bell points out "the only way to deal with sin is therefore to deal with the sinner himself."[222] The solution is for God to deal with the sinful nature rather than the sin itself.[223] We conclude therefore that the atonement is about dealing with the very *being*, the very *existence* of humanity.

Genesis 3 recounts the disobedient act of Adam and Eve and in Rom 5:12ff. Paul highlights its consequences, namely that "sin came into the world through one man, and death came through sin, and so death spread to all because all have sinned" (Rom 5:12). Through Adam, sin entered the world and because "the story of Adam is projected into the present as the story of the I [humankind] is implicated in the story of Adam."[224] Paul uses four terms to describe 'sin' and the 'sinful man': ἁμαρτία / ἁμαρτωλός,

---

222. Bell, *Deliver Us from Evil*, 192.

223. Hofius explains: "Der Gedanke der kultischen Sühne setzt nämlich ein Vertständnis von Sünde voraus, das in der Sünde entschieden mehr sieht als bloß die einzelne sündige *Tat* [. . .] Die Sünde ist vielmehr eine Größe, die den Sünder in seinem *Sein* betrifft und zeichnet. Sie ist die vom Menschen her vollzogene Zerstörung der personalen Verbundenheit mit dem ihm zugewandten Gott und als solche die fundamentale Verfehlung der Daseinsbestimmung, von Gott her und für Gott zu leben," in Hofius, "Sühne und Versöhnung," 41f.

224. Käsemann, *Commentary on Romans*, 196.

ἀσέβεια / ἀσεβής, ἄδικος / ἀδικία and ἔχθρα εἰς θεόν / ἐχθρός. Paul sees sin as a power that rules over humanity and thus (1) humanity becomes a slave to sin (Rom 3:9; 6:16f.; 6:20; 7:14)[225] and (2) sin lives or resides in a person, dwelling in his innermost being and governing him from within (Rom 7:17, 20).[226] Sin for Paul is not primarily a moral term, but a theological one, and this means that first and foremost sin is not an act but, rather, is something that affects the being and nature of a person. Sin is a reality that not only affects the sinner's outward behavior, but also penetrates his whole nature.[227] Sin is a degeneration of the whole of human nature and therefore Paul talks about the existence of the sinful person as a σῶμα τῆς ἁμαρτίας (Rom 6:6) and σώματος τοῦ θανάτοτυ (Rom 7:24). It is an existence of death,[228] according to which the whole of humanity is already spiritually dead and is going towards total condemnation since they are all trapped in the *Tun-Ergehens-Zusammenhang* of cause and effect, sin and death.[229]

Furthermore, sin in the Old Testament should also be seen ontologically rather than simply from a moral or forensic perspective. Moberly's close reading of the account of the fall shows that in a literal sense, 'the serpent got it right,' which is a dilemma, and must lead to some re-evaluation of sin.[230] Moberly's solution is to redefine the 'death' promised in Gen 2:17 to mean death in terms of *relationship*.[231] The "relationships [that] have been poisoned by the act of disobedience"[232] are between God and humanity (Gen 3:10), human beings (Gen 3:12) but also between humanity and nature (Gen 3:16–19). The real problem of sin is not that it must inevitably lead to the punishment of bodily death; it is that sin will inevitably lead to death in the relationships humanity cherishes. This does not minimise the significance of sin's seriousness, for human beings are in many ways defined by their relationships and if these relationships are damaged by sin, then

---

225. See Hofius, "Sühne und Versöhnung," 44.

226. See Hofius, "Der Mensch im Schatten Adams," 130.

227. See Hofius, "Sühne IV," 344. See also Stolina, "Tod und Heil. Zur Heilsbedeutung des Todes Jesu," 94ff. and his 'relational ontology' in regard to sin. See also Maurer, "'Für uns': An unserer Stelle hingerichtet. Die Herausforderung der Versöhnungslehre," who writes that "die menschliche Existenz in der Sünde selbstbezogen [ist]," 191.

228. See Hofius, "Sühne und Versöhnung," 44.

229. See Koch, *Um das Prinzip der Vergeltung in Religion und Recht des Alten Testaments*, XI.

230. See Moberly, "Did the Serpent Get It Right?." I am indebted to Michael Bigg for directing me to this essay.

231. See ibid., 13–18.

232. Ibid., 17.

the very essence of humanity is marred. Moberly's conception of the nature and problem of sin offers a different view of the atonement. The solution to this is not retributive, but restorative; sinners are not in need of further punishment, but of restoration. His reading of Gen 3 accounts for this by building retribution into the nature of sin itself. The consequence of sin is the destruction of relationship, which in turn leads to destruction of the fullness of humanity that exists at its best when engaged in unbroken relationship. This explanation frees the path for the atonement to become a task of restoration, of healing relationships, and of rebuilding true humanity.

Within this understanding, the act of atonement is not so much about paying a debt to a God who is offended by humanity's sins. Instead, humanity is understood as a victim of her own sins.[233] Humanity in and of herself—her entire being—is the cause of the broken relationship with God. It is humanity that bars fellowship with God, standing in her own way, 'blocking' communion with God. Paul understood this when in Rom 7:24 he cries out "Wretched man that I am! Who will deliver me from this body of death?" Luther also understood this when he said "I am thy sin."[234] What needs to change is the entire nature and being of a person.[235] It is not that something needs to be taken away, but that the whole person needs to die, because sin resides within that person, to be resurrected again in order to be with God. We have already seen that the cultic death is not a negative act simply of removing sin but a sanctifying and purifying death resulting in fellowship with God. What becomes clear is that Jesus frees the sinner from sin, lifting (*nāśāʿ ʾāwôn*) and removing the transgression.

What exactly happens on the cross? What happens to sin if Jesus does not bear it in the way Christians are traditionally led to understand? How then could he be thought to conquer the powers of death? And if it is just that Jesus bears sin by forgiving it, why did he have to die at all?

5.2. *Sin Removal*

McCormack argues that, for Barth, the doctrine of election has replaced the notion of double imputation, and that forensicism has become "the

---

233. See Stolina, "Tod und Heil. Zur Heilsbedeutung des Todes Jesu," who writes that "die unwiderstehliche Macht der Sünde zeigt sich darin, daß der Mensch darin ihr Opfer ist, daß er ihr Täter ist und von sich her sein muß," 96.

234. Luther, *A Commentray on St. Paul's Epistle to the Galatians*, 283.

235. See Hofius who writes: "Die Sünde greift deshalb ins Zentrum der *Person des Sünders*. Weil die Zerstörung des Gottesverhältnisses vom Sünder her eine totale und irreparable ist und weil das Sein des Sünders gottfernes Sein ist, deshalb hat der Sünder sein Leben definitive verwirkt," in Hofius, "Sühne und Versöhnung," 42.

frame of reference that is basic to the whole of his soteriology."[236] Barth's over-forensicism creates a number of problems which may be illustrated by examining one problematic New Testament verse, 2 Cor 5:21, which will become a paradigm for the interpretation of other passages.

Adopting the cultic perspective of the atonement and the concept of *Existenzstellvertretung*, it is as already apparent that in 2 Cor 5:21 Paul also talks about Christ's death as a *Stellvertretung*, with the ὑπέρ prepositions indicating the soteriological intention of Christ's atoning death.[237] Verse 21 "For our sake he [God] made him [Jesus] to be sin who knew no sin, so that in him we might become the righteousness of God"—includes the problematic phrase ἁμαρτίαν ἐποίησεν, which has been the subject of various interpretations and translations. Barth calls 2 Cor 5:21, Christ becoming 'sin' for us, a statement which is "almost unbearably severe."[238] However, in the LXX, the ḥaṭṭā't is seen as the "primary expiatory offering in the Levitical system of offerings"[239] and is translated here as περὶ ἁμαρτίας (see Lev 5:6, 7, 11) or simply ἁμαρτία (Lev 4:21, 24; 5:12).[240] Therefore, ḥaṭṭā't can mean both 'sin' and 'sin offering.' Because of this, some exegetes translate the first ἁμαρτία in verse 21 as 'sin' and the second, "leaning on an Old Testament testimony, namely, Isaiah 53:10"[241] as 'sin offering.'[242] However, what is most significant for Wilkens is that 2 Cor 5:21 shows the atonement context of the καταλλαγή of verse 18f. Here, the cultic correlation becomes explicit:[243] the idea that God would have made the crucified one sin 'for us' would have been an alien one to Greek ears and can only be explained with the cultic rite in Lev 4. Wilkens sees 2 Cor 5:21 as derivative from the declaration formula חַטָּאת הוּא, where the priest announces in Lev 4:21 of the LXX that ἁμαρτία συναγωγῆς ἐστιν.[244] This notion that Jesus should be seen as a 'sin offering' in verse 21 is affirmed by Dunn, who points out that the phrase περὶ ἁμαρτίας is regularly used in the LXX to translate the Hebrew ḥaṭṭā't (*inter alia* Lev 5:6–7.11; 16:3.5.9; Num 6:16; 7:16).[245] The phrase denotes a technical expression from the language of sacrifice. In this way, Paul refers

---

236. McCormack, "Justitia Aliena," 192.

237. See Knöppler, *Sühne im Neuen Testament*, 157.

238. *CD* IV/1, 165.

239. Averbeck, "Sacrifices and Offerings," 720.

240. Stuhlmacher, *Biblische Theologie des Neuen Testaments*, 290.

241. Martin, *2 Corinthians*, 137.

242. See Harris, *The Second Epistle to the Corinthians*, 452.

243. See Wilckens, *Der Brief and die Römer*, 240.

244. See ibid., 240.

245. See Dunn, *Romans 1–8*, 422.

to Jesus as the sacrificial *ḥaṭṭāʾt* that has passed through death, *stellvertretend* for the sinner accompanying him.[246]

A close parallel to 2 Cor 5:21 is Rom 8:3, which describes the Father sending the Son περὶ ἁμαρτίας. Just as we read in Gen 22, when God commanded Abraham to sacrifice his son Isaac, Rom 8:3 also shows God sending his own Son to be a sin offering in order to condemn sin in the flesh.[247] Paul uses a *sending formula*[248] to describe the incarnation of the pre-existent Son of God (see Gal 4:4, John 3:16f.; 1 John 4:9) as the salvation of the world.[249] Christ came in the concrete likeness, the form, of σαρκὸς ἁμαρτίας, not simply in resemblance of it (though Paul does emphasise that Jesus entered fully into the human condition (Phil 2:6ff.)).[250] He came as a human "knowing the same mortality, the same human appetites,"[251] sharing fully the weakness of destructive sin, and yet he did not sin but was obedient to God until death (see Rom 5:18f.).[252] The death sentence on the ἁμαρτία is the verdict on the human κατα σάρκα. This κατάκριμά, which according to Paul "hung over human beings because of sin (v. 1), falls not upon them—or at least not upon those 'in Christ'—but upon sin itself."[253] However, it is not the Son who is condemned—it is sin. The phrase περὶ ἁμαρτίας highlights the purpose of the incarnation and the way condemnation of sin is executed, that is, through the *stellvertretenden* death of the righteous one.[254] Since Jesus identifies himself with the σάρξ (see the *sĕmîkâ*-rite), the human σάρξ becomes the σάρξ of Christ and thus it encounters the fatal κατάκριμά that humanity deserves.[255] Thus, on the cross a judgment *is* executed—but it is not Jesus who is judged. Instead, Jesus is the one who judges and condemns sin (Rom 8:3). Dunn puts it very aptly that God deals with sin in its own domain, in the σάρξ "by having it put to death, that is, by destroying it, since flesh without life is flesh destroyed."[256] In condemning sin in the flesh, God breaks sin's power and enables new life.[257] Again, describing Jesus' death on

---

246. See Stuhlmacher, *Revisiting Paul's Doctrine of Justification*, 59.
247. See Stuhlmacher, *Paul's Letter to the Romans*, 120.
248. See Breytenbach, "Versöhnung, Stellvertretung und Sühne," 71.
249. See ibid., 216f.
250. See Wilckens, *Der Brief and die Römer*, 125.
251. See Dunn, *Romans 1–8*, 439.
252. See Stuhlmacher, *Paul's Letter to the Romans*, 119.
253. Byrne, *Romans*, 237.
254. See Söding, "Sühne durch Stellvertretung," 392.
255. See Knöppler, *Sühne im Neuen Testament*, 173.
256. Dunn, *Romans 1–8*, 439.
257. See Breytenbach, "Versöhnung, Stellvertretung und Sühne," 71.

the cross as the θάνατος ὑπὲρ πάντων (see 2 Cor 5:14), Paul presupposes that identification has taken place. In the atoning crucifixion, it is God himself who identifies with the sinner (whose existence is forfeited by sin) in Christ.[258] In Paul's understanding, it is not simply that "Christ takes our place in death"[259] or that "Christ and the believer change places, but rather that Christ, by his involvement in the human situation, is able to transfer believers from one mode of existence to another."[260]

Barth points out that 'flesh' in the biblical usage refers "frequently and primarily" to the "general sense of human existence or the human mode of being."[261] It does of course have a negative connotation especially in the Pauline letters—Paul does not see the human σάρξ as evil but "simply weak and corruptible."[262] Barth refers to a negative situation and describes the "condition of man in contradiction, in disorder and sickness, man after Adam's fall."[263] He understands the 'flesh' as a human consisting of soul and body "without the Logos."[264] In the incarnation the Bible talks specifically about the *Logos* taking on flesh. Barth seeks to explain that "something happens for and in the flesh"[265] for all humanity when the *Logos* enters flesh. Though "in itself [it] is disobedient," Barth sees the flesh as a "purposeful instrument" which *becomes* obedient through the *Logos* entering it, attaining both a "determination and hope."[266] The *Logos* becoming flesh shows that the human Jesus "has and is spirit and life, and the flesh itself becomes quickening and living and meaningful."[267] Therefore, in order for it to benefit humanity, all the deeds of Jesus had to take place in the flesh. It was only by virtue of his identity with the human condition that Jesus could redeem those enslaved by sin and allow them to become partakers of the divine sonship.[268] Barth concludes that it is in the flesh that "victory is won, or in positive terms the transformation of the fleshly nature achieved. The flesh now becomes the object and subject of saving passion and action. In the flesh the reconciliation of the flesh is completed. This is the triumph of the

---

258. See Knöppler, *Sühne im Neuen Testament*, 157.
259. Denney, *The Death of Christ*, 88.
260. Hooker, *From Adam to Christ*, 5.
261. *CD* III/2, 335.
262. Dunn, "Paul's Understanding of the Death of Jesus as Sacrifice," 37.
263. *CD* III/2, 335.
264. *CD* III/2, 335.
265. *CD* III/2, 336.
266. *CD* III/2, 336.
267. *CD* III/2, 336.
268. See Dunn, "Paul's Understanding of the Death of Jesus as Sacrifice," 38.

meaning of the human existence of Jesus."[269] In our Old Testament analysis we saw that God is not the receiver or the object of the sacrifice but the subject of an act that was performed in his name by the priest.[270] Now in 2 Cor 5:21 and Rom 8:3, God once again is not the receiver of the sacrifice, but just as he was the one making the sacrifice possible in the Old Testament, here too Jesus himself is simultaneously "*Opfer und Opfernder.*"[271] Therefore, this sacrifice not only indicates the price love is willing to pay, but is in fact love itself.[272] In condemning sin in the flesh, God breaks sin's power and enables new life.[273]

The task of the next section will be to give answers to the questions raised in sections 3 and 4. Furthermore, we will question Barth's case for prioritizing the forensic view of the atonement over the cultic. We will also consider whether Barth's analysis amounts to a proper account of the cultic atonement as described in Scripture or whether it reduces the rich imagery of the cultic sacrifice.

6. *Existenzstellvertretung* in the New Testament

In our treatment of Barth's exegesis in *CD* II/2 we used the concept of *Existenzstellvertretung* (a model that focuses on the participation of the sinner in the sacrifice)[274] as a paradigm to guide our thinking on the atonement. We will now contrast this approach with Barth's views on the atonement. In the New Testament the notion of *Existenzstellvertretung* is expressed by various prepositions such as ἀντί, δία, περί and ὑπέρ. These terms express the idea that one person has suffered or done something 'in place of' [*an Stelle*] another person or persons, and are similar to the Old Testament understanding of *Existenzstellvertretung*, expressed with the preposition תַּחַת.[275] Paul's repeated phrase ὑπὲρ ἡμῶν is a short form of the so-called *dying formula* of 1 Cor 15:3, which states that Χριστὸς ἀπέθανεν ὑπὲρ τῶν ἁμαρτιῶν ἡμῶν (see also: Rom 5:6.8; 2 Cor 5:14f.). He sees the death of

---

269. *CD* III/2, 336.
270. See Koch, "חטאת," 316.
271. Söding, "Sühne durch Stellvertretung," 392. Italics mine.
272. See ibid., 393.
273. See Breytenbach, "Versöhnung, Stellvertretung und Sühne," 71.
274. See Bell, *Deliver Us from Evil*, 190-92, who explains the concept of *exkludierender* and *inkludierender Stellvertretung* (p. 191f.) and the concept of *Existenzstellvertretung* (190-211 passim).
275. See Janowski, "He Bore Our Sins: Isaiah 53 and the Drama of Taking Another's Place," 53.

Christ as *Existenzstellvertretung*: the ὑπέρ ἡμῶν ἀπέθανεν expression in Rom 5:8 shows that the death was 'for us,' and according to 2 Cor 5:14f., it is an act of identification for all, insofar as in the death of the crucified Christ the death of the πάντες is also performed.[276] It is in Christ's identifying himself with the sinner in his death that the sinner becomes inextricably tied to Christ: "Jesus became one with man in order to put an end to sinful man in order that a new man might come into being."[277]

Morna Hooker believes that it is Paul's fundamental notion of participation in Christ which is not only the key for Paul's understanding of his Christology[278] but also for his understanding of salvation.[279] The concept of interchange, which is better described as a 'mutual participation,' offers "the real clue to Paul's understanding of the atonement."[280] Christ took the individual's sinful existence with him into death, establishing a covenant between himself and humanity through the act of spiritual circumcision in baptism. Through Christ's sacrifice, the sinful nature and thus sin itself was cut off, freeing the sinner from the body of death and making him alive in Christ (Col 2:11ff.). Only in this way can the "destruction of the sinful flesh, the body of death, be accomplished without destroying the believer at the same time."[281] Romans 6:6–7 states that "We know that our old self was crucified with him so that the body of sin might be destroyed, and we might no longer be enslaved to sin. For whoever has died is freed from sin."

Paul conceives of Jesus dying as representative human in "terms of cultic sacrifice."[282] Thus the background to the notion of identification is the Old Testament cultic atonement rite of the *sĕmîkâ*,[283] through which the person identified himself with the dying animal and participated in its death. There we also saw that it was not simply a transferal of sin but a *Subjektübertragung*—the death of the animal became the person's own death.[284] Christ's destiny becomes the destiny of humankind because what happened to the sacrificial animal in the cultic atonement was also meant for the person identifying with the animal. Through the blood (which contained

---

276. See Gaukesbrink, *Die Sühnetradition bei Paulus*, 151.

277. Dunn, "Paul's Understanding of the Death of Jesus as Sacrifice," 36.

278. See Hooker, *From Adam to Christ*, 4.

279. See ibid., 9.

280. Ibid., 22.

281. Dunn, "Paul's Understanding of the Death of Jesus as Sacrifice," 48.

282. Ibid., 44.

283. See Knöppler, *Sühne im Neuen Testament*, 151.

284. See also Bell, *Deliver Us from Evil*, who writes that "this is an act of *identification* such that the Israelite participates in the death of the sacrificial animal," 191.

the soul) sprinkled onto the *kappōret* in the Holy of Holies the sinner was brought into contact with God. Likewise, the crucified Christ representing the holy God has justified the sinner through his blood (Rom 5:9) and has tied himself to the godless sinner in order that the godless sinner is inextricably tied to him.[285] Christ did not simply die to take away sin and guilt but rather identified with the sinner in order to bring him into contact with God through his offering up of his life by his blood, in order to establish the new covenantal fellowship with God. As explained in chapter 2, the cross becomes the new *kappōret*,[286] the place where humanity can meet the transcendent God through the mediation of Jesus Christ. God made the cross on Golgotha his kingly throne.[287] Through this identification on the cross, God with Christ (2 Cor 5:19) and Christ with the sinner, the sinner dies and is able to come through Christ into contact with God, becoming a καινὴ κτίσις.[288]

According to 2 Cor 5:15, the efficacy of Christ's death is of universal scope. Does this mean, however, that because the πάντες have died with Christ, they will also be resurrected and live with Christ? Dunn shows that although Christ died and thus all died, "beyond death he no longer represents [. . .] all men, fallen man."[289] He goes on to explain that in his risen life Christ "represents only those who identity themselves with him, with his death through baptism, only those who acknowledge the Risen One as Lord (2 Cor 5:15). Only those who identify themselves with him in his death are identified with him in his life from death."[290] Therefore, according to Dunn, for Paul union with Christ is not a "once-for-all event of initiation now past and gone for the believer [. . .] identification with Christ in his death is a *process* as well as an *event*."[291] Through participating not only in Christ's death but also in his resurrection, a new existence is bestowed on the person and he becomes a a καινὴ κτίσις—Jesus' resurrection becomes the very basis of humanity's righteousness (2 Cor 5:21).[292] The concept of *Existenzstellver-*

285. See Hofius, "Sühne IV," 32:344.
286. See Knöppler, *Sühne im Neuen Testament*, 116.
287. See *CD* IV/1, 345.
288. See Hofius, "Sühne und Versöhnung," 47.
289. Dunn, "Paul's Understanding of the Death of Jesus as Sacrifice," 40.
290. Ibd., 40.
291. Ibid., 47. Dunn explains that "the believer has been nailed to the cross of Christ, and is still hanging there! This is simply a vivid way of saying that the death of 'the old nature,' of 'the body of sin' is not accomplished in an instant. Rather it is a lifelong process, only completed in the resurrection of the body."
292. See Hooker, *From Adam to Christ*, 39.

tretung should therefore be seen in the light of an inclusive Christology, as participation *in* and *with* the salvific work of Christ, and can therefore be called a 'participatory substitution' model of the atonement. Therefore the emphasis is on both the substitutionary aspect as well as the participatory one. Substitution highlights that it is not humanity's work but exclusively the complete work of Christ alone (in fact it is God in Christ) that makes the reconciliation possible. Participation clearly highlights that the human agent needs to partake in the event; she needs to die as well, and be freed from her sinful nature in order to be removed from the sphere of death and brought into the sphere of life.

In the *CD* this notion is not entirely absent. Barth also talks about an "inclusive Christology which embraces the *existence* of men"[293] and has a similar notion to Gese's understanding of 'inclusive' and 'exclusive' *Stellvertretung*. In fact he says "*Es gibt dann also gerade keine exklusive, sondern nur eine inklusive Christologie*"[294] and goes on to say that an exclusive Christology would be "*geradezu falsch*"[295] in the light of the *Versöhnungslehre*. Only in relation to "Him as my Substitute [*Stellvertreter*] do I know [*erkenne*] myself as the man who is also smitten by this judgment."[296] Barth sees Christ as our *Stellvertreter*, as both our substitute as well as our representative and understands the atonement from the view of an 'inclusive Christology.' Neder writes that "Barth brings participation and substitution together in such a way that neither can be described apart from the other: substitution is participatory and participation is substitutionary."[297] Barth uses these participatory terms as early as *CD* II/2: "In the death which the Son of God has died for them, they themselves have died as sinners."[298] Although superficially there may seem to be similarities between the concept of *Existenzstellvertretung* and Barth's model of atonement with a Christology that embraces the *existence* of all humanity, there are a number of significant differences. Some of these are explicit differences based on Barth's own stated views, and some arise from conclusions which can be legitimately drawn from his comments. These are as follows:

1. According to Barth's view, Christ's death on the cross was God's 'negative act' that, in light of Easter, was undertaken with a 'positive intention.' The notion of an act that was both 'negative' and 'positive'

---

293. *CD* IV/1, 354. Italics added.
294. *KD* IV/1, 387.
295. *KD* IV/1, 385.
296. *CD* III/3, 307.
297. Neder, *Participation in Christ*, 23.
298. *CD* II/2, 125.

suggests the primary aim of the cross was to deal with sin. But the true emphasis of the New Testament understanding of the cross is to reconcile humanity to God—not merely to deal with the barrier of sin—"in Christ God was reconciling the world to himself" (2 Cor 5:19). Although Barth's conclusion about the new status of humanity is in line with our interpretation of the cross-event (the "turning of man"[299] and "his positing afresh"[300] [*seine neue Setzung*] into a new and positive relationship with God) we have seen that the whole Christ-event should not be seen as an act that was both negative and positive but rather was a wholly positive act by Jesus that brought humanity into fellowship with God.

2. A second, linked criticism relates to Barth's positioning of the cross-event as a 'negative act.' In so doing, Barth implies something very specific about the nature of the reconciliation that occurred. For Barth to say that the aim of the atonement was to remove the barrier between God and humanity is to imply a *shift* or *change* in the previously existing relationship between the two. However, Barth's understanding of the atonement is narrow here. In fact, it is clear that this reconciliation through the cross was not merely a matter of repairing a broken relationship. Rather, it was a complete annulment of the negative relationship that determined the existence of the sinner before God.[301] Through the cross, God annulled the enmity and rebellion of humanity and placed her into a right relationship with him, that is, a relationship of 'peace with God' (Rom 5:1).[302]

3. Another troubling implication that follows from the above is that it might be suggested that God has two wills towards humanity—God's *No* (the negative act) and *Yes* (the positive act). The idea is that "God took the initiative and loved those whom he hated."[303] This idea is resonant of Augustine's paradoxical statement: "even when He hated us, He loved us,"[304] a notion we also see in Calvin when he writes that "[n]o one will ever feel that God is favourable

---

299. *CD* IV/1, 310.

300. *CD* IV/1, 310.

301. Hofius, "Sühne und Versöhnung," 37.

302. See Hofius, "Erwägungen zur Gestalt und Herkunft des paulinschen Versöhnungsgedankes," 4.

303. Peterson, *Calvin and the Atonement*, 23.

304. Augustine, "Homilies on the Gospel of John," Tractate CX.6, John 17:21–23, 411.

to him unless he understands that God is appeased in Christ."[305] The sense here is that God is angry with humanity in the first person of the Trinity but loving in the second person. However, any model of the atonement that is truly Trinitarian must reject this apparently changeable model of God with his 'split personality.' Paul does not say that God loved us when he hated us, but that he loved us while we were still sinners (Rom 5:8)! The Father loves humanity in the same way that the Son loves humanity and the Son hates sin with the same wrath that the Father is wrathful towards it. A genuinely Trinitarian understanding of the cross must be that it was the work of a God with internal harmony and consistency, and of one will—the work of the Father, through the Son, in the power of the Spirit.

4. One difficulty that is explicit in Barth's 'negative' view of the cross lies in the notion that the Son takes the Father's wrath. According to Barth, "the New Testament says that the Son of God [. . .] stands under the wrath and judgment of God, He is broken and destroyed on God."[306] This implies that God was punishing God. However, the concept of punishment is entirely absent from the biblical conception of atonement (in both Leviticus and the Pauline texts). Therefore, Jesus' death should not be seen as an appeasing sacrifice to God; instead, we should understand, with Paul, that "God is the subject of the action; it is God who provided Jesus as a *hilasterion*."[307] Since the Father and Jesus are one, the act of reconciliation on the cross is a godly act *for us*, not an act to appease an angry God. It is God's own act, occurring out of love for humanity (Rom 5:8). Because God was present in the crucified one, the death of Christ is not merely the *medium* or *enabling* of reconciliation—it is the *realization* of the act. Therefore it is not the *do ut des* principle that is applied on the cross, but the principle of *Tu solus omnia dedisti*—you (God) alone have given everything. As 2 Cor 5:18 states: "All this is from God, who reconciled us to himself through Christ, and has given us the ministry of reconciliation."

5. The fifth problem is that Barth conceives of Jesus' death in forensic terms. He applies a dialectical method, God's *Yes* and *No* (which seems methodologically very close if not related to the Lutheran

---

305. Calvin's Commentary on John 17:23, *CNTC*, vol. 5, 150.
306. *CD* IV/1, 175.
307. Dunn, "Paul's Understanding of the Death of Jesus as Sacrifice," 48f.

simul). This theological approach permeates his entire theology, as we have demonstrated in our examination of Barth's treatment of the doctrines of election, creation, and reconciliation. However, if we are to see the atonement in terms of the concept of *Existenzstellvertretung*, then the forensic model of *imputation* has been proved to be misleading. Preference must be given to the cultic model of *participation*, which is fluent and seems to do more justice to Barth's own actualistic ontology. In doing this we do not abrogate the negative aspect of the cross, God's *No*—indeed, we hold firm to the double aspect (God's *Yes* and *No* in the cross). But the *No* of the Father is not spoken against the Son—instead it is spoken through the Son against sin. This understanding is more in harmony with a Trinitarian understanding of God's work in the atonement.

Moreover, even allowing for Barth's reliance on the forensic model, he is inconsistent in his deployment of it and at times dives into cultic imagery and terminology if it seems to suit his purpose. In fact, he regularly mixes forensic and cultic imagery when talking about the death of Christ and even uses both in the same sentence: "He who is in the one person the electing God and the one elect man is as the rejecting God, the God who judges sin in the flesh, in His own person the one rejected man, the Lamb which bears the sin of the world that the world should no longer have to bear it or be able to bear it, that it should be radically and totally taken away from it."[308]

6. The most fundamental problem with Barth's doctrine of the atonement is the way that he relates the cross to sin. Although Barth talks about an inclusive *Stellvertretung*, seeing Jesus as the substitute, he undermines his own position by continuing to use terminology that implies sin transferal onto Jesus. Barth sees Jesus as taking humanity's place and bearing her sin, which thereby ceases to be her own. However, sin cannot simply be taken away from a person, since "*Schuld is ebensowenig abnehmbar und übertragbar wie der Tod.*"[309] Even if this were possible, one would have to question whether this would really constitute divine justice. Our conclusion is that the New Testament model is not one depicting the transferal of sin. Rather the New Testament depicts Jesus dying for our sins

---

308. *CD* IV/1, 237.
309. See Hofius, "Sühne und Versöhnung," 42.

by taking sinful humanity with himself into death and, since he has tied himself to humanity in death, humanity will also be tied to him in his resurrection (Rom 6:3–4). If we accept Hartmut Gese's concept of atonement as 'a coming to God through death,' then we can conclude that Christ has passed through death for sinners and that they have gone with him.[310] On this basis, the death of Christ should be seen from the perspective of *Existenzstellvertretung*—Jesus overcoming death and sin and identifying and annihilating the sinful existence of the sinner, bringing about a new creation.[311]

Conclusion

We saw that the transformation that is effected by the atonement is not in God but rather in sinful humanity. The theory of Penal Substitution only tackles the issue of sinful actions (what human beings have done) and not the issue of who human beings are (a sinful humanity estranged from God). According to Paul our complete nature is sinful and needs to be dealt with (Rom 7:24). This took place through the Christ-event on the cross, bringing about a 'new creation' (2 Cor 5:17f.). Furthermore, on the cross, Jesus is not the 'Judge Judged in Our Place' but he is the active Judge, judging sin and condemning and conquering it once and for all.

Thus we have not abrogated the negative aspect of the cross but taken seriously the fact that the act of God speaking a *Yes* towards humanity also meant that Jesus actively speaks a *No* against sin. Therefore the dialectical *Yes* and *No* can still be brought into a synthesis and be seen as united together in Christ; but the *No* is not a *No* spoken against the Son—it is a *No* of the Father over against sin, executed by and through the Son's vicarious and victorious death. Again, the double aspect is not abrogated, but God's *Yes* is always a *Yes* to and for something—and this automatically indicates a *No* against something else. The *Yes* and *No* come together perichoretically (unity-in-distinction) in the way that God's *Yes* towards humanity automatically speaks God's *No* against sin. In fact, God's *Yes* executes and performs the *No*. The *No* is executed by the Son in a perichoretical relationship with the Father and the Spirit. This notion seems to be reflected in John 5 where we read in verse 19 that "the Son can do nothing by himself; he can do only what he sees his Father doing, because whatever the Father does the Son also does." This seems to conform with a Trinitarian model of the

---

310. See Stuhlmacher, *Revisiting Paul's Doctrine of Justification*, 59.
311. See Breytenbach, "Versöhnung, Stellvertretung und Sühne," 68.

atonement much more satisfactorily than Barth's model does. The Father's *Yes* to humanity is affirmed by the Son's *Yes* to the Father in the incarnation, and is further seen by the Son's obedience in going to the cross and saying *No* against sin, a *No* against sin that is echoed by the Father. This is the obedience of Christ that is continually emphasized in the New Testament—we see in John 5:30, "By myself I can do nothing; I judge only as I hear, and my judgment is just, for I seek not to please myself but him who sent me."

Bearing this in mind, to speak of the cross as an event of punishment (the Father punishing the Son) seems wholly inappropriate. It also seems inappropriate to suggest that Jesus was abandoned on the cross, since this is surely inconsistent with the traditional dogma that in one person the two natures of Christ were united in the hypostatic union. The logical conclusion of this position is that the covenant that was established in the incarnation was suddenly broken on the cross and then re-established in the resurrection! This suggests that the Father forsook the Son. But if the two natures work out salvation together in one person, producing a single effect, how can it be suggested that there was a 'separation' on the cross, since in this one person, God and humanity are united?

Thus we must conclude that Jesus' death is not about the Father punishing the Son, and therefore the Father and the Son are not separated in the cross event, but rather the cross is about humanity coming back to God through death. Since Jesus did not bear sin, he is not a covenant-breaker. The death on the cross not only highlights humanity's sinfulness, but also reveals and bears witness to the fact that not even death can separate and destroy the covenant with God that has been established in Jesus Christ. The cross can then come to symbolise that *death* has been overcome and conquered and has lost its sting (1 Cor 15:54–56). The cross becomes a sign that nothing can break the covenant between God and the person of Jesus Christ. If Jesus had been abandoned and rejected on the cross then sin would have won, because it would have succeeded in separating Jesus and the Father (which would leave Jesus is the same predicament as the rest of humanity). But with Christ as the Victor on the cross, not the victim, he is not 'The Judge Judged in Our Place' but the 'Judge Judging sin' on our behalf, making humanity co-workers in the fight against sin and evil.[312] This is in line with the Fathers who saw a two-sidedness in the doctrine of atonement, not only an act "wrought by God on our behalf; [but] also a sense in which something is offered to God in the Humanity of Christ."[313] This two-sidedness is also something that Aulén and Torrance both repeatedly

---

312. See chapter 3.
313. Turner, *The Patristic Doctrine of Redemption*, 22.

highlight, and is clearly stated by Irenaeus: "For unless man had overcome the enemy of man, the enemy would not have been legitimately vanquished. And again: unless it had been God who had freely given salvation, we could never have possessed it securely. And unless man had been joined to God, he could never have become a partaker of incorruptibility."[314] Consequently, the atonement must be seen in light of the unity between the person and work of Christ and in the hypostatic union of both divine and human natures, *in one person*. He acts as God from the side of God and as man from the side of Man and in this way fulfils the covenant from both sides.[315] What he has done in his human nature, he has done on behalf of humanity *coram Deo*. It is not, however, possible to categorise the various acts as either human acts or divine acts. What happened on the cross is one divine-human act in the one person Jesus Christ.

---

314. Irenaeus, "Against Heresies," III.18.7, 448.
315. See Torrance, *Incarnation*, 56.

5

Election, Atonement, and the Holy Spirit

When the perishable has been clothed with the imperishable, and the mortal with immortality, then the saying that is written will come true: "Death has been swallowed up in victory."
    (1 Cor 15:54)

Introduction

HAVING CONCLUDED CHAPTER 2 BY SAYING THAT JESUS IS ONLY THE ELECT and not the rejected, and highlighted in chapter 4 that the cross was neither an active rejection of Jesus nor a passive rejection inflicted upon him, but instead an active rejection and condemnation of sin by Jesus the Judge, we will now consider the meaning and ramifications of these conclusions for humanity. What does it mean for humanity—for everyday life—that Jesus is only the elect, and is not judged on the cross? Do these conclusions alter humanity's state of existence? In the first section of this chapter we will once again turn our focus to the doctrine of election and ask: what happens with the rejection aspect of election? What happens to the 'double' aspect in predestination? And what are the implications for humanity that Jesus was not judged and did not 'bear' sin? Can we still contend, with Barth, that the sinner who lives a life as a *'Verworfener'* is also one of the elected ones in Christ? Is 'rejected man' simply, as Barth describes, a fleeting shadow, and is there a final *apokatastasis*? Alternatively, would this mean that the election of Christ was a static event rather than a dynamic actualistic one? So we need to address the question of whether there is a difference between being 'in Christ' and being outside Christ, and if so, whether Barth collapses the individual election of a person into the election of the God-man Jesus in such a way that no distinction exists between the two? Finally we will give an answer to the problem raised in the introduction, of the relationship between Christ's death and sin removal which, we saw, logically appears to lead either to limited atonement or universalism, two alternatives that we considered problematic.

The second section highlights the role of the Holy Spirit in the saving work and discusses the subjective and objective side of God's works *ad extra*. We will focus on Christian particularity in the Spirit in order to safeguard that "Christian faith is not subsumed under the objective reality of God's work of salvation in the person of Christ,"[1] and once more revisit the problem of rejection in light of the Spirit's involvement in the saving work.

In the last section of this chapter, we will look at human faith and how *metanoia*, the divine change through which a person is freed to be faithful to God in freedom, is brought about. The focus is on Barth's understanding of divine-human correspondence between *Geistestaufe* and *Wassertaufe*, human freedom for God and the faith and obedience necessary for humanity to respond to God's call to follow in Christ's footsteps.

1. Election and Universalism

We saw that Barth looks at election through the lens of the doctrine of God in Jesus Christ and his pastoral concern of being able to reassure people of their salvation very much permeates his theology. His main worry with the doctrine of election and salvation is a *Deus absconditus*, a hidden God, a problem not properly addressed in the history of the Church. Barth rules out this possibility with a pre-emptive strike, when he depicts Jesus not only as the historical Mediator of the covenant but also actively involved and eternally ordained as the electing God as well as the elected human.[2] As chapter 1 showed, it was in Barth's doctrine of election that he first expounded the idea of Christ as the *subject* of election, which is inseparably connected to the person of Jesus. We saw that we cannot talk about God's *Yes* in abstract terms—when we talk about God's *Yes* in Jesus Christ we must include humanity.[3] And God's *Yes* in his eternal decision in Christ to be *pro nobis* and to enter into a covenant-fellowship with humanity remains a *Yes* even though all that humanity deserves is his *No*.[4] Thus for Barth, it is the person of Jesus who is the subject of election and not an "indeterminate (or

---

1. Greggs, *Barth, Origen, and Universal Salvation*, 131.
2. See Kreck, *Grundentscheidungen in Karl Barths Dogmatik*, 194.
3. See ibid., 193.
4. See *CD* II/2, 162.

'absolute') *Logos asarkos*."[5] However, election in Jesus Christ should not only be seen as an eternal decision in the Godhead, but an event in both time and eternity, before the foundation of the world yet simultaneously occurring in history.[6] Hence election involves not only a divine decision in eternity but also a human answer in faith and obedience in history, an "autonomy of the creature which is constituted originally by the act of eternal divine election."[7] God elects humanity in order that humanity may elect God. As Barth states, "The purpose and meaning of the eternal divine election of grace consists in the fact that the one who is elected from all eternity can and does elect God in return."[8] This has happened and is happening in Jesus Christ, as an on-going event in time and eternity.[9] The living Word, Jesus Christ, is the "*Klammer*"[10] that encompasses both eternity and time in an on-going actualistic event of election.[11] In this way the actuality of the person of Jesus is placed centre stage.

We saw that another point of contention in Barth's dialectic is that he rules out a view of condemnation as an equal counterpart to election and in this way the traditional understanding of double predestination undergoes a complete metamorphosis.[12] It is God who takes condemnation and rejection in order that humanity may encounter bliss and be brought into fellowship with God.[13] For Barth, God in Christ took on flesh in order to be judged on the cross, becoming the one and only rejected person. By seeing Jesus as the *Seinsgrund* of election, both the subject and object of election, Barth makes the term *election* a positive one.[14] God's *Yes* is dominant over and above any *No*. Chapter 1 explained that Barth argues that the *No* is only spoken for the sake of God's grace and mercy in his *Yes*. He writes:

> And we introduce the first and most radical point with our thesis that the doctrine of election must be understood quite

5. McCormack, "Grace and Being," 95.
6. See Kreck, *Grundentscheidungen in Karl Barths Dogmatik*, 197.
7. *CD* II/2, 177.
8. *CD* II/2, 178.
9. See Kreck, *Grundentscheidungen in Karl Barths Dogmatik*, 197.
10. Ibid., 198.
11. At the Geneva congress of 1936 Peter Barth proposed his thesis, an "aktuellen Prädestination gegenüber der überkommenen statischen Auffassung." Karl Barth picks this up and includes it in his doctrine of election. See Kreck, *Grundentscheidungen in Karl Barths Dogmatik*, 198.
12. See ibid., 198.
13. See *CD* II/2, 163.
14. See Kreck, *Grundentscheidungen in Karl Barths Dogmatik*, 190.

> definitely and unequivocally as Gospel; that it is not something neutral on the yonder side of Yes and No; that it is not No but Yes; that it is not Yes and No, but in its substance, in the origin and scope of its utterance, it is altogether Yes.[15]

At that stage we had not looked closely at Barth's dogmatic exposition of the doctrine of atonement and God's *No* spoken on the cross. All we said until then was that the *No* is the negative side of election, the rejection on the cross. Initially this appeared to be in harmony with our exegesis that Jesus is the ultimate *Yes* of God spoken towards humanity. However, we need to consider whether it is also in accord with our exegesis of chapter 4 where the parallel structuring and the synthesis of *Yes* and *No* in election and reprobation is given up and only election (and not rejection) is based on Jesus Christ. By disagreeing with Barth on the synthesis of *Yes* and *No* in Christ, we have not denied the negative aspect in chapter 4 but have said that we could not follow Barth's interpretation of the *No*. Before we deal with the subjective side (the role of the Spirit and human faith) of God's *Yes* and *No* further, we need to consider one more aspect of Barth's thought that is related to the doctrines of election and atonement. This is the question of *apokatastasis*, an examination of which will deepen our understanding of Barth's view of election and atonement in Christ.

1.1. *Election, Rejection, and the Question of Apokatastasis*

For Barth, election in Christ includes humanity's autonomy to elect God in return. The Bible appears silent on the reason *why* a person might refuse the offer of God. But will the person who rejects the offer finally be without God? What is the relationship between Barth's doctrine of election, rejection, and the notion of *apokatastasis*?

Barth finishes his study of 'The Condemnation of Man' by questioning whether or not we can be sure that this threat of condemnation will finally be executed. For Barth, the 'man of sin' is a liar, a "man who goes forward to his condemnation."[16] Yet in what Jesus has accomplished on the cross, a work that no human being could have accomplished, the word of reconciliation and truth spoken upon all of humanity is a word of pardon and is as follows: "Thou art no longer the man of sin whose figure and role thou dost still assume. That man is set aside and overcome. He is dead. Thou canst be that man no longer, not just because thou hast put him to death, but because

---

15. *CD* II/2, 13.
16. *CD* IV/3, 462.

thou hast done so in My death and passion."[17] This for Barth is the word of the cross in the light of Jesus Christ, the word of reconciliation, and the promise of the Spirit "whether it pleases him or not, whether it cheers or startles him, this is its substance, promise and claim."[18] No person can turn and dissolve this truth into untruth and therefore he "is what he has to be in contradiction between his subjective and objective reality,"[19] though "*es bleibt dabei, daß die Wahrheit auch für ihn gilt.*"[20] For Barth, the reality of God in the human Jesus Christ is "superior [*überlegen*] to the pseudo-reality" of the man of lies.[21]

So coming back to our concerns in chapter 1: is Brunner's charge against Barth justified? Does Barth advocate an *apokatastasis*?[22] Over and over again Barth has been charged with universalism,[23] and yet, as Greggs points out, "while the tenor of Barth's soteriology clearly points in a universalist direction, Barth on a number of occasions specifically and emphatically rejects the doctrine of universalism or *apokatastasis*."[24] In fact, he even gives a warning about promoting the idea of *apokatastasis*:

> We should be denying or disarming that evil attempt and our own participation in it if, in relation to ourselves or others or all men, we were to permit ourselves to postulate a withdrawal of that threat and in this sense to expect or maintain an *apokatastasis* or universal reconciliation as the goal and end of all things.[25]

Though 'theological consistency' might seem to lead towards this thought, he argues, "we must not arrogate to ourselves that which can be given and received only as a free gift."[26] He goes on to say that therefore "[n]o such

---

17. *CD* IV/3, 463.
18. *CD* IV/3, 464.
19. *CD* IV/3, 474.
20. *KD* IV/3, 546.
21. *CD* IV/3, 477.
22. See Nimmo, "Election and Evangelical Thinking," 34–35.
23. See Berkouwer, *The Triumph of Grace in the Theology of Karl Barth*, 111–22.
24. Greggs, "Jesus is Victor," 197. See also *CD* II/2, 417 and 476–77 as well as *CD* IV/3, §70.3, 'The Condemnation of Man.' On the claim that Barth tends in a 'universalist direction' see also Hunsinger, *How To Read Karl Barth*, 128–35.
25. *CD* IV/3, 477.
26. *CD* IV/3, 477.

postulate can be made even though we appeal to the cross and resurrection of Jesus Christ."[27]

Greggs goes on to explain that commentators on Barth—those defending Barth as well as his opponents—often miss the radical newness and re-description of Barth's interpretation of the doctrine of election. Barth's rejection of universalism or *apokatastasis* is not rooted in a notion of God's limitation of his own ultimate work of salvation, but rather with some problematic concepts or principles within universalism. Election, both for the individual and the community, is only understood 'in Christ.' It thus finds its meaning and purpose solely in him. There is a dialectic here between the particular and the universal, that it is the original universal election of Jesus Christ which "gives particular truth to individual election (II/2, p. 310)."[28] The final section of this chapter will show that what Barth wants to do is to "affirm the particularity of the Christian in the Holy Spirit, but this does not limit the ministry of the Holy Spirit."[29] Nevertheless, it is easy to see how Barth's all-inclusive election has caused some commentators to charge him with universalism.

One such commentator is Berkouwer, in *The Triumph of Grace in the Theology of Karl Barth*. Though Barth acknowledges Berkouwer's criticism by saying that "Berkouwer has undoubtedly laid his finger on an important point,"[30] in *CD* IV/3 he rejects Berkouwer's charge of universalism on the grounds of the book's title and its implications. Barth asserts that for him Christianity is not simply a 'triumphant affair' and Berkouwer's criticisms are predicated on a confused understanding of Barth's position as exemplified by the title of Berkouwer's book:

> If I am in a sense understood by its clever and faithful author, yet in the last resort I cannot think that I am genuinely understood for all his care and honesty, this is connected with the fact that he tries to understand me under this title.[31]

For Barth it is not the "triumph of grace" but the "triumph of the person Jesus Christ";[32] it is not a christological 'principle' that undergirds his work

27. *CD* IV/3, 477.
28. Greggs, "Jesus is Victor," 202.
29. Greggs, *Barth, Origen, and Universal Salvation*, 135.
30. *CD* IV/3, 173.
31. *CD* IV/3, 173.
32. See Gloege, "Zur Versöhnungslehre Karl Barth," who writes: "Jesus ist Sieger! In dem ‚ist' des Satzes [. . .] verbirgt sich eine Geschichte, ein Drama. Das ‚ist' ist nicht statisch, sondern dynamisch zu verstehen. Leben, Bund, Versöhnung ‚sind,' indem sie sich ereignen [. . .] Ihr Triumph ist ausschließlich *sein* Triumph und nicht der ‚der

(Barth accuses Berkouwer of misrepresenting him here) because "we are not dealing with a Christ-principle, but with Jesus Christ Himself as attested by Holy Scripture."[33] Hence Barth says that the work should be retitled *Jesus is Victor*.[34] It is not that Barth rejects the final victory of Christ as such, but rather that he rejects a particular (and in his view incorrect) understanding of the way and means by which this victory comes to its completion and is fulfilled. In his reinterpretation, Barth carefully removes the "negative charges involved with an ultimate salvation of all humanity, while still allowing for and pointing towards that ultimate salvation."[35] So far, we might summarize (with Greggs) that "Barth rejects universalism because 'universalism' itself can never be the victor: this victory is Jesus Christ's."[36]

Furthermore, we need to consider Barth's understanding of time and eternity. Barth speaks in his theology of a pre-, supra-, and post-temporal eternity, which he sees as biblical since God who is omnipresent and omnipotent can exist before, above and after time.[37] This understanding of eternity is worked out in its (positive) relation to time. Eternity does not destroy time—instead it enables and safeguards it. Christ's election is an election in time and history of the life of Jesus:

> before all created reality, before all being and becoming in time, before time itself, in the pre-temporal eternity of God, the eternal divine decision as such has as its object and content the existence of this one created being, the man Jesus of Nazareth, and the work of this man in His life and death, His humiliation and exaltation, His obedience and merit. It tells us further that in and with the existence of this man the eternal divine decision has as its object and content the execution of the divine covenant with man, the salvation of all men.[38]

Gnade,'" 140.

33. *CD* IV/3, 174.

34. See *CD* IV/3, 173. It is interesting to note that nowhere in *CD* IV/3 does Barth object to Berkouwer's charges of universalism, nor indeed does he even mention them. What he *does* reject, however, are the implications drawn from Berkouwer. These four points of objection by Barth against Berkouwer's charges are precisely highlighted by Greggs, "Jesus is Victor," 204–6.

35. Ibid., 206.

36. Ibid., 206.

37. See *CD* II/1, 169.

38. *CD* II/2, 116.

Barth does not believe that it is possible "entirely [to] separate the ultimate and penultimate."[39] For Barth, the Christian is a penultimate sign of the ultimate, from which he cannot be separated.[40] The ultimate sign is *Jesus is Victor*. In contemporary Christianity, the Christian faith and "the Christian himself is not the end of the ways of God but only the preliminary sign of this end,"[41] since when we speak of faith "we are speaking of most important penultimate things, but not of ultimate things."[42] The Christian lives in anticipation of his own awaited completion as well as in the "anticipation of what is truly and finally purposed in what God has done and revealed in Jesus Christ, namely, the liberation of all men."[43] It is this notion of the penultimate in Barth's theology that allows room in history for human freedom. The basis for human freedom in history is Jesus' victory and this is the way in which one should understand Barth's doctrine of election and its ramifications, including rejection.

Barth's emphasis on the ultimate in the assertion that *Jesus is Victor* undoubtedly displays a strong universalistic tendency. We saw that Barth's rejection of *apokatastasis* is grounded in the rejection of a principle, a conceptual framework, rather than in the rejection of a hope for the salvation of all: "I don't believe in universalism, but I do believe in Jesus Christ, the reconciler of all."[44] If commentators are to charge Barth with universalism, they have to be careful not to accuse him of something that he himself rejects so earnestly, and sees as bringing about limitations and problems. According to Barth, to put one's faith in universalism would be to put one's faith in something that is greater than Christ and consequently the concept of universalism would undermine the sovereignty of God. By placing one's faith in Jesus Christ, the 'reconciler of all,' and believing that 'Christ is victor,' God is truly affirmed as the subject of salvation. Thus, by affirming the particularity of Christ in election for humanity's salvation, Barth wants to free and transform radically the doctrine of election from its 'horrible' binary division of humanity into two camps, making way for the positive message of election and salvation in Christ. For Barth, the Church is the kingdom of God in action in the world for the salvation of the 'many.' The

---

39. Greggs, *Barth, Origen, and Universal Salvation*, 127.

40. See *CD* IV/3, 351–52.

41. *CD* IV/3, 675.

42. *CD* IV/1, 767.

43. *CD* IV/3, 675.

44. Karl Barth, Conv. IX: Conversations with Swiss Methodist preachers, 16 May 1961 and representatives of the pietists, 6 October 1959, cited from Busch, *Karl Barth: His Life from Letters and Autobiographical Texts*, 394.

'many' must be seen as a dynamic and open number and not a determinate one. He points to passages such as 1 Tim 2:4 and says that the will of God is directed to the salvation of all of humanity as well as being sufficient for all. He writes:

> we cannot follow the classical doctrine and make the open number of those who are elect in Jesus Christ into a closed number to which all other men are opposed as if they were rejected. Such an assumption is shattered by the unity of the real and revealed will of God in Jesus Christ. [...] And yet it is not legitimate to make the limitless many of the elect in Jesus Christ the totality of all men. For in Jesus Christ we have to do with the living and personal and therefore the free will of God in relation to the world and every man.[45]

Thus, for Barth, election is not a static event, but must be understood dynamically. He does not speak of any subjective certainty of a person's own salvation but only of the objective work of Jesus Christ, who is the Redeemer of all. It seems that Barth advocates universal atonement, and the possibility of universal election and salvation in Christ, without actually saying that all *will* be saved, thus denying the thought of *apokatastasis*. Having said that, Barth does very much encourage the *apokatastasis* as something that every Christian should hope for, even pray for. He says that "there is no good reason why we should not be open to this possibility," posing the question of whether or not the reality of God and humanity in Jesus Christ points plainly in the "direction of the work of a truly eternal divine patience and deliverance and therefore of an *apokatastasis* or universal reconciliation?"[46] He finishes by saying that though we are forbidden to count on it "we are surely commanded the more definitely to hope and pray for it as we may do already on this side of this final possibility."[47]

1.2. Limited Atonement vs. Universalism

The issues of election and universalism are affected by yet another matter: the scope of the atonement. The historical outworking of the election and the covenant is the cross, but we have to ask: 'Who did Christ die for?' 'Only for the elect or for all?' It is the question of limited (or 'definite') versus

---

45. *CD* II/2, 422.
46. *CD* IV/3, 478.
47. *CD* IV/3, 478.

universal atonement: whether Christ died only for some (the elect few who are finally saved) or for everyone.

Traditionally, Calvinists (i.e., those who adhere to the *Westminster Confession of Faith*) have sought to defend God's sovereignty, arguing for limited atonement,[48] which is linked to the doctrine of unconditional election,[49] and for no libertarian human free will.[50] Those Calvinists would contend that though Christ's death was sufficient for all (sufficient to cover all the sins of humanity), it was effective only for the elect—those chosen by God before the beginning of the world. Though Christ's death was potentially sufficient to save tens of worlds if necessary, it would nonetheless

---

48. Limited Atonement: "6. As God hath appointed the elect unto glory, so hath he, by the eternal and most free purpose of his will, foreordained all the means thereunto. Wherefore, they who are elected, being fallen in Adam, are redeemed by Christ, are effectually called unto faith in Christ by his Spirit working in due season, are justified, adopted, sanctified, and kept by his power, through faith, unto salvation. Neither are any other redeemed by Christ, effectually called, justified, adopted, sanctified, and saved, but the elect only." (chapter III, art. 6). "4. God did, from all eternity, decree to justify all the elect." (chapter XI, art. 4)

49. Unconditional Election: "3. By the decree of God, for the manifestation of his glory, some men and angels are predestinated unto everlasting life; and others foreordained to everlasting death. 4. These angels and men, thus predestinated, and foreordained, are particularly and unchangeably designed, and their number so certain and definite, that it cannot be either increased or diminished. 5. Those of mankind that are predestinated unto life, God, before the foundation of the world was laid, according to his eternal and immutable purpose, and the secret counsel and good pleasure of his will, hath chosen, in Christ, unto everlasting glory, out of his mere free grace and love, without any foresight of faith, or good works, or perseverance in either of them, or any other thing in the creature, as conditions, or causes moving him thereunto; and all to the praise of his glorious grace." (chapter III, art. 3, 4 and 5).

50. The *Westminster Confession of Faith* expresses 'no libertarian human free will' through the doctrine of irresistible grace: "1. All those whom God hath predestinated unto life, and those only, he is pleased, in his appointed and accepted time, effectually to call, by his Word and Spirit, out of that state of sin and death, in which they are by nature, to grace and salvation, by Jesus Christ; enlightening their minds spiritually and savingly to understand the things of God, taking away their heart of stone, and giving unto them a heart of flesh; renewing their wills, and, by his almighty power, determining them to that which is good, and effectually drawing them to Jesus Christ: yet so, as they come most freely, being made willing by his grace. 2. This effectual call is of God's free and special grace alone, not from anything at all foreseen in man, who is altogether passive therein, until, being quickened and renewed by the Holy Spirit, he is thereby enabled to answer this call, and to embrace the grace offered and conveyed in it. 4. Others, not elected, although they may be called by the ministry of the Word, and may have some common operations of the Spirit, yet they never truly come unto Christ, and therefore cannot be saved." (chapter X, art. 1, 2 and 4).

be wrong to say that Christ died for each human being.[51] "Since the work of God is always efficient, those for whom atonement was made and those who are actually saved must be the same people."[52] Thus, Torrance correctly summarizes the Calvinist view on Christ's intention when he says that Jesus died sufficiently for all but not effectively, as his death was not applied to all human beings "since Christ did not die with the intention that his death should be applied to all."[53]

---

51. See also Steele, Thomas, and Quinn, *The Five Points of Calvinism, Defined, Defended, and Documented*, "Christ's redeeming work was intended to save the elect only and actually secured salvation for them. His death was a substitutionary sacrifice of the penalty of sin in the place of certain specified sinners. In addition to putting away the sins of His people, Christ's redemption secured everything necessary for their salvation, including faith, which united them to Him. The gift of faith is infallibly applied by the Spirit to all for whom Christ died, thereby guaranteeing their salvation," 6–7. "Thus, Christ's saving work was limited in value, for it was of infinite worth and would have secured salvation for everyone if this had been God's intention," 40.

We have already shown in chapter 4 that the atonement's biblical scope must be seen as universal and unlimited. Election and atonement (salvation) are achieved and completed 'in Christ.' Therefore the atonement's value is not limited to certain elect individuals, excluding others; instead, Christ's offer of salvation with his call to follow him *truly* extends to all of humankind, without any hidden clauses. This allows for the *possibility* of salvation for all.

52. Boettner, *The Reformed Doctrine of Predestination*, 155.

53. Torrance, *Atonement*, 186. On the role of the Holy Spirit see also Steele, Thomas and Quinn, *The Five Points of Calvinism, Defined, Defended, and Documented*, "The gospel *invitation extends a call* to salvation to every one who hears its message. It invites all men without distinction to drink freely of the water of life and live. It promises salvation to all who repent and believe. But this outward general call, extended to the elect and nonelect alike, will not bring sinners to Christ. Why? Because men are by nature dead in sin and are under its power. They are of themselves unable and unwilling to forsake their evil ways and to turn to Christ for mercy. Consequently, the unregenerate will not respond to the gospel call to repentance and faith. No amount of external threatenings or promises will cause blind, deaf, dead, rebellious sinners to bow before Christ as Lord and to look to Him alone for salvation. Such an act of faith and submission is contrary to the lost man's nature. Therefore, the *Holy Spirit*, in order to bring God's elect to salvation, extends to them *a special inward call* in addition to the outward call contained in the gospel message. Through this special call the Holy Spirit performs a work of grace within the sinner which inevitably brings him to faith in Christ. [. . .] Although the general outward call of the gospel can be, and often is, rejected, the special inward call of the Spirit never fails to result in the conversion of those to whom it is made. This special call is not made to all sinners but is issued to the elect only. The Spirit is in no way dependent upon their help or cooperation for success in His work of bringing them to Christ. It is for this reason that Calvinists speak of the Spirit's call and of God's grace in saving sinners as being 'efficacious,' 'invincible,' or 'irresistible.' The grace which the Holy Spirit extends to the elect cannot be thwarted or refused; it never fails to bring them to true faith in Christ," 52–54. The

But this raises numerous further concerns as behind this reasoning lie two concepts: a strictly logical, mathematical, and analytical concept in relation to the bearing of sin, and a metaphysical or philosophical concept of irresistible grace. The first is trying to safeguard the sufficiency of the cross. If Christ indeed died for all the sins of humanity, and yet not all are saved (and according to the biblical witness some people are thrown in the lake of fire to suffer the gnashing of teeth) the cross would not emerge as totally sufficient, or rather, we would have to question God's omnipotence; though he wanted to save all, he is nevertheless unable to do so. Since this cannot be, the Calvinist response is to posit another idea, which contends that God's will was for Christ to die only for those who were predestined to be saved—the elect. In order to safeguard the sufficiency of the cross and take seriously those passages of Scripture that speak about hell and destruction, they argue that Christ did not die for the sins of the reprobate. The second concept is the metaphysical or philosophical concept of irresistible grace and absolute divine causality. Torrance points out that it "could not but be held that all for whom Christ died efficaciously must necessarily be saved" and the doctrine of absolute predestination "appears to supply a notion of causal efficacy to the death of Christ"[54]—only the elect are saved. Yet this raises an important question about divine freedom and the transcendence of God. Furthermore, it either calls into question the relationship between God's action and being in the atonement or it questions God's loving nature altogether. Either it attacks the notion that the atonement flows out of God's nature (essentially arguing that the atonement flows out of some arbitrary divine will); or, if it affirms that the atonement does flow out of God's nature (John Owen), then it attacks God's being, making God's love arbitrary

---

fact that a strong separation is placed here between the Gospel's *general* outward and Holy Spirit's *special* inward call is important for our discussion in section 2 the role of the Holy Spirit in the atonement as well as human freedom and the human response in sections 3.1. and 3.4., respectively. The flawed logic of this position is exposed by the fact that Christ's call to repentance is made to all people, and not just to a few elect. Jesus calls every person to the banquet (Matt 22 and Luke 14) and the invite to "Come, for everything is now ready" (Luke 14:17) must therefore be seen as universal. This becomes apparent in the second half of the parable. In Luke 14:21, the invitation is explicitly extended to "the poor, the crippled, the blind and the lame," and in Matt 22:9 it is to "*anyone* you [the servants] find." The words of the Gospel message (the objective content of the atonement) and the Holy Spirit's work in a person (the subjective side) work hand in hand (see chapter 5, section 2.3. and 3.4. for a discussion of the objective and subjective sides of the atonement). Thus Word and Spirit cannot be seen as separate in the way described above.

54. Torrance, *Atonement*, 186.

because he would be seen to love some and not others (some would be saved, whilst others condemned).

Furthermore, they go on to argue that

> the Arminian limits the atonement as certainly as does the Calvinist. The Calvinist limits the extent of it in that he says it does not apply to all persons (although as has already been shown, he believes that it is efficacious for the salvation of the large proportion of the human race); while the Arminian limits the power of it, for he says that in itself it does not actually save anybody. The Calvinist limits it quantitatively, but not qualitatively; the Arminian limits qualitatively, but not quantitatively.[55]

However, here we have to contend, with Barth, that the atonement is not a 'principle' that saves humanity, but that it is the unity of the person and work of Jesus Christ who is *Versöhnung*. When referring to Christ's death, the New Testament writers are not interested in speculating about who is and who is not saved in abstract terms, but rather, they highlight that it is Jesus who became the sin offering and ransom, the place of redemption. To limit the extent or the power of the person of Jesus Christ in his saving work would have the effect of limiting the extent of God's unconditional love towards humanity or the power of his omnipotence.

In order to safeguard the sufficiency of the cross, Calvinists settled on the concept that the cross was only efficacious for the chosen elect. However, this means that Christ's work on the cross is separated from God's love, since "Christ's love for all mankind is not translated into action."[56] There might appear to be a fatal weakness in this position, because it would predicate the separation of Christ's person from Christ's work and this undermines not only the atonement but also the incarnation.[57] The argument that Christ died only for the sins of the chosen elect is made more problematic by the fact that this would mean that God's judgment against sin on the cross was only a partial judgment and therefore only a partial victory over evil, sin, and death. But what are the implications of this argument for the finished work of Christ in the atonement? It must mean that on the cross God did not speak a final *No* against sin and death, but only enacted a partial substitution.[58] In this way it is actually the Calvinist who appears to limit the power of the saving work of God on the cross. We have already shown that this kind of logic was refuted by the concept of *Existenzstellvertretung*,

55. Boettner, *The Reformed Doctrine of Predestination*, 153.
56. Torrance, *Atonement*, 187.
57. See ibid., 187.
58. See ibid., 185.

which highlights that in the Old Testament atonement, the animal[59] did not bear sin (as in a penal model of atonement) and thus there is no need to 'limit' the atonement just to the elect. It can therefore affirm the universal notion that *Jesus Christ is Victor* and point to a universal offer of salvation without logically leading into universal salvation as such.

Implications and Criticism

Barth developed his doctrine of election in the context of his concern that the traditional Reformed doctrine was not faithful to the whole of Scripture, and also caused pastoral difficulties in assuring Christians of their salvation. However, in the light of our exegesis and examination of Barth's ideas, we have to ask whether Barth himself is truly faithful to Scripture and whether his ideas raise further pastoral problems in themselves.

In any examination of the doctrines of election in eternity and eternal salvation, we have to acknowledge the limitations of the Christian understanding of God as revealed in Scripture. Ultimately, the Christian has to affirm that God has to have the final word when it comes to a person's individual salvation. Thus to begin with, we have to agree with Barth and say that no Christian could with absolute certainty affirm an *apokatastasis*, though no Christian should not *not* hope and pray for it either. Both are extremes that might be perceived as unbiblical or even un-Christian. However, since Barth will not rule out an *apokatastasis* or universal salvation, we have to press Barth and ask whether this might create a threefold problem: (1) Would it be faithful to Scripture to ignore those passages that clearly talk about rejection of the sinner? (John 3:36); (2) Would it not again create exactly what Barth tried to avoid with his entire undertaking of the doctrine of election—a special kind of *Deus absconditus*, a God about whom at the end nothing is fully revealed and certain?; and finally (3) since to see Jesus is to see the Father's will, does the condemnation and punishment of Jesus not also undermine the revelation of God in Jesus Christ on the cross?

Barth asserts that the election of humanity takes place in the eternal decision and the historical life of the incarnate Son. Salvation for humanity is achieved and offered in the election of Christ, 'in Christ' who is Victor. We saw that, for Barth, the election of Christ does not mean the election of a principle but of a person. In this election, human freedom is secured and given space in a way that a principle could never provide. This is the main reason for Barth's rejection of universalism, because he wants to safeguard the particularity of the person of Jesus, and sees this particularity

---

59. See chapter 4: 4.6. *Existenzstellvertretung* in the New Testament.

undermined by a principle in place of a person. As Webster points out, for Barth election is centred on the person Jesus Christ and thus, "human reality, and therefore human agency, are '*enhypostatically* real,' drawing their substance from the human reality of Jesus Christ."[60] Yet it is not only humanity's freedom that is guarded in the particularity of Jesus in election, but also God's freedom and sovereignty. Once more, for Barth, God is not limited or constrained by a Christ-principle but rather, in his free sovereign choice, God decided to embrace this self-limitation, he chose to become Jesus of Nazareth. Barth is very clear that God does not have to elect at all—he is under no obligation, but chose to do so in Christ.[61]

In this way, Barth's theology insists that God is not binding himself to an arbitrary principle of election but rather is emphasizing the person of Jesus. The mysterious sovereign will of God revealed in the person of Jesus is the eternal will of God incarnate, "the Prophet who knows and proclaims the will of God which is done in His existence."[62] Thus Barth stresses the sovereignty of God, a sovereignty in which God in his eternal election of the person of Jesus Christ demonstrates his will to be *for* humanity.

However, Barth's doctrine of election is a double predestination of election and rejection in which God's *No* in rejection is not his final but only his penultimate word. The ultimate word is the final *Yes* of God's election, which rejection cannot in any way undo. Thus for Barth the rejected are ultimately also elected in Christ. Here we see the implications of Barth's separation of the cross and the resurrection, the cross as the Father's negative *No* and the resurrection as his positive *Yes*. For Barth, God in Christ took on flesh in order to be judged on the cross, becoming the one and only rejected person.

Despite this apparent duality, the cross and the resurrection should not be seen as two distinct events happening sequentially, but as one and the same positive event, the Christ-event, working out the redemption in Jesus Christ. Our exegesis concluded that Jesus is only the elect and not the rejected. But where does this leave the rejection side of election on the cross and what happens to the 'double' aspect of predestination? In considering the Old Testament cult, we argued against the idea of the sacrificial animal (*ḥaṭṭā't*) (which should be seen as a type of Christ) bearing sin and being judged for it. Our exegesis demonstrated that only the Azazel-goat bore sin. We saw in chapter 4 (which dealt specifically with the notion of sin bearing) that this was also the case with Jesus' death on the cross. In the same way

---

60. Webster, *Barth*, 89.
61. See *CD* II/2, 101.
62. *CD* IV/3, 180.

that 'sin bearing' or 'sin removal' is pivotal for the doctrine of atonement, it is likewise a crucial concept for the doctrine of election. One's understanding of sin bearing alters everything.

Therefore, we must again ask Barth whether the rejected are ultimately also elected in Christ. Even though this would seem to convey certainty in the sense that 'all' would be saved, salvation would in practice still remain an uncertainty, because it would not be something revealed through Christ on the cross. Instead, it would ultimately be a decision of the *eschaton*, one that, from the perspective of created time, God makes later. Although the New Testament depicts salvation as ultimately a matter for God (Matt 25:31–46), it would still be a decision that has not been revealed in Jesus Christ. This therefore would make salvation a hidden reality for humanity, even if it were a positive one; that is to say, it is a matter about which God conceals certain knowledge from humanity. This would also render the cross only a penultimate decision, an idea that relegates the chief supremacy of revelation of Christ on the cross. Thus, this would again create a choice of God behind Jesus Christ and therefore another *Deus absconditus*—exactly that which Barth so strongly opposed in Calvin's theology. To argue that God might eventually choose to be gracious to those who have lived a life as 'sinful man as a liar' in opposition of God, throws doubt on the reliability of God's Word. How is it possible to know that such an unpredictable God is trustworthy and that he might not, in turn, then choose to deny his grace to others who have faithfully followed him? Despite this apparent duality, the cross and the resurrection should not be seen as two events happening sequentially (a penultimate and an ultimate one) but as one and the same positive event, the Christ event, where both a final election and rejection occur in and through Christ. Together they are a revelation *of* and a window *to* the ultimate decision made in front of the judgment seat at the *eschaton*, because to assert otherwise would be to create another *Deus absconditus*.

2. The Eternal Spirit and the Mortal Soul

We heard from Barth that the doctrine of creation is the beginning of all God's works distinct from himself. One might argue that the doctrine of reconciliation is the doctrine that talks about how this distinction is overcome by and in Jesus Christ through the Holy Spirit. Barth posits neither an abstract concept of God nor an abstract concept of humanity. Instead, for Barth, the historical Jesus of Nazareth is the sole basis of election—the "electing God and the elect human."[63] He is not, as Augustine and Calvin

---

63. McCormack, "Grace and Being," 93.

saw him, merely a mirror—Barth argues that this would make Jesus into an "instrument" independent and separated from the primordial divine decision. In *The Humanity of God* Barth claims that "one cannot speak of God without speaking of man."[64] He continues in *The Gift of Freedom* to say that one can "speak about man only by speaking about God."[65] Thus God and humanity must be seen together as a unity from the "vantage point"[66] of Jesus Christ. God in his downward movement has "attached Himself to another,"[67] bound himself to humanity and made her a covenant partner in Jesus Christ. Barth says that in "Jesus Christ there is no isolation of man from God or of God from man"[68] but that in him we can see the history in which "God and man meet together and are together, the reality of the covenant mutually contracted, preserved, and fulfilled."[69] Jesus Christ is the person who is both a "loyal partner"[70] to humanity from God's side and to God from humanity's side.

2.1. Christ the Mediator

In this way Jesus Christ, in his hypostatic union, represents both parties and is not only the Mediator (μεστίης) and reconciler of the covenant between God and humanity, establishing justice and peace between both parties, but is also the eternal covenant personified. Barth sees Jesus Christ as a series of correspondences: the lion of Judah as well as the lamb slain before the foundation of the world; the king of the tribe of Judah as well as the High Priest from the tribe of Levi; God as well as human.[71] These dual aspects

---

64. Barth, *The Humanity of God*, 56.
65. Ibid., 70.
66. Ibid., 55.
67. Ibid., 49.
68. Ibid., 46.
69. Ibid., 46.
70. Ibid., 46.
71. See *CD* IV/3, 5. Here Barth seems to get the *munus duplex* of Christ wrong, which also leads to his different account of the *munus triplex* in comparison with Calvin. Whereas the Priesthood of Christ is normally attributed to the humanity of Christ, Barth attributes it to his divinity, which is also seen in his attribution of Christ's humanity to kingship and not to his divinity. Barth wants to attribute soteriology of the priesthood to God and opts out for a Christology in which the humanity is exalted in her kingly role. However, in Hebrews we read that it is the *man* Jesus Christ that is after the order of Melchizedek and in the Old Testament the king of Israel was the Son of God, or rather the representative of God (see Ps 72). This notion of God being the one who sacrifices himself is seen in *CD* IV/1 in the downward movement of the Son

constitute the framework and content of the christological-soteriological doctrine of reconciliation.[72] For Barth, reconciliation signifies the Emmanuel, the God of peace with humanity.[73] Jesus Christ is thus the "actualisation of the covenant between God and man, both on the side of God and also on that of man."[74] In the first part of the work of reconciliation there is a "mighty movement from above to below [. . .] from God to man, the reconstitution and renewal of the covenant between God and man under the sign of the first element in the gracious saying of the Old Testament: 'I will be your God.'"[75] "[T]he second element in that gracious saying of the Old Testament: 'Ye shall be my people,'"[76] which is the reconciled man in Jesus Christ. The entire divine work of God's grace in the atonement can be summed up by saying that "as God condescends and humbles Himself to man and becomes man, man himself is exalted, not as God or like God, but to God, being placed at His side, not in identity, but in true fellowship with Him, and becoming a new man in this exaltation and fellowship."[77] Thus the event of the atonement is both, "wholly and utterly a movement from above to below, of God to man [. . .] and utterly a movement from below to above, the movement of reconciled man to God."[78]

Barth says that these two aspects of God and of humanity in the atonement are represented in the incarnation, where we read in John 1:14 that the *Logos* became flesh. If we put the emphasis on "flesh," Barth says that this is a statement about God who went into the far country; but if we put the emphasis on the "Logos" that was incarnate, then this is a statement about humanity, who is brought back home.[79] Barth sees these two movements reflected in the Greek word ἀποκαταλλάσσειν—to reconcile—which in its original meaning carries the notion of 'to exchange.' Therefore, as already argued, the renewal of the covenant between God and humanity involves the 'exchange,' both the *exinanitio* seen in the humiliation of God, as well as the *exaltatio* seen in the exaltation of humanity. Barth maintains that it was

---

of God and that it is man that is exalted as the king in the upward movement in *CD* IV/2. However, rather than separating the two natures of Jesus we have to see them together as Scripture does.

72. See *CD* IV/3, 6.
73. See *CD* IV/3, 4.
74. *CD* IV/3, 4.
75. *CD* IV/2, 4
76. *CD* IV/2, 5.
77. *CD* IV/2, 6.
78. *CD* IV/2, 6.
79. See *CD* IV/2, 20.

"God who went into the far country, and it is man who returns home. Both took place in the one Jesus Christ. It is not, therefore, a matter of two different and successive actions, but of a single action in which each of the two elements is related to the other and can be known and understood only in this relationship."[80] We have to understand God's going out "only as it aims at the coming in of man [and] the coming in of man only as the reach and outworking of the going out of God."[81] These two movements happen only in its original form "as the being and history of the one Jesus Christ."[82] Thus for Barth, the content of the doctrine of reconciliation *in nuce* is the human Jesus Christ, the fulfiller of the covenant and reconciler of the world.[83] Therefore in Jesus Christ reconciliation is not simply achieved, rather he *is* reconciliation.

However, it is only from the completed standpoint of the prophetic and mediating work of Christ that we see the fulfilment of the eternal covenant; the downward movement of the Son of God and the upward movement of the Son of Man. These two events coincide, perfectly resulting in the sealing and fulfilment of the covenantal promise from both sides, thus effecting peace: "I will be your God, and ye shall be my people."[84] It is here, from the central perspective of the prophetic office, that we see the unity of the twofold movement, which is actually just one "whole history in which God gives to man salvation but also causes man to give Him glory."[85] It is only from this midpoint that we see the content of reconciliation in perfect simultaneity, two ontologically distinct covenant partners in perfect harmony.[86] Barth says that we are first compelled to look downward from God to humanity and then also upward from humanity to God. Only then do we see this unity of God and human, embodied in Jesus Christ who in his being enacts this event of reconciliation. Nothing in terms of content is added in the prophetic office in *CD* IV/3 to the doctrine of reconciliation but it is here that we see that not a truth but *the* truth of the event "mediates and reveals

---

80. *CD* IV/2, 21.
81. *CD* IV/2, 21.
82. *CD* IV/2, 21.
83. See *CD* IV/3, 4.
84. See *CD* IV/3, 6.
85. *CD* IV/3, 7.

86. For further insight into the prophetic office in *CD* IV/3 I am indebted to Robert Leigh who deepened my understanding of the Mediator role of Christ and highlighted various aspects of Barth's understanding of the subjective side both being grounded in the objective work of Christ and simultaneously flowing out of Christ.

itself."[87] Truth is neither conditioned upon humanity's reception (but rather is the basis of all reception) nor is it "dark and dumb but perspicuous and vocal, [so] that it may and will therefore be received."[88] For Barth, reconciliation is thus not simply something Christ did on the cross but an ongoing event, a reality that "summons to conscious, intelligent, living, grateful, willing and active participation"[89] in this event. This event contains both God's action and being because Jesus Christ enacts *who* he is and *what* he does in himself—*Versöhnung*—and through history draws humanity deep into the Christ-event.

Thus, the entire doctrine of reconciliation has at its centre and *telos* the covenant fellowship, the union of God and humanity. This we might also call the question of the angels (see 1 Pet 1:12): 'How can the (sinful) mortals become immortal and have fellowship with a holy God?'

2.2. *From Perishable to Imperishable: The Spirit's Role in the Atonement*

Our discussion of Barth's theological anthropology in chapter 3 revealed his view that a human being exists by having '*Geist*' and thus being "*grounded, constituted and maintained* by God *as soul of his body [Seele seines Leibes]*."[90] The statement that humanity has '*Geist*' logically requires that she cannot exist in body and soul without God but depends upon the "ever new act of God."[91] The Spirit is the relation of God and humanity in the covenantal fellowship, or in the most general sense, God's "operation" [*Wirkung*] upon his creation, in particular the movement towards humanity.[92]

(A) THE SPIRIT AS CREATOR AND SUSTAINER

For Barth, to be human is not only to be a soul, but a "soul of a spatial body."[93] Barth's thought is reflected in the Genesis narrative of God creating 'man' by breathing into man's nostrils the breath (*rûaḥ*) of life (Gen 2:7). Through

---

87. *CD* IV/3, 8.
88. *CD* IV/3, 8.
89. *CD* IV/3, 8.
90. *CD* III/2, 349. Italics mine.
91. *CD* III/2, 356.
92. See *CD* III/2, 356.
93. *CD* III/2, 349. Barth emphasizes the when we speak about the human soul we highlight that the soul always belongs to a physical body.

Election, Atonement, and the Holy Spirit   219

God's breath man became a *"living soul"* (Gen 2:7), thereby imparting to humanity *some measure* of his own spiritual nature.[94] Thus a body without a soul would not be alive and so for Barth "'Soul' is a determination of earthly being. As it can only be the soul of a physical and therefore a material body, from which it cannot be parted, this settles the fact that man belongs to the earth and therefore to the lower side of created reality."[95] Barth explains that it is the Spirit who is

> God Himself in His creative movement to His creation. It is God who breathes specially upon man (Gen. 2:7), thus living for him, allowing him to partake of His own life, and therefore making him on his side a living being. From the standpoint of man, He is thus his possibility of being a 'living soul' (Gen. 2:7, ψυχὴ ζῶσα, 1 Cor. 15:45), and as such a body.[96]

In the Spirit, God moves towards all his creatures in the fullness of his own life. The fact that they live depends upon this movement and insofar as they live at all, they live by the Spirit. For the manner and measure of their life corresponds to the manner and measure in which this movement of God is of benefit to them and as such, it could be of benefit to man in the most perfect manner and measure. It is, however, of only transitory and partial benefit to man and hence his life is only transitory and partial: transitory, since it comes only to go; partial, since death and corruption are always near it.[97]

Insofar as the Spirit not only originates in, but also proceeds from God, the Spirit is "identical with God."[98] Therefore rather than suggesting that someone *has* the Spirit, a better description would be that the Spirit

---

94. See Pannenberg's emphasis on "without measure" and the "resting" of the Spirit. He writes: "The Spirit's work is always in some measure linked to an imparting [*Mitteilung*] of his dynamic even though he is not in the full sense always imparted and received as gift. [. . .] [O]nly to the degree that the Son is manifested in creatutrely life does the work of the Spirit in creation take on the form of gift. This is definitely so only in trelation to the incarnation of the Son. Hence it is said of Jesus Christ that the Spirit is given him 'without measure,' i.e. without restriction (John 3:34). For believers, then, the Spirit as gift is related to their becoming sons and daughters in baptism by fellowship with Jesus Christ (Rom. 5:15; 6:3ff.). In an extended sense the breath of life that is already given to all of us at creation (Gen. 2:7) may be seen as endowment with God's Spirit," in *Systematic Theology III*, 9.

95. *CD* III/2, 351.
96. *CD* III/2, 333f.
97. See *CD* III/2, 334.
98. *CD* III/2, 356.

"takes place"[99] in a person, as an "action and attitude"[100] of the Creator. Thus, humanity exists by and through God, and even in her fallen state of "*Geist*entfremdung"[101]—in death and under judgment—she remains human and "within the hand and power of God."[102] Barth affirms that God sustains humanity: not only did God create humanity, but he continues to sustain her in an "ever new act of divine creation."[103] Barth therefore calls God the living and active basis [*Urgrund*] of humanity, which is her hope, even in death.[104] Humanity would immediately cease to exist and perish eternally if God were to withdraw and cease to be the living God.[105] Therefore, "man is, as God is for him,"[106] and it is humanity's destiny to be God's covenant partner. Thus human existence rests wholly upon the free creative grace [*Schöpfergnade*] of God.

(B) The Spirit as Reconciler and Redeemer

God's *Yes* towards humanity can be summed up in his giving life through his *rûaḥ*, his impartation of some measure of his spiritual nature, as well the *Schöpfergnade* of sustaining humanity, through his "*Schöpferwirken als creatio continua.*"[107] However, in the book of Acts, we read about Pentecost and the Old Testament prophecy of the book of Joel being fulfilled, where it was promised that God's Spirit would be poured out on all human flesh. Barth calls this God's 'second Yes,' "which creates and gives them new life: a Yes which He did not owe them, but which He willed to speak, and which was the gracious confirmation of His own original will to create and His act

---

99. *CD* III/2, 356.

100. *CD* III/2, 356.

101. Joest points out that "[d]arum wird gerade da, wo Gott den ihm abgekehrten Menschen ‚heimsuchen' beginnt, exemplarisch in seiner Geschichte mit Israel, zunächst die Geistentfremdung dieses Menschen offenbar. [...] Auch über die Abkehrung des Menschen vor Gott ist die Schöpfung nicht einfach vom Wirken seines Geistes verlassen. Darin, daß Gott das geschaffene Leben nicht preisgibt, sondern auf das Ziel seiner Heimholung in Christus hin erhält, geht sein Schöperwillen beständig gegen die ihm entgegenwirkende Macht der Zerstörung an," in Joest, *Dogmatik Bd:1 Die Wirklichkeit Gottes*, 304.

102. *CD* III/2, 347.

103. *CD* III/2, 348.

104. See *CD* III/2, 348.

105. See *CD* III/2, 348f.

106. *CD* III/2, 349.

107. Joest, *Dogmatik Bd:1 Die Wirklichkeit Gottes*, 284.

Election, Atonement, and the Holy Spirit 221

of creation."[108] This second or "new 'Yes' is life because it calls forth the One who died in complete and utter solidarity with sinful and lost humanity."[109] For Barth, Pentecost is the Holy Spirit "bridging the gulf between Jesus' past and present. One looks back to Christ's coming on earth and forward to His coming in glory, but He is known in the present through the Holy Spirit: the Spirit is Christ's *geschichtliche Selbstmitteilung*."[110] Once again, rather than an act of positive and active possession by the believer, the coming of the Spirit at Pentecost is in fact a state of passive receiving, the result of the active giving by God of his Spirit. So when we read about the nature of humanity in Scripture, what is signified by a person's 'having' the Spirit is not something from her own innate capacity or ability, but something foreign to her nature that has come from God. God's gift of the Holy Spirit is his initiative and movement towards humanity to create covenantal fellowship, a meeting of Creator and creature.[111] We saw this symbolized in Leviticus

108. *CD* IV/1, 308. We do well to remember, however, that as Joest points out, the Spirit as 'Creator and Sustainer' is not *different* to the Spirit as 'Reconciler and Redeemer because "[d]er Leben wirkende Geist des Schöpfers ist kein anderer als der in und durch Christus wirkende Geist des Erlösers. [. . .] Der Geist des Schöpfers ist in seiner Macht, das Zerstörende zu überwinden, auch der Geist des Versöhners und Erlösers. Und der Geist des Versöhners und Erlösers is kein anderer als der Geist des dem von ihm geschenkten Leben die Treue haltenden Schöpfers. [. . .] Was der Geist der Versöhnung wirkt is *neues* Leben. Aber das Neue dieses Lebens sollte nicht verstanden werden als die Negation des natürlichen, geschaffenen Lebens, sondern als die Negation und das Abtun der *Zerstörung* dieses Lebens," Joest, *Dogmatik Bd:1 Die Wirklichkeit Gottes*, 304f. Genesis 2:7 describes God 'breathing out,' his *rûaḥ* going forth and thereby creating and sustaining all of creation. In light of this, the 'second yes' of reconciliation and new life 'in Christ' can be seen as God's 'breathing in'; the Spirit's "Heimholung" of lost and fallen humanity in her state of alienation, the Spirit's bringing about the *metanoia* (see chapter 5, section 3.2) *in* the person who was in a state of "Geistentfremdung." A Christian is therefore a person who ceases to work against the Spirit, 'turns around' (*šûb* or *metanoia*) and aligns herself with God's will and starts to 'battle' against the desires of the flesh, guided by the power of the Spirit in the footsteps of Christ. We can therefore conclude that God's 'breathing out' in creation and his 'breathing in' in the "Heimholung" represent two movements of the same Spirit (just like the two connected movements of recapitulation in *CD* IV/1 (*exinanitio*) and *CD* IV/2 (*exaltatio*)). They have the same purpose or result—covenantal fellowship between God and humanity.

109. Rodin, *Evil and Theodicy in the Theology of Karl Barth*, 213.

110. Greggs, *Barth, Origen, and Universal Salvation*, 126.

111. See Pannenberg who says that "the mediating of the gift of the Spirit by the Son and its eschatological content as participation in the death-defeating life of God go hand in hand. The gift of the Spirit to humanity at creation and the charisms of the old covenant as well are simply anticipatory signs of this eschatological gift. By this gift alone the Spirit binds himself to the lives of the recipients in such a way that

on the *kappōret*-rite: it is never a movement towards God initiated by Israel but rather something that proceeds from God—Israel is simply allowed to respond and imitate God's movement through the cultic rituals.[112] This is a vital observation, because it precludes any notion of appeasement of God. God—and never humanity—is always the initiator of reconciliation. He sends his Spirit of peace to bring about covenantal fellowship, something that humans can never initiate, but only receive. We see this notion represented in the Old Testament cult where it is YHWH who wants to come down and dwell amongst his people and bestow blessing upon them. Similarly, in the New Testament we read in Romans 5 that "While we were still sinners, Christ died for us" and that "God's love has been poured out into our hearts through the Holy Spirit, who has been given to us" (vv. 8 and 5).

This covenantal fellowship, established by the Spirit of peace through which *humanity* is changed, is revealed in history in the reconciling work of Christ, in both his death and resurrection. The two components of the Christ-event need to be seen together. It is not the death itself nor the event of the resurrection, but it is the person of Christ that is central. It is by the action of Holy Spirit that a person is drawn into the Christ event. "As the Holy Spirit is the agent of this union of man with Jesus Christ, therefore the work of the Holy Spirit belongs inseparably to the death and resurrection of Jesus Christ and to the happening portrayed in baptism,"[113] as we shall see later in section 3. It is by the Spirit that the person participates 'in Christ' in the cross event as well as in the resurrection and is thereby transformed into the likeness of Christ, the new *imago Dei*, which is "defined by Barth as the relationship within the covenant of grace which God has established with humanity."[114] "The centrality of the atonement is thus not the centrality of a doctrine of the Atonement, but the centrality of the act of Atonement in which God is God."[115] Therefore Barth can say "*Jesus Christus ist die Versöhnung.*"

---

even death can no longer separate these lives from his creative power," in *Systematic Theology III*, 12.

112. We will see this notion of correspondence [*Entsprechung*] more clearly explained in the later discussion of Barth's understanding of *Geistestaufe* und *Wassertaufe* (Section 3).

113. Barth, *The Teaching of the Church Regarding Baptism*, 12.

114. Rodin, *Evil and Theodicy in the Theology of Karl Barth*, 216.

115. Sykes, "Barth on the Centre of Theology," 40.

(c) The Spirit, Jesus, and 'Sinful' Flesh

It is the Spirit resting on Jesus who brings about a new order, subsuming the old disorder of the relationship between the body and the soul, which had stood in opposition to each other. For Barth 'sinful flesh' thus means the struggle of body and soul, a struggle overcome by the Spirit who brings peace and creates the right order of soul over body.[116] In the meeting of "willing spirit" and "weak flesh" (Matt 26:41) it is the Spirit in Jesus that brings victory and triumphs over the flesh.[117] This relationship of body and soul, with the body serving the soul, reminds us of Jesus' supreme particularity, that this "true man is primarily and at the same time the true God Himself. It is in this way, this higher unity of His existence with that of God Himself, that He is whole man, a meaningfully ordered unity of soul and body."[118] This image of his composition as a human being resembles the relationship and order of his being fully God and fully man, and thus soul and body are "clearly related to one another in the man Jesus, as His being as Son and Word of God the Creator is related to His creaturely constitution as soul and body of this man."[119] We conclude with Barth that the *analogia relationis* of soul and body of Jesus "are mutually related to one another as are God and man in His person, and Himself and His community."[120]

In the oneness and wholeness of Jesus' life and death, we see the soul and body in order, which again resembles the proper created order of the relationship between God and man.[121] Thus for Barth, Jesus' body is "used and governed"[122] for the specific purpose of his suffering action, and serves the function of the soul—his body is therefore "the body of His soul, not *vice versa*."[123] Yet it is not that Jesus' suffering is the end *per se*—instead his suffering should be seen as a means to an end. Suffering does not bring all threads of soteriology together but the real end here is the obedience of the Son (we read in Heb 5:8 that he "learned obedience"), the eternal *Logos*, in spite of his suffering. It is this theme of obedience—despite humanity's disobedience, and despite the suffering, even unto death (Phil 2:6)—that can be traced through the New Testament corpus as the hope for humanity. We

---

116. See *CD* III/2, 338.
117. See *CD* III/2, 338.
118. *CD* III/2, 340f.
119. *CD* III/2, 341.
120. *CD* III/2, 343f.
121. See *CD* III.2, 341.
122. See *CD* III/2, 399.
123. *CD* III/2, 339.

have to see suffering through the lens of the 'battle' between the Spirit and the flesh; Jesus does not give up hope in Gethsemane, nor is he overcome by despair but he puts his faith in his God, both in Gethsemane and on the cross. The psalms Jesus cites in the time between the garden and the cross are psalms of hope and trust in God (Pss 42 and 22). These prayers he prays are windows that reveal first the intimacy between Father and Son and secondly the divine comfort provided at this time of distress by the Holy Spirit. It is here that we understand the nature of the Spirit's power upon Jesus and the implication that Jesus is first and primarily God as well as man.[124] And it is in this way that Jesus' obedience cancels out the disobedience of Adam (Rom 5). Barth says that the fidelity of the Son towards the Father is seen in the "obedience [and] supreme freedom, [when] He gave up His soul and also His body, giving Himself to the service of the mercy of God towards men."[125] This obedience of Jesus results in the exaltation of humanity in the form of body and soul.

Some might see the fallen Adam as lacking Spirit [*geistlos*] or rather remaining without "*Geist*" and that therefore the *Logos*, the second Adam, came "in the flesh" to firstly give Geist to humanity and secondly to transform it and bring humanity back to God.[126] In this case, "the formation and ordering, which come on the flesh when the Logos becomes flesh and the Spirit rests upon this man, is and creates something quite new in and out of the flesh."[127] This is the slaying and cutting off of the old flesh through death and its renewal and transformation through the resurrection; or, in the language of Paul, the abolition of the old Adam and the coming of the new being, the second Adam, in a new bodily form of the second Adam (Rom 5; 1 Cor 15).

---

124. Barth sees this picture of order, of first and second, God and humanity, soul and body also reflected in the relationship between Christ and his Church, which is his body. Where Christ is not exalted there the Church is dead, the same way as the body is dead without the soul, yet where the Church is alive, there she is obedient to Christ. The *analogia relationis* between Christ and Church is particularly interesting when it come to election. Barth writes: "The one divine act of election is the election of this head and this body. As Jesus' soul and body are inseparably one, so are He and His people. And as order rules in the one case, so also in the other," *CD* III/2, 342. In this way, the Church is co-elect in Christ and belongs to him. This is a strong emphasis that God does not want to be without humanity. That does not mean that God needs humanity but that this is the created order he has established and his faithful to in regard to his own being.

125. *CD* III/2, 338.

126. See *CD* III/2, 338.

127. *CD* III/2, 336.

(D) The Spirit's Saving Action: Soul and Body[128]

It is essential to understand the close relationship between the incarnation (in which the divine *Logos* took on flesh and incorporated himself into humanity) and the atonement (whereby humanity was incorporated into Christ through the Spirit).[129] At the heart of this mutual incorporation stands the hypostatic union, which is carried out through the life, death and resurrection of Christ, reconciling humanity to God. This reciprocal incorporation of God into humanity and humanity into God, as achieved in the hypostatic union in Jesus Christ, is the fulfilment of the Old Testament covenant in Lev 26:12.[130] In this way, Jesus' incarnation, life and death represent 'God hidden in Man,' and the resurrection, ascension and Pentecost represent 'Man hidden in God' (see Col 3:1-3). Christ's atoning work (incarnation, life, death and resurrection) can be summarized with the 'exchange-formula': 'God in man' in order that 'man in God.'[131] Paul says in 2 Cor 8:9: "For you know the grace of our Lord Jesus Christ, that though he was rich, yet for your sake he became poor, so that you through his poverty might become rich." Furthermore, in Philippians Paul talks about Christ's voluntary and humble *kenosis* and exaltation. This motif of *recapitulation* that Christ did something for humanity or came towards her in order for her to become rich or dwell with God (a notion found in St. Irenaeus, St. Athanasius, St. Gregory of Nyssa) is neatly summarized by the Russian theologian Vladimir Lossky who says that "[t]he descent (*katabasis*) of the divine person of Christ makes human persons capable of an ascent (*anabasis*) in the Holy

---

128. This is not to suggest that the Spirit's saving action is limited to soul and body alone. There is strong biblical evidence that the Spirit's role encompasses the redemption of the entire creation (see Rom 8:19-23). However, the focus of this particular study is the Spirit's role in the redemption of the individual.

129. We saw that the individual's incorporation into the 'holy' was also part of the cultic atonement; when the blood (the life-substance or the 'soul') was "brought into contact with the 'holy' the Israelite is thereby able to have fellowship with God," Bell, *Deliver Us from Evil*, 199.

130. See *CD* IV/2, 5.

131. Irenaeus had the first 'exchange-formula': "For it was for this end that the Word of God was made man, and He who was the Son of God became the Son of man, that man, having been taken into the Word, and receiving the adoption, might become the son of God," in, "Against Heresies," III 19.1. Canlis points out that what being "exchanged is not humanity for divinity (a common misreading of the Irenaean exchange), but an alienated humanity for a *koinōnia*-humanity. Note carefully that humanity is not just given this altered relationship *ex nihilo*, but receives it only has 'having been taken into the Word.' Adoption is being taken into the Son, the progress, his ascent to the Father," in Canlis, *Calvin's Ladder*, 206.

Spirit."[132] Thus "Christian life is the new life in hope begotten of the Holy Spirit. Seeing that the Christian man is hidden with Christ in God, he has always a conscience that is leading him into all truth."[133]

For Sarah Coakley, the Spirit is "catching up and incorporating the created realm into the life of God."[134] Similarly, Bell writes that "in Christian faith our very soul is taken (by God) into the reality of Christ."[135] It is only through this mutual incorporation of Christ into humanity and *vice versa* that humanity is redeemed and the atonement can be fully understood as God bringing "our soul together with that of Christ."[136] God in Christ in the incarnation 'clothed' himself with earthly, human, and thus perishable flesh in order to transform this human body into a heavenly, spiritual, and imperishable one (1 Cor 15:42–44) in Christ's resurrection.[137] Through the resurrection the human body was transformed, and made into a body clothed with the divine, or as Paul states it in 1 Cor 15:54: "the perishable has been clothed with the imperishable, and the mortal with immortality." Furthermore, Paul talks about being 'sealed' or 'marked' by the Spirit until the day of redemption and the Spirit being the guarantor, deposit or down payment of the future day of salvation when humanity will be given resurrection bodies. Thus the Holy Spirit is the eschatological promise that guarantees that humanity will share in this new creation. Already, the human soul is clothed by the divine Spirit, and thus human beings are embodied souls,[138]

---

132. Lossky, "Redemption and Deification," 97.

133. Barth, *The Holy Spirit and the Christian Life*, 2.

134. Sarah Coakley, "Why Three? Some Further Reflections on the Origins of the Trinity," 36.

135. Bell, *Deliver Us from Evil*, 229.

136. Ibid., 222.

137. Athanasius writes: "Wherefore, the Word, as I said, being Himself incapable of death, assumed a mortal body, that He might offer it as His own place of all, and suffering for the sake of all through His union with it," in, *On The Incarnation*, §20, 49.

138. The background to this 'clothing' of the soul is the Old Testament notion of identification. In the cultic atonement rite of the *sĕmîkâ* the person identified himself with the animal and participated in its death through the *Subjektübertragung*. Bell in *Deliver Us from Evil* writes: "in these Old Testament sin offerings (and in the death of Christ) there is an *ex opere operato*, not in the negative sense of 'securitas' but in a positive sense! The positive sense of this *ex opere operato* is as follows. When the animal dies the soul of the animal, the essential being, lives on in the blood. Therefore, the 'substance' which is transferred from the Israelite to the animal is the 'soul,'" 198. Bell talks here about 'soul,' not 'subject,' arguing that this is a more appropriate term to use in biblical discussions, the background of which being "found in the Old Testament understanding of the soul as the person," 203. Because the soul stands for all of human life (see pp. 193–95), the soul is "fundamental for the atonement," 203.

hidden in Christ by the Holy Spirit, God's *Geist*. Here we see again the pattern of double incorporation at work: because the *Logos* was made flesh and was united to humanity, humanity is also united to him in his death as well as his resurrection, making Christ the first fruit of the new creation (1 Cor 15). In Jesus' identification with the human condition, he redeemed those enslaved by sin and made them partakers of the divine sonship.[139]

Thus Paul can also talk about his body as an earthly 'tent' and the longing of his soul to be clothed not by an earthly tent but instead by a heavenly dwelling. He calls this clothing of the soul by the Spirit the mortal being swallowed up by life (2 Cor 5:1–4). "If we are united to Christ through our soul and if this soul is related both to his humanity and his divinity, then in some sense our inner person is related not only to the 'world' but also to 'God.' In the words of Col 3.3, our life 'is hidden with Christ in God.'"[140] When a person puts her faith in Christ, the Spirit enters the person and by dwelling in a person 'clothes' the human soul.

Thus the mortal soul is no longer trapped in the sinful "body of death" (Rom 7:24) but clothed with the immortal Spirit. So when the person dies her human soul is not lost and does not depart from God, but is instead safely hidden in the Spirit who dwells within. The person will thus be drawn into the divine fellowship. This hope of the resurrection is, according to the letter to the Hebrews, the "anchor for the soul," that which "enters the inner sanctuary behind the curtain" (Heb 6:19). This thought is reflected in the Old Testament atonement ritual, where the soul (life) which was in the blood, was brought on *Yom Kippur* behind the curtain of the Holy of Holies and sprinkled on the Ark of the Covenant, and in this way was brought into contact with the transcendent God.

However, this it is not simply a 'saving of the soul' that occurs here; Paul goes on to say in Romans 8:11 that "if the Spirit of him who raised Jesus from the dead dwells in you, he who raised Christ Jesus from the dead will also give life to your mortal bodies through his Spirit who dwells in you." Thus the body will also be given new life—this is seen in the resurrection of Christ, where he is given a new 'spiritual' body. For Paul, "[p]articipation was a sharing in the corporeality (*Leiblichkeit*) of Christ."[141] Thus according to Paul, our bodies will also be transformed into new resurrection bodies.[142]

---

139. See Dunn, "Paul's Understanding of the Death of Jesus as Sacrifice," 38.

140. Bell, *Deliver Us from Evil*, 226.

141. Stowers, "Matter and Spirit, or What is Pauline Participation in Christ?," 93.

142. For a discussion of Barth's understanding of the resurrection of the body in *CD* IV/1–3, see Hitchcock, *Karl Barth and the Resurrection of the Flesh*, especially chapters 4 (109–46) and 5 (147–82).

This is humanity's hope of salvation—not simply Christ's death and resurrection, but humanity's participation in that death and resurrection.

Therefore Paul can say that "We always carry around in our body the death of Jesus" (2 Cor 4:10) and that the persecution Christians suffer must be seen in the relation to Christ's suffering. Thus he writes that "though our outer self is wasting away, our inner self is being renewed day by day" (2 Cor 4:16), which, to refer to John 12:24, is the kernel falling into the ground in order to break open and bring about new life. Athanasius writes:

> Have no fears then. Now that the common Savior of all has died on our behalf, we who believe in Christ no longer die, as men died aforetime, in fulfillment of the threat of the law. That condemnation has come to an end; and now that by the grace of the resurrection, corruption has been banished and done away, we are loosed from our mortal bodies in God's good time for each, so that we may obtain thereby a better resurrection. Like the seeds cast into the earth, we do not perish in dissolution, but like them shall rise again, death having been brought to nought by the grace of the Savior.[143]

Like the kernel of a seed (which represents the flesh—that which is perishable and sown in the earth, the sinful flesh that needs to be circumcised through death), so too was the *Logos* 'sown' when Christ 'clothed' himself with an earthly body and died in order to be resurrected. He shot forth and bore much fruit, drawing the believers into him to become part of his body, the Church. In this way the Christian who is now 'in Christ' is not only a part of Christ's Church like the ear of the corn, but will in the final consummation of all things be completely 'clothed' by God when God is 'all in all.'

2.3. Revisiting the Problem of Rejection

On the one hand, Barth emphasizes that the individual is not dissolved in the collective mass, but that the good news allows a person to be an individual,[144] and safeguards and confirms human particularity.[145] On the other hand, he argues that what has already been decided in eternity in Jesus Christ is now revealed in history. One might ask what is the purpose of preaching the good news if, as Barth suggests, the decision over *being* has already been

---

143. Athanasius, *On The Incarnation*, §21, 50.
144. See Kreck, *Grundentscheidungen in Karl Barths Dogmatik*, 208.
145. See Greggs, *Barth, Origen, and Universal Salvation*, 123–50 passim.

Election, Atonement, and the Holy Spirit 229

made in Christ. In this context, how can the concept of rejection have any validity?

Greggs points out that Barth "does not wish to divide humans into binary categories of saved or lost, elect or damned, but categorizes humans as Christians or non-Christians based upon the activity of the Holy Spirit in a believer—not their salvific end."[146] It is in the Spirit, according to Barth, that we find the "particularity of the elect whose lives are part of the movement of God towards humanity in the event of Christ's election—a movement to which humans are called to respond."[147] Barth says that "[b]etween the being of the elect and his life as such there lies the event and the decision of the reception of the promise. It is not for his being [*Sein*] but for his life [*Leben*] as elect that he needs to hear and believe the promise."[148] Non-Christians therefore do not lack "Christ and in Him the being of man reconciled to God. What they lack is obedience to His Holy Spirit."[149] He goes on to say that to *hear* means "to be aware that in Jesus Christ this decision has been made concerning him"[150] and to *believe* means "to accept the situation which has been created by this decision. The godless man makes that transition as and to the extent that he hears and believes the promise."[151] And thus, the concluding definition of the election of the individual is that "the election in Jesus Christ of the godless man who is shown to be elect in the fact that as a hearing and believing recipient of the promise of his election he may live the life of the elect."[152] In this way obedience to God's promise becomes the defining characteristic for the Christian. This however, "provides the identity of the Christian with the world as those in whom this promise is yet to be completely fulfilled, but it also provides particularity as those who have the promise and are given hope."[153]

For Barth, the role of the Holy Spirit, which establishes Christian particularity and identity, is part of—or worked out within—a universalist soteriology.[154] And thus to be rejected eventually becomes an objective impossibility because Jesus has borne all sin and guilt on the cross.[155] A person

---

146. Greggs, *Barth, Origen, and Universal Salvation*, 132.
147. Ibid., 133.
148. CD II/2, 321.
149. CD IV/1, 93.
150. CD II/2, 322.
151. CD II/2, 322.
152. CD II/2, 323.
153. Greggs, *Barth, Origen, and Universal Salvation*, 132.
154. See Ibid., 124.
155. As Greggs explains, though, according to Barth, the "Spirit brings newness

can only live the life of a condemned person and yet cannot alter the fact that Jesus died for him on the cross and dealt with his sin. The individual can thus only display the life of a condemned person but cannot annul God's decision in his '*Gnadenwahl.*'

However, we have seen that, since election is based upon God's eternal decision in Jesus Christ to be the *Deus pro nobis*, it is neither an arbitrary will nor a mysterious will of God; instead, in Jesus, God's will is incarnate, lived and fully revealed. We saw that it was on the cross and in Jesus' resurrection that humanity recognizes God as the Emmanuel, the God with us, and understands that God wants all people to come to salvation. We have also noted that when Jesus died for the sins of all humanity, he did not 'bear sins' in the way that is normally understood by the term—by bearing them and being judged for them. But when Jesus died on the cross he conquered humanity's sin in his own body, triumphing over death in the power of the Spirit and bringing his soul (his life) into contact with God by shedding his blood (Heb 9:14). Through Christ's death and resurrection, the transformation of the earthly body into a new spiritual body, God made it possible for sinful humans to inherit their own new spiritual bodies, free from sin and death through participation. An yet if Jesus did not deal with sin on the cross by bearing it all away but instead by triumphing and conquering over it and on the cross, making sin something that has no more authority over him, then this means that the person 'outside' Christ is still trapped in her own sin.

This might imply that Jesus merely provided a possibility for atonement and freedom from sin but has not actually achieved it for humanity. However, the New Testament is clear that the cross does not simply offer the possibility of salvation but that atonement is fully achieved in Jesus Christ, who is salvation personified (Heb 5:9). He embodies fellowship with God because in him, in his hypostatic union, God and man are forever united. He is the second Adam who has conquered sin and death and is given a new immortal body. Atonement is complete in him and this makes fellowship with God possible, but only for those who are 'in Christ' (2 Cor 5:17).

Returning to Barth's own typology of election and rejection, we saw that the story of Cain and Abel in Genesis 4 was paradigmatic for Barth's doctrine of election. One is elected and the other is rejected. In this story

---

of Christian particularity" it takes place in the "universal eternal salvation in Christ that Barth's *CD* presents: the economy of the Holy Spirit is the operation of God which allows for the place of faith and Christian existence within a universalist soteriology based strongly on the objective work of Christ; the Spirit allows this objective reality to reach the individual community," in Greggs, *Barth, Origen, and Universal Salvation*, 123–24.

we read that YHWH accepted one offering and rejected the other. In this way, Cain becomes a picture of the scapegoat, who, hidden from the presence of God, becomes an aimless wanderer, a man without a place, bearing (*nāśāʿ*) his punishment. Those people who have not changed their ways of Cain (Jude 11f.) and rejected the offer of salvation in Christ, belong like the scapegoat and Cain to the evil one (1 John 3:12). They are thus hidden from the presence of God and outcasts, aimless wanderers bearing their own sin, which remains trapped in them and for which they will eventually bear punishment.

The good news is that for those 'in Christ,' who have accepted the gift of forgiveness offered through Christ's sacrifice, their scapegoat-like existence is cancelled by Christ; not as the goat did by bearing the sins which are laid upon it, but by taking them away and forgiving them through his atoning death on the cross. The individual who participates in Christ's own death through faith and baptism also therefore dies 'with Christ' (Rom 6:8) to sin and punishment. Again, it is 'in Christ' that God has affirmed that he is the *Deus pro nobis*, speaking his *Yes* over humanity. Salvation is achieved in Christ once and for all (Heb 9:26)—the one died for the many (2 Cor 5:15) and nothing can be added.[156]

However, even though salvation is final and completed in Christ and nothing can be added to this salvation, this does not alter two biblical contentions:

1. The individual person has 'in Christ' the freedom as well as the responsibility to submit to Jesus' obedience to the Father and align herself with this decision to follow the will of the Father in Christ. Christ's obedience in his life and death towards the Father becomes the paradigmatic example to follow. Though salvation from a biblical view needs to be seen as collective (in the same way as election), salvation is achieved 'in Christ' for all; the one died for the many, and nothing can be added (especially no human act). Thus there is a particularity in the universality of it. Because "only those who identify themselves with him in his death are identified with him in his

---

156. It might be argued that according to 2 Cor 5:15, all humanity has died 'in Christ' and in this way, all humanity is already objectively 'in Christ.' However, as Dunn points out, although Christ died and thus all died, "beyond death he no longer represents [. . .] all men, fallen man." Instead, Dunn explains, Christ in his risen life "represents only those who identify themselves with him, with his death through baptism, only those who acknowledge the Risen One as Lord (2 Cor 5:15)," in Dunn, "Paul's Understanding of the Death of Jesus as Sacrifice," 40.

life from death,"[157] the Christian is commanded to follow in Christ's footsteps. The individual is personally challenged to respond to Jesus' call to take up one's cross to follow him (Matt 16:24)—not alone, but through the power of the Spirit. This does not require any human *cooperatio* nor does it add anything to what Christ has already done, but it is necessary for individuals to respond to Christ's call by 'remaining' in him. This is especially important since, according to John 15, it is possible for those who fail to remain 'in Christ' to 'fall away' or be 'cut off.'

2. Jesus is simultaneously both the salvation as well as also the means of salvation for humanity, both the source of light in himself as well as the light that illuminates others. He has opened a door, and is himself the door to salvation for all who believe in him. Thus Barth can say that Jesus Christ is both the objective side as well as the subjective side of the atonement—or rather the objective side contains in itself the subjective principle of Christ's making himself known. It is not so much that humanity receives Christ but rather that because Jesus gives himself to be known by the Holy Spirit, humanity participates in the Christ-event. Here Barth picks up the theme of light in the Johannine 'I am' saying—Jesus being the light of the world. Just as light cannot be given to somebody or be contained by somebody but rather is something that a person encounters, likewise the subjective side of the atonement flows (breaks out) like light from Christ to humanity, and it is in this way that Christ reveals himself and makes himself known to a person.[158] What is important is not so much that a person *knows* God, but the event of being *known* by God himself.[159] For Barth, reconciliation is identical with God's revelation because God always reveals himself. Thus revelation of reconciliation is a communicative event which "moves out and communicates itself,"[160] a self-declaration of its origin, content and subject, Jesus Christ, the *Versöhnung*.

---

157. Ibid., 40.

158. See *CD* IV/3, 9.

159. See also Bell, who discusses the difference of "theoretical knowing" and "practical knowing" and argues for the idea of being "localized in the object of knowledge," in Bell, *Deliver Us from Evil*, 250.

160. *CD* IV/3, 8.

Torrance puts this in a slightly different way—that Christ is both the agent and content of humanity's salvation.[161] The act of atonement is complete and final and, from God's perspective, the work of salvation is "accomplished in the Son."[162] However, when looked at from the side of sinners and a fallen world, the work of salvation does not yet appear to be completed, "not in such a way that the perfect and finished work of reconciliation is fully actualised" in humanity.[163] What we see is that the atonement is fully completed by the pouring out of the Spirit by Christ at Pentecost. It is through the sacrifice of Christ and by the shedding of his blood that we are bought for a price (1 Cor 6:20 and 7:23) and freed from sin, and our consciences are cleansed.

Yet how does one participate in Christ's salvation? The short answer is 'by faith in Christ.' We said that though Christ has died for all, only those who have faith in him participate in his resurrection. A person has thus to be united with Christ in order to participate in the Christ-event. As already seen in chapter 4, Dunn points out that for Paul, union with Christ is not a "once-for-all event of initiation now past and gone for the believer [. . .] identification with Christ in his death is a *process* as well as an *event*."[164] Atonement is thus an on-going actualistic event in which humanity participates by faith in baptism and in the Eucharist,[165] the symbols of the covenant in Christ. Thus it is through the application of the Spirit that humanity's possession of Christ is realized,[166] since it is by the Spirit that the effect of the atonement is applied to a person, who becomes a partaker of the divine life and is incorporated into the triune fellowship.[167]

161. See Torrance, *Atonement*, 173.
162. Ibid., 174.
163. Ibid., 174.
164. Dunn, "Paul's Understanding of the Death of Jesus as Sacrifice," 47.
165. Bell, *Deliver Us from Evil*, 200, notes that the believer is "identified with Christ in his death through faith and baptism" and that this union with Christ is "also celebrated in the Lord's Supper" (see 1 Cor 10:16).
166. See Torrance, *Atonement*, 180.
167. See Pannenberg who writes: "The Augustinian suggestion that we view the Spirit as gift in which the fellowship of Father and Son finds fulfillment in mutual love achieves its full biblical depth, the depth of the intratrinitarian divine life, only when seen in the light of this giving and giving back of the Spirit that takes place between Father and Son. The gift of the Spirit to believers in which the Father and the Son work together follows only from its mediation by the fact that believers, linked by faith and baptism to the Son revealed in Jesus Christ, become members of his body, so that sonship in relation to the Father finds manifestation in them, too, as participation in the sonship of Jesus and therefore in the intratrinitarian life of God, in the reception of the Spirit by the Son and in the giving back of the Spirit to the Father," in *Systematic*

This raises the question, however, of divine sovereignty and human freedom. Is faith a gift only given to some and not all? Is there genuine human freedom to make a choice and make a decision for God? And if so, what does this decision to follow Christ by faith look like?

3. Humanity, Freedom, and Faith

In *The Humanity of God* and later in *CD* IV/4, Barth gives us a brief glimpse into how he views the question of human faith. Here he asks about the miracle and mystery of the event of faith: How is it that a person becomes a willing and active subject of this event of faith in God, becoming alive instead of dead? What kind of divine possibility is it that makes the human act of faithfulness to God possible?[168] For Barth what is at issue here is really a question about humanity: not a humanity that is shielded off as under a "*Glasglocke*"[169] but a humanity that can be touched, affected and altered in her most inner being—humanity as a covenant partner standing in an 'I-Thou' relationship with God. The core question that Barth asks is "how a man becomes a Christian."[170] For Barth this possibility is not some kind of "magical infusion of supernatural powers"[171] into a person who then is given the willingness and possibility to be faithful to God; instead, the willingness for God is a divine change brought about by the "work of the Holy Spirit."[172]

3.1. Human Freedom for God

For Barth, God is the "*free* One in whom all freedom has its ground."[173] What this means is that God as the source of all freedom is "determining Himself to be Father and the Son in the unity of the Spirit."[174] In this way he is the source of human freedom. In Jesus "man's freedom is wholly enclosed

---

Theology III, 11.
168. See *CD* IV/4, 4.
169. *KD* IV/4, 4
170. *CD* IV/4, 4
171. *CD* IV/4, 4.
172. *CD* IV/4, 27.
173. Barth, *The Humanity of God*, 48.
174. Ibid., 71.

in the freedom of God,"[175] because "[h]is deity *encloses humanity in itself.*"[176] What God wants is to be humanity's covenant partner and savior and thus, "God in His own freedom bestows human freedom."[177] However, one fundamental aspect of freedom to understand is that, for Barth, God's freedom is "essentially not freedom *from*, but freedom *to* and *for*."[178] Thus, God does not exist without humanity because he "wants in His freedom actually not to be without man but *with* him and in the same freedom not against him but *for* him."[179] Barth concludes that "God's freedom is and remains above and beyond human freedom"[180] which has its beginning in the divine freedom.[181] For Barth, the "freedom of God in which is grounded man's becoming free to be faithful to God' is itself grounded in the 'condescension [demonstrated] in the history of Jesus Christ."[182] It is God's freedom *for* humanity; despite human sinfulness, God in his grace bestows on humanity the gift of human freedom in Jesus Christ, in order that humanity might be free *for* God. In this way, God makes himself available for humanity, freeing them to respond to him, which leads to salvation.[183]

Thus, to "call man free is to recognize that God has *given* him freedom."[184] For Barth, the concept of an unfree person is a contradiction in terms.[185] Humanity cannot earn freedom or obtain it by her own efforts—it is something that can only be received and appropriated as a gift. The event of humanity's freedom can therefore only be understood as the "event of her thankfulness for the gift"[186] that was given to her by God.

However, we then need to ask why the particular history, of this one man Jesus Christ, can have universal ramifications. "How can that which He was and did *extra nos* become an event *in nobis*?"[187]

---

175. Ibid., 48. In chapter 1 we saw that for Barth election is as an event in which God 'encloses' the human being (see *CD* II/2, 180f.).

176. Ibid., 50.

177. Ibid., 75.

178. Ibid., 72.

179. Ibid., 50.

180. Ibid., 74.

181. See ibid., 74.

182. *CD* IV/4, 13.

183. See Barth, *The Humanity of God*, 75.

184. Ibid., 75.

185. See ibid., 76.

186. Ibid., 76.

187. *CD* IV/4, 18.

Barth sees two factors (or rather, he sees two forms of the one factor) as the divine basis on which humanity becomes faithful to God: the act of God in the resurrection of Jesus Christ from the dead as well as the work of the Holy Spirit in which its revelation reaches certain persons in such a way that they are opened up for it.[188] He continually re-emphasizes that God does not put humanity into the situation of making a decision (such as Hercules at the crossroads with a *liberum arbitrium*).[189] For Barth, the opposite is true: "God frees man from this false situation [and] lifts him from appearance to reality."[190] Though Barth affirms that human freedom is a 'choice' or 'decision' he immediately clarifies that it is a "genuine decision and act in the right direction."[191]

In *Karl Barth's Table Talk* a student asked a question about the nature of human freedom—as to whether a person can say *Yes* or *No* to God. Barth gave an illuminating account of what he understood to be the concept of human freedom:

> The decisive point is whether freedom in the Christian sense is identical with the freedom of Hercules: choice between two ways at a crossroad. This is a heathen notion of freedom. Is it freedom to decide for the devil? The only freedom that means something is freedom to be myself as I am created by God [. . .] We are confused by the political idea of freedom. [. . .] Being a slave of Christ means being free.[192]

What Barth seems to say is that whereas on the crossroads Hercules has the freedom to either go left or right, towards the right or wrong path, true human freedom only allows us to walk on one, the right path. How are we to understand this? For Barth, there are not two ways for humanity to be free but only one—the way that God has predestined, to be in a covenantal relationship. Freedom is not a "choice of alternatives [. . .] but [of] being in the marvellous light of Christ. Only those who are not blind but can see have freedom worthy of the name."[193]

---

188. See *CD* IV/4, 29f.
189. See Barth, *The Humanity of God*, 76.
190. Ibid., 76.
191. Ibid., 76.
192. Godsey and Barth, *Karl Barth's Table Talk*, 37.
193. Couvenhoven, "Karl Barth's Conception(s) of Human and Divine Freedom(s)," 247. In the fall, Adam and Eve did not actualize their freedom but lost it.

3.2. Metanoia: The Correspondence between Geistestaufe and Wassertaufe

Barth considers how this 'Wendung' or metanoia—through which a person is freed to be faithful to God in freedom—is brought about, where this freedom comes from and where it is grounded. For Barth, the history of Jesus Christ is the "origin and beginning of the Christian life, the divine change [göttliche Wendung] in which the impossible thing that there is [. . .] faithfulness of God [. . .] is not only possible but actual."[194] The reason that this freedom is grounded in Jesus is that "Jesus Christ is the One elected from eternity to be the Head and Saviour of all men, who in time responded to God's faithfulness with human faithfulness as the Representative of all men."[195] Hence Barth sees a Christian as someone "from whom it is not hidden that his own history took place along with the history of Jesus Christ. As a word spoken to him and received by him in the living power of the Holy Spirit."[196] A Christian is somebody "whose life Jesus Christ has entered as the subject of that history of His [. . .] whose acknowledged, recognised and confessed Lord He has become. He is a man to whom Jesus Christ has given not just a potential but an actual share in that history of His."[197]

We saw that the individual's participation in, and identification with, the Christ-event is by faith: "[t]he nature of this identity is grounded in Barth's concept of correspondence (*Entsprechung*)."[198] Baptism and the Eucharist are two corresponding sacraments, which show "*menschliche Ereignisse, daß die Menschen anredende Verkündigung der Kirche Antwort auf Gottes Wort ist und als Antwort diesem entspricht. Taufe und Abendmahl zeigen das, indem sie ihrerseits als Antwort geschehen.*"[199] Thus the divine change, Barth writes,

194. CD IV/4, 17.
195. CD IV/4, 13.
196. CD IV/4, 13.
197. CD IV/4, 14.
198. Greggs, *Barth, Origen, and Universal Salvation*, 124. Greggs explains: "the Spirit is not only the divine mode of being who establishes *Christian* identity and particularity, but also the person who establishes *human* identity and particularity," 124.
199. Jüngel, "Karl Barths Lehre von der Taufe," 281. Both Jüngel and Barth follow the biblical witness of Acts 10:44–48, the correspondence between God's Word being preached and the human response, and the model of *Wassertaufe* following *Geistestaufe*: "While Peter was still speaking these words, the Holy Spirit came on all who heard the message. The circumcised believers who had come with Peter were astonished that the gift of the Holy Spirit had been poured out even on the Gentiles. For they heard them speaking in tongues and praising God. Then Peter said, 'Can anyone keep these people from being baptized with water? They have received the Holy Spirit just as we have.' So he ordered that they be baptized in the name of Jesus Christ. Then

takes place by the "baptism with the Holy Ghost."[200] It constitutes the foundation of the Christian life, and "manifests itself in obedience to Christ" and therefore necessarily "brings with it an ethical command."[201] The term *Geistestaufe* [baptism of the Spirit] thus becomes the "epitome [*Inbegriff*] of the divine change which founds the whole Christian life,"[202] and is for a believer the "*Anfang seiner christlichen Existenz*."[203] Barth sums this up with the single sentence: "In the work of the Holy Spirit the history manifested to all men in the resurrection of Jesus Christ is manifest and present to a specific man as his own salvation history [*Heilsgeschichte*]."[204] Whereas a person could previously only say *No* through being 'grasped' [*ergriffen*] by the Spirit, he or she is now 'opened up' to say *Yes* to God's grace. Barth uses the illustrations of *Geistestaufe* and *Wassertaufe*—two actions of two subjects that have the same *Ereignis*—[205] to explain the togetherness and distinctness of divine freedom and sovereignty in relation to human freedom. He sees the divine change and the human decision both as a necessary part yet subordinating

---

they asked Peter to stay with them for a few days." The stories in Acts sometimes also differ in the sequencing of *Geistestaufe*, *Wassertaufe* and faith (see Acts 8:14–17; and Acts 19:1ff). Despite these irregularities however, it should be said that "grundsätzlich erscheint im Neuen Testament der Heilige Geist in festem Zusammenhang mit dem Geschehen der Verkündigung und des Glaubens, den sie weckt—er ist es, der dieses Geschehen wirkt," in Joest, *Dogmatik Bd:1 Die Wirklichkeit Gottes*, 293.

200. *CD* IV/4, 30.

201. Greggs, *Barth, Origen, and Universal Salvation*, 134. He writes that "Christian obedience proceeds 'from the election and call which constitutes a Christian; from participation in Jesus Christ; from the gift and operation of the Holy Spirit.' [III/3, 261] The gift of this Holy Spirit is that He brings obedience to the Christian in her own environment from without," 134. Furthermore, Jüngel points out the following: "Man muß sich, wenn es hier «auf der ganzen Linie» um «das christliche (menschliche!) Werk in seinem korrespondierenden und also eigenständigen Charakter gegenüber dem [...] göttlichen Versöhnungswerk» (ebd.) gehen soll, auf der ganzien Linie darüber klar sein, daß für Barth die Ethik ein Kapitel der *Dogmatik* ist," in Jüngel, "Karl Barths Lehre von der Taufe," 254.

202. *CD* IV/4, 31.

203. *KD* IV/4, 35.

204. *CD* IV/4, 27.

205. Jüngel explains: "So wenig «Gott» und «Mensch» unter einen gemeinsamen Oberbegriff fallen, so wenig lassen sich die «Taufe mit dem Heiligen Geist» und die «Taufe mit Wasser» unter einen beide Begriffe umgreifenden Oberbegriff «Taufe» subsumieren. Es handelt sich zwar bei beiden Phänomenen um zwei Taten zweier verschiedener Subjekte in *einem*, in *demselben* Ereignis» (45). Aber zu diesem einen und selben Ereignis kommt es erst auf Grund der die «Taufe mit Wasser» ermöglichenden und fordernden «Taufe mit dem Heiligen Geist»," in Jüngel, "Karl Barths Lehre von der Taufe," 256.

the human decision and giving priority to the divine change.[206] Barth says that "the baptism of the Spirit certainly calls for the baptism with water [. . .] but it is not identical with this."[207] The divine change itself brings about the possibility of—in fact it demands—a corresponding human act, a decision.[208] However, he emphasizes that the human decision is not what brings forth the divine change. Rather, the possibility of a free human act to be faithful to God is God's own work; God gives himself in his work to a person as a gift in the form of the Holy Spirit. Barth writes that it is baptism by the Holy Spirit that is the "origin, beginning and initiation of the faithfulness of man which replies and corresponds to the faithfulness of God."[209]

Nevertheless, whilst Barth prioritizes the divine act, he does emphasise the importance of the human response as well, saying that a person "becomes a Christian *in* his human decision [. . .] but he does not become a Christian *through* his human decision or his water baptism."[210] It is *in* the person's request to receive water baptism that she acknowledges and reveals to the community that the prior divine change has taken place. In this way, for Barth, "baptism with water is what it is only in relation to baptism with the Holy Spirit."[211] Yet, we need to remember that "[d]ie Wassertaufe its ebenso exklusiv menschliche Tat, wie die Geisttaufe exklusiv göttliche Tat ist."[212] Thus in "correspondence to the grace of God in the power of the Holy Spirit, the Christian is able to become one for whom it is possible to be faithful to God."[213] Barth writes: "What God does in Jesus Christ through the Holy Spirit is exclusively His action. Similarly, what man can and should do in

---

206. See Jüngel: "Barths eigene Antwort in dieser Sache besteht in der These, daß allein die in der Geschichte Jesu Christi bereits geschehene göttliche Wendung einem Menschen als die ihn befreiende Kehre so widerfahren kann, daß es dabei zur von diesem Menschen selbst vollzogenen Umkehr kommen kann. Auf Grund einer Tat Gottes kommt es zu einer ihr entprechenden Tat des Menschen, und beide Taten beider Subjekte zusammen machden das «Ereignis echten *Verkehrs* zwischen Gott und Mensch» (25) aus," in Jüngel, ibid., 257.

207. *CD* IV/4, 32

208. This correspondence must be seen as involving both a response as well as an act of participation. I am grateful for the input of Ashley Cocksworth in deepening my understanding of the divine-human correspondence. For further insights into why this correspondence involves both a response as well as an act of participation, see his forthcoming article "Revisiting Karl Barth's Doctrine of Baptism from the Perspective of Prayer," in *SJTh*.

209. *CD* IV/4, 3.

210. *CD* IV/4, 32f.

211. *CD* IV/4, 42.

212. Jüngel, "Karl Barths Lehre von der Taufe," 258.

213. Greggs, *Barth, Origen, and Universal Salvation*, 138.

face of the divine action is wholly his own human action."[214] In this way the Holy Spirit is the "economic action of God that protects both the Creator as Creator and the creature as creature."[215]

3.3. Faith and Obedience

The *Heilsgeschichte* records God bestowing freedom upon humanity. But how does this occur? In section 2.3. of this chapter we looked at the Gospels' regular challenge to the individual to obey Jesus' call to take up one's cross and to follow him,[216] following the paradigmatic example Christ showed in his own obedience to the Father in his life and death.

Barth also links human freedom with obedience. For Barth, human freedom is the "God-given freedom to obey [and] *faith* is the obedience of the *pilgrim* who has his vision and his trust set upon God's free act of reconciliation."[217] To illustrate this, Barth uses the example of the Israelites in the wilderness. Barth says that Deuteronomy 30 is often misunderstood as Israel having 'freedom' to decide to follow God and chose life, or not to do so. However, Barth maintains that a failure to choose God does not result in freedom but death. Additionally, the biblical text (Deut 30:16) makes clear that YHWH commands the people to love God and walk in obedience according to the decrees and laws of the covenant given to Israel at Mount Sinai. Before the covenant was established between God and Israel, Moses read God's will and the rules written in the Book of the Covenant (the conditions of the covenant) to the people, who agreed to them by responding: "We will do everything the LORD has said; we will obey." (Exod 24:3 and 7).

We recall that Barth sees *Wassertaufe* as the "*Akt des Gehorsams gegen das Gebot Jesu Christi und als Akt der Hoffnung auf Grund der Verheißung Jesus Christi.*"[218] Thus for Israel to turn their hearts away from God is not a decision that leads to freedom—the command is a prophetic word of warning that disobedience will lead only to destruction. There is only one way into the Promised Land—to follow the pillar of fire and remain obedient to God. By doing so Israel is free to worship and follow YHWH and experience his blessing. If Israel does choose to disobey she is not exercising freedom but remains in captivity, since "trying to escape from being in accord with

---

214. CD IV/4, 72.

215. Greggs, *Barth, Origen, and Universal Salvation*, 145.

216. Matt 4:19.; 8:22; 9:9; 10:38; 16:24; 19:21; Mark 1:17; 2:14; 8:34; 10:21; Luke 5:27; 9:23, 59; 14:27; 18:22; John 1:43; 10:27; 12:26; 21:19, 22.

217. Barth, *The Humanity of God*, 82.

218. Jüngel, "Karl Barths Lehre von der Taufe," 261.

God's own freedom is not human freedom."[219] What Barth is saying is that "man becomes free and is free by choosing, deciding, and determining himself in accordance with the freedom of God."[220] We saw that for Barth, both the freedom of God as well as the freedom of an individual is above all a freedom *for* rather than a freedom *from* something. The choice to disobey is therefore not one made in or *for* freedom since it results in slavery. Instead, true human freedom is the "venture of obedience whereby man reflects in his own life God's offer and his own response. This is the life of obedience, allowed for by man's freedom"[221]—humanity's desire to be God's covenant partner, agreeing to God's holy will. Thus for Barth freedom must be understood not as an independent freedom but a "being in activity in line with God's own goodness."[222]

The reason why Barth denies that freedom not to choose God (as exemplified by the Hercules motif) is true freedom, is that this freedom would give humanity the possibility to make a decision against God. God would be an object that can be either accepted or rejected. But although God gives himself for humanity and is free for her, he gives himself only as a gift. Barth's concept of freedom is therefore "'normative,' meaning that it is an asymmetrical way of speaking about freedom."[223] To use yet another illustration: humanity does not stand free on the road to make a choice between left or right. Instead, she is trapped in a ditch or chained in a prison cell from which she cannot free herself. What God offers in the atoning work of Christ is the free gift of a rope out of the ditch or, better, freedom from the chains of captivity. On the cross and in his resurrection Jesus has achieved and completed atonement once and for all, and humanity's decision *for* Jesus is, as already said, the only freedom she is given by God. An important reference point here is the parable in Luke 15, where the Good Shepherd picks up the hundredth sheep. Jesus as the Good Shepherd takes the individual from the ditch or prison and leads him or her out of entrapment into freedom. Jesus invites a person to leave slavery and bondage behind and to be in covenantal fellowship with God.[224] In the parables of the

---

219. Barth, *The Humanity of God*, 77.

220. Ibid., 76.

221. Barth, *The Humanity of God*, 80.

222. Couvenhoven, "Karl Barth's Conception(s) of Human and Divine Freedom(s)," 248.

223. Ibid., 248.

224. See Jesus' parable of the great banquet in the Gospel of Luke 14:15–24 or the similar yet different parable of the wedding banquet in the Gospel of Matthew 22:1–14, where it talks about an invitation by God.

banquets in Luke 14 and Matthew 22, we read about the servant who went out to tell those who had been invited, "Come, for everything is now ready" (Luke 14:17) but the people paid no attention and just made excuses. There was no response to the call at all. Not to accept this invitation with gratitude (not to grab the rope or leave the prison) is not a decision made *for* human freedom, because this rejection does not lead to freedom, but instead leaves him or her in captivity. In fact, to refuse the invitation does not represent a true choice, and thus a decision not to follow God cannot be regarded as a decision *for* human freedom. True human freedom is "liberation bestowed upon us"[225] (God's offer in Jesus Christ to be in covenantal fellowship with him) and not something intrinsic to us. All God wants is humanity's thankfulness and gratitude and for her to be with him in covenantal fellowship. This does not represent a human/divine synergism; it is God's own divine act, just as it is the shepherd who enacts the change in the sheep's situation when he searches for it, finds it, picks it up and carries it home.

3.4. Faith and Human Response

Once again, exactly *how* is this freedom bestowed upon humanity? In section 2.3 of this chapter we mentioned another biblical contention—that Jesus is simultaneously both the salvation as well as the means of salvation for humanity, both the objective side as well as the subjective side of the atonement.

We said that Jesus has both opened the door to salvation and at the same time is the door of salvation. Barth picks up the theme of light, another biblical metaphor for Christ's objective and subjective saving action, saying that Jesus is both the source of light in himself as well as the light that illuminates others. Light, we said, cannot be given nor can it be contained, but instead it is something that a person encounters. This encounter is the work of the Holy Spirit, the subjective side of the atonement, which flows out or radiates from the cross of Christ (the symbol of human freedom from slavery of sin) into the human darkness of captivity. This is how Christ reveals himself and makes himself known to a person, and thus being *known* by God is a communicative event—the revelation of reconciliation in Jesus Christ. This being 'grasped' [*ergriffen*] by the Spirit, to be 'opened up' to say *Yes* to God's grace, is the light of the cross, radiating upon the person in darkness. It is *in* obeying God's call to follow, *in* this decision and act to walk out of darkness *to* light, that the person becomes a Christian. It is in

---

225. Couvenhoven, "Karl Barth's Conception(s) of Human and Divine Freedom(s)," 247f.

this way, that the freedom bestowed upon humanity to make a decision *for* God is grounded in the salvation, which is achieved by the objective and subjective divine work of Jesus Christ through the Holy Spirit, without any human *cooperatio*.

The understanding of the objective and subjective sides of baptism correspond to Barth's understanding of the salvific side of revelation. In chapter 1 we noted Barth's understanding of the objective as well as the subjective side of revelation. We saw that for Barth, there is a twofold movement in God's self-revelation: "objectively, proceeding from God by His Word; and subjectively, moving towards man by His Holy Spirit."[226] Therefore the purpose of the work of the Holy Spirit in "subjective revelation is in order that there can be no division of the objective nature of revelation from its subjective reception."[227] Thus it is the Spirit who "maintains the uniqueness of revelation as the only possibility of humanity being open to God, such that, for Barth, the presence of God comes not only from above but also from *within* the human. This means that, through the Spirit, 'man is also there for God' [I/1, 480]."[228] Barth is affirming that the Word of God must be heard by a person through the Holy Spirit and 'happen' within him or her; the person needs to respond in order to participate in the Christ-event.

This is the individual's thankful *Yes* to the divine *Yes* already spoken over him or her in Jesus Christ, the acceptance of an invitation to the heavenly meal. Barth writes:

> Man is, of course, purely receptive as regards the movement from God, but he is also purely spontaneous in the movement to God. He is not merely a partial function in a dynamic whole. He is not a mere function at all. In this matter, God is Subject, but over against God and in relation to Him man is also subject. I imply that I am subject by saying: "I will."[229]

However, Barth sees both the objective and subjective elements "individually and also in correlation"[230] as the one work of salvation. The totality of the event would be misunderstood if they were "either separated from or, instead of being distinguished, mixed together or confused with the other."[231] These two elements—the objective and the subjective—build the foundation

---

226. *CD* III/3, 142.
227. Greggs, *Barth, Origen, and Universal Salvation*, 128.
228. Ibid., 128.
229. *CD* III/2, 180.
230. *CD* IV/4, 41.
231. *CD* IV/4, 41f.

of the Christian life, both in their correlation and in their distinction. Just as *Wassertaufe* can only follow the *Geistestaufe* and is always *"menschliche Tatantwort auf Gottes Gnadentat und Gnadenwort,"*[232] so the human response in accepting the invitation (grabbing the rope or leaving the prison) is only possible because of God's prior invitation to freedom. The human response to God's offer to be in a covenant through Jesus Christ is therefore not a human *coopertio*, just as an invitation to the celebratory meal does not indicate that the guest is called upon to prepare the food. There is no synergism between God and humanity in the work of salvation. As Jüngel points out, we need to be careful not to confuse God's *Allwirksamkeit* with some sort of *Alleinwirksamkeit* of God. He writes: "*Mit der Ablehnung der These von der Alleinwirksamkeit Gottes ist eine positive Aussage über den Menschen als Subjekt seiner selbst gemacht.*"[233] The divine change "makes possible and demands human decision as conversion from unfaithfulness to faithfulness to God"[234] and the human decision has its "origin wholly and utterly in the divine change."[235] Yet only when the two are seen together in 'differentiated unity' [*differenzierten Einheit*] does the mystery of faith become clear. We must also remember that it is called the *mystery* of faith; Barth does not 'lift' a veil that is impossible to be lifted.

Conclusion

God's commandments to humanity, the rules and regulations of the covenant, are expressed in Jesus' two words: 'Follow me,' to follow in Christ's footsteps in loving God and loving one's neighbor. We saw that the human response to God's call in Christ, the offer to be in covenantal relationship with God, is a human decision *for* freedom rather than a decision made *in* freedom. The objective and subjective side of the cross is freedom *for* humanity, freedom from the bondage of sin and darkness and fellowship with the triune God. To make a decision to follow Jesus by 'bearing one's one cross daily' is the only possible free human response. It is in and through the act of following Christ that human freedom is exercised. Not to make a decision to follow Christ necessarily involves remaining in the prison of darkness, but the decision to follow Christ involves walking out of darkness into God's radiant light of salvation. Human freedom is therefore not a human possession of freedom, but rather the freedom of God bestowed

---

232. Jüngel, "Karl Barths Lehre von der Taufe," 253.
233. Ibid., 255.
234. *CD* IV/4, 32.
235. *CD* IV/4, 41.

Election, Atonement, and the Holy Spirit 245

upon humanity, the light of the cross of Christ, the symbol of freedom from captivity of darkness, radiating salvation. Again, it is God's light shining from the cross upon humanity into the darkness of the prison, and so this freedom is, as Barth contends, "freedom of God in which is grounded man's becoming free to be faithful to God."[236] To walk out of the prison of darkness into the freedom of light is a decision, as Barth says, *for* freedom *in* the freedom of Christ's radiant light. However, the human response in accepting God's invitation is only possible because of God's prior invitation into his freedom, God's *Yes* manifested 'in Christ,' which we saw also mirrored in the correspondence between *Wassertaufe* following *Geistestaufe*.

One of the best illustrations of human captivity is the parable of the cave, told by the classical philosopher Plato. Those in the cave only have one exit, and to refuse to go out is to stay in bondage and a shadowy existence. However, to go out of the cave is to be lifted, as Barth says, from "appearance to reality."[237] Jesus has 'opened' the door of the prison and his light shines into the darkness (John 1:5). We saw that Barth said that God wants to be humanity's covenant partner and savior. By Jesus saying "I am the light of the world. Whoever follows me will never walk in darkness, but will have the light of life," (John 8:12), Jesus reveals himself as this covenant partner and savior. Furthermore, according to Luke 4:18, where Jesus reads the prophecy in Isa 61 of the Suffering Servant of God and Matt 4:12–17, Jesus fulfills the OT prophecies of the prophet Isaiah for the day of salvation.[238] God's promises in Isa 9, that "the people walking in darkness have seen a great light" (v. 2) and in Isa 42, to make the servant of God "a covenant for the people and a light for the Gentiles" (v. 6) in order to "open eyes that are blind, to free captives from prison and to release from the dungeon those who sit in darkness" (v. 7), are fulfilled in Christ. To obey the command of Jesus to "Follow me" means for the captives to "Come out" and "Be free" from the prison of darkness (Isa 49:9) and walk towards this light in order to be free.

---

236. *CD* IV/4, 13.

237. Barth, *The Humanity of God*, 76.

238. Pannenberg writes: "Again, the herald of joy in Isa. 61:1 says of himself that the Spirit of the Lord rests on him because the Lord has anointed him. Luke's Gospel sees this saying as a promise that finds fulfillment in the coming of Jesus (4:18), and Matthew's (12:18; cf. 12:28. 31) finds in the healing ministry of Jesus a fulfillment of the promise in Isa. 42:1 that the Servant of the Lord will be equipped with God's Spirit. Confirmed here is the link between endowment with the Spirit and sonship that comes to definitive representation in the person of Jesus Christ," in *Systematic Theology III*, 10.

For Barth, the relationship that election and atonement have with human freedom is the joy whereby a person acknowledges and confesses the divine saving work of Christ. The believer thereby appropriates God's election in Jesus Christ, "deciding, and determining himself to be the echo and mirror of the divine act."[239] The reason for joy is that freedom is the unmerited gift of God which "awakens the receiver"[240] and brings the person who was "separated and alienated from God"[241] into discipleship and covenantal fellowship. "By acknowledging and confessing Jesus Christ as the creation and revelation of God's freedom, this community is incorporated into the body of Christ and becomes the earthly and historical form of His existence."[242] Thus the community, the Church, is an expression of God's covenant in Jesus Christ and corresponds to God's freedom given to humanity. Therefore Barth can state: *extra ecclesiam nulla salus*.[243]

---

239. Barth, *The Humanity of God*, 79.
240. Ibid., 78.
241. Ibid., 78.
242. Ibid., 74.
243. See *CD* I/2, 215.

Conclusion

For no matter how many promises God has made, they are "Yes" in Christ.
   (2 Cor 1:20)

IN THE *CHURCH DOGMATICS* BARTH UNDOUBTEDLY OPENS UP A NEW UNderstanding of the doctrine of election, which avoids the dilemma of the 'horrible decree' of God choosing some people for heaven and others for hell. He uses Eph 1:4 as the hermeneutical key for his entire doctrine of election and explains it christologically, as rooted in the primal decision in the Godhead. In this way, Barth places election (like salvation) solely on the God-man Jesus Christ and argues that Jesus is both electing God as well as elected human. Barth argues that it is only because Jesus is both elected human and also electing God that we can know that God is truly the *Deus pro nobis*, and that only by knowing Jesus, who elected himself, can we know about God. Thus Barth affirms that Jesus is the full revelation of God and through him, humanity can know that God loves us. Furthermore, Barth links this idea with his understanding of the atonement, arguing that on the cross we see that Jesus is both elected as well as rejected. In this way, election and atonement are events happening in Christ: all of creation participates in the Christ-event through the divine *Logos*, through whom the entire world was created. Thus, for Barth, it is not a *doctrine* of universal salvation that the New Testament teaches but universal salvation is achieved in the *person* of Jesus Christ.

1. Problems with Barth's Exegesis

Barth revolutionized the Reformed doctrine of election by placing election solely upon Christ, seeing him as both the elect as well as the rejected. Nevertheless, it could be argued that Barth did not bring what he had started to its logical conclusion (we saw this for both election and atonement). This might have been because, despite wanting to escape Calvin's binary divisions of elect or rejected, saved or damned, Barth nonetheless limited himself to a Calvinistic framework of double predestination. He continued to use binary categories when talking about humanity, divided it into two simultaneous groups—Christian and non-Christian alongside each other in the world. As Greggs points out: "It is not an 'either-or' situation which the Christian faces with regard to the world, but rather a 'both-and' situation which she recognizes in her relationship to the grace of God in Jesus Christ through the Holy Spirit."[1]

First of all, although Barth understands the relationship between the Christian and non-Christian in regard to the world, God and the receiving of the Holy Spirit, in an eschatological sense—"in relation to the *eschaton*, the eternal reality of the divine fulfilment and consummation"[2]—we still have to ask whether the distinction of Christian and non-Christian is, at least in some way, also a binary distinction in the 'here and now.' Furthermore, by trying to remove the binary distinction from humanity, Barth places it onto Jesus Christ, and therefore creates an even more problematic binary distinction, in seeing Jesus both as the elect as well as the rejected.

In his systematic outworking of the doctrine of election Barth follows Calvin's understanding of the two natures of Christ on the cross. He divides Jesus' two natures into two separate functions rather than highlighting the unity of the one person Jesus. The result is that he again arrives at a binary relation. Whereas Calvin contends that it is only the human nature that suffers and dies on the cross (highlighting the immutability of God), Barth, though he strikes a careful balance between the two-natures of Christ, inverts this and maintains that it is not man who is condemned but God himself. God takes condemnation upon himself as the 'Judge judged in our place.' In his shortest formula, Barth says that God (who assumes condemnation) loses in order that man (who is exalted to the fellowship with God) wins. The 'Son of God' takes the judgment upon himself and loses in order that the 'Son of Man' (and with him all of humanity) can be exalted to the triune communion of God. Barth writes, "He predestined His own Son to existence as the Son of David," and continues, "[i]n the election of Jesus Christ, which is the eternal will of God, God has ascribed to man the former, election, salvation and life; and to Himself He has ascribed the latter, reprobation, perdition and death."[3]

---

1. Greggs, *Barth, Origen, and Universal Salvation*, 199.
2. Ibid., 148.
3. *CD* II/2, 163.

However, Barth's approach is not consistent. His typological exegesis of Lev 16 reveals another interpretation. He associates the goat 'for YHWH' with the divine nature of Christ and his once-and-for-all sacrifice on the cross (as stated in the letter to the Hebrews). And he associates the goat 'for Azazel' with Jesus' humanity, which suffers and bears sin. So when describing the sin-laden goat being sent away, he contradicts himself and follows Calvin's exegesis in writing that "according to his human nature as the Son of David, he must be Rejected"[4] as the second goat, the sin-laden one which is cast out into the wilderness, explaining that it is according to his divine nature that Jesus is the sinless, sin offering.

However, to divide Jesus' nature into human and divine means employing an unhelpful binary distinction when it comes to Jesus' work on the cross. In contrast, we argued that seeing Jesus as 'rejected man' contradicts the fact that he is elected and that instead we should focus on the unity of the person of Jesus. Though we understand that what Barth means by the rejected man is the old adamic man, it is not actually humanity that is rejected but sin in sinful flesh (Rom 8:3). This is crucial. The question that permeates the atonement is therefore 'How can sin be rejected without the sinner being rejected?' We saw that the concept of *Existenzstellvertretung* has provided a solution to this problematic.

2. Beyond the Binary Impasse of the *Yes* and *No* in Christ

We saw that for Barth the story of Jesus Christ is identical with the story of the reconciliation of God and humanity, and the inner dialectic of the doctrine of reconciliation is encapsulated in the downward movement of the Son of God (God's humiliation) and upward movement of God and Son of Man (humanity's exaltation). These occur simultaneously and are grounded in the person Jesus, who in the hypostatic union is true deity and true humanity.[5] God does not leave humanity alone or abandon her in her state of contradiction, which would end any relationship with God. Instead, he confronts humanity in her sinful state and brings salvation for his own glory in the reconciling work of Jesus Christ.

> In God's Yes to man, in the reconciliation of the world with God, it is a matter of this One, and therefore of His deity and humanity, of God's humiliation and man's exaltation, of the justification

---

4. See *CD* II/2, 365.
5. See *CD* IV/3, 4.

and sanctification of man, of faith and love. A doctrine of reconciliation which does not present both these aspects with equal seriousness is incomplete, one-sided and erroneous.[6]

We agreed with Barth's understanding of the twofold movement—God's humiliation and humanity's exaltation—but questioned Barth's systematic outworking and his exegesis on *how* this is worked out. We took up Barth's challenge by trying to give an alternative typological exegesis. The outcome of this new exegesis required Barth's doctrines of election and atonement to be altered. We followed Barth in his christological alteration of Calvin's doctrine of election and argued that Christ is both electing God as well as elected human. However, our exegesis differed from Barth in that we said that Jesus Christ is only the elect and that, over Jesus, the Father has only spoken a *Yes* from all of eternity. Jesus is only a picture of the sin offering and not the condemned goat for Azazel.

Through the concept of *Existenzstellvertretung* we argued that when looking at the death of Christ in the New Testament, a cultic framework advocating participation should be preferred over a forensic one of imputation. This challenged the entire concept of sin bearing that Barth proposes when he propounds God's judgment of wrath and the notion that on the cross God is "against Himself,"[7] the Father punishing the Son. Thus the concept of *Existenzstellvertretung* differs from Barth's approach on one important issue: Jesus does not bear sin and is not substitutionally judged for it. For the atonement, this meant that Christ was not condemned on the cross. We concluded that Christ did not bear humanity's sins in the way that the Azazel-goat did (driven into abandonment and thus taking God's punishment upon himself). Instead, we argued that Christ took *away* the sins of the people, by lifting them from them and forgiving humanity.

Although Barth might succeed in combining the Victor and the Victim model, the concept of *Existenzstellvertretung* and our exegesis of cultic texts have questioned the propriety of this combination. Instead, Jesus is the Victor on the cross, and the 'Victim' model of sin transferal is therefore discredited as unbiblical. The way that sinful humanity is freed from her body of death is by participating in the sanctifying and 'to-God-bringing' death through baptism. Furthermore, through Jesus who, in his death offered himself up through the eternal Spirit to God (Heb 9:14), the human soul was incorporated into the divine, just as in the Old Testament cult where the *nepeš* in the blood was incorporated into the holy by being sprinkled

---

6. *CD* IV/3, 5.
7. *CD* IV/1, 184.

on the *kappōret*. In this way, Christ as the Mediator represents God to man (God hidden in the flesh) as well as man to God (soul hidden in the Spirit).

Barth's dialectic, the *No* of rejection and the *Yes* of election synthesized in Jesus Christ, is problematic. We have demonstrated that Jesus should be seen only as the elect and not the rejected. The atonement is not simply the negative aspect of election, God's *No* on the cross to deal with sin, but is rather God's electing love in action, re-establishing the covenant of grace. It is the prolonged arm of God's *Yes* in Jesus Christ that reaches into history and brings humanity back into fellowship with the divine in eternity. And therefore, in God's divine election and the covenant of grace, God speaks only a *Yes* over Jesus Christ and through him over humanity. As affirmed by Paul in 2 Cor 1:18–20:

> But as surely as God is faithful, our message to you is not 'Yes' and No.' For the Son of God, Jesus Christ, who was preached among you [. . .] was not 'Yes' and 'No,' but in him it has always been 'Yes.' For no matter how many promises God has made, they are 'Yes' in Christ."

This study has therefore argued that both the cross and the resurrection must be seen as God's wholly positive *Yes* in Jesus Christ and not simply as a negative act (the cross) albeit with a positive intention (the resurrection).

Some might argue that those following a Calvinist framework put their trust primarily in an abstract principle—the decision they believe God made in eternity to elect some and not others—rather than in the Gospel. In contrast, we have shown that, since Christ is only the elect and not the rejected (it was *sin* that was rejected on the cross) it is not the case that some people are elect and others are rejected. Salvation and forgiveness of sins do not involve turning the cross into a 'principle,' but rather rely wholly upon the person and saving work of Jesus Christ. A person's salvation depends on participation in the cross-event through faith. From a New Testament perspective, salvation is not contingent on whether or not the individual is part of an 'elect,' but instead must be viewed as a free invitation to be in covenantal fellowship with God. Likewise, it is not contingent on whether or not Christ bore a person's sins, but rather on a person's response to the work of Christ, trusting in God's decision over Christ that he or she is elected 'in Christ.'

Furthermore, we saw that Barth safeguards human particularity: "The particularity of the Christian's identity is a particularity in correspondence with the particularity of the work of God in Jesus Christ. It is through the Holy Spirit that the correspondence of human faith to the divine act of revelation takes place."[8] Thus the *Yes* spoken by God over humanity needs to be followed by a corresponding *Yes* from humanity. Though salvation has been fully accomplished on the cross, it is only through the application of the Holy Spirit, by being 'born from above' (John 3:7), that the individual participates through faith in the Christ-event and the kingdom of God. Therefore, Jesus' cross-event is not just a means to an end but the end to humanity's needs. If a person participates in Christ, she participates in the divine fellowship. The person who is 'in Christ' becomes co-elect and a co-heir with Christ.

In contrast, the person who does not believe in the Son remains under God's *No*—this *No* is outside Christ and is spoken against sin and death. Picking up again the picture of Lev 16, it is the goat of the sin offering that mirrors God's *Yes* in Christ's election to save humanity and bring her back into covenantal fellowship, and it is the picture of the scapegoat, the goat sent to Azazel, that is sent into the wilderness (into nothingness), mirroring God's *No* in condemning sin and conquering death on the cross. In this way, the goat for Azazel, upon which the *No* rests, trapped in its own sins and driven out in the desert of chaos, becomes a picture for the person who does not believe in the Son and thus remains under the wrath of God (John 3:36).

To disagree with this approach requires a better explanation, one which does not amount to conventional Calvinistic thinking, falling back into the error of creating a *Deus absconditus* who makes arbitrary choices. Everything we can know about God is revealed in Jesus Christ and witnessed in Scripture. The Calvinistic approach is speculative and creates a picture not of a more loving God but a more arbitrary God. Jesus came to reveal the will of the Father and in doing so to fulfill and hold in tension both views of Scripture—that of divine sovereignty and human free choice.

3. Pastoral Implications: Limited Atonement and Universalism

What are the implications for the doctrine of election and atonement if we say that only Jesus is the elect of God? We saw that God's being (election) and God's action (atonement) have to be taken together, as united in the one person and work of Christ: Christ as the elect of God who brings about salvation. In our introduction, we said that this notion of the unity of the person and work of Christ has always been a point of disagreement in the history of the Church. This disagreement was built on wrong presuppositions tied to the notion of how sin is dealt with in the atonement. Broadly

---

8. Greggs, *Barth, Origen, and Universal Salvation*, 137.

speaking, those who follow a strictly logical approach to the atonement take one of two extreme positions: (1) limited (definite) atonement: Christ died only for the sins of the elect, hence only those who are elect are saved; and (2) universalism: Christ died for the sins of all, thus all are saved. We saw that though Barth never explicitly makes the claim himself, he falls into the second camp. The way he propounds his doctrines of atonement and election in the *Church Dogmatics* means that the two lines of his approach, Christ dying for all and all being saved in Christ, will eventually cross each other when followed to their logical conclusions. Barth's logical presupposition amounts to some sort of universalism (Christ the Victor of all).

This raised the question as to whether it is possible to hold a doctrine of universal atonement without leading to the obvious conclusion of universal salvation, or whether it is contradictory to say that Christ died for all but not all are saved. We saw, however, that this question itself rests on a false dichotomy. The notion of sin bearing, which was the *Dreh- und Angelpunkt* for our answer, was also fundamental for the doctrine of limited atonement. We then provided a new exegetical approach and showed how an understanding of the atonement through the lens of *Existenzstellvertretung* (a participatory atonement model) frees both limited atonement as well universalism from its logical conclusions. In our exegesis we highlighted how Christ's death was substitutionary not in that he bore all of humanity's sin, but in that he died for all of humanity.

We showed that what Jesus does is not take our sins and bear them away. Instead (to use a phrase that is perhaps inelegant but nonetheless best expresses what occurs) he 'puts to death' the old adamic nature by dying on the cross, taking humanity with him in order that humanity is dead to sin and can become a new creation. (By 'putting to death' we mean that in Jesus' death, sinful flesh dies—this is distinct from both the idea of simply dying for us as well as that of 'killing' our humanity for us.) As Barth puts it "[i]t is in Him that He judges us."[9] Or rather, it is Jesus who brings about justice in himself for our sinfulness. He judges sin in his own flesh (Rom 8:3). However, since it is 'in him' through whom the sinful flesh is circumcised (Col 2), humanity is also united with Christ because "[i]n Him He has bound Himself to us, before he bound us to Himself, and before we bound ourselves to Him. In Him He has decided Himself for us before all our decisions, before we recognized ourselves as His servants."[10] Thus it is in Jesus Christ that God shows his grace, the "divine decision about our whole

---

9. *CD* II/2, 736.
10. *CD* II/2, 736.

being."[11] Jesus is the one who brings humanity into relationship with God, who reconciles sinful *humanity*—the real problem—to God. It is humanity's sinful existence that needs redemption. Christ takes humanity's sinful existence with him into his extraordinary death and in this way makes an end to sinful humanity. However, because humanity is united with him in death, she is also united with him in his resurrection and thus, even though the body dies, the person 'in Christ' will be given a new resurrection body and be brought into contact with God.

Calvin connected the death of Christ with the specific sins of individuals, arguing that Christ bore only the sins of the elect on the cross—thus dying only for a few and not all and making his death beneficial only for a few elect (on the basis that otherwise Christ would have died in vain for those who did not believe in him). In contrast, the doctrine of participatory atonement highlights that Christ's death is not linked to any specific sins of individuals, but argues that Christ did not in fact bear any sins. This therefore does not limit the people saved to a specific number and frees both limited atonement as well as universalism from their logical conclusions. In this way, we could argue for a universal atonement (Christ died for the entire world) without logically having to end up at a universal salvation (logically, not all are saved). We showed that we can take seriously the passages that talk about God wanting all of humanity to be saved, without rejecting the passages that talk about God's judgment upon sinners.

Furthermore, we have seen that both universalism and limited atonement create something of a *Deus absconditus*. A person's decision corresponds to a person's salvation because this is an affirmation of what God has already said and done in Jesus Christ—God's eternal *Yes*. This also means that God does not overrule the decision of those who do not believe or in obedience accept his invitation to covenantal fellowship with Christ. Therefore, it is not God who condemns them, and neither is his ability to save in any way limited; those who do not believe already stand condemned (John 3:18) because God has given us true freedom in Christ to respond to God's eternal *Yes*. God has invited everybody to the Heavenly Feast, but he does not force anybody to the meal. Everybody who attends will do so as a result of her own decision (for and in the freedom that Christ has achieved on the cross), a decision that leads to the true human freedom for which Christ has set us free (Gal 5:1). We saw throughout this study that the theme of 'obedience' towards the will of God is key to understanding (1) Christ's suffering on the cross as well as (2) human faith as a response of covenantal obedience to follow Christ's example and to agree to God's will. For Barth, the doctrine

---

11. *CD* II/2, 632.

of reconciliation is God's 'active and superior' *Yes* to humanity "as it is the fulfilment of the eternal election in which God has determined, determines and will again determine Himself for man to be his God, and man for Himself to be His man."[12] The superior *Yes* of God's mercy is the overcoming of contradiction and disruption of the *No* in which humanity finds herself, because God does not "permit to execute this No of his."[13] Obedience, we saw, was the link between the *Yes* of God and its corresponding counterpart, the human *Yes* said in faith and obedience. As the *Geistestaufe* has to be followed by *Wasstertaufe*, so God's *Yes* has to be followed by the human *Yes*, to follow Christ's example in obedience towards the will of God.

If we agree with this exegesis of Leviticus, then Christ's death—in which he died for humanity's sins not by bearing them but by opening up a way for every individual to be freed from sin—can be seen as a genuine saving event for the *entire* world. Christ not only opens up a door but himself becomes a door or 'gate' (John 10), and any of the sheep entering through him and accepting his invitation to follow him and pick up their cross will be saved. We saw that Barth does not 'lift' a veil that is impossible to be lifted—we cannot know why somebody would reject this invitation. Some mysteries of God and faith remain. According to Barth, however, what also remains is the good news: that in Christ, God is the *Deus pro nobis*, the savior of the entire world.

4. Systematic Implications: The Economic and Immanent Trinity

Furthermore, we saw that for Barth, God the Father and God the Son are never without the Holy Spirit, who is the *vinculum caritatis* between the two.[14] But what happens on the cross? Is the 'inner' relationship between Father, Son, and Holy Spirit, which is reflected in eternity, also reflected in history on the cross? Barth does emphasize that it is not an *analogia entis* but an *analogia relationis*, a correspondence [*Entsprechung*] of relationship that reflects the immanent Trinity and the way God as Creator acts with his creatures. He says that "[t]here is an *analogia relationis* [and] the freedom in which God posits Himself as the Father, is posited by Himself as the Son and confirms Himself as the Holy Ghost, is the same freedom as that in which

12. *CD* IV/3, 3.
13. *CD* IV/3, 3.
14. See *CD* IV/1, 209.

He is the Creator of man."[15] It is in this freedom that the "Creator-creature relationship is established by the Creator."[16] Barth continues:

> The correspondence and similarity of the two relationships consists in the fact that the eternal love in which God as the Father loves the Son, and as the Son loves the Father, and in which God as the Father is loved by the Son and as the Son by the Father, is also the love which is addressed by God to man. The humanity of Jesus, His fellow-humanity, His being for man as the direct correlative of His being for God, indicates, attests and reveals this correspondence and similarity. It is not orientated and constituted as it is in a purely factual and perhaps accidental parallelism, or on the basis of a capricious divine resolve, but it follows the essence, the inner being of God. It is this inner being which takes this form *ad extra* in the humanity of Jesus, and in this form, for all the disparity of sphere and object, remains true to itself and therefore reflects itself.[17]

In the light of all that we have considered in this study, can we, with Rahner, conclude that the economic Trinity is the immanent Trinity?[18] What Rahner is trying to express is the notion that God communicates himself to humanity and interacts in the world in his 'economic' Trinity, in the same way as he is in the divine communion of the triune God in the 'immanent' Trinity. Thus we have seen that for this study the real question is less an ontological one about the Trinity and God's being *per se*, but rather about the work of the economic and immanent Trinity. The questions are whether we can say that God's action is his being, and his being his action, and whether God's action in the economic Trinity is congruent with the being and action of the immanent Trinity.[19]

We concluded that the idea that the love between Father and Son in eternity is reflected in the history between the Father and Jesus, particularly on the cross, does not correlate with Barth's doctrine of election and atonement. We asked, with Luther, 'Is Christ's death on the cross a mirror of the fatherly heart of God?' Is the way that Barth portrays God's work *ad intra*

---

15. CD III/2, 220.
16. CD III/2, 220.
17. CD III/2, 220.
18. See Rahner, *The Trinity*, 99–103.
19. Paul Nimmo has shown that for Barth there is no "ontic distinction between the being of God in the incarnation and the being of God in eternity," in Nimmo, "Barth and the Christian as Ethical Agent," 225. It is the concept of Christ's obedience which is the dominant moment in this conception of God.

congruent with God's work *ad extra* and in line with Trinitarian thought? Barth would not disagree with the idea that the same love between Father and Son in eternity is reflected in the history between the Father and Jesus on the cross. However, when placing our analysis of what sacrifice means alongside our examination of Barth's understanding of election and atonement, we see that the two do not harmonize. When Barth speaks about election he sees Jesus as both electing God as well as elected human being. He goes on to say that Jesus is both elected as well as rejected human, the rejection side of election being revealed on the cross. On the cross God's *Yes* and God's *No* are spoken over him, Moreover, we saw that Barth is almost as radical as to separate the cross and the resurrection, making the cross the *No* and the resurrection the *Yes*. But, as we argued in chapter 4, the cross is a wholly positive Trinitarian act in history that reflects the love between Father and Son in eternity. Yet Barth sees the cross as a negative act in history and projects the same understanding onto his interpretation of Rev 13:8, "the lamb who was slain before the foundation of the world." However, it is only when both the cross and the resurrection are seen as God's *Yes* to humanity within the context of an understanding of *Existenzstellvertretung* that we can say that the cross is a loving act in history reflecting the Father-Son relationship in eternity. This 'participatory substitution' model of the atonement is consistently Trinitarian, highlighting the close relationship of Father and Son in the work of the cross as well as a consistency between the person and the work of Christ. God was in Christ and therefore Jesus acts on the cross as the God who actively judges sin. Barth's understanding of the cross is insufficiently Trinitarian.

Let us return for one final time to the topic of the immanent and the economic Trinity in light of what has been said above about obedience. Nimmo has highlighted that there is another dynamic of the Father-Son relationship—namely, the obedience of the Son in eternity and the obedience of the Son of history.[20] This is a helpful lens through which to see the Father-Son relationship, a theme that runs through the Gospel narratives. The Son humbled himself to become incarnate and again humbled himself to death on a cross. But this obedience is always an active obedience of wanting to fulfill the will of the Father. We therefore have to ask whether it was the will of the Father to judge the Son, or rather, whether it was the will of the Son to be judged. Surely a Trinitarian understanding demands that the Father and Son work together in the salvific act, particularly as this is what the Gospel of John repeatedly states?[21] The Son became incarnate out of his free will, in

---

20. See Nimmo, "Barth and the Christian as Ethical Agent," 229.
21. John 3:16–18; 5:19–23, 36; 6:57; 8:54; 10:30; 12:49; 14:11; 15:1–17; 16:15; 17:21.

obedience to the Father. In this way, the crucifixion represents an act not of passive obedience by the Son, but of active obedience to the Father, as well as the Father's active execution of his own will in judging 'sin in the flesh' (Rom 8:3). Thus it is not that the Father judges the Son, but that the Father and the Son actively remain one in the cross-event. As Paul states, it is God in Christ who reconciles the world to himself (2 Cor 5:19). We highlighted that, rather than remaining over and against the Son, on the cross the Father judges sin in and through the Son.

We saw that in order for the atonement to be a truly Trinitarian act—an act of Father, Son, and Spirit in complete unity—the immanent Trinity and the economic Trinity must be congruent. What we say about the immanent Trinity when we say that Jesus is the electing God as well as elected human from eternity must also be reflected in what we say about the economic Trinity. In history, on the cross, Jesus is both rejecting God as well as rejecting human in the sense that he condemns sin in the flesh. We have to argue that on the cross it is the work of both God and man, or rather God as man, which condemns sin and in this way frees humanity from sin.

Suggesting that Jesus is only the elect and not the rejected fits much better with Rahner's statement that the 'economic Trinity is the immanent Trinity.' Indeed, a Penal Substitution understanding of the atonement (however nuanced) combined with the notion of double predestination, might actually be seen to stand in contradiction to Rahner's statement. This is because it makes Jesus on the cross not the active electing God from eternity but rather a passive 'instrument,' the one who is acted upon. Furthermore, it makes the action of the Father different to the action of the Son—on the cross, the Father and the Son and their actions are depicted as opposed to each other. In contrast, if we see the cross not as a negative rejection but part of the positive work of election, the Son's work on the cross is seen to be fully harmonised with the work of the Father. There is perfect unity between Father and Son not only in their being but also in their action in the world—it is the Father working out salvation through the Son in the power of the Spirit.

Therefore, in order to maintain the congruency of the immanent and economic Trinity we have to say that Jesus is both "electing God and elected human" in eternity as well as "rejecting God and rejecting man" in history. On the cross Jesus is the Judge who judges sin, and humanity, who has been elected in Christ and thus has been made a covenant partner in the incarnation, participates in this rejection of sin. Once humanity is elected and joined with God in a hypostatic union in the incarnation, she becomes a co-worker with God in the work of redemption and the "battle against sin," as seen in the life and death of Christ (see 1 Cor 9:25; 2 Cor 10:4; Phil

3:12; 1 Tim 6:12). Thus this book has argued that the atonement should be seen neither as an act of appeasement nor an act of punishment (the Father punishing the Son) but as a perichoretical act of Father and Son in the unity of the Holy Spirit, who is the *vinculum amoris* between Father and Son. It is through the Spirit that humanity participates in Christ's divine election from eternity, making humanity co-heirs with Christ (Rom 8:17). Furthermore, chapter 5 argued that distinguishing between a penultimate and ultimate decision of God risks the creation of a new kind of *Deus absconditus*, that which Barth so fervently attempts to avoid and seeks to correct in Calvin. Though God has to have the final word in salvation, his final decision over humanity is seen already on the cross (and not just in the verdict of the Father in the resurrection) where we see the *Deus revelatus*, that God is love.

Concluding Remarks

The wider contribution that Karl Barth's *Church Dogmatics* has made to theology and the Church has been immeasurable, and on the doctrine of election (*CD* II/2) and atonement (*CD* IV/1) he has provided for us an astute and critical dialogue partner. This book has sought both to engage with Barth's systematic reflection and exegesis and to bring a critique from within. Where it has been critical, it has always been in the spirit of Barth's own challenge to the reader to interrogate and surpass his analysis, and this is only possible because of the breadth and depth Barth brings to his interpretation of the reconciling work of Christ. And so, to take up the musical theme from our introduction, we conclude by saying that, weaving together the harmonies of election and atonement, we can only hope that this contribution adds one note to the wider symphony of God's saving work of humanity in Christ to which Karl Barth himself contributed so profoundly in the crescendo of the covenant of grace.

Bibliography

Primary Sources

Barth, Karl. "4. Vorlesung: *Creatorem coeli et terrae*." In *Credo: Die Hauptprobleme der Dogmatik, dargestellt im Anschluß an das Apostolische Glaubensbekenntnis. 16 Vorlesungen, gehalten an der Universität Utrecht im Februar und März 1935*, 29-37. Zollikon-Zürich: Evangelischer Verlag, 1948.

———. "The Christian's Place in Society." In *The Word of God and the Word of Man*, translated by Douglas Horton, 272-27. Gloucester, MA: Smith, 1978.

———. *Dogmatics in Outline*. Translated by G. T. Thomson. London: SCM, 1949.

———. "II. Dogmatik und Exegese. Anhang: Fragebeantwortung am 5. und 6. April 1935." In *Credo: Die Hauptprobleme der Dogmatik, dargestellt im Anschluß an das Apostolische Glaubensbekenntnis. 16 Vorlesungen, gehalten an der Universität Utrecht im Februar und März 1935*, 153-54. Zollikon-Zürich: Evangelischer Verlag, 1948.

———. *The Epistle to the Romans*. Translated by Edwyn C. Hoskyns. London: Oxford Univesity Press, 1933.

———. "7.Vorlesung. Gottes Entscheidung und des Menschen Erwählung (Art.7-8.)." In *Gotteserkenntnis und Gottesdienst nach reformatorischer Lehre. 20 Vorlesungen (Gifford-Lectures) über das Schottische Bekenntnis von 1560*, 94-103. Zollikon: Verlag der evangelischen Buchhandlung, 1938.

———. *Gottes Gnadenwahl*. München: C. Kaiser, 1936.

———. "Hegel." In *From Rousseau to Ritschl: Being the Translation of Eleven Chapters of* Die Protestantische Theologie im 19. Jahrhundert. Translated by Brian, 268-305. London: SCM, 1959.

———. *The Humanity of God*. Translated by John Newton Thomas and Thomas Wieser. Richmond, VA: John Knox, 1960.

———. *JA und NEIN-Karl Barth zum Gedächtnis*. Ein Nachruf von Heinz Knorr. Interview: Rudolf Rohlinger. Stuttgart: Calwer Verlag, 1967.

———. *Karl Barth's Table Talk*. Edited by John Godsey. Richmond: John Knox, 1963.

———. *Der Römerbrief*. Zollikon-Zürich: Evangelischer Verlag, 1922.

———. *The Teaching Of The Church Regarding Baptism*. Translated by Ernest A Payne. London: SCM, 1948.

———. "The Word of God and the Task of Ministry." In *The Word of God and the Word of Man*, translated by Douglas Horton, 183-217. Gloucester, MA: Smith, 1978.

Other Sources

Aland, Kurt and Barbara Aland. *Novum Testamentum Graece*. Stuttgart: Deutsche Bibelgesellschaft, 1993.
Anselm, von Canterbury. *Cur Deus Homo. Warum Gott Mensch geworden*. Darmstadt: Wissenschaftliche Buchgesellschaft, 1970.
Athanasius. "On The Incarnation of the Word." In *Nicene and Post-Nicene Fathers, Second Series, Volume 4*, edited by Philip Schaff, 36–67. Grand Rapids: CCEL, 1891.
Augustine. "Confessions." In *Nicene and Post-Nicene Fathers, First Series, Volume 1*, edited by Philip Schaff, 45–207. Grand Rapids: CCEL, 1886.
———. "Homilies on the Gospel of John." In *Nicene and Post-Nicene Fathers, First Series, Volume 7*, edited by Philip Schaff, 7–452. Grand Rapids: CCEL, 1888.
———. "Reply To Faustus The Manichaean." In *Nicene and Post-Nicene Fathers, First Series, Volume 4*, edited by Philip Schaff, 155–345. Grand Rapids: CCEL, 1887.
Aulén, Gustaf. *Christus Victor: An Historical Study of the Three Main Types of the Idea of the Atonement*. Translated by Arthur Hebert. London: SPCK, 1970.
Averbeck, Richard E. "כפר." In *NIDOTTE* 2:688–710.
———. "Sacrifices and Offerings." In *DOTP* 706–733.
Bächli, Otto. *Das Alte Testament in der Kirchlichen Dogmatik von Karl Barth*. Neukirchen-Vluyn: Neukirchener Verlag, 1987.
Bailey, Daniel P. "Concepts of Stellvertretung in the Interpretation of Isaiah 53." In *Jesus and the Suffering Servant: Isaiah 53 and Christian Origins*, edited by William H. Bellinger, Jr. and William R. Farmer, 223–50. Harrisburg, PA: Trinity, 1998.
———. "Jesus as the Mercy Seat: The Semantics and Theology of Paul's Use of Hilasterion in Romans 3:25." PhD diss., University of Cambridge, 1999.
Bakker, L. A. R. "Jesus als Stellvertreter für unsere Sünden und sein Verhältnis zu Israel bei Karl Barth." *ZDTh* 2 (1986) 39–59.
Balthasar, Hans Urs von. *The Glory of the Lord: A Theological Aesthetics Vol. VII: Theology: The New Covenant*. Translated by B. McNeill. Edinburgh: T. & T. Clark, 1989.
———. *Mysterium Paschale: The Mystery of Easter*. Translated by Aidan Nichols. Edinburgh: T. & T. Clark, 1990.
———. *The Theology of Karl Barth: Exposition and Interpretation*. Translated by Edward T. Oakes. San Francisco: Ignatius, 1992.
———. *The Von Balthasar Reader*. Edited by M. Kehl and W. Löser, translated by R. J. Daly and F. Lawrence. Edinburgh: T. & T. Clark, 1985.
Barnabas. "The Epistle Of Barnabas." In *Ante-Nicene Fathers, Volume 1*, edited by Schaff Philip, 137–49. Grand Rapids: CCEL, 1885.
Bell, Richard H. *Deliver Us from Evil: Interpreting the Redemption from the Power of Satan in New Testament Theology*. Tübingen: Mohr Siebeck, 2007.
———. "Sacrifice and Christology in Paul." *JThS* 53.1 (2002) 1–27.
Berkouwer, Gerrit Cornelius. *The Triumph of Grace in the Theology of Karl Barth*. Translated by Harry R. Boer. Grand Rapids: Eerdmans, 1956.
Blocher, Henri A. G. "Atonement." In *DTIB* 72–76.
Boettner, Lorraine. *The Reformed Doctrine of Predestination*. Phillipsburg: P. & R., 1991.
Bremmer, Jan. "Scapegoat Rituals in Ancient Greece." *HSCP* 87 (1983) 299–320.
Breytenbach, Cilliers. "Versöhnung, Stellvertretung und Sühne." *NTS* 39 (1993) 59–79.

Bromiley, Geoffrey W. *An Introduction to the Theology of Karl Barth*. Edinburgh: T. & T. Clark, 1979.
Brunner, Emil. *The Christian Doctrine of God: Dogmatics Vol.I.* Translated by Olive Wyon. London: Lutterworth, 1949.
Buckley, James J. "Christian Community, Baptism, and Lord's Supper." In *The Cambridge Companion to Karl Barth*, edited by John Webster, 195–211. Cambridge: Cambridge University Press, 2000.
Busch, Eberhard. *Karl Barth: His Life from Letters and Autobiographical Texts*. Translated by John Bowden. London: SCM, 1976.
Butin, Phil. "Two Early Reformed Catchisms, The Threefold Office, and the Shape of Karl Barth's Christology." *SJTh* 44 (1991) 195–214.
Büttner, Matthias. *Das Alte Testament als erster Teil der christlichen Bibel: Zur Frage nach theologischer Auslegung und 'Mitte' im Kontext der Theologie Karl Barths*. Gütersloh: Gütersloher Verlagshaus, 2002.
Byrne, Brendan. *Romans (SP)*. Collegeville, MN: Liturgical, 1996.
Cane, Anthony. *The Place of Judas Iscariot in Christology*. Aldershot, UK: Ashgate 2005.
Canlis, Julie. *Calvin's Ladder: A Spiritual Theology of Ascent and Ascension* Grand Rapids: Eerdmans, 2010.
Chilton, Bruce. *The Isaiah Targum: Introduction, Translation Apparatus and Notes*. Edinburgh: T. & T. Clark, 1987.
Coakley, Sarah. "Why Three? Some Further Reflections on the Origins of the Trinity." In *The Making and Remaking of Christian Doctrine: Essays in Honour of Maurice Wiles*, edited by Sarah Coakley and David Pailin, 29–56. Oxford: Clarendon, 1993.
Cortez, Marc. "Body, Soul, and (Holy) Spirit: Karl Barth's Theological Framework for Understanding Human Ontology." *IJST* 10.3 (2008) 328–45.
———. *Embodied Souls, Ensouled Bodies: An Exercise in Christological Anthropology and Its Significance for the Mind/Body Debate*. London: T. & T. Clark, 2008.
Couvenhoven, Jesse. "Karl Barth's Conception(s) of Human and Divine Freedom(s)." In *Commanding Grace: Studies in Karl Barth's Ethics*, edited by Daniel L. Migliore, 239–55. Grand Rapids: Eerdmans, 2010.
Crisp, Oliver D. "The Election of Jesus Christ." *JRTh* 2.2 (2008) 131–50.
———. "'I Do Teach It, but I Also Do Not Teach It': The Universalism of Karl Barth." In *"All Shall Be Well": Explorations in Universal Salvation and Christian Theology, from Origen to Moltmann*, 305–24. Eugene, OR: Cascade, 2001.
Daly, Robert J. *Christian Sacrifice: The Judaeo-Christian Background before Origen*. Washington, DC: Catholic University of America Press, 1978.
Davies, W. D., and Dale C. Allison. *A Critical and Exegetical Commentary on The Gospel according to Saint Matthew*. Edinburgh: T. & T. Clark, 1997.
Denney, James. *The Death of Christ*. London: Tyndale, 1951.
De Roo, Jacqueline C. R. "Was the Goat for Azazel Destined for the Wrath of God?" *Biblica* 81.2 (2000) 233–42.
Dowey E. A. *The Knowledge of God in Calvin's Theology*. Grand Rapids: Eerdmans, 1994.
Drury, John L. "The Priest Sacrificed in Our Place: Barth's Use of the Cultic Imagery of Hebrews in Church Dogmatics IV/1, §59.2." *1st Annual Barth Conference: 'Thy Word is Truth: Reading Scripture Theologically with Karl Barth.'* Center for Barth Studies, Princeton Theological Seminary, 2006.

Dunn, James D. G. "Paul's Understanding of the Death of Jesus as Sacrifice." In *Sacrifice and Redemption: Durham Essays in Theology*, edited by Stephen W. Sykes, 35–56. Cambridge: Cambridge University Press, 1991.

———. *Romans 1–8*. WBC. Dallas: Word, 1988.

Ford, David F. *Barth and God's Story: Biblical Narrative and the Theological Method of Karl Barth in the Church Dogmatics*. Frankfurt am Main: Lang, 1981.

———. "Barth's Interpretation of the Bible." In *Karl Barth: Studies of his Theological Method*, edited by Stephen W. Sykes, 55–87. Oxford: Clarendon, 1979.

———. "Epilogue: Twelve Theses for Christian Theology in the Twenty-first Century." In *The Modern Theologians: An Introduction to Christian Theology since 1918*, edited by David F. Ford et al., ed., 760–61. Malden, MA: Blackwell, 2005.

———. "Introduction to Modern Christian Theology." In *The Modern Theologians: An Introduction to Christian Theology since 1918*, edited by David F. Ford et al., 1–15. Malden, MA: Blackwell, 2005.

Freedman, Willoughby, Fabry, Ringgren. "נשׂא." In *TDOT* 10:24–40.

Gane, Roy. *Cult and Character: Purification Offerings, Day of Atonement, and Theodicy*. Winona Lake, IN: Eisenbrauns, 2005.

Gaukesbrink, Martin. *Die Sühnetradition bei Paulus: Rezeption und theologischer Stellenwert*. Würzburg: Echter, 1999.

Gerleman, Gillis. "דם." In *TLOT* 1:337–39.

Gese, Hartmut. "The Atonement." In *Essays on Biblical Theology*, translated by Keith Crim, 93–116. Minneapolis: Augsburg, 1981.

———. "Die Sühne," In *Zur biblischen Theologie: Altestamentliche Vorträge*, 85–106. München: Kaiser-Verlag, 1977.

Gibson, David. *Reading the Decree: Exegesis, Election and Christology in Calvin and Barth*. London: T. & T. Clark, 2009.

Gignilliat, Mark S. *Karl Barth and the Fifth Gospel*. Aldershot, UK: Ashgate, 2009.

Gill, Theodore A. "Barth and Mozart." *Theology Today* 43.3 (1986) 403–11.

Gloege, Gerhard. "Zur Prädestinationslehre Karl Barths." In *Theologische Traktate. Erster Band: Heilsgeschehen und Welt*, 77–132. Göttingen: Vandenhoeck & Ruprecht, 1965.

———. "Zur Versöhnungslehre Karl Barth." In *Theologische Traktate. Erster Band: Heilsgeschehen und Welt*, 133–73. Göttingen: Vandenhoeck & Ruprecht, 1965.

Gockel, Matthias. *Barth and Schleiermacher on the Doctrine of Election: A Systematic-Theological Comparison*. Oxford: Oxford University Press, 2006.

Goebel, Hans Theodor. *Vom freien Wählen Gottes und des Menschen: Interpretationsübungen zur »Analogie« nach Karl Barths Lehre von der Erwählung und Bedenken ihrer Folgen für die Kirchliche Dogmatik*. Frankfurt am Main: Lang, 1990.

Grabbe, Lester L. "The Scapegoat Tradition: A Study in Early Jewish Interpretation." *JSJ* 18.2 (1987) 152–67.

Graf, Daniel. *Unterwegs zu einer Biblischen Theologie: Perspektiven der Konzeption von Peter Stuhlmacher*. Göttingen: Vandenhoeck & Ruprecht 2011.

Greggs, Tom. *Barth, Origen, and Universal Salvation: Restoring Particularity*. Oxford: Oxford University Press, 2009.

———. "'Jesus is Victor': Passing the Impasse of Barth on Universalism." *SJTh* 60.2 (2007) 196–212.

Gundry, Robert Horton. *Matthew: A Commentary on his Literary and Theological Art.* Grand Rapids: Eerdmans, 1982.
Gunton, Colin. *The Barth Lectures.* Edited by Paul Brazier. London: T. & T. Clark 2007.
———. "Karl Barth's Doctrine Of Election as Part of His Doctrine of God." *JThS* 25.2 (1974) 381–92.
———. "Salvation." In *The Cambridge Companion to Karl Barth*, edited by John Webster, 143–58. Cambridge: Cambridge University Press, 2000.
Hagner, Donald A. *Matthew 1–13.* WBC. Dallas: Word, 1993.
Härle, Wilfried. *Sein und Gnade: Die Ontologie in Karl Barths Kirchlicher Dogmatik.* Berlin: De Gruyter, 1975.
Harris, Murray J. *The Second Epistle to the Corinthians: A Commentary on the Greek Text (NIGTC).* Grand Rapids: Eerdmans, 2005.
Hartley, J. E. "Day of Atonement." In *DOTP* 54–61.
Hays, Christopher B. "'Blessed be Egypt my people': Karl Barth and the Election of the Outsider in the Old Testament." *PTR* X.1 (2003) 30–41.
Hector, Kevin W. "God's Triunity and Self-Determination: A Conversation with Karl Barth, Bruce McCormack and Paul Molnar." *IJST* 7.3 (2005) 246–61.
Helm, Robert. "Azazel in Early Jewish Tradition." *AUSS* 32.3 (1994) 217–26.
Hitchcock, Nathan. *Karl Barth and the Resurrection of the Flesh: The Loss of the Body in Participatory Eschatology.* Eugene, OR: Pickwick, 2013.
Hofius, Otfried. "Der Mensch im Schatten Adams." In *Paulusstudien 2 (WUNT 143),* edited by Otfried Hofius, 104–54. Tübingen: Mohr Siebeck, 2002.
———. "Erwägungen zur Gestalt und Herkunft des paulinischen Versöhnungsgedankes." In *Paulusstudien. WUNT 51,* edited by Otfried Hofius, 1–32. Tübingen: Mohr Siebeck, 1989.
———. "Sühne und Versöhnung. Zum paulinischen Verständnis des Kreuzestodes Jesu." In *Paulusstudien, WUNT 51,* edited by Otfried Hofius, 33–49. Tübingen: Mohr Siebeck, 1989.
———. "Sühne IV (Neues Testament)." In *TRE* 32:342–477.
Hooker, Morna. *From Adam to Christ: Essays on Paul.* Cambridge: Cambridge University Press, 1990.
Hübner, Hans. "Sühne und Versöhnung: Anmerkungen zu einem umstrittenen Kapitel Biblischer *KuD* 29 (1983) 284–305.
Hunsinger, George. *Disruptive Grace: Studies in the Theology of Karl Barth.* Grand Rapids: Eerdmans, 2001.
———. "Election and the Trinity: Twenty-Five Theses on the Theology of Karl Barth." In *Trinity and Election in Contemporary Theology,* edited by Michael T. Dempsey, 91–114. Grand Rapids: Eerdmans, 2011.
———. *How To Read Karl Barth: The Shape Of His Theology.* Oxford: Oxford University Press, 1991.
———. "A Tale of Two Simultaneities: Justification and Sanctification in Calvin and Barth." In *Conversing with Barth,* edited by John C. McDowell and Mike Higton, 68–89. Aldershot, UK: Ashgate, 2004.
Ignatius. "The Letters of Ignatius: Ephesians." In *Early Christian Fathers,* edited by Cyril C. Richardson, 87–93. London: SCM, 1953.
Irenaeus. "Against Heresies." In *Ante-Nicene Fathers, Volume 1,* edited by Philip Schaff, 315–578. Grand Rapids: CCEL, 1885.

Irenäus von Lyon. *Gegen die Häresien*. Translated by Norbert Brox. Freiburg: Herder, 1995.

Janowski, Bernd. "Atonement." In *EncChr*, Volume 1: A–D 152–54.

———. "He Bore Our Sins: Isaiah 53 and the Drama of Taking Another's Place." In *The Suffering Servant: Isaiah 53 in Jewish and Christian Sources*, edited by Bernd Janowski and Peter Stuhlmacher, 48–74. Grand Rapids: Eerdmans, 2004.

———. *Sühne als Heilsgeschehen: Traditions- und religionsgeschichtliche Studien zur Sühnetheologie der Priesterschrift*. Neukirchen-Vluyn: Neukirchener Verlag, 2000.

Janowski, Bernd and Peter Stuhlmacher, eds. *The Suffering Servant: Isaiah 53 in Jewish and Christian Sources*. Translated by Daniel P. Bailey. Grand Rapids: Eerdmans, 2004.

Janowski, Bernd, and G. Wilhelm. "Der Bock, der die Sünden hinausträgt: Zur Religionsgeschichte des Azazel-Ritus Lev. 16,10.21–22." In *Religionsgeschichtliche Beziehungen zwischen Kleinasien, Nordsyrien und dem Alten Testament*, edited by Bernd Janowski et al., 109–69. Göttingen: Vandenhoeck & Ruprecht, 1993.

Jenson, Matt. *The Gravity of Sin: Augustine, Luther and Barth on 'Homo Incurvatus In Se.'* London: T. & T. Clark 2006.

Jenson, Philip Peter. *Graded Holiness: A Key to the Priestly Conception of the World*. Sheffield, UK: JSOT, 1992.

Jenson, Robert W. *Alpha and Omega: A Study in the Theology of Karl Barth*. Reprint. Eugene: Wipf and Stock, 2002.

Jeong, Sung Min. *Nothingness in the Theology of Paul Tillich and Karl Barth*. Lanham, MD: University Press of America, 2003.

Joest, Wilfried, *Dogmatik Bd:1 Die Wirklichkeit Gottes*, 4. durchges. Aufl. Göttingen: Vandenhoeck & Ruprecht, 1995.

Jones, Paul Dafydd. *The Humanity of Christ: Christology in Karl Barth's Church Dogmatics*. London: T. & T. Clark, 2008.

———. "Karl Barth on Gethsemane." *IJSTh* 9.2 (2007) 148–71.

Jüngel, Eberhard. "Einführung in Leben und Werk Karl Barths." In *Barth-Studien*, edited by Eberhard Jüngel, 22–60. Zürich-Köln: Benzinger Verlag, 1982.

———. "Das Opfer Jesu Christi als Sacramentum et Exemplum." In *Wertlose Wahrheit. Theologische Erörterungen*, edited by Eberhard Jüngel, 261–71. München: Kaiser, 1990.

———. "Die Möglichkeit theologischer Anthropologie auf dem Grunde der Analogie. Eine Untersuchung zum Analogieverständnis Karl Barths." *Evangelische Theologie* 22 (1962) 535–57.

———. *God's Being Is in Becoming: The Trinitarian Being of God in the Theology of Karl Barth. A Paraphrase*. Translated by John Webster. Edinburgh: T. & T. Clark, 2001.

———. "Karl Barths Lehre von der Taufe." In *Barth-Studien*, edited by Eberhard Jüngel, 246–90. Zürich-Köln: Benzinger Verlag, 1982.

Käfer, Anne. *Inkarnation und Schöpfung: Schöpfungstheologische Voraussetzungen und Implikationen der Christologie bei Luther, Schleiermacher und Karl Barth*. Berlin: De Gruyter, 2010.

Käsemann, Ernst. *Commentary on Romans*. Translated by Geoffrey W. Bromiley. Grand Rapids: Eerdmans, 1980.

Kedar-Kopfstein, Benjamin. "דם." Im *TDOT* 3:234–250.

Kennedy, Darren M. "A Personalist Doctrine of Providence: Karl Barth's *Church Dogmatics* III.3 in Conversation with Philosophical Theology." PhD diss., University of Edinburgh, 2007.
Kiuchi, Nobuyoshi. *The Purification Offering in the Priestly Literature: Its Meaning and Function*. Sheffield, UK: Sheffield Academic Press, 1987.
Klappert, Bertold. *Die Auferweckung des Gekreuzigten: Der Ansatz der Christologie Karl Barths im Zusammenhang der Christologie der Gegenwart*. Neukirchen-Vluyn: Neukirchener Verlag, 1981.
———. "Gott in Christus–Versöhner der Welt: Die Christologie Karl Barths als Anfrage an die Christologie der Gegenwart." In *Versöhnung und Befreiung: Versuche, Karl Barth kontextuell zu verstehen*, 141–65. Neukirchen-Vluyn: Neukirchener Verlag, 1994.
Knöppler, Thomas. *Sühne im Neuen Testament: Studien zum urchristlichen Verständnis der Heilsbedeutung des Todes Jesu*. WMANT 88. Neukirchen-Vluyn: Neukirchener Verlag, 2001.
Koch, Klaus. "חטאת." In *TDOT* 4:309–319.
———. *Um das Prinzip der Vergeltung in Religion und Recht des Alten Testaments (Wege der Forschung)*. Darmstadt: Wissenschaftliche Buchgesellschaft, 1972.
Kohlbrügge, Hermann Friedrich. *Auslegungen zu 3. Mose 1 bis 3. Mose 26*. Elberfeld: Schröer, 1911.
Kreck, Walter. *Grundentscheidungen in Karl Barths Dogmatik: Zur Diskussion seines Verständnisses von Offenbarung und Erwählung*. Neukirchen-Vluyn: Neukirchener Verlag, 1978.
Krötke, Wolf. "The Humanity of the Human Person in Karl Barth's Anthropology." In *The Cambridge Companion to Karl Barth*, edited by John Webster, 159–76. Cambridge: Cambridge University Press, 2000.
———. *Sin and Nothingness in the Theology of Karl Barth*. Translated by Philip Gordon Ziegler and Christina-Maria Bammel. Princeton: Princeton Theological Seminary, 2005.
———. *Sünde und Nichtiges bei Karl Barth*. Neukirchen-Vluyn: Neukirchener Verlag, 1983.
Lang, Bernhard. "כפר." In *TDOT* 7:288–303.
Levine, Baruch A. *In the Presence of the Lord: A Study of Cult and some Cultic Terms in Ancient Israel*. Leiden: Brill, 1974.
Lewis, Alan E. *Between Cross and Resurrection: A Theology of Holy Saturday*. Grand Rapids: Eerdmans, 2001.
Lewis, David. "Do We Believe in Penal Substitution?" In *Oxford Readings in Philosophical Theology: Volume 1: Trinity, Incarnation, Atonement*, edited by Michael Rea, 309–313. Oxford: Oxford University Press, 2009.
Lossky, Vladimir. "Redemption and Deification." In *In the Image and Likeness of God*, edited by John H. Erickson and Thomas E. Bird, 97–110. Crestwoo, NY: St Vladimir's Seminary Press, 1974.
Luther, Martin. *A Commentray on St. Paul's Epistle to the Galatians*. Translated by Philip S. Watson. London: James Clarke, 1953.
Maass, Fritz. "רפא." In *TLOT* 2:624–35.
Maccoby, Hyam. "Jesus and Barabbas." *NTS* 16 (1969/70) 55–60.
———. *Revolution in Judaea*. London: Ocean, 1973.

Maclean, Jennifer K. Berenson. "Barabbas, the Scapegoat Ritual, and the Development of the Passion Narrative." *HThR* 100.3 (2007) 309–34.
Mangina, Joseph L. *Karl Barth: Theologian of Christian Witness.* Aldershot, UK: Ashgate, 2004.
Martin, Ralph P. *2 Corinthians.* WBC. Waco, TX: Word, 1986.
Maurer, Ernstpeter. "'Für uns': An unserer Stelle hingerichtet. Die Herausforderung der Versöhnungslehre." *ZDTh* 18 (2002) 190–210.
Maury, Pierre. "Election et foi." *Foi et Vie* 37 (1936) 203–23.
———. *Prädestination.* Translaed by Rudolf Pfisterer. Neukirchen: Neukirchener Verlag, 1959.
———. *Predestination and Other Papers.* Translated by Edwin Hudson. London: SCM, 1960.
McCormack, Bruce L. "The Actuality of God: Karl Barth in Conversation with Open Theism." In *Engaging the Doctrine of God: Contemporary Protestant Perspectives*, edited by Bruce L. McCormack, 185–242. Grand Rapids: Baker Academic, 2008.
———. "Election and the Trinity: Theses in Response to George Hunsinger." In *Trinity and Election in Contemporary Theology*, edited by Michael T. Dempsey, 115–37. Grand Rapids: Eerdmans, 2011.
———. *For Us and Our Salvation: Incarnation and Atonement in the Reformed Tradition.* Princeton: Princeton Theological Seminary, 1993.
———. "Grace and Being: The Role of God's Gracious Election in Karl Barth's Theological Ontology." In *The Cambridge Companion to Karl Barth*, edited by John Webster, 92–110. Cambridge: Cambridge University Press, 2000.
———. "Justitia Aliena: Karl Barth in Conversation with the Evangelical Doctrine of Imputed Righteousness." In *Justification in Perspective: Historical Developments and Contemporary Challenges*, edited by Bruce L. McCormack, 167–96. Grand Rapids: Baker Academic, 2006.
———. *Karl Barth's Critically Realistic Dialectical Theology: Its Genesis and Development, 1909–1936.* Oxford: Clarendon, 1995.
———. "Seek God where he may be found: a response to Edwin Chr. van Driel." *SJTh* 60.1 (2007) 62–79.
McDonald, H. D. *The Atonement of the Death of Christ: In Faith, Revelation, and History.* Grand Rapids: Baker, 1985.
McDonald, Suzanne. *Re-Imaging Election: Divine Election as Representing God to Others and Others to God.* Grand Rapids: Eerdmans, 2010.
McDowell, John C. "Contriving Creation Eschatologically under Christological Control: The Doctrine of Election (*CD*, II-III)." In *Hope in Barth's Eschatology: Interrogations and Transformations beyond Tragedy*, 123–46. Aldershot, UK: Ashgate 2000.
———. "'Mend your speech a little': Reading Karl Barth's *das Nichtige* through Donald MacKinnon's Tragic Vision." In *Conversing with Barth*, edited by John C. McDowell and Mike Higton, 142–72. Aldershot, UK: Ashgate, 2004.
McFayden, Alistair. *Bound to Sin: Abuse, Holocaust and the Christian Doctrine of Sin.* Cambridge: Cambridge University Press, 2000.
McLauchlan, Richard. "Poems from Holy Saturday: Encountering Divine and Human Silence in the Poems of R. S. Thomas." PhD diss., University of Cambridge, 2014.
McMaken, Travis. "Election and the Pattern of Exchange in Karl Barth's Doctrine of Atonement." *JRTh* 3 (2009) 202–18.

Mikkelsen, Hans Vium. *Reconciled Humanity: Karl Barth in Dialogue*. Grand Rapids: Eerdmans 2010.
Milgrom, Jacob. *Leviticus 1-16: A New Translation with Introduction and Commentary*. New York: Doubleday, 1991.
———. *Studies in Cultic Theology and Terminology*. Leiden: Brill, 1983.
Moberly, Robert W. L. "Did the Serpent Get It Right?." In *From Eden to Golgotha: Essays in Biblical Theology*, 1-27. Atlanta: Scholars, 1992.
Molnar, Paul. "Can the Electing God Be Without Us? Some Implications of Bruce McCormack's Understanding of Barth's Doctrine of Election for the Doctrine of the Trinity." In *Trinity and Election in Contemporary Theology*, edited by Michael T. Dempsey, 63-90. Grand Rapids: Eerdmans, 2011.
———. "The Trinity, Election, and God's Ontological Freedom: A Response to Kevin W. Hector." In *Trinity and Election in Contemporary Theology*, edited by Michael T. Dempsey, 47-62. Grand Rapids: Eerdmans, 2011.
Muller, Richard A. *Christ the Decree: Christology and Predestination in Reformed Theology from Calvin to Perkins*. Grand Rapids: Baker Academic, 2008.
Neder, Adam. *Participation in Christ: An Entry into Karl Barth's Church Dogmatics*. Louisville, Kentucky: Westminster John Knox, 2009.
Nimmo, Paul T. "Barth and the Christian as Ethical Agent." In *Commanding Grace: Studies in Karl Barth's Ethics*, edited by Daniel L. Migliore, 216-38. Grand Rapids: Eerdmans, 2010.
———. *Being in Action: The Theological Shape of Barth's Ethical Vision*. London: T. & T. Clark, 2007.
———. "Election and Evangelical Thinking: Challenges to Our Way of Conceiving the Doctrine of God." In *New Perspectives for Evangelical Theology: Engaging with God, Scripture, and the World*, edited by Tom Greggs, 29-43. London: Routledge, 2010.
Nolland, John. *The Gospel of Matthew: A Commentary on the Greek Text*. Grand Rapids: Eerdmans, 2005.
Origen. *Homilies on Leviticus: 1-16*. Translated by Gary Wayne Barkley. Washington, DC: Catholic University of America Press, 1990.
———. "Origen Against Celsus." In *Ante-Nicene Fathers, Volume 4*, edited by Philip Schaff, 395-669. Grand Rapids: CCEL, 1885.
Pannenberg, Wolfhart. *Systematic Theology Vol. 3*, translated by Geoffrey Bromiley. Grand Rapids: Eerdmans, 1991.
Peterson Sr., Robert A. *Calvin and the Atonement: What the Renowned Pastor and Teacher Said about the Cross of Christ*. Fearn, UK: Mentor, 1999.
Polen, Nehemia. "Leviticus and Hebrews . . . and Leviticus." In *The Epistle to the Hebrews and Chrsitian Theology*, edited by Richard Bauckham et al., 213-25. Grand Rapids: Eerdmans, 2009.
Prenter, Regin. "Karl Barths Umbildung der traditionellen Zweinaturlehre in lutherischer Beleuchtung." *Studia Theologica* 11.1 (1957) 1-88.
Rendtorff, Rolf. *Studien zur Geschichte des Opfers im alten Israel*. Neukirchen-Vluyn: Neukirchener Verlag, 1967.
Rodin, Scott R. *Evil and Theodicy in the Theology of Karl Barth*. New York: Lang, 1997.
Ruddies, Hartmut. "Christologie und Versöhnungslehre bei Karl Barth." *ZDTh* 18 (2002) 190-210.
Rudman, Dominic. "A Note on the Azazel-goat Ritual." *ZAW* 116.3 (2004) 396-401.

Scarlata, Mark. *Outside of Eden: Cain in the Ancient Versions of Genesis 4.1–16*. London: T. & T. Clark, 2012.

Schwartz, Baruch J. "The Bearing of Sin in the Priestly Literature." In *Pomegranates and Golden Bells: Studies in Biblical, Jewish, and Near Eastern Ritual, Law, and Literature in Honor of Jacob Milgrom*, edited David P. Wright et al.,3–22. Winona Lake, IN: Eisenbrauns, 1995.

Söding, Thomas. "Sühne durch Stellvertretung: Zur zentralen Deutung des Todes Jesu im Römerbrief." In *Deutungen des Todes Jesu im Neuen Testament, WUNT 181*, edited by Thomas Söding, 375–96. Tübingen: Mohr Siebeck, 2005.

St. Athanasius. *On the Incarnation: The Treatise De Incarnatione Verbi Dei*. Translated and edited by a Religious of C.S.M.V. London: Mowbray, 1982.

Staubli, Thomas. "Die Symbolik des Vogelrituals bei der Reinigung von Aussätzigen (Lev 14,4–7)." *Biblica* 83 (2002) 230–37.

Steele, David N., et al. *The Five Points of Calvinism, Defined, Defended, and Documented*. Phillipsburg: P. & R., 2004.

Stoevesandt, Hinrich. "Karl Barths Erwählungslehre als Rahmen einer geschichtsbezogenen Theologie." In *Gottes freie Gnade. Studien zur Lehre von der Erwählung*, edited by Michael Beintker, 119–40. Wuppertal: Foedus-Verlag, 2004.

Stökl Ben Ezra, Daniel. "The Biblical Yom Kippur, the Jewish Fast of the Day of Atonement and the Church Fathers." *Studia Patristica*, edited by M. F. Wiles and E. J. Yarnold, 493–502. Leuven: Peeters, 2001.

———. "The Christian Exegesis of the Scapegoat between Jews and Pagans." In *Sacrifice in Religious Experience*, edited by Albert I. Baumgarten, 207–32. Leiden: Brill, 2002.

———. *The Impact of Yom Kippur on Early Christianity: The Day of Atonement from Second Temple Judaism to the Fifth Century*. Tübingen: Mohr Siebeck, 2003.

Stolina, Ralf. "Tod und Heil. Zur Heilsbedeutung des Todes Jesu." *NZSTh* 44.1 (2002) 89–106.

Stolz, F. "גוא." In *TOLT* 2:769–74.

Stoltzfus, Philip E. *Theology as Performance: Music, Aesthetics, and God in Western Thought*. London: T. & T. Clark, 2006.

Stowers, Stanley. "Matter and Spirit, or What is Pauline Participation in Christ?" In *The Holy Spirit: Classic and Contemporary Readings*, edited by Eugene F. Rogers, Jr., 91–105. Malden, MA: Wiley-Blackwell, 2009.

Stuhlmacher, Peter. *Biblische Theologie des Neuen Testaments, Band 1: Grundlegung Von Jesus zu Paulus*. Göttingen: Vandenhoeck & Ruprecht, 2005.

———. "Existenzstellvertretung für die Vielen: Mk 10,45 (Mt 20, 28)." In *Versöhnung, Gesetz und Gerechtigkeit: Aufsätze zur biblischen Theologie*, edited by Peter Stuhlmacher, 27–42. Göttingen: Vandenhoeck & Ruprecht, 1981.

———. *Paul's Letter to the Romans: A Commentary*. Edited by Scott J. Hafemann. Louisville, Kentucky: Westminster/John Knox, 1994.

———. "Recent Exegesis on Romans 3:24–26." In *Law, Reconciliation, & Righteousness: Essays in Biblical Theology*, translated by Everett R. Klain, 94–109. Philadelphia: Fortress, 1986.

———. *Revisiting Paul's Doctrine of Justification: A Challenge to the New Perspective*. Edited by Donald A. Hagner. Downers Grove, IL: InterVarsity, 2001.

Sykes, Stephen W. "The Study of Barth." In *Karl Barth, Studies of His Theological Method*, edited by Stephen W. Sykes, 1–16. Oxford: Clarendon, 1979.

Tawil, Hayim. "Azazel the Prince of the Steepe: A Comparative Study." *ZAW* 92.1 (1980) 43–59.
Thomas, Günter. "Der für uns gerichtete Richter. Kritische Erwägungen zu Karl Barths Versöhnungslehre." *ZDTh* 18 (2002) 211–25.
Torrance, James B. *Worship, Community and the Triune God of Grace*. Downers Grove, IL: InterVarsity, 1997.
Torrance, Thomas F. *Atonement: The Person and Work of Christ*. Edited by Robert T. Walker. Milton Keynes, UK: Paternoster, 2009.
———. *Incarnation: The Person and Life of Christ*. Edited by Robert T. Walker. Milton Keynes, UK: Paternoster, 2008.
———. *Karl Barth: Biblical and Evangelical Theologian*. Edinburgh: T. & T. Clark, 1990.
———. *The Trinitarian Faith: The Evangelical Theology of the Ancient Catholic Church*. Edinburgh: T. & T. Clark, 1988.
Trebilco, Paul. "דם." In *NIDOTTE* 1:963–66.
Turner, David L. *Matthew*. Grand Rapids: Baker Academic, 2008.
Turner, Henry E. W. *The Patristic Doctrine of Redemption: A Study of the Development of Doctrine During the First Five Centuries*. London: Mowbray, 1952.
Vetter, Isolde. "Mozarts Nachschrift des Allegrischen *Miserere*: Ein Gedächtnis 'wunder'?" In *Musik als Text. Bericht über den Internationalen Kongress der Gesellschaft für Musikforschung, Freiburg im Breisgau 1993*, edited by Hermann Danuser, Tobias Plebuch et al., 144–47. Kassel: Bärenreiter 1998.
Vondey, Wolfgang. "The Holy Spirit and the Physical Universe: The Impact of Scientific Paradigm Shifts on Contemporary Pneumatology." *Theological Studies* 70.1 (2009) 3–36.
Wallace, Mark I. "Karl Barth's Hermeneutic: A Way beyond the Impasse." *JR* 68.3 (1988) 396–410.
Ward, Graham. "Barth, Hegel, and the Possibility for Christian Apologetics." In *Conversing with Barth*, edited by John C. McDowell and Mike Higton, 53–67. Aldershot, UK: Ashgate, 2004.
Webster, John B. *Barth*. London: Continuum, 2004.
Welker, Michael. "Barth und Hegel. Zur Erkenntnis eines methodischen Verfahrens bei Barth." *Evangelische Theologie* 43 (1983) 307–28.
Wendel, François. *Calvin: Origins and Development of His Religious Thought*. Grand Rapids: Baker, 1997.
Westbrook, Raymond and Theodore J. Lewis. "Who Led the Scapegoat in Leviticus 16:21?." *JBL* 127.3 (2008) 417–22.
Wilckens, Ulrich. *Der Brief and die Römer (EKK)*. Neukirchen-Vluyn: Neukirchener Verlag, 1978–82.
Williams, Rowan. "Barth on the Triune God." In *Karl Barth: Studies of his Theological Method*, edited by Stephen W. Sykes, 147–93. Oxford: Clarendon, 1979.
———. *Silence and Honey Cakes: The Wisdom of the Desert*. Oxford: Lion, 2003.
Wood, Donald. *Barth's Theology of Interpretation*. Aldershot, UK: Ashgate, 2007.
Wright, David P. *The Disposal of Impurity: Elimination Rites in the Bible and in Hittite and Mesopotamian Literature*. Atlanta: Scholars, 1987.
———. "The Gesture of Hand Placement in the Hebrew Bible and in Hittite Literature." *JAOS* 106.4 (1986) 433–46.
Young, Frances M. *Sacrifice and the Death of Christ*. London: SPCK, 1975.

———. *The Use of Sacrificial Ideas in Greek Christian Writers*. Philadelphia: The Philadelphia Patristic Foundation, 1979.

Zatelli, Ida. "The Origin of the Biblical Scapegoat Ritual: The Evidence of Two Eblaite Texts." *VT* 48.2 (1998) 254–63.

Subject Index

abandonment, 9, 61, 112, 183, 250
actualistic, 7, 16, 17, 156, 195, 199, 201, 233
ad extra, 3, 18, 20, 39, 44, 105, 136, 172, 200, 256, 257
ad intra, 3, 44, 136, 256
analogia entis, 19, 255
analogia fidei, 19
analogia relationis, 223, 224, 255
anhypostatic/anhypostasia, 33, 95, 117, 151, 152
anthropology/anthropological, 26, 31, 34, 100, 112–17, 120, 218
antithesis, 96, 114, 123, 125–26, 137, 141–42, 149
apokatastasis, 9, 199, 202–4, 206–7, 212
appeasement, 75, 151, 154, 222, 259
Ark of the Covenant, 48, 51, 72, 227
Arminian, 211
assumptio carnis, 156
assurance (pastoral), 13, 15
atonement (doctrine of), 4–5, 8, 64, 170, 197, 202, 214
Azazel, 3, 8, 48–49, 51–52, 56–57, 65–67, 75, 78–81, 83–85, 87–90, 92–93, 95, 98–99, 213, 249–50, 252

baptism, 162, 190–91, 219, 222, 231, 233, 237–39, 243, 250
βασιλεία τοῦ θεοῦ, 22
bearing (sin), 2–3, 9, 38, 67–68, 79, 82–83, 88–91, 99, 112, 145–46, 150, 167, 182–83, 195, 210, 213–14, 230–31, 244, 250, 253, 255

Bible, xii–xiv, 2, 17, 21–22, 26, 44, 54, 57, 62, 80, 87–88, 98, 101, 104, 128, 173–74, 188, 202
binary, 6–7, 12, 39, 41, 46, 64, 96, 99, 206, 229, 248–49
bird, 48–49, 53–54, 56, 61, 64, 72, 77, 80, 84–86
blood, 8, 48, 50–55, 67–69, 71–76, 78–82, 84–86, 89, 93, 145, 154, 175–77, 182, 190–91, 225–27, 230, 233, 250

Calvinist, 1, 11, 28, 208–11, 248, 251–52
Christology/christological, 5, 7, 10–11, 17, 24, 26, 31, 36, 39–40, 47, 59, 88, 101, 105–7, 112, 115–16, 124, 143, 148, 151, 157–58, 160, 165–66, 190, 192, 204, 215–16, 247, 250
Christus Victor, 8, 148–50, 174
Church, xii–iii, 1, 4, 6–8, 10–11, 14, 19, 21, 28, 32, 37, 41–42, 60, 88, 119, 146–48, 156, 200, 206, 224, 228, 246, 252, 259
Church Fathers, 7, 59, 63, 87, 94, 123, 148,
clean/unclean, 48, 56, 69–70, 72, 80–82, 85, 89–90, 233
co-belligerent, 126
communicatio apotelesmatum, 152
communicatio idiomatum, 151
communicatio operationum, 152
condemnation, 11–12, 25, 39, 43, 105, 112, 156, 163–64, 167, 171, 184, 187, 199, 201–3, 212, 228, 248,

condescension, 135, 158–61, 166, 235
consummation, 102, 127, 228, 248
correspondence, 131–32, 137, 200, 215, 222, 237, 239, 245, 251, 255–56
covenant/covenantal, 5, 8, 23–25, 27–31, 34–35, 41–42, 51, 69–70, 72, 75–77, 81–82, 93, 100–117, 123 134–35, 137, 13–19, 141, 145, 157, 165–66, 168, 175–78, 180, 190–91, 197–98, 200, 205, 207, 215–18, 220–22, 225, 233–36, 240–42, 245–46, 251–52, 254, 258–59
Creator/creation, 10, 17–18, 20, 24, 31 41–42, 56, 81, 84, 100–107, 111, 113–14, 116, 118, 120, 122–27, 130, 133–38, 140–44, 149, 167, 172, 195–96, 214, 218–21, 223, 225–27, 240, 246–47, 253 255–56, 259
cross, 1–5, 7–9, 12, 20, 36, 38–44, 64, 88–90, 92–96, 101, 103, 110–12, 115, 121, 124, 126–27, 133, 142–46, 149–50, 152–54, 156–57, 159, 161–72, 179, 181–83, 185, 187–88, 191–99, 201–4, 207, 210–14, 218, 222, 224, 229–32, 240–42, 244–45, 247–59
crucifixion, 11, 36, 63–64, 149, 161, 188, 258
cultic, 3, 5, 7–9, 45–47, 56, 58, 65–69. 72–74, 76–77, 82, 84–86, 97, 146, 161, 173–76, 179, 181, 185–86, 189–90, 195, 222, 225–26, 250
Cur Deus Homo, 9, 148, 150–51, 156, 170, 173
curse, 130, 139, 150, 164, 167

damnation, 16, 25, 38, 130
Day of Atonement, 8, 48, 51–52, 77, 81, 88, 93,
death, 1, 3, 6–9, 16, 36–41, 43–45, 50–58, 61, 63–64, 67–69, 72, 75–77, 79–80, 82, 84–86, 88–93, 99, 107, 111–12, 121–22, 127, 129–31, 133, 140–42, 144–51, 153–56, 160–61, 163–64, 166–67, 169–71, 173–74, 177–80, 182–92, 194–200, 202–3, 205, 208–11, 213, 219–28, 230–33, 240, 248, 250, 252–58
decretum absolutum, 7, 11, 15, 28
decretum concretum, 15, 28, 32
decretum horribile, 15
depravity, 153, 155
determinism, 25
dereliction, 112
Deus dixit, 21
Deus pro nobis, 3, 5, 15, 27, 102, 109, 115, 136, 164, 230–31, 247, 255
Deus absconditus, 4, 9, 11, 21, 28, 200, 212, 214, 252, 254, 259
Deus revelatus, 4, 21, 259
devil/Satan/Evil One, 130, 149, 168–69, 174, 231, 236
dialectic/dialectical, 8, 12, 20, 37, 39–40, 43, 63–64, 95–97, 107, 111, 114, 123–26, 133, 137, 143, 194, 196, 201, 204, 249, 251
disobedience, 106, 138, 149–50, 184, 223–24, 240
Docetism, 152, 166
dogmatics, 5, 19, 21, 97, 119, 161, 173
double imputation, 4, 185
double predestination , 1–3, 7, 12, 14, 25, 36, 38, 201, 213, 248, 258
Doppelbewegung, 158
do ut des, 72, 74, 154, 177, 194

election (doctrine of), xiv, 1–2, 4–8, 10–21, 24–26, 28–31, 35, 37–40, 42–43, 45–49, 55, 60, 62–67, 87, 94, 96–97, 100, 103–4, 107, 111, 115, 159, 165–66, 185, 199–202, 204, 206, 212–14, 230, 247–48, 250, 252, 256, 259
enhypostatic, 95, 117, 151, 213
Entsprechung, 222, 237, 255
Erwählung, 12–13, 16, 24–25, 44, 120
eschaton, 214, 248
eternity, 5, 7, 17, 21, 26–27, 29, 31, 33, 38, 42, 94, 95, 100, 108–9, 156–57, 165, 170, 201, 205, 208, 212, 228, 237, 250–51, 255–59
Eucharist, 87, 123, 148, 233, 237

evil, 40, 42, 52, 63, 79–80, 88, 90, 98, 103, 110, 123, 130, 133, 136, 142, 149–50, 158, 163, 166, 168–69, 183, 188, 197, 203, 209, 211, 231
exaltation, 6, 61, 107, 141, 158–59, 166, 181, 205, 216, 224–25, 249–50
excursus, 46–47, 55, 61, 173–74
exegesis, 3, 5, 7–9, 12–13, 37, 46–48, 59–68, 70, 72, 84–87, 94–99, 102, 145, 173, 181, 189, 202, 212–13, 249–50, 253, 255, 259
Existenzstellvertretung, 8–9, 66, 68–69, 76, 80, 82, 84–86, 93–94, 121, 146, 165, 186, 189–90, 192, 195–96, 211–12, 249–50, 253, 257

faith, 1, 4, 9–10, 13, 19, 44, 57, 59–60, 63, 101, 119–20, 152, 157, 200–202, 206, 208–9, 224, 226–27, 230–31, 233–34, 237–38, 240, 242, 244, 250–52, 254–55
fall, 114, 139, 147–48, 162, 184, 188, 236
fellowship, 5, 8–9, 23, 29, 34, 39, 41–42, 69–70, 75–77, 82, 95, 100–102, 106, 110, 112–13, 115–16, 119, 123, 137, 151, 165, 172, 175, 182, 185, 191, 193, 200–201, 216, 218–19, 221, 222, 225, 227, 230, 233, 241–42, 244, 246, 248, 251–52, 254
flesh, 9, 31, 33, 60, 81, 108, 113, 115, 117, 148, 150, 155–56, 160, 162, 166–67, 187–90, 195, 201, 208, 213, 216, 220–21, 223–28, 249, 251, 253, 258
forensic, 4, 5, 7–9, 149, 151, 153, 161, 170, 173–74, 181, 184–86, 189, 194–95, 250
forgiveness, 83, 178, 181, 231, 251
fourfold *pro nobis*, 8, 156, 173, 181
free will, 207–8, 257
freedom, 24–25, 28, 30–31, 35, 39, 47, 49, 53–54, 57, 61, 64, 77, 80, 84, 106, 131, 149, 156, 166, 180–81, 200, 206, 210, 212–13, 215, 224, 230–31, 234–38, 240–46, 254–56

fulfilment, 17, 25, 42, 60–64, 87, 103, 107–8, 110–11, 156–57, 170, 176–78, 217, 225, 228, 233, 245, 248, 255

Geist, 120–22, 200, 218, 220–22, 224, 227, 238
Geistestaufe, 200, 222, 236–38, 244–45, 255
Gethsemane, 163, 165–69, 224
Gnadenwahl, 11, 24, 230
goat, 3, 8, 48–54, 56, 60, 63, 65–67, 70, 75, 78–81, 83–93, 95, 98–99, 176, 213, 231, 249–50, 252
Golgotha, 93, 95, 97, 111, 182, 191
Gottes Gnadenwahl, 11, 24
Göttingen Dogmatics, 16

ḥaṭṭāʾt/חַטָּאת, 4, 68, 70–73, 75, 78, 80–82, 84–86, 88–89, 93, 186–87, 213
Heilsgeschichte, 37, 106, 149, 177, 238, 240
hell, 1–2, 5, 43, 130, 210, 247
High Priest, 48, 50, 75, 78, 82, 84–85, 89, 173–79, 181, 215
hilasterion, 177, 194
history (of the Church), 1, 28, 146, 200, 252
Holy of Holies, 48, 71, 78, 81, 89, 93, 191, 227
Holy Spirit, xiv, 6, 9, 16, 19–22, 24, 178, 200, 204, 208–10, 214, 221–22, 224, 226–27, 229–30, 232, 234, 236–40, 242–43, 248, 251–52, 255, 259
horrible decree, 5, 247
humiliation, 6, 61, 95, 107, 141, 156, 158–61, 205, 216, 249–50
hypostatic union, 8. 95, 117, 145, 148, 151, 155, 197–98, 215, 225, 230, 249, 258

ἱλαστήριον, 48, 78
imago Dei, 116, 222
immortality/immortal, 9, 121–23, 148, 199, 218, 226–27, 230
impasse, 58, 249

Subject Index

imperishable, 123, 128, 199, 218, 226
impossibility, 110, 114, 229
impure/impurity, 51, 53, 61, 72, 74, 79–81, 86
imputation, 4, 153, 185, 195, 250
incarnation, 22, 31–33, 106–8, 110–11, 115, 117, 141–42, 148–52, 157, 159–60, 167, 187–88, 197, 211, 216, 219, 225–26, 228, 256, 258
Israel, 6, 8, 41, 49–52, 54–55, 57, 61, 63, 70–71, 73–79, 81–82, 84–86, 88, 100, 108–9, 153, 161–63, 166, 169–70, 177, 190, 215, 220, 222, 225–26, 240
iustitia distributive, 171

judge, 8–9, 51, 136, 145, 156, 160–65, 167–68, 170–71, 173–77, 179, 181, 196–97, 199, 248, 257–58
judgment, 3, 24, 38–39, 41, 43–44, 51–52, 56, 59, 85, 111–12, 135–36, 153–54, 156, 159, 161–67, 170–73, 176–77, 182, 187, 192, 194, 197, 211, 214, 220, 248, 250, 254
judicial/ juridical, 5, 153, 156, 161, 173–76, 179, 181

kappōret, 48, 75, 78–79, 81–82, 84, 86, 93–94, 191, 222, 251
kenosis, 225
kipper, 8, 68–69, 70–71, 75, 83
kōper/כֹּפֶר, 69, 71, 74–75, 86

legal, 49–50, 69, 149, 151, 153, 155
leitmotif, 5, 28, 41
Leviticus, 7, 12, 45–50, 53, 61, 65, 67–68, 70, 73, 77, 81, 87, 90, 97, 166, 175, 194, 221, 255
lex credendi, 146
lex orandi, 146
liberum arbitrium, 236
Logos, 31, 33, 44, 107, 110, 115, 117, 142, 147, 153, 156, 188, 216, 223–25, 227–28, 247
asarkos, 28, 32–33, 201
ensarkos, 32–33
lordship, 23, 105–6, 127, 132, 137

Lutheran, 13, 46, 194

Mediator, 6, 27–29, 31, 109, 111, 145, 151, 159, 175, 180, 200, 215, 217, 251
mercy seat, 48, 78
Messiah, 87, 90–91
Metanoia, 200, 221, 237
Miserere, xi
munus triplex, 157, 159, 215

nāśā' 'āwôn, 83, 99, 185
nepeš, 73, 75–76, 79, 84, 86, 250
new covenant, 31, 93, 108, 145, 165, 176–77, 191
New Testament, 2, 32, 60, 62–63, 72, 88–89, 97–99, 115, 123, 146, 151, 153, 173–75, 186, 189, 193–95, 197, 211–12, 214, 222–23, 230, 247, 250–51
das Nichtige, 8, 100, 112, 124, 126–34, 136–37, 139, 142, 169
nothingness, 60, 100, 110, 114, 118, 123–44, 164, 167, 169, 252

obedience, 3–4, 36, 45, 61, 106, 111, 115, 138–39, 149–50, 155–56, 158–60, 163, 165, 168, 179, 184, 197, 200–201, 205, 223–24, 229, 231, 238, 240–41, 254–58
object, 7, 12, 17, 22, 25–27, 31, 35–36, 38, 50–51, 72, 76, 84, 94–95, 127, 133, 135, 152, 161–62, 183, 188–89, 201, 205, 232, 241, 256
Old Testament, 3, 45, 47, 49, 55, 58–61, 63–64, 66, 68–69, 74, 77, 83, 87, 88–90, 97–99, 146, 151, 162, 175, 177, 184, 186, 189–90, 212–13, 215–16, 220, 222, 225–27, 250
ontology/ontological, 7–8, 16, 19, 20, 34, 100, 102, 110, 114, 116, 118, 122, 125, 129, 133–34, 137, 151, 156, 184, 195, 217, 256
omnipotence, 103, 131, 164, 210–11
Opfer, 77, 138, 174, 177, 179, 185, 189
opus alienum, 135–36
opus proprium, 135–36
original sin, 122, 153, 155–56

orthodox, xiii–ix, 26, 105, 117, 147, 152

participation, 40, 108–9, 189–90, 192, 195, 203, 218, 221, 228, 230, 233, 237–39, 250–51
particularity, 30, 200, 204, 206, 212–13, 223, 228–31, 237, 251
patristic, 20, 33, 87, 117, 145, 149, 158–59
paschal lamb, 87, 89, 92, 177
Passover, 88, 91–92
Penal Substitution, 89, 150, 153–55, 171, 183, 196, 258
penalty, 91, 150, 154, 171, 209
Pentateuch, 77
Pentecost, 151, 220–21, 225, 233
penultimate, 4, 64, 111, 143, 206, 213–14, 259
perichoresis/ perichoretical, 9, 20, 21, 196, 259
perishable, 199, 226, 228
pharmakos, 88–89
prayer, 167–68, 224
predestination, 1–3, 7, 11–14, 16, 18, 23, 25, 28, 31, 35–36, 38–39, 42, 46, 104–5, 124, 142, 172, 199, 201, 210, 213, 248, 258
propitiation, 71, 175
providence, 98, 103–6, 134, 137
punishment, 2, 3, 9, 36, 52, 69, 72, 83, 95, 111–12, 150, 153, 155, 159, 164, 168–72, 184–85, 194, 197, 212, 231, 250, 259

ransom, 69, 73–74, 86, 174, 211
recapitulation, 6, 149, 221, 225
reconciler/reconciliation, 6, 20–21, 24, 42, 50, 52–53, 60, 70, 75, 85, 93, 95 122, 130, 133, 139, 157–61, 165, 167–68, 170, 173–75, 178, 180, 182–83, 188, 192–95, 202–3, 206–7, 214–12. 232–33, 240, 242, 249–50, 255
reconciliation (doctrine of), 6, 21, 133, 158–60, 173–74, 214, 216–18, 249–50

Redeemer/redemption, 6, 20, 31, 39, 69, 102, 105, 107, 122–23, 146–49, 152, 176, 207, 209, 211, 213, 220–21, 225–26, 254, 258
Reformed, xiv, 8, 12–14, 16, 24–26, 29, 31, 42, 46, 105, 151–55, 159, 212, 247
Reformation, xii, 1, 46, 158
rejection, 6–7, 9, 12, 36–45, 48, 55, 57, 60, 64–65, 95–99, 131, 134–35, 142, 144, 163, 165, 167–69, 199–202, 204, 206, 212–14, 229–30, 242, 251, 257–58
removal (sin), 8–9, 44–45, 50, 67, 70, 76, 80, 100, 112, 123, 163, 182–83, 185, 200, 214
representative, 35, 38, 45, 52, 73, 78, 82, 85, 156, 171, 175, 190, 192, 206, 215, 237
reprobation, 11–12, 35–38, 43–45, 94–95, 111, 124, 140, 166, 169, 202, 248
resurrection, 3–4, 9, 40, 54–55, 61, 63–64, 93, 96, 107, 121, 123, 126, 140, 142–43, 148–49, 151, 161, 165, 167, 191, 196–97, 204, 213–14, 222, 224–28, 230, 233, 236, 238, 241, 251, 254, 257, 259
revelation, xii, 7, 19–23, 27–28, 30, 42, 44, 57, 62, 93, 101, 109, 113, 124–25, 138, 156–57, 212, 2142, 232, 236, 242–43, 246–47, 252
righteousness, 36, 98, 154–55, 172, 180–81, 186, 191
Römerbrief, 10, 25, 63
rûaḥ, 218, 220–21

sacrifice, 45, 52–54, 56–57, 60–61, 68, 70–72, 74–77, 79, 82–85, 88–89, 91–93, 115, 151, 154, 170, 173–81, 186–87, 189–90, 194, 209, 215, 231, 233, 249, 257
salvation, 1–4, 7, 9, 12–15, 28, 41–42, 51, 54, 56, 60–61, 67, 72, 84–85, 90, 98, 103, 106–9, 111, 125, 128, 149, 152, 154, 158–60, 162, 168, 177, 181, 187, 190, 197–98, 200, 204–9, 211–12, 214, 217, 226,

228, 230–33, 235, 238, 242–44, 247–49, 251–54, 258–59
sanctification, 51, 82, 179, 250
σάρξ, 167, 187, 188
satisfaction, 150, 153, 170–72
scapegoat, 48, 80–81, 87–92, 231, 252
Schöpfergnade, 220
Scripture, xi–iv, xvii, 1, 14, 19, 21–22, 46, 59, 62–63, 97–98, 119–20, 124, 152, 189, 205, 210, 212, 216, 221, 252
Seinsgrund, 30, 201
Seinsweisen, 23
Selbstbestimmung, 26, 29
self-determination, 20, 26–27, 29–30, 35
self-unveiling, 21, 94
sĕmîkâ/סְמִיכָה, 67, 75–77, 80, 84–86, 187, 190, 226
Septuagint, 89
shadow side/*Schattenseite*, 137, 140–44
Shekinah, 78, 86
Sin as *pride, sloth, falsehood*, 133, 168
sinless, 3, 39, 44, 60, 61, 67, 74, 86–87, 93, 97, 111, 154, 182, 249
sinner, 2–3, 38–39, 42, 51, 70–72, 74–77, 83–84, 86, 90, 93–94, 112, 139, 143–44, 154, 161–65, 171, 178–79, 183–85, 187–94, 196, 199, 209, 212, 222, 233, 249, 254
sin offering, 3, 8, 45, 65–69, 71–72, 76, 78–79, 87, 89–90, 92–93, 95, 186–87, 211, 226, 249–50, 252
Son of God, 17, 34, 39, 61, 95, 105, 108, 142, 149–50, 153–54, 156, 159–61, 163, 167, 187, 192, 194, 215, 217, 225, 248–49, 251
Son of Man, 39, 45, 94–95, 142, 149, 158–59, 217, 225, 248–49
soteriology/soteriological
soul, 73, 86, 120–23, 153, 188, 191, 218–19, 223–27, 230, 250–51
Spirit, 9, 20, 22, 55, 89, 103, 119, 122–23, 145–46, 151, 155, 177, 182, 194, 196, 200, 202–3, 208–10, 218–27, 229–30, 232–34, 237–39, 242–43, 245, 250–51, 258–59

Stellvertretung, 40, 75–76, 161–62, 170–73, 186, 192, 195
subject, xii, 7, 9, 17, 21–22, 25–28, 36, 38, 44, 46, 58–60, 63, 70, 72, 74–75, 115, 129, 141, 152, 157, 159–61, 166, 181, 188–89, 194, 200–201, 206, 226, 232, 234, 237, 243
substitute/substitution, 8, 38–40, 68–69, 74–77, 80, 82, 84, 112, 150, 153 155–56, 161, 171, 183, 192, 195, 209, 211, 250, 253, 257
suffering, 3–4, 39, 44–45, 51, 64, 83, 85, 111, 155, 163–64, 170–71, 223–24, 226, 228, 245, 254
Suffering Servant, 89, 153, 245

תַּחַת, 69, 189
theologia crucis, 44, 147, 161
transcendent, xii, 68, 75, 79, 84, 86, 113, 115, 122, 191, 227
Trinity, 3, 9, 20, 44, 103, 146, 157, 172, 182–83, 194, 255–58
immanent and economic, 3, 9, 20, 172, 255–58
triumph, 139, 141, 158, 188, 204, 223
Tun-Ergehens-Zusammenhang, 184
typology/typological, 3, 7–8, 12, 47, 59, 61–66, 68, 87–90, 94, 97–99, 230, 249–50

Ubi et quando Deo visum est, xii
ultimate, 4, 15, 64, 98, 108, 111, 143, 202, 204–6, 213–14, 259
unbelief, 110
unde malum, 128
union with Christ, 191, 233
universal atonement, 1, 3, 207–8, 253–54
universalism, 2–4, 200, 203–7, 212, 252–54
Urentscheidung, 15, 28

vere Deus et vere homo, 60, 107, 152
Versöhnung, 109, 157, 161, 165, 175, 180, 204, 211, 218, 221–22, 232
vicarious, 8, 39, 44, 68, 84, 86, 161, 196

victim, 8, 97, 111, 138, 143–44, 150–51, 164, 179, 185, 197, 250
Victor (Jesus), 126–27, 137, 142, 150, 197, 205–6, 212, 250, 253
vinculum amoris, 172, 259
vinculum caritatis, 255

Wassertaufe, 200, 222, 237–40, 244–45
Westminster Confession of Faith, 208

wrath, 3, 9, 13, 38, 51, 53–54, 112, 128, 135–36, 150–51, 153–54, 161–63, 165, 169–72, 182–83, 194, 250, 252

YHWH, 55, 72–75, 77–79, 81–82, 85–86, 92–93, 222, 231, 240, 249
Yom Kippur, 68, 71, 75, 77–81, 86–89, 91–93, 227

Name Index

Aaron, 50, 66, 80, 176
Abel, 46–47, 49, 52, 61, 64, 230
Adam, 114, 149, 155, 170–71, 183–84, 188, 208, 224, 230, 236, 249, 253
Aland, Barbara, 91
Aland, Kurt, 91
Allegri, xi
Anselm (of Canterbury), 8, 14, 22, 145, 153, 156, 169–70, 172–73
Athanasius, 148, 225–26, 228
Augustine (of Hippo), 14–15, 55, 150, 193, 214
Aulén, Gustaf, 148, 150, 197
Aquinas, Thomas, 14, 18, 24, 28, 153
Averbeck, Richard, 70, 73, 186

Bächli, Otto, 47, 67, 76, 97
Bailey, Daniel, 68, 94
Bakker, L. A. R., 161–63, 166, 169–70
Barabbas, 90–93
Barnabas, 88–89
Bell, Richard H., 68, 183, 189–90, 225–27, 232–33
Berkouwer, Gerrit Cornelius, 203–5
Blocher, Henri A. G., 146
Boettner, Lorraine, 2, 209, 211
Bremmer, Jan, 88
Breytenbach, Cilliers, 187, 189, 196
Bromiley, Geoffrey W., 138
Brunner, Emil, 27, 32–33, 43–44, 101, 119–20, 203
Buckley, James J., 119
Burney, Charles, xi
Busch, Eberhard, 96, 206
Butin, Phil, 159
Büttner, Matthias, 47

Byrne, Brendan, 187

Cain, 46–47, 49, 52, 55, 61, 64, 98–99, 230–31
Calvin, John, 4, 6–8, 11–16, 25, 40, 43, 46, 50, 60, 87, 103–6, 146, 151–55, 159, 169, 182, 193–94, 208–11, 214–15, 225, 248–52, 254, 259
Canlis, Julie, 225
Chilton, Bruce, xiii
Coakley, Sarah, xviii, 146, 226
Cocksworth, Ashley, 239
Cortez, Marc, 120, 122
Couvenhoven, Jesse, 236, 241–42
Crisp, Oliver D., 24, 43

Daly, Robert J., 81
David (king), 46–47, 55, 97
Davies, W. D. and Dale C. Allison. A, 90
Denney, James, 188
De Roo, Jacqueline C.R., 79, 88
Dowey E. A., 105
Drury, John L., 181–82
Dunn, James D.G., 186–88, 190–91, 194, 227, 231, 233

Emmanuel, 216, 230
Einstein, Albert, xi, xiv

Ford, David F., xii, 5, 22, 27, 43, 46–47, 50, 57, 59, 61–65, 97–99, 106, 123, 128
Freedman, David Noel, 83

Name Index

Gane, Roy, 78–79
Gaukesbrink, Martin, 190
Gese, Hartmut, 68–69, 73, 75–76, 79, 82, 192, 196
Gibson, David, 11, 13–15, 37, 46
Gill, Theodore A., 6
Gloege, Gerhard, 10, 15, 26, 28, 32, 34, 40, 44, 46, 99, 204
Gockel, Matthias, 10–12, 16, 23, 26, 28–29, 33–36
Goebel, Hans Theodor, 12–13, 16–17, 27, 36, 40, 43
Grabbe, Lester L., 49, 80, 88
Graf, Daniel, 68
Greggs, Tom, 33, 36, 39–41, 45, 64, 200, 203–6, 221, 228–30, 237–40, 243, 248, 252
Gregory (of Nyssa), 225
Gundry, Robert Horton, 90
Gunton, Colin, 14, 16, 18–20, 22, 39, 149

Hagner, Donald A., 90
Härle, Wilfried, 102–3, 108, 114–15, 118, 125, 128, 130–34, 137, 139–40
Harris, Murray J., 186
Hartley, J. E., 77
Hays, Christopher B., 13–14, 43, 46
Hector, Kevin W., 20
Hegel, Georg Wilhelm Friedrich, 95–97, 121
Helm, Robert, 49, 80
Hercules, 236, 241
Hitchcock, Nathan, 227
Hofius, Otfried, 68, 76–77, 84, 154, 172, 183–85, 191, 193, 195
Hooker, Morna, xii, 188, 190–91
Hübner, Hans, 79, 82
Hunsinger, George, 20, 35, 107, 111, 117, 203

Ignatius, 123, 148
Irenaeus/Irenäus, 123, 148–50, 198, 225

Janowski, Bernd, 68–9, 71, 73–79, 81, 88–89, 161, 189

Jenson, Matt, 133
Jenson, Philip Peter, 80–81
Jenson, Robert W., 101–2
Jeong, Sung Min, 134
Jesus of Nazareth, 17, 27, 31, 33–34, 92, 111, 115–17, 152, 156, 172, 205, 213–14
Joest, Wilfried, 220–21, 238
Jones, Paul Dafydd, 11, 26–29, 32–33, 107, 160–61, 165–69
Jüngel, Eberhard, 17–23, 29–30, 33–34, 159, 174, 237–40, 244
Judas (Iscariot), 61, 97–98
Joel (prophet), 220

Käfer, Anne, 102, 131, 140–41, 143
Käsemann, Ernst, 183
Kedar-Kopfstein, Benjamin, 74
Kennedy, Darren M., 104–6, 134, 136, 142
Kiuchi, Nobuyoshi, 84
Klappert, Bertold, 135, 156, 158, 161–62
Knöppler, Thomas, 73–74, 93, 186–88, 190–91
Koch, Klaus, 71–72, 184, 189
Kohlbrügge, Hermann Friedrich, 48, 50, 53–55, 58, 60
Kreck, Walter, 13, 17, 28, 30, 32–33, 44, 97, 120, 200–201, 228
Krötke, Wolf, 113–14, 116, 120, 122–24, 129, 133, 135

Lang, Bernhard, 70–71, 73
Levine, Baruch A., 69
Lewis, Alan E., 3–4
Lewis, David, 155
Lewis, Theodore J., 88
Lombard, Peter, 18
Lossky, Vladimir, 225–26
Luther, Martin, 48, 94, 112, 135, 185, 256

Maass, Fritz, 69, 79
Maccoby, Hyam, 92
Maclean, Jennifer K., 92
Mangina, Joseph L., 14, 24, 107, 113, 115, 165

Martin, Ralph P., 186,
Maurer, Ernstpeter, 162, 164, 168–69, 184
Maury, Pierre, 7, 10–12, 36, 38
McCormack, Bruce L., 4–5, 10–11, 14, 16–17, 19–21, 28, 33, 104–5, 151–55, 185–86, 201, 214
McDonald, H.D., 146
McDonald, Suzanne, 24
McDowell, John C., 33, 128, 135
McFayden, Alistair, 133
McLauchlan, Richard, 3
McMaken, Travis, 39, 64, 170
Melchizedek, 176, 215
Mikkelsen, Hans Vium, 107–8, 114, 117, 134, 143
Milgrom, Jacob, 71–72, 79–80, 82
Moberly, Robert W. L., 184–85
Molnar, Paul, 20
Mozart, Wolfgang Amadeus, xi, 6, 141
Muller, Richard A., 13

Neder, Adam, 40, 45, 114, 118, 192
Newton, Sir Isaac, xiv
Nimmo, Paul T., 11, 14–17, 27, 33, 203, 256–57
Nolland, John, 90

Origen, 90, 147, 149
Owen, John, 210

Pannenberg, Wolfhart, 18, 32, 55, 94, 165, 219, 221, 233, 245
Paul (apostle), 44–45, 88, 175, 183–91, 193–94, 196, 224–28, 233, 251, 258
Parmenides, 125, 128
Peterson Sr., Robert A., 154, 193
Pilate (Pontius), 91–92
Polen, Nehemia, 82–83
Prenter, Regin, 107

Rendtorff, Rolf, 70–71
Rodin, Scott R., 129, 131, 135, 221–22
Ruddies, Hartmut, 157, 160
Rudman, Dominic, 81

Saul (king), 46–47, 55, 97

Scarlata, Mark, 99
Schleiermacher, Friedrich D. E., 55
Schwartz, Baruch J., 83
Söding, Thomas, 174, 187, 189
Staubli, Thomas, 54, 77, 80, 85
Steele, David N., 209
Stoevesandt, Hinrich, 11, 35, 64, 97
Stökl Ben Ezra, Daniel, 87–89, 91–92
Stolina, Ralf, 184–85
Stolz, F., 83
Stoltzfus, Philip E., 6
Stowers, Stanley, 227
Stuhlmacher, Peter, 68, 89, 93–94, 186–87, 196
Sykes, Stephen W., 62, 222

Tawil, Hayim, 49
Thomas, Günter, 135, 171–72,
Torrance, James, 149
Torrance, Thomas F., 108–9, 117, 148–49, 152, 158, 197–98, 209–10, 233
Trebilco, Paul, 73
Turner, David L., 90
Turner, Henry E.W., 146–47, 149–51, 197

Vetter, Isolde, xi
Von Balthasar, Hans Urs, 4–7, 17, 23–25, 31, 37–38, 41, 102, 112
Vondey, Wolfgang, xiv

Wallace, Mark I., 63
Ward, Graham, 96
Webster, John B., 24, 26, 29–31, 102–3, 107, 110, 114, 117, 157–58, 160–62, 213
Welker, Michael, 95–97
Wendel, François, 105
Westbrook, Raymond, 88
Wilckens, Ulrich, 186–87
Wilhelm, G., 88
Williams, Rowan, xv, 16, 19–22
Wood, Donald, 97
Wright, David P., 75, 80

Young, Frances M., 88, 146

Zatelli, Ida, 79

Scripture Index

Old Testament

Genesis

1–2	102
1:26	116
1	102
2	102
2:7	218–19, 221
2:17	184
3	183, 185
3:10	184
3:12	184
3:16–19	184
4	47
9:3–5	73
9:6	74

Exodus

21:30	69, 71
24:3	240
24:7	240
24:15f.	81
25:17	85
25:22	78, 93
30:11–16	73

Leviticus

4	186
4:3	72
4:4	80
4:5–7	73
4:15	80
4:16	73
4:18	73
4:21	186
4:24	186
4:25	71, 73
4:26	70
4:30	71, 73
4:31	70
4:34	71, 73
4:35	70
5:2–3	72
5:6	70, 186
5:6–7	186
5:11	186
5:10	70
5:12	186
5:13	70
5:18	70
5:26	70
5:11–13	79
10:17	74, 81
11:44	109, 177
12:6–8	72
14	5, 12, 46–50, 53–64, 67–70, 72, 80, 84–86, 94
14:4–7	47
14:18	70, 72
14:20	70, 72
15:15	70
16	5, 12, 46–50, 52, 53–60, 62–63, 67–68, 70, 72, 78, 84–87, 89, 91–94, 252
16:3	186
16:5	186
16:5–6	47, 48
16:6–10	92
16:8–9	66
16:9	186

Scripture Index

16:13	78
16:14	78
16:15	78
16:18	71
16:18–19	78
16:21	81
16:22	90
16:27	81
17:10–14	73
17:11	71, 73, 74
17:13	73
19:22	70
26:12	109, 177, 225

Numbers

6:16	186
7:16	186
16:46	71
25:11	71
25:13	71
27:18	75
27:23	75

Deuteronomy

12:23	73, 74
30:16	240
34:9	75

1 Kings

13	46, 47, 55

Psalms

22	224
40:7	179
42	224
72	215
110:4	176

Isaiah

9:2	245
42:1	55, 245
42:6	55, 245
42:7	245
43:1	36
43:10	55
49:6	55
49:9	245
53	89–90, 153
53:4	90
53:6	153
53:10	186
53:12	153
61	245

Jeremiah

31:33	100

New Testament

Matthew

4:12–17	245
4:19	240
8:12	2
8:17	90
8:22	240
9:9	240
10:28	122
10:38	240
12:18	245
12:28	245
12:31	245
13:42	2
13:50	2
16:24	232, 240
19:21	240
22	210, 242
22:1–14	241
22:9	210
22:13	2
24:51	2
25:30	2
25:31–46	214
25	99
26:41	223
27:11ff.	91
27:15–23	90
27:15–26	92
27:17	91

Mark

1:17	240

2:14	240	10:30	257
8:34	240	12:24	228
10:21	240	12:26	240
10:45	174	12:49	257
14:32–42	166	14:9	3
15:6–15	92	14:11	257
		15	232

Luke

		15:1–17	257
		16:15	257
4:18	245	17:21	257
5:27	240	18:39–40	92
9:23	240	19:14	92
9:59	240	19:28	179
13:28	2	21:19	240
14	210, 242	21:22	240
14:15–24	241		
14:17	210, 242	## Book of Acts	
14:21	210		
14:27	240	8:14–17	238
15	158	10:44–48	237
18:22	240	19:1ff.	238
23:16	91		
23:18–25	91	## Romans	
23:21	91		
24:27	1	2:7	148
		3:9	184

John

		3:25	177
		4:25	61
1:1	32, 108	5	224
1:5	245	5:1	193, 224
1:14	32	5:5	222
1:29	89, 177	5:6	189
1:43	240	5:8	189–90, 193, 222
3:7	252	5:9	191
3:16f.	187	5:12ff.	149, 183
3:16–18	257	5:15	219
3:18	254	5:18f.	187
3:34	219	6:3ff.	219
3:36	44, 212, 252	6:3–4	196
5:19–23	257	6:4	61
5:22	vi	6:6	184
5:30	197	6:6–7	190
5:36	257	6:8	231
6:57	257	6:16f.	184
8:12	245	6:20	184
8:54	257	7:14	184
10	255	7:17	184
10:17–18	168	7:20	184
10:27	240	7:24	184–85, 196

8:3	72, 187, 189, 249, 253, 258
8:11	227
8:17	151, 259
8:19–23	225
9–11	37, 46

1 Corinthians

1:1	44
5:7	88–89, 177
6:20	233
7:23	233
9:25	258
10:11	90
10:16	233
15	224
15:3	189
15:42–44	226
15:45	219
15:53f.	148
15:54	199, 226
15:54–56	197

2 Corinthians

1:18–20	251
1:20	247
4:3f.	44
4:10	228
4:16	228
5:1–4	227
5:14	188–90
5:15	191, 231
5:17	230
5:17f.	196
5:18	194
5:19	160, 191, 193, 258
5:21	9, 72, 89, 153, 186, 189, 191
8:9	225
10:4	258

Galatians

4:4	187
4:7	151
5:1	254

Ephesians

1:4	32, 34, 247
1:4–5	10
3:9–11	32

Philippians

2	45
2:6	223
2:6ff.	158–60, 187
3:12	258f.

Colossians

1:15	109
1:20	158
2	253
2:11ff.	149, 190
3	227
3:1–3	225

1 Timothy

2:4	2
2:5	175
6:12	259

2 Timothy

1:10	148

Titus

3:7	151

Hebrews

4:14	176
4:16	175
5:6	176
5:8	223
5:9	230
6:19	227
6:20	175
8:5	176
9:11–12	182
9:12	176
9:14	177, 182, 230, 250
9:14–15	145
9:24	175
9:26	88, 231
10:1	90, 177

10:8f.	179	3:12	99, 231
10:10	88	4:9	187
10:20	175		
13:12	60	***Jude***	

1 Peter

		11	99
		11f.	231
1:12	218		
2:24	89	***Revelation***	

1 John

		13:8	38, 257
1:5	98		

www.ingramcontent.com/pod-product-compliance
Lightning Source LLC
Chambersburg PA
CBHW061430300426
44114CB00014B/1619